Using Microsoft Office for W... SO-AXT-721

Quick Start to Microsoft Office Success!

Standard equipment for Microsoft Office windows

If you've never used Windows or Microsoft Office before (or even if you have!), here's some basic stuff you need to know before you get started.

Main menu bar
Anything you can do in Office, you can do by choosing from one of these menus. Just click on any of the menu choices to see the menu.

Title bar
Which program are you using? What is the name of the document you have open? Look here to find out.

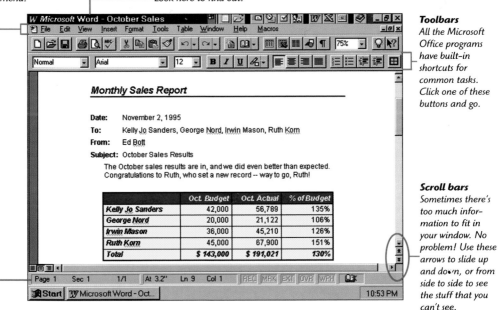

Toolbars
All the Microsoft Office programs have built-in shortcuts for common tasks. Click one of these buttons and go.

Scroll bars
Sometimes there's too much information to fit in your window. No problem! Use these arrows to slide up and down, or from side to side to see the stuff that you can't see.

Status bar
Information Central for your Office programs: What page am I on? What does that button do? Double-click in each area to find even more time savers.

Office Shortcut bar
The buttons on the OSB work just like elevator buttons to shuttle you straight to the individual Office programs. You can add or remove as many shortcut buttons as you need.

Schedule+ Shortcuts
Office 95 makes scheduling easy!

Click here to add a new appointment to your calendar
Click here to enter a new task to your to-do list
New client? Click here to add her vital statistics to your address book

Answer Wizard
Not sure what to do? Click the Answer Wizard, and type in your question

QUE
201 W. 103rd Street • Indianapolis, IN 46290 • (317)581-3500
Copyright© 1994 Que Corporation

Mouse techniques

General Office techniques	How do I do it?
Display a pull-down menu.	Click on the menu choice in the menu bar.
Display a shortcut menu.	Right-click where you need the menu to appear.
Find out what a button does.	Move the mouse pointer over the toolbar button to display a ToolTip.
Display the Office Manager menu.	Click on the Office Manager button on the MOM toolbar.

Selecting stuff	How do I do it?
Select an icon or picture.	Point at it and click.
Select two things that aren't right next to one another.	Hold down the Ctrl key as you select the first one, and keep holding it down as you move from place to place, marking the selections with the mouse.
Deselect something.	Point somewhere outside the highlighted area and click.

Selecting text in Word	How do I do it?
Select a word.	Point to the word and double-click.
Select an entire sentence.	Hold down the Ctrl key, point to the sentence, and double-click.
Select an entire paragraph.	Move the mouse pointer to the left margin until it turns into an arrow, position it alongside the paragraph, and double-click.
Select the whole document.	Move the mouse pointer to the left margin until it turns into an arrow, and then triple-click.

Working with a single cell in Excel	How do I do it?
Select a cell.	Point and click.
Position the insertion point in a cell.	Point and double-click.
Select characters in a cell.	Double-click in the cell, then drag through the characters you want to select.
Select a word in a cell.	Double-click the word. (This also works with cell addresses, formula arguments, and other things that aren't "words."

Selecting multiple cells in Excel	How do I do it?
Select a range.	Click in the cell at one corner of the range and drag the pointer to the opposite corner.
Select a group of unconnected cells.	Select the first cell or range, then hold down the Ctrl key and select the next cell or range. Continue holding the Ctrl key down until you've selected all the cells you want.
Select an entire row or column.	Click on the letter or number in its heading.
Select multiple rows or columns.	Select the first row or column and hold down the mouse button while dragging through the rest.

Using

Microsoft® Office for Windows® 95

Using

Microsoft® Office for Windows® 95

Ed Bott

Using Microsoft® Office for Windows®95

Library of Congress Catalog No.: 95-70639

ISBN: 0-7897-0176-6

97 96 95   4   3   2   1

Interpretation of the printing code: the rightmost double-digit number is the year of the book's printing; the rightmost single-digit number, the number of the book's printing. For example, a printing code of 95-1 shows that the first printing of the book occurred in 1995.

Credits

President
Roland Elgey

Vice President and Publisher
Marie Butler-Knight

Associate Publisher
Don Roche, Jr.

Editorial Services Director
Elizabeth Keaffaber

Director of Marketing
Lynn E. Zingraf

Managing Editor
Michael Cunningham

Acquisitions Editors
Jenny L. Watson
Nancy Stevenson

Product Directors
Lisa D. Wagner
Robin Drake
Lorna Gentry

Technical Editor
Frank Gamino

Senior Editor
Nancy E. Sixsmith

Editor
Charles K. Bowles II

Novice Reviewer
Beth Lucas

Assistant Product Marketing Manager
Kim Margolius

Technical Specialist
Cari Skaggs

Acquisitions Coordinator
Tracy M. Williams

Operations Coordinator
Patricia J. Brooks

Editorial Assistant
Carmen Phelps

Book Designer
Ruth Harvey

Cover Designer
Dan Armstrong

Production Team
Mary Ann Abramson
Angela D. Bannan
Carol Bowers
Georgiana Briggs
Michael Brumitt
Terrie Deemer
George Hanlin
Louisa Klucznik
Bob LaRoche
Kevin Laseau
Paula Lowell
Donna Martin
Brian-Kent Proffit
Bobbi Satterfield
Tina Trettin
Mark Walchle
Karen York

Indexer
Cheryl Dietsch
Jeanne Clark

Composed in *Stone* and *MCPdigital* by Que Corporation

Dedication

To my father, who patiently answered all my questions when I was a child, and then had a few hundred questions of his own—all about computers—when I became an adult.

About the Author

Ed Bott, the author of Que's *Using Microsoft Office 4* and *Using Windows 95*, is Senior Contributing Editor of *PC/Computing* magazine. With two monthly columns and frequent cover stories on Microsoft Windows and other topics, his is one of the most recognized "voices" in the computing industry.

Acknowledgments

There may be only one name on the cover, but it took a hard-working and dedicated team of professionals to bring this book to life. Literally dozens of people—editors, designers, proofreaders, technical reviewers, and others—worked on this book. It's impossible to thank them all personally, so let me single out a handful of individuals whose efforts were truly heroic.

Three Product Development Specialists—Lisa Wagner, Robin Drake, and Lorna Gentry—tackled different sections of the book. Their questions, comments, and suggestions during the many months we worked together helped ensure that every chapter was genuinely useful.

I can't imagine what this book would have been without the work of Senior Editor Nancy Sixsmith, whose attention to detail and command of the English language are rare indeed.

Acquisitions Editor, Nancy Stevenson, drew the unenviable task of pulling all the pieces together and made it look effortless. Bruce Hallberg and Sue Plumley pitched in with invaluable additions. Eric Maloney made major improvements to the Word sections. Technical Editor Frank Gamino helped stomp out errors and inconsistencies. Thank you, one and all.

I owe a special debt of gratitude to Robin Drake at Que Corporation and Yael Li-Ron, my colleague at *PC Computing*. In the face of impossible deadlines, they delivered polished, professional work—and in some cases they said it better than I could have.

Finally, a heartfelt thank you to Associate Publisher, Don Roche, Jr., without whose enthusiasm and support this book would not exist.

Trademarks

We'd like to hear from you!

As part of our continuing effort to produce books of the highest quality, Que would like to hear your comments. To stay competitive, we *really* want you, as a computer book reader and user, to let us know what you like and dislike about this book or other Que products.

You can mail comments, ideas, or suggestions for improving future editions to the address below, or send us a fax at (317)581-4663. For the on-line inclined, Macmillan Computer Publishing now has a forum on CompuServe (**GO QUEBOOKS** at any prompt), through which our staff and authors are available for questions and comments. The address of our Internet site is **http://www.mcp.com** (World Wide Web).

In addition to exploring our forum, please feel free to contact me personally to discuss your opinions of this book. On CompuServe, I'm at 74404,3307; on the Internet, I'm **lwagner@que.mcp.com**.

Thanks in advance—your comments will help us to continue publishing the best books available on computer topics in today's market.

Lisa D. Wagner
Product Development Specialist
Que Corporation
201 West 103rd Street
Indianapolis, IN 46290
USA

Contents at a Glance

Table of Contents

Part I: Getting Started

Part II: Using Word

6 Creating a New Document

7 Opening and Editing Documents

8 The Secrets of Great-Looking Documents

9 Let Word Do Your Work for You

10 Lists and Tables

11 Letters by the Dozen

12 Fancy Word Tricks

13 Putting It on Paper

Part III: Using Excel

14 Creating a New Worksheet

15 Get the Most Out of Your Worksheets

16 Making Great-Looking Worksheets

17 Fancy Excel Tricks

18 Chart Your Progress, Map Your Future

19 Printing Your Worksheets

20 Using Word with Excel, and Vice Versa

Part IV: Using PowerPoint

21 Creating a New Presentation

22 Making Great-Looking Presentations

23 Using Word and Excel with PowerPoint

24 It's Showtime! Giving a Great Presentation

Part V: Beyond the Basics

25 Wrapping Everything Up with Office Binders

26 Making Office Work the Way You Do

Part VI: Troubleshooting

Troubleshooting Office 95

Part VII: Indexes

Action Index

Introduction

I wrote this book for my father, the small business owner. And for my brother, the teacher, and my cousin, the biologist, and my insurance agent, and my accountant, and the UPS driver, and the guy who runs the Italian restaurant on Main Street, and a bunch of other people just like them.

What do these folks have in common? Well, all of them are bright, well-educated, and successful (especially my father). They've mastered the really hard stuff in life, like raising kids, running a business, killing crabgrass, and programming a VCR. They're all experienced computer users, but they're not computer experts. And at one time or another, each of them has asked me the exact same question:

What do I do now?

If you're like a few million other people, you've been asking that question a lot lately, ever since a huge collection of Windows programs called Microsoft Office appeared on your PC. Maybe it was just there when you bought a new PC. Maybe it showed up on your department's network one day, along with a terse note telling you it's time to switch from WordPerfect or Lotus 1-2-3 or Harvard Graphics to these new programs.

What do I do now?

You could start pulling down menus, clicking mouse buttons, and pressing key combinations until you stumble on the right ones.

Or you could look in the manuals. *If* you could find them. And *if* they were written in plain English. And *if* you had the time to scour through several hundred pages of technotrivia in search of the answers you need.

Or you could look in this book, which was written specifically to answer one question:

What do I do now?

What makes this book different?

You don't need an advanced degree in engineering or computer science to read this book. If you can tell the difference between the left and right mouse buttons, you've got all the technical background you need.

It's written in plain English, too. I promise not to bury you in detailed explanations and three-letter acronyms (TLAs). After all, you're not studying for a degree in computer science—you're trying to get some work done, with the help of some incredibly powerful and occasionally baffling computer programs.

With Office, as with all Windows programs, there are always *at least* four different ways to do everything. If you were planning to become a computer expert, you'd expect a computer book to give you step-by-step instructions for each of them. Not this book.

In this book, I focus on results. That means I'll tell you the best way to get each job done. There might be three other ways to do the same thing, but for most people, most of the time, the technique I describe is the one that will get results most quickly.

Oh, and there won't be a quiz.

How do I use this book?

This isn't a textbook. You don't have to start at page 1 and read all the way to the end. It's not a mystery novel, either, so if you want to skip to the last chapter first, be my guest.

You'll probably be surprised at some of the things the programs that make up the Microsoft Office can do. That's why, if you have the time, it's worth flipping through the chapters, looking at the headings, and searching out references to the things you do at work. The people who published this book went to a lot of trouble to make sure that those interesting ideas would leap off the page and catch your attention as you browse. (It shouldn't take that long—after all, this isn't one of those 1200-page monster books that helps you build up your biceps every time you lift it.)

This book will come in especially handy when you have a big job to do and you're not sure where to begin. And if you get stuck, you'll probably find the way out in these pages.

How this book is put together

Some people will use all the programs in Office 95. Others will spend most of their time in one. It doesn't matter which type you are—you'll find exactly what you're looking for. You could look at this book as a sort of Dagwood sandwich, with three big chunks of information, one for each of the big three Office programs, stuffed between two slices of general information. These five parts are divided into chapters that get into the specifics of each program. And inside each chapter, you'll find tips, hints, and step-by-step instructions for getting your work done faster without having to ask what to do next.

Part I: Getting Started

What is this thing called Office? It's four powerful programs (plus a bunch of little ones you get for free). Look here to discover all the things these programs have in common, like menus, toolbars, dialog boxes, and helpful wizards. If you're upgrading from Microsoft Office 4, check out the "Office 95 Upgraders' Guide."

Part II: Using Word

It's official—Microsoft Word is now the world's most popular software program. Word is filled with shortcuts and features—like an automatic spelling checker that flags your errors as you type, and lots of features that practically read your mind and just do things for you without being asked (like replacing your common typos automatically). Word comes with several ready-made templates that let you put together memos, letters, invoices, and brochures without breaking a sweat. So, for you and the 20 million or so other people who use Word, here's all you need to know to create a simple letter or your own professional-looking newsletter.

Part III: Using Excel

There are all sorts of accounting genes in my family, but I didn't get any of them, which is why I use Excel all the time. With Excel worksheets, I can type in row after row, and column after column of numbers—with full confidence that Excel will add, subtract, multiply, divide, and generally crunch them correctly. Check out these chapters for details on how to build budgets, turn numbers into great-looking graphs, and print out dazzling reports guaranteed to impress even non-accountants. Turn straight to Chapter 20 if you want pointers on using Excel and Word together.

Part IV: Using PowerPoint

How many times have you sat in a darkened room while someone else stands at an overhead projector, droning on and on and flipping boring black-and-white foils? Drone, flip, drone, flip, snore.... The next time *you* stand up in front of a crowd, use PowerPoint to help keep your audience awake and on the edge of their seats. If you ever have to sell anything—products, services, or ideas—you'll find PowerPoint's dazzling electronic slide shows irresistible.

Part V: Beyond the Basics

And then there's the rest of Office (the proverbial last but not least). New in Office 95 are Binders, which let you assemble projects from several Office documents, easily and painlessly. Need to create a marketing plan which includes a few Word documents, some Excel worksheets, and a couple of PowerPoint slides? Just drag those documents to the Binder, and it's done. And Schedule+, the group scheduler and personal information manager, keeps you organized, timely, and on good terms with other members of your workgroup.

Also in this section: helpful advice on using Office with your company's electronic mail and a brief introduction to all the little Office programs, including one that lets you manage the collection of clip art you didn't even know you had, and another that lets you create official-looking organizational charts showing who's who in your company. If you want to rework any part of Office to match the way you work, check out Chapter 26.

Part VI: Troubleshooting

Problems with hardware? Software? Find answers to thorny questions in "Troubleshooting Office 95."

Part VII: Indexes

Everything...yes, everything you want to look up is found here, including tasks and commands.

Special book elements

This book contains a number of special elements and conventions to help you find information quickly—or skip information you don't want to read right now.

TIP **Tips either point out information often overlooked in the** documentation, or help you use your software more efficiently, like a shortcut. Some tips help you solve or avoid problems.

CAUTION **Cautions alert you to potentially dangerous consequences of a** procedure or practice, especially if it could result in serious or even disastrous results, such as loss or corruption of data.

Q&A *What are Q&A notes?*

Cast in the form of questions and answers, these notes provide you with advice on ways to avoid or solve common problems.

 Plain English, please!

These notes explain the meanings of technical terms or computer jargon.

Throughout this book, we'll use a comma to separate the parts of a pulldown menu command. For example, to start a new document, you'll choose File, New. That means "Pull down the File menu, and choose New from the list."

And if you see two keys separated by a plus sign, such as Ctrl+X, that means to press and hold the first key, press the second key, then release both keys.

Sidebars are interesting nuggets of information

Sidebars provide interesting, nonessential reading, side-alley trips you can take when you're not at the computer or when you just want some relief from "doing stuff." Here you may find more technical details, funny stories, personal anecdotes, or interesting background information.

Office 95 Upgraders' Guide (So You've Used Office Before?)

● In this chapter:

- **What's new and exciting in Office 95?**

- **Introducing the Shortcut Bar**

- **New programs: Microsoft Binder, Answer Wizard, and Schedule+**

- **Great new features in familiar programs**

You may feel like a rookie with Office 95 at first, but it won't be long before you're perfectly comfortable with your new team . . . . ●>

T he end of summer is an exciting time of year for football fans. That's when they start pouring over their favorite teams' rosters to find out who's out, who's in, and which fresh-out-of-college hotshot has been recruited. The question on everybody's mind, of course, is: will this new ensemble take us to the Super Bowl?

Office 95 is a winning team of world-class players. Office 4 users will be delighted to find their old favorite stars in the lineup, as well as some new ones. And, while the old coach did a good job, the new one is true Super Bowl material.

The lineup

Here are the applications in Office 95:

- Word
- Excel
- PowerPoint
- Schedule+ (new)
- Binder (new)

Last but not least: the coach, which used to be called Microsoft Office Manager (MOM), has been replaced with the Microsoft Office Shortcut Bar.

What's new in Office 95?

Beyond the new Office application programs, there are lots of new features in Office. Word is a lot more powerful, much easier to use, and so are Excel and PowerPoint. And team spirit is unprecedented. The applications are better integrated than ever before, and they've even learned to *share* better, which is an important trait for any team.

Let's look at what's new in Office 95.

It's a Windows 95 suite

Before you say, "duh," let's examine what being a Windows 95 program means. It means that you can use long file names when you save files. Long, easy-to-decipher names, like *First draft of the 96-97 budget* (see fig. 1). And, yes, spaces are allowed. It also means that you can use drag-and-drop almost anywhere, for anything, and right-click on almost any part of your screen to get context-sensitive menus.

Fig. 1
In Office 4, you might have named this file WRLDSR96.DOC. I don't know about you, but I think that's a bit cryptic.

I miss my MOMmy!

MOM, or the Microsoft Office Manager, has been replaced by the **Microsoft Office Shortcut Bar** (see fig. 2). This new toolbar provides handy shortcuts to anything on your system: the different Office 95 applications, other applications, shortcuts on the Desktop, and so on.

The buttons on the Shortcut Bar work like regular shortcuts in Windows 95. For example, right-clicking on a button brings up a context menu. You can customize the Shortcut Bar to your heart's content; add, delete and move the buttons, or choose other toolbars in addition to the standard Office toolbar.

Fig. 2
Meet your new Office Manager.

Document Centric? What's that?

Beyond new features, Office 95 has changed its fundamental philosophy. In the old days of Office 4, you used to work in application programs. You'd launch Word to type a memo, or open Excel to check out last year's figures. Office 95 has turned this around, so that now the *task* is more important than the *tool*. This is called a **Document Centric** approach. That's why you have two new items on your Start menu: New Office Document and Open Office Document. (You even have buttons for these items on the Shortcut Bar.) Need to work on a new proposal? Select New Office Document, and pick a template from the New dialog box you see in figure 3.

Fig. 3
The document or project, not the program, is the important part of your work.

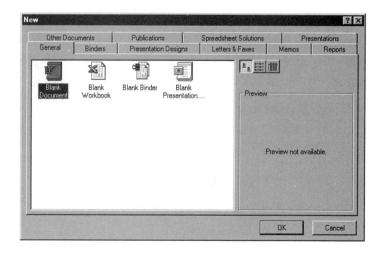

File/Open: more power to you

The File/Open dialog box—which is identical in all of Office 95's programs, except for Schedule+—has been rebuilt from the ground up. First of all, it looks and acts like a regular Windows 95 folder. That means that you can create, rename, delete, copy, or move folders and files right here, without having to switch to Explorer—all by right-clicking. Are you going to use this file regularly? Just add it to your Favorites folder from inside the File/Open dialog box. When you click on the Favorites folder button, you'll get a listing of all the files you've designated as *favorite*, for frequent access.

Thanks to the new Fast Find tool, you can locate your files, whether they're on your hard disk or on a network drive. Don't know what the file is called, but remember a few words in it? Don't worry. That's all Fast Find needs. Found a file, but you aren't sure it's the right one? Check out the Preview thumbnail, which lets you peek into the file without actually opening it (see fig. 4).

File/Save is a lifesaver

Just like File/Open, the File/Save dialog box is common to all Office 95 applications, except for Schedule+. You're bound to save lots of time and effort if you take advantage of the File/Save dialog features. For example, how many times have you attempted to save a file in Office 4, and realized that you didn't have an appropriate directory to place that file in? As you see in figure 5, now you can create a new folder from the File/Save dialog box, and proceed to save.

Fig. 4
The File/Open dialog box can do much more than just open files. It's a powerful file-management tool, saving you the need to switch over to Explorer or My Computer.

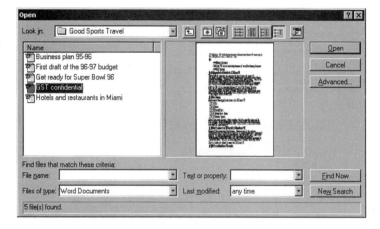

Fig. 5
No folder? No problem. Make one now, and save your file in it.

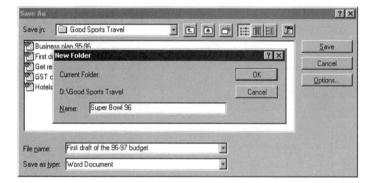

Better team spirit

Office applications now share a common dictionary (for spell-checking) and AutoCorrect entries. AutoCorrect, which is a great shorthand and error-correction tool, used to be available only in Word, but now you can type *hte* in Excel and get *the*, just as you do in Word. When you add an entry to the AutoCorrect list in one application, it becomes available to other Office applications. Note that there's no AutoCorrect in Schedule+. And, as shown in figure 6, now you can spell-check your Excel worksheets and PowerPoint presentations as well.

Put it all together with the Binder

The new Office 95 program called **Binder** creates a master document that combines several documents into one cohesive project. Add documents from Word, Excel, or PowerPoint by dragging-and-dropping their icons into the Binder. This is a great tool for proposals and reports, which usually combine text, graphics, and numbers. The pages inside a Binder document are numbered automatically, according to the order in which the documents are placed. Move one PowerPoint slide from the beginning to the end, and it'll get a new page number. See figure 7.

Fig. 6
You can check your spelling in Excel and PowerPoint.

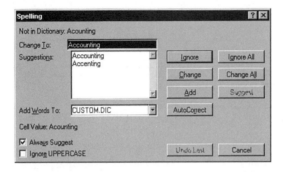

Fig. 7
To rearrange documents in the Binder, just drag their icons around.

Answer Wizard

Online help is a great feature, but it's sometimes hard to find the answer to your question, especially if you're not sure how to ask. The new **Answer Wizard** makes it easier to find help. Just click the Answer Wizard button on the Shortcut Bar, and type in your question. In plain English. You know, like, "How do I embed an Excel graph in a Word document?" As you see in figure 8, the Answer Wizard looks at your query and displays all kinds of help topics that are appropriate to your problem. If that's not enough, Answer Wizard can even hold your hand and show you step-by-step how to complete a task.

Fig. 8
Think of the Answer Wizard as your own $0-per-hour consultant/trainer. This is much easier than picking up the phone and asking a question, especially because the response is immediate. And the Answer Wizard has a great attitude, too.

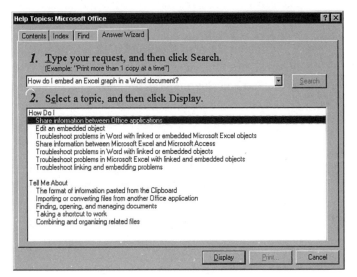

The players

Let's look at the new features in the different Office 95 components.

Sprint through your worksheets with Excel

Excel 5 was no slouch when it came to crunching numbers, but it's even faster now. Lots of **IntelliSense** has been poured into Excel.

Plain English, please!

IntelliSense is Microsoft's term for the clever technology that reads your mind (well, almost) and does a lot of the dirty work for you. Type a short line, press Enter twice, and Word will assume that it's a paragraph heading and format it accordingly. Or type an asterisk (*) before a paragraph, and Word will convert it to a stylish "bullet." Just like that.

Just look at these new features:

- **AutoCalculator keeps the score.** If you need a quick sum (or count, or several other quick calculations) of the numbers in any range, click once, and Excel does it for you. Yes, you can auction off that desktop calculator now.

- **Easier number formatting.** You can quickly assign fancy formatting, such as different colors for different values, and more.

- **Type less with AutoComplete.** Here's the perfect preventative medicine for your aching wrists. Type the first few characters of a cell entry, and Excel completes the rest. How? Excel stores what you've typed already in a list, and picks the most likely candidate from there. Or, pick the entry you want by right-clicking and selecting Pick from the menu that shows up.

- **AutoFilter with Top Ten**. Who were the top producers last quarter? In Excel 5 you had to do some fancy footwork to figure that out. But with AutoFilter with Top Ten, you can get a list of the top 5, 10, 100, or whatever number you want. Painlessly.

- **Enhanced drag-and-drop**. Now you can drag-and-drop cells (or a range of cells) between worksheets and workbooks. To drag-and-drop to a worksheet in the same workbook, hold the Alt key down and drag to a sheet tab. This brings up the target worksheet and lets you drop your stuff exactly where you want to.

- **ScrollTips.** Scrolling up and down a large document used to be a "shot in the dark" experience. But now, when you click on the scroll bar, it displays a tiny label with the current page number. Keep scrolling until you get to the page you're looking for, and let go of the mouse button.

- **CellTips.** When you share a worksheet with others, it's easy to get confused. Why was this value entered here? Who changed this figure? With CellTips, your questions are answered. These are cell annotations that pop up when you move your pointer over the cell, and you can even attach sound clips to that annotation to make it more interesting.

- **Data Maps.** Sure, you can analyze your data by looking at row after row of numbers. But an easier way is to look at graphic representation. Like a map, with demographic breakdown of your clients. Or a state-by-state comparison of this year's sales against last year's. And it's easier to do than typing all those numbers in. The Data Map in Excel takes your existing data and converts it to a map.

- **Work together with Shared Lists**. Thanks to the new Shared Lists feature, Excel is a great workgroup application, allowing several users to work on the same worksheet, at the same time, across a network.

- **New templates.** There are new templates for home and business use in Excel, too. Look under the Spreadsheet Solutions tab by clicking on New Office Document.

Word reads your mind

Many new features help automate and speed up common tasks, making Word easier than ever to use. How easy, you ask? Sometimes it just does it all for you, and lets *you* get all the praise. Check these out:

- **Automatic Borders.** You've got to try this: type three dashes (-) in a row, and press Enter. Word creates a thin border. Cool, no? And how about this: type three equal signs (=) in a row, and press Enter… whoa! Word slams a double-line border on your document faster than you can say, "How do I create a line?"

- **AutoCorrect**. Oh, sure, AutoCorrect was here before. But could it draw happy faces on your screen? And how about arrows, legal symbols, and other things you always had to dig through the Symbol dialog box to get? Try this: type two hyphens followed by a greater than symbol (-->). Pretty ugly, right? But AutoCorrect takes that primitive combination and turns it into → in a fraction of a second.

- **Automatic headings.** Type a short line, and press Enter twice. What are you trying to create? A heading? Word understands that, and formats that line with a Heading style.

- **Automatic numbered lists and bullets**. Need to type a numbered list? Or a bulleted one? No sweat. Just type a number, followed by a period, and type a paragraph. When you hit Enter, you'll switch to a perfectly-formatted numbered list. If you type something like **a)** or **I.** before a paragraph, Word will continue the list just the way you'd expect it to: with a b) or II. For bulleted lists, type an asterisk in front of the line. For square bullets, use a hyphen.

- **TipWizard helps you along.** While you slug it out in Excel or Word, you have a friendly personal trainer working with you at all times. The TipWizard looks at what you're doing; if it thinks there's a better way to do whatever you're trying to achieve, it'll tell you so.

- **WordMail.** Have you ever sent a poorly spelled e-mail message to your boss? No? Well, I have. Most people make mistaks, especially when theyr on a deadlinne. Like I amm now. WordMail, simply put, is the marriage of Word and your e-mail program, Microsoft Exchange. When you compose a new message, you'll notice those squiggly red lines under your misspelled words. Anything you can do in Word, you can do in WordMail. It's that powerful.

PowerPoint is more to the point

Just like everywhere else in Office 95, Intellisense has affected PowerPoint, too. So you have access to AutoCorrect and Answer Wizard. But there's more to help your slides dazzle the audience.

- **Presentation conferencing.** As a true team player in the Office suite, Office lets you run presentations across a network. And it's not merely a passive experience for audience members. They can send you feedback by annotating and drawing on the slides during the presentation.

- **Pack and Go Wizard.** Now you can take your presentations *to-go*. The Pack and Go Wizard does it all for you, preparing all the files that make up the presentation and assembling them into one portable package, which you can run on any system, even where PowerPoint isn't installed. Do you want fries with that?

- **Multiple Undo.** This terrific tool was first introduced in Word 6, and is now available in PowerPoint. You can undo anything, even a template selection.

See the top of your desk with Schedule+

New in Office 95 is Schedule+, the organizer/appointment book/personal information manager (PIM)/group scheduler. Schedule+ can organize your work and personal life, so you can throw away all those sticky notes that cover your screen, your keyboard, and any space on your desk that's not taken by computer peripherals.

- **Maintain a to-do list**. Schedule+ will remind you, doggedly, that you have to complete a task.

- **Keep a contact list**. Phone numbers, addresses, even birthdays, they're all within your reach. Now you can surprise a client with a birthday card and maybe even close that deal.

- **Schedule meetings.** Invite other members of your workgroup to meetings, set aside conference rooms, and get confirmations, all without lifting a phone or writing a single note.

Part I: Getting Started

1

What Is Microsoft Office?

● In this chapter:

- What is Office, what can it do for me, and why should I care?

- Standard? Professional? CD-ROM? Which version do I need?

- Starting Office

- How do I know which version of Office I have?

- What do all these programs do?

When you're in a foreign country and you want to communicate with the natives, you pull out your Berlitz phrase book, right? Windows lets you do the same thing. . . . . ❯

Every time I turn on my PC, I remember that scene in the classic horror film *Frankenstein*. You know the one: Igor pulls the switch, the monster begins to twitch, Dr. Frankenstein's eyes light up, and he exclaims, *"It's alive!"*

The trouble with Frankenstein's monster, of course, is that the parts didn't match up very well. Arms and legs from here, a heart from there, and a brain from who-knows-where. It's no wonder the poor beast couldn't put one foot in front of the other without scaring the poor townspeople.

Sometimes it seems like the average computer has the same problem. You pick up a word processor from here, a spreadsheet program from there, a cool chart-making program from somewhere else, and your productivity grinds to a halt. The problem? All those programs were never designed to work together, so you get hopelessly lost every time you switch from one to another.

Fortunately, there's a solution: Microsoft Office. In one box, you get all the business software you need. The programs look alike, work alike, and talk to one another in exactly the same language.

Gee... do you suppose if Dr. Frankenstein had had a copy of Office, the movie would have had a happy ending?

A shelfful of software

There's a lot more to Office than just a bunch of programs in the same box. As the name suggests, Microsoft Office includes a team of powerful business applications that handle words, numbers, and images with style and grace.

But the real appeal of Office is the glue that ties all those applications together. All the programs share common menus and rows of buttons that look remarkably similar. When you learn how to use one application, you've got a big head start on learning the others. You even get an easy-to-use control center that lets you start and stop the individual programs, or get detailed instructions and hands-on help just by clicking a mouse button.

Plain English, please!

What's the difference between a **program** and an **application**? Nothing, really. Computer experts use the terms interchangeably. Applications are usually big programs that do a wide variety of tasks. Tiny programs that do just one thing are sometimes called **applets**.

In this book, I'll show you how to use all the pieces of Microsoft Office—individually and together—to become more productive with your PC. You'll learn how to create great-looking letters and reports, crunch numbers faster than the most dedicated bean counter, and tie it all together in presentations that'll win the hearts and minds of customers and coworkers alike.

If you wanted, you could buy a bunch of programs and try to glue them together yourself. But you'd wind up with the same headache you'd get if you tried to put together a killer audio/video system using a bunch of individual components. To play a video, you press Start; but to listen to a cassette, you have to press Play. The VCR's Eject button is on the right, but the CD's Open/Close button is on the left. And have you ever looked at the back of a stereo amplifier and tried to figure out which wire goes where?

Whether you're working with a PC or a home theater, the glue that ties the components together is the most important part. When your computer's programs look and act the same way, it's less confusing for you to switch back and forth. It's also easier to install and upgrade.

Which version of Microsoft Office is right for me?

There are three distinct versions of Office.

Standard edition

For most people, this is the right choice. You get a word processor for letters and reports, a spreadsheet for numbers and lists, a graphics program that lets you create colorful slide shows on your PC, and a scheduler/contact/time management program that helps you enter and organize all sorts of personal information—from small details, like your travel agent's phone number, to genuinely important ones, like the values around which you organize your life. You also get a handful of little programs you can use to create graphs, organization charts, and other useful, snazzy additions to business documents. And it costs a lot less than the individual pieces would cost on their own.

Professional edition

This is just like the Standard edition, but with a powerful data-management program called Access. Not for everyone, but useful for experts and computer users who don't mind thinking like computer programmers.

CD-ROM edition

Both Office editions come on floppy diskettes, and on CD-ROM. If you don't have a CD-ROM drive, this is a great reason to get one. Thanks to the CD-ROM's huge storage capacity, you get more software for your money—the CD-ROM version of Office Professional edition, for example, includes the entire Microsoft Bookshelf, which is a collection of seven complete reference books, including an encyclopedia and *The World Almanac*.

CAUTION **What if you don't have enough space on your hard drive to install** Office? Don't even think about running it directly from the CD-ROM. You'll save a few megabytes of hard disk space, but you may end up waiting minutes to complete even the simplest tasks. Better to buy a new hard drive, or try doubling your disk's storage capacity by using a disk-compression utility like Windows 95's DriveSpace (to find it, click on the Start menu, then follow the cascading menus through Programs, Accessories, and System Tools).

How do I start up Office (and shut it down safely)?

How do you start up Office and all the Office programs? That depends. When you (or someone else) installed Microsoft Office, it added an assortment of icons to the Start menu (see fig. 1.1). To start any of the Office programs, just click on the appropriate entry on the menu. If you're comfortable with the Windows Start menu, you can use the Programs menu to find and start any of the Office programs. Here's how:

• Click the Start button and point to the <u>P</u>rograms entry.

• After a brief pause, a new menu will unfold (the Windows 95 term is **cascade**) to the right. Move the mouse pointer to the right to highlight any option there.

• Click on the application you want to work with.

Fig. 1.1
You can start each of the Microsoft Office programs by clicking its entry on the Start menu.

But Office also includes its own toolbar, called the Office Shortcut Bar. Like the Windows taskbar, it lets you start up programs and switch between them with a single click. You can even add your own icons and folders if you really want to customize your workspace. It's a cool control center that's never more than a mouse click away. Taskbar or Shortcut Bar? Take your choice.

When you ran the Office installation program, the OSB icon should have landed in your StartUp folder so that OSB starts automatically (and you see the OSB toolbar) every time you start Windows. For more details on how to use the Office Shortcut Bar, see Chapter 5.

**CAUTION** **Always close the Office programs and shut down Windows** properly before you turn off your PC. If you don't, you run the risk of losing data, and maybe even making such a mess out of Windows or Office that neither one will start up properly. Why take chances? To shut down the right way, click the Start button, choose Sh<u>u</u>t Down, select one of the options from the Shut Down Windows dialog box, and then click <u>Y</u>es.

How do I know which version of Microsoft Office I have?

The easy way to figure this out is to watch your screen when you first start up your computer. As the Microsoft Office Shortcut Bar loads, you'll see a title screen like the one in figure 1.2, which unmistakably details the version number.

Fig. 1.2
Which version of Office is installed on your PC? Watch for this title screen just before the Microsoft Office Shortcut Bar appears.

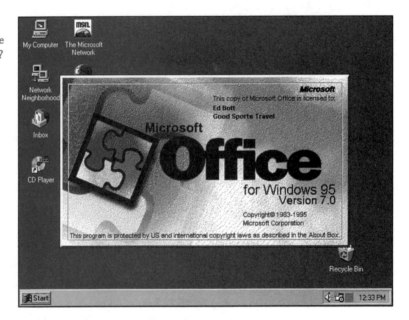

Meet the Office applications

So what's inside the Office package? Plenty. But before I get to that, let me ask a fundamental question: What kind of person are you? No, this isn't some kind of psychological test. There's no right or wrong way to work. It's really a lot simpler than that: how you work will help define which of the big three Office programs you're most likely to call home.

In the Office package you get ...

- **Big applications**

    Word is a powerful word processor that lets you quickly create everything from simple memos to slick newsletters and brochures. We'll cover Word in detail in Part II.

Excel does for numbers what Word does for nouns and verbs. Anyone who lives or dies by the numbers probably will live in Excel—at least at the office. Use Excel to create budgets and financial reports, turn numbers into easy-to-follow charts and graphs, perform "What If?" analyses of just about any question, and sort through lists in seconds. Read all about using Excel in Part III.

PowerPoint lets you create a professional-looking presentation, complete with snazzy graphics and step-by-step bulleted lists of arguments. Best of all, you can turn a Word document into a presentation with just one click. If your work depends on convincing other people that your products, ideas, and dreams are right for them, you'll love PowerPoint. Read more about PowerPoint in Part IV.

Schedule+ helps you manage your own time, tasks, and personal contacts. If others in your office use Schedule+, you can share calendars and contact lists, and even coordinate meetings automatically. Surprisingly, Schedule+ even includes a serious personal-growth program based on the life-management strategies outlined in Stephen R. Covey's best-selling book, *The Seven Habits of Highly Effective People.*

Access (Office Professional Edition only) is a powerful data-management program that's mostly for programmers. If someone in your office has created an Access program, you may need this to run it.

- **A bunch of little applications**

  Let's see, there's **Graph**, which lets you enter a few numbers and quickly turn them into a chart. **Organization Chart** helps you find your place on the corporate ladder (give yourself a promotion and see how it feels). **Equation Editor** is pretty boring, unless you're a professor of mathematics. **WordArt** lets you twist letters and numbers into creative shapes you can use for logos and headlines. **Data Map** takes a boring list of addresses and plots each one on a map so you can see where the action *really* is. There's even a **ClipArt Gallery** that lets you browse through a few hundred drawings in search of the perfect illustration for your newsletter or presentation. We'll look at these "applets" in more detail in Part V.

- **Some great help aids**

  Office (and the Office applications) are stuffed with helpful hints and step-by-step instructions for getting work done. **Tip Wizards** watch how you do something, and offer helpful advice on how to accomplish the same task a little faster or smarter. **Answer Wizards** listen while you ask a question in plain English, and then offer up a list of possible solutions. Wizards walk you step-by-step through complex tasks. Sometimes the Office applications even help out quietly in the background; for example, Word constantly checks your spelling while you type, correcting words that are obviously misspelled and marking others for you to review later. We'll look at all the Help options later in this section.

- **And, of course, OSB.**

  The **Office Shortcut Bar**, or **OSB**, is the starting point for all the Office applications. If you like it enough, you can use it to run nearly everything on your computer. We'll look at OSB in detail in Chapter 5.

Microsoft Office programs share common menus and buttons that look remarkably similar. When you learn to use one application, you've got a big head start on learning the others.

What do those version numbers really mean?

Until recently, my PC had more numbers on it than a roulette table. Microsoft Office Version 4.3, it used to say when I started up. Inside, I had Word 6.0c, Excel 5.0c, and PowerPoint 4.0c. Of course, all those programs ran with the help of MS-DOS 6.22 and Microsoft Windows 3.11.

Today, all those programs share a single version number—in Microsoft Office for Windows 95, I have Word 7.0, Excel 7.0, PowerPoint 7.0...well, you get the idea.

Why bother with version numbers in the first place? Because that's the only way to tell whether your Office software is up-to-date. The number to the left of the decimal point (7, in this case) identifies **major releases**, filled with hot new gee-whiz features. The numbers to the right of the decimal point identify **minor upgrades**, new versions with just a few little changes—nothing to write home about. In this case, the zero means these are the first releases in a new line of Office programs.

Those little letters at the far right of some version numbers? Each one represents a **bug fix**—a new edition of the program that Microsoft publishes to correct problems that people complained about in the previous version.

Frankly, the whole notion of labeling software with version numbers is a relic of the Dark Ages, when the only people who used computers were absolute nerds. You know the kind. They survive on Twinkies and Jolt cola, and are only dimly aware of the outside world.

Can you imagine how confusing life would be if these people had been responsible for making some of the other products we take for granted every day? You might be driving a Cadillac Seville, version 7.0b. Your kids would be begging you to take them to McDonald's for a Big Mac 4.25 and a Coca-Cola Classic (version 2.0). And you'd probably drive there on Interstate 10.11.

Fortunately, version numbers are a dying species, like hula hoops and pet rocks. Windows 95 is named after the year in which it was introduced, for example, instead of adopting an arbitrary version number. If future versions of Office follow the same pattern, there won't be a version 8 of any of these programs—instead, we'll have Office 96, Office 97, and so on. And we'll all have an easier time figuring out which version is the latest and greatest.

Common Office Features: Menus, Toolbars, and More

● In this chapter:

- **What can I do with the main menus?**

- **I have too many choices! Show me a shorter list.**

- **What are these rows of buttons for?**

- **I wonder what this button does...**

Word, Excel, and PowerPoint, the three big Office programs, are designed like a Holiday Inn—no surprises. When you know your way around one, you've learned the basic layout of the others, too. . . . . **>**

Everyone knows that "Where am I?" feeling you get when you spend the night away from home. You wake up in the middle of the night, but can't find the light switch. So you grope around in the dark and bash your shin against the coffee table. Ouch!

One way to avoid bumps and bruises is to stay in a Holiday Inn, where the motto is "No surprises." Every room is laid out exactly the same, so whether you're in Topeka or Timbuktu, you'll know where that coffee table is.

Word, Excel, and PowerPoint, the three big Office programs, are designed just the same as a Holiday Inn—no surprises. When you learn your way around one, you've learned the basic layout of the others, too. When you switch programs, the menus are right where you expect them to be, and buttons that do similar things have identical pictures.

The applications in Office don't always work *exactly* alike. But they get close most of the time. In this chapter, we'll look at the pieces of Office that you'll use most often: menus, toolbars, and the Office help system.

What's on the menu?

No matter where you are in Office, you have a choice of menus when you want to do something. Some stay right in front of you all the time; others remain hidden until you ask them to pop up.

Try the main menu first

Every Office program has nine pull-down menus that you can use to do nearly anything. Each of the menus on the menu bar is identified by a single word, and they're arranged in a neat row just below the title bar, as shown in figure 2.1. No surprises—eight of the nine choices are absolutely identical in each program. When you want to save your work, for example, you'll always use the File menu.

Because each program handles a different kind of data, the choices that appear when you pull down menus with the same name will vary slightly from program to program. And every program has one choice that's reserved for that program alone.

Fig. 2.1

No matter which Office program you use, the top menu choices always appear in the same place. That means you always know just where to go to get any job done.

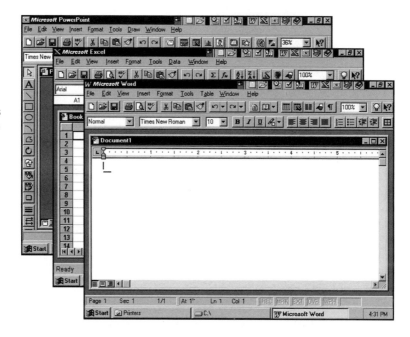

Here's a sampling of some of the options available under each menu choice:

- **File.** Save your work; find files you've saved previously; send work to the printer.

- **Edit.** Move, copy, and delete text or objects; search for words and phrases.

- **View.** Look at whatever you're working with in different ways—zoom in for a super close-up view, for example. Also the place you go to show or hide toolbars.

- **Insert.** Add special information (like today's date or page number) to whatever you're working on. Also lets you add objects, such as a picture or a graph.

- **Format.** Make your work look more attractive by changing the typeface, page size, colors and shading, and more.

- **Tools.** Do specialized tasks like checking for spelling mistakes. This is also the place where you can change program options, like where your data files are automatically stored.

- **Table/Data/Draw.** The only "uncommon" menu choices. Here's where you go to work with Word tables, Excel lists, and PowerPoint drawings.

- **Window.** Switch from one document window to another, or rearrange the windows that are already open.

- **Help.** Here you'll find all sorts of information that can get you back to work when you're not sure what to do next.

Check the shortcut menus for quick advice

Throughout the Office programs (and, in fact, throughout Windows 95), you're rarely more than one mouse click away from a special **shortcut menu**. It's like having a personal Office assistant following along one step behind you. You snap your fingers—well, actually, you click the right mouse button—and you get a short, easy-to-read list of options. Best of all, whoever puts together these shortcut menus must be psychic, because they contain only the things you're most likely to want to do right now.

Anytime you want to do something, and you're not sure how to do it, it's a good idea to press the right mouse button. There's an excellent chance that the choice you're looking for is right there (see fig. 2.2 for examples of these shortcut menus).

Fig. 2.2
Click the right mouse button to pop up one of these handy shortcut menus. For the three main Office applications, the menus start the same, but change a little to reflect the different things each program lets you do.

Word

Excel

PowerPoint

TIP **When people talk about the right mouse button, they really mean** the button that *isn't* the main one. On most computers, that's the right button. Left-handers (or anyone who just prefers to roll the mouse around with that hand) can switch the functions of the left and right mouse buttons using the Windows Control Panel. If you've done that, you'll have to mentally swap the directions when reading this book.

Or skip the menus and use keyboard shortcuts instead

Menus sometimes get in the way of productivity. Let's say you're working on a long, complicated, important report. Because you don't want a power failure to wipe out your work, you save what you've done every 10 minutes. (Very wise of you.) You *could* take your hand off the keyboard, grab the mouse, pull down the File menu, and click Save. Or you could just press Ctrl+S, which does exactly the same thing in one smooth motion.

There are literally thousands of keyboard shortcuts in the Office programs. No one expects you to memorize them all, but there are a few special keyboard shortcuts for activities you do over and over again. Use them regularly, and you can save enough mouse clicks to maybe go home 10 minutes early one day a week. These ten shortcuts, listed in table 2.1, are worth knowing, because they work the same in all the Office applications. In some cases, they're easy to remember because the command (Save) starts with the same letter as the shortcut (Ctrl+S).

Table 2.1 Top ten keyboard shortcuts

Keyboard shortcut	What does the shortcut do?
Alt+F4 or Ctrl+F4	Closes a program window or closes a document window, respectively.
Ctrl+C or Ctrl+X or Ctrl+V	Cuts, copies, or pastes whatever the mouse is pointing at.
Ctrl+Z	Oops! Undoes whatever I just did!
Ctrl+B	Makes it **bold**.
Ctrl+I	Makes it *italic*.
Ctrl+S	Saves whatever I'm working on right now.
Ctrl+N	Starts a new document/worksheet/presentation using default formats.
Ctrl+F6	Shows me the next window.
Ctrl+F	Finds some text in the current document.
Ctrl+A	Selects all (the whole document/worksheet/presentation I'm working with).

Toolbars: one-click shortcuts

Everywhere you turn in Microsoft Office, you run into long rows of buttons just waiting to be clicked. Fortunately, these button collections, called **toolbars**, share the same pictures and descriptions. So whichever program you're working with, the toolbars all look pretty much the same, and they're organized in similar ways, too. When you learn how one toolbar works, you've got a big head start on all the Office programs.

TIP **Toolbars start out in a neat row along the top of the screen, but** you can move them around if you'd prefer to see them elsewhere. Just use the mouse to "grab" a portion of the toolbar where there are no buttons, and drag the entire toolbar. If you move it to a side or the bottom of the program window, the toolbar will snap into position along that edge. If you move it somewhere other than an edge, the toolbar turns into a window that floats over whatever you're working on.

Standard toolbar

If you're like most people, there are certain things you do over and over again. When you have a few phone numbers that you dial repeatedly, you can save time by programming them into your telephone's speed dialer. The **Standard toolbar**, shown in figure 2.3, works the same way, offering one-button shortcuts for the things you're most likely to do every time you start up Office, like opening and saving files.

Fig. 2.3
In Microsoft Office programs, the Standard toolbar at the top of the window works just like the speed dialer on your telephone. Each button acts as a shortcut for one of the menu choices you make most often.

Here are some of the most useful buttons on the Standard toolbar:

Toolbar button	What does the button do?
	Creates a new file, opens a saved file, saves the file I'm working with now.
	Cuts whatever I'm pointing at now, makes a copy of it, or pastes whatever I just copied into the spot I'm pointing at now.

Toolbar button	What does the button do?
	Sends this job to the printer.
	Fixes those <u>embarrasing</u> and annoying misspelled words.
	Oops! Undoes whatever I just did!

Formatting toolbar

The other toolbar, right under the Standard one, works the same way. Should you have to pull down a bunch of menus and click through a maze of dialog boxes to do common things? Of course not. It's much easier to just click a button on the **Formatting toolbar** (see fig. 2.4).

Fig. 2.4

Use the buttons on the Formatting toolbar to make your words and numbers look bigger, bolder, and better.

Here are some of the most useful buttons on the Formatting toolbar:

Toolbar button	What does the button do?
Arial	Change to a different font, please.
10	I'd like these letters to be bigger or smaller, please.
B *I* <u>U</u>	Make it **bold**, *italic*, or <u>underline</u>.
	Please center these words on the page (or push them to the left or to the right).

Other toolbars

Each Office program has at least five toolbars, plus the two greatest-hits collections we've already talked about. Most of these buttons handle special jobs you don't do that often, like drawing or charting, or working with databases. When you first start up Office, they're out of sight.

You *could* put all seven toolbars on the screen at the same time, but you wouldn't like the results. Too many toolbars cover up the space you need to work in, as if you'd backed up a dump truck full of buttons and spilled them all over your PC's monitor.

You're better off popping up the other toolbars only when you need them. To show one of these hidden toolbars (like Excel's floating set of Drawing tools, shown in fig. 2.5), point to one of the toolbars you can see, and then click the right mouse button. On the list that pops up, click the name of the toolbar you want to show. When you're finished using the toolbar, right-click on it, then click its name on the shortcut menu to make it disappear.

Fig. 2.5

This is the Drawing toolbar from Excel, one of many extra toolbars that can come in handy for special jobs.

 Q&A   *I can't see any toolbars at all! Where did they go? How do I get them back?*

They're not gone, they're just hidden. When you can't see the regular toolbars, you can't pop up the Toolbars menu by clicking the right mouse button. Instead, pull down the <u>V</u>iew menu, and choose the <u>T</u>oolbars option. Check the Standard and Formatting boxes to bring back the default toolbars.

 TIP   **How can you tell whether a toolbar is hidden or visible?**
Look for a checkmark next to the toolbar's name on the shortcut menu.

What does that button do?

If you're not sure what the picture on that button is supposed to mean, just point the mouse at the button and leave the arrow there for a few seconds. After a brief pause, you'll see a little yellow label called a **ToolTip** (see fig. 2.6), that pops up to tell you, in English, what the button does.

Fig. 2.6

When you're not sure what a button's for, let the mouse pointer rest over it. After a few seconds, one of these ToolTips will pop up to tell you in plain English.

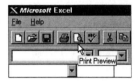

Other look-alike features

Besides menus and toolbars, there are a few other parts of the individual Office programs that look and act alike.

- **Properties sheets** include titles, author names, summary information, and descriptions of what's inside a document, worksheet, or presentation. You can add or update this information anytime you save a file, then use it to find files later.

- **Status bars** include tidbits like today's date and time, the current page number, and whether the CAPS LOCK button is on.

- **Rulers** help you position words, tabs, pictures, and margins exactly where you want them.

Have it your way: rearranging toolbars

For most people, the toolbars that come with Office are good enough just the way they are. But if they're not arranged exactly the way you prefer to work, give your toolbars a makeover. You can take buttons off a toolbar, add new ones, rearrange the buttons, even reposition each toolbar off the screen.

To delete a button. If you use a button so rarely that it's more of a distraction than a helper, take it off the toolbar. Point to the toolbar, click the right mouse button, and choose Customize from the shortcut menu. With the Customize dialog box on the screen, point to the button you want to zap, click the left mouse button and hold it down, then drag the button off the toolbar. As soon as you let go of the button, poof—it's gone!

To add a new button. Use the same technique to call up the Customize dialog box, but this time drag a button from the dialog box onto the toolbar. Buttons are arranged into categories, so you may need to hunt a bit to find the right one. If you're not sure what a button really does, click on it and you'll see a description.

To rearrange toolbar buttons. Pull up the Customize dialog box, then click and drag the buttons to the positions you prefer. To add a thin space between buttons, leave an imaginary gap between the buttons you want separated. To put two buttons *thisclosetogether*, drop one right onto the side of another.

When you're through adding and zapping buttons, press the Close button.

Help is Just a Mouse Click Away

● **In this chapter:**

- **Where can I find help?**

- **Sometimes the program will just do it for you**

- **I need help just for this problem**

- **Migrating from WordPerfect or Lotus 1-2-3**

- **You can go online to get help**

Learn to rely on the built-in Help features in Office 95, and you'll be on your way . . . . ⊘

Why is it that when you need help with your computer, you end up calling your neighbor's kid? The problem with that kid is, he presses five keys faster than David Copperfield can pull an elephant out of a hat, says an ancient curse, solves the problem, and disappears. Do you learn from the experience? No. Will you need his services again tomorrow? You bet.

Ready for a better system? Try the Help feature in Office 95. Whatever your problem, wherever you're stuck or baffled, Office can help you. And not just in one way, but in many different ways.

When in doubt, press F1

In Office 95 applications, just like anywhere else in Windows, you can press F1 to activate the **Help system**. That's always a good place to start. Help is a straightforward tool. Use it whenever you're trying to do something and for the life of you, you can't remember which keys to press or what the thing is called.

Help is **context-sensitive**; that means that you get Word help when you press F1 in Word, and the Excel Help screens pop up when you press F1 inside a worksheet. The Office-specific help (that is, not for individual applications, but for the whole suite) is accessible by clicking the Answer Wizard button on the Shortcut Bar.

Open any Office application and press F1. The Help menu you get is made up of four different tabs:

- Contents
- Index
- Find
- Answer Wizard

Now click on the Contents tab. The screen you see in figure 3.1 is a table of contents to all the Help screens in that program. Each book icon represents a category. Double-click on a book icon, and you'll get a listing of topics, or Help screens, available for that category.

Fig. 3.1

Double-click on one of the question-mark icons, and an informative screen will pop up.

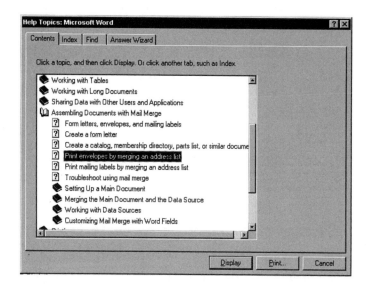

Do I just read these screens?

The Help screens are made up of more than just text. (If you want to read, you have this book, right?) The Help screens go one step further than any book can, because they're **interactive**. A book can tell you to press a key or select a menu, but an interactive Help screen can do it for you. Look at figure 3.2 for an example.

 Plain English, please!

An interactive program accepts input from the user and acts on it. For example, you can watch a screen saver of football players running and catching balls—that may be entertaining for a while, but it soon gets old, because you're passive. But when you start up a game that lets you play quarterback and score points by reacting to events on the screen, you're interacting with the program. And that's fun. 🙰🙰

Fig. 3.2
The buttons on this
screen are **hot**, or **live**.
Meaning, if you click
on them, they'll take
you to the task you're
trying to achieve.

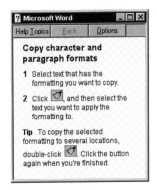

These categories aren't helping me

Want to print an envelope, and don't know under which category that
information is buried? You'll find a much more detailed screen under the
Index tab. The Help index works just like the index in the back of this
book—you find important topics listed in alphabetical order. Click on the
Index tab, and you'll switch to the screen you see in figure 3.3.

Type the first few characters of whatever you're looking for in the top box,
and your pointer will "jump" to the first match. If you type **e**, you'll go to the
beginning of the E entries, but typing **env** will take you to envelopes.

Fig. 3.3
Now that you've
highlighted the topic
you want to study,
double-click on it to
open its Help screen.

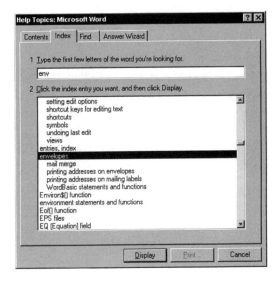

I don't *know* what it's called!

Sometimes you have a vague idea of what you want, but you have no idea what it's called, which makes it hard to search the Help file. The Index finds topics in the Help file, but that doesn't help you when you don't know exactly what you're looking for. For example, you want to take a pie chart in Excel and pull out one of the slices, to make it stand out. What's the thing called? Would you have guessed "Explosion"? Probably not. Pies and bombs don't usually have too much in common…

So press F1 from within Excel. Next click on the Find tab, because there you can search the entire contents of the Help file, not just topic titles. Here's how it works: In box 1, type the word or phrase you're searching for. For example, **slice**. You'll get a few topics in box 2, and a few more in box 3. Here's how that works: Every line in box 2 points to a few help topics, which are presented in box 3. Click on each line in box 2, until you see the topic you're looking for (or something pretty close) in box 3. As you see in figure 3.4, the road from slices to explosions is a three-step search.

Fig. 3.4

Click on each line in box 2 until you find what you're looking for, in box 3.

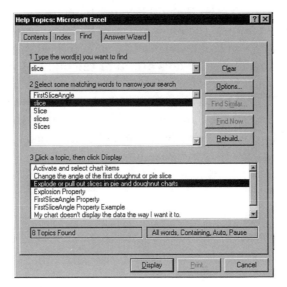

TIP   **If this is your first time using Find, you'll get a screen telling you** that you need to build an index. Click next to Minimize Database Size (Recommended), and then click Finish. In a few minutes, the Help program will gather all the words from the entire Help file and place them alphabetically, like a regular index.

To include every possible word or phrase in your Find index, select Maximize when you build the index. The process will take longer and will result in a larger file on your disk, but you'll leave no stone unturned.

How to ask in plain English

If these techniques don't feel natural to you, there's a good reason. People just don't go around asking things like, "slice?" "spell?"—and thanks to the **Answer Wizard** you don't have to. Click on the Answer Wizard tab. Now type a question in any form you're comfortable with. For example, **Where's Jimmy Hoffa?** (The question mark is optional.)

While Office can't solve the unsolved mysteries of the century, it'll help you with things it knows. The Answer Wizard looks for familiar words in the phrase you type in box 1, and displays appropriate topics. As you can see in figure 3.5, when I typed **Who's afraid of the big, bad wolf?**, I got six different topics. How's that possible? The Answer Wizard recognized the word "big" in the question, and searched for topics containing that word. Note that figure 3.5 is showing the Office Answer Wizard (from the Shortcut Bar), and I would have received different options had I typed that question in a Word or Excel Answer Wizard.

Fig. 3.5
This isn't Jeopardy. You can phrase your question in the form of an answer, and you'll still score some points.

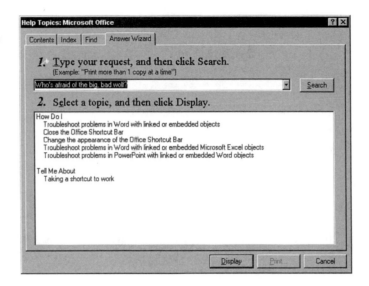

 TIP **Select the Options menu in any Help screen, select Keep Help on Top,** then click on On Top, and the Help screen will stay on top of any open application or window, so you can keep referring to it. To move it out of the way temporarily, minimize it.

Can I print these screens?

Have you heard of the Paperless Office? In this futuristic vision, office workers won't waste paper because all information will be shared electronically. It's going to happen real soon. Yeah, right. As soon as the Chicago Cubs win the World Series.

At least the online Help in Microsoft Office is one step in the right direction, because it's comprehensive enough to do away with the paper-based manuals. But sometimes you just need a printout of a Help screen—for example, when you know you're going to need the information again tomorrow or when you want to share it with a colleague. Within any Help screen, click on the Options menu, and select Print Topic (see fig. 3.6).

Fig. 3.6
The printed version of the Help screen is not as useful as the electronic version because it loses the links to other screens and all other interactive elements.

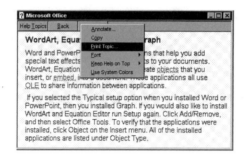

Can't I just get answers as I work?

No problem. Your wish is our command. The Office genie will just sit next to you as you work and point out things you can do better, and explain to you what you're looking at.

Think I'm kidding? It's the truth. Office has a few hidden treasures that act as your personal tutors, always available, always friendly and helpful.

The TipWizard

TipWizard is a new feature in Word and Excel. If you haven't activated the TipWizard box yet, do it now: Click on the light-bulb button on your toolbar (in either application), and you'll see the box shown in figure 3.7. This is where you get ongoing advice on whatever you're doing.

Don't understand the advice? Click on the Show Me button to the right, and the genie will just do it for you.

Fig. 3.7
Click the up or down arrows to the right of the TipWizard to scroll back and forth between tips you've seen already.

💡 3) To keep the proportions of an object constant, hold down SHIFT while dragging a corner.

What are all these buttons?

Not sure which button does what you're looking for? Move your pointer over it, and a tiny "Post-it" note, called a **ToolTip**, will pop up and identify each button for you (see fig. 3.8).

Fig. 3.8
ToolTips are available for any type of toolbar. Just move your pointer around to discover all the hidden labels.

Shortcut menus use all the right clicks

Most users can't memorize what's inside each menu. A common routine for many users is to move from menu to menu, drilling down to submenus, until they find the option they're looking for. But there's a better way.

One of the great hidden helpers in Office is your right mouse button. Give it a try. Right-click anywhere, on anything. What you get are **shortcut menus** specific to whatever you're doing, which is much more efficient than wandering about aimlessly between the different menus. Right-click inside a table, and you'll get table-specific commands. Right-click on a chart, and most of the things you can do with the chart will be at your fingertips. As you see in figure 3.9, you can even use the right-click as a mini-help utility, because sometimes you'll see a What's this? label, which leads you to a brief description of the object you're right-clicking on. The What's this? label isn't available everywhere, but right-clicking on any part of the screen is guaranteed to yield some buried treasures, so don't be bashful—do the right-click.

Fig. 3.9
Don't be shy! Right-click anywhere to get more information, specific menus, or help.

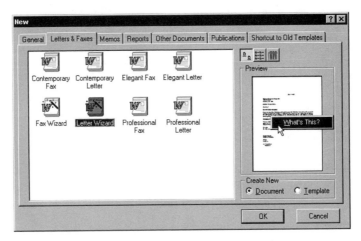

TIP **When I say "right-click," I'm talking about the clicking on the** secondary mouse button. To most people, the secondary button is the right one, but if you're a lefty and have configured the mouse so that the right button is your primary one, then replace any mention of right-click in this chapter with left-click. Don't know how to swap the buttons? From the Start menu, select Settings, Control Panel, and double-click on the Mouse icon.

The little Help that could

 In addition to the regular Help menu, there's a Help button on the Excel and Word toolbars that lets you point to almost anything on the screen and get additional information. Click on that button, and the pointer changes to the shape of an arrow and question mark. Now click on anything on the screen (buttons on the toolbar, text in a document, and so on), and you'll get a tiny pop-up note like the one in figure 3.10. This feature offers more detail than a standard tooltip without taking you out of the program and into a complicated help screen.

Fig. 3.10
What a difference a Help button makes! This is really just a tooltip on steroids.

TIP **In Word, click the Help button, then click on any part of a** document, and you'll get paragraph and font formatting information. This is a great tool when you can't figure out why your text doesn't look the way you want it to.

To turn off the Help pointer, just press the Esc key or click the Help button again.

Off to see the wizards

While you go through this book, you'll notice copious mentions of various **wizards**. Wizards don't just tell you how to do stuff. They do it for you, after you tell them exactly what you're trying to achieve. It's pretty much a fill-in-the-blanks process. See figure 3.11 for an example of a wizard.

Fig. 3.11
Remember, a good manager knows how to delegate. So tell the wizard to make you a good-looking table, and give yourself a promotion.

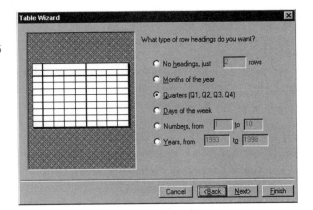

I'm used to WordPerfect and I keep hitting the old keys!

WordPerfect and Lotus 1-2-3 veterans (DOS versions) are familiar with some keystrokes, and press them without thinking. If that's the case, go to the Help menu in Word or Excel, select WordPerfect Help or Lotus 1-2-3 Help, respectively. The Lotus 1-2-3 Help screen will tell you which keys to press or which menus to select in Excel to achieve what you're trying to do.

WordPerfect users get an extra helper, which lets them press the same old navigation keys in Word. Choose Help, WordPerfect Help, click the Options button, and select Navigation keys for WordPerfect users from the dialog box you see in figure 3.12. Now you can press Home, up arrow to go to the top, just like you're used to.

Fig. 3.12
Here's a neat trick: Check the option Help for WordPerfect users, then click next to Demo. Now press any WordPerfect keystroke (for example, Ctrl+F10 to record a macro), and Word will show you how to achieve the task you're attempting.

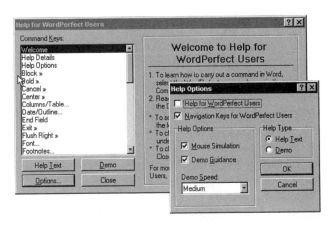

What about technical support?

Sometimes, even the help menus don't have the answer to your problem. So you call the support hotline mentioned in your documentation. And then the fun begins. Don't you just love being put on hold for hours, listening to somebody else's idea of relaxing music?

Well, you don't have to. If you own a modem and are a member of the Microsoft Network (MSN), you can go online to find help. Click on Help, The Microsoft Network, select the forum you want to go to from the dialog box you see in figure 3.13, and get help faster than you can spell Muzak.

Fig. 3.13
Can't wait for a consultant or the customer-support hotline? Go online to get quick answers to your questions.

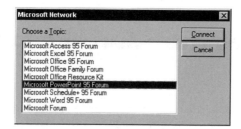

 TIP **MSN is Microsoft's own online service, but there's plenty of help** on other online services as well. If you're a member of CompuServe, America Online, or Prodigy, you can find answers to most of your questions there. And these answers are also widely available on the Internet and the World Wide Web, of course. As long as you know where to go and who to talk to.

Saving Your Work (and Finding It Again)

● **In this chapter:**

- How do I create a new file?

- Naming files

- Why did Windows beep when I gave my file a name?

- I want to work with the file I put away yesterday!

- Hey, where did that file go?

What happens if you don't bother organizing your files? Eventually, you'll spend so much time looking for stuff that you won't have time to get any real work done! . . . . ⊖

Imagine what a mess you'd have on your hands if you simply threw every scrap of paper in your office into the nearest file cabinet without bothering to label it. Junk mail, annual reports, confidential memos, paycheck stubs—just toss 'em into whichever drawer is open, and keep doing the same thing until the cabinet is full. Eventually you'll spend so much time looking for old pieces of paper that you won't have time to get any real work done.

If you're not careful, the same thing will happen inside your PC. Your computer lets you save your work, so you can pick up tomorrow where you left off today. You can even reuse old data files—changing a few words here and a few numbers there to do an hour's worth of work in just a few minutes.

But you can't reuse your work if you don't save it first. And you can't save any time if you can't find those saved files. In this chapter, I'll tell you secrets for saving files so you can find them *fast*.

How do I keep my files organized?

When we talk about a file, we're not referring to a sheet of paper inside a manila folder—we're talking about a data file stored on a disk inside your computer. Fortunately, these electronic files are as easy to organize as stacks of paper. To make it easier to find files fast, you can collect them in groups and store each group in its own folder.

What's a file?

As far as your computer is concerned, a **file** is just a collection of information. If it were a file on your desktop, it might contain a piece of paper or a Polaroid picture. On your computer, a file can hold almost anything—a memo, a report, a budget, or a bunch of charts and graphs. If you have a multimedia PC, a file can even hold a recording of Clint Eastwood saying "Go ahead, make my day."

Every file on your computer has a name, and your computer's operating system keeps track of details like how big it is and when you last saved it.

What's a folder?

What would happen if you took every piece of paper in your office and just threw it into a huge cardboard box? You'd never be able to find anything, right? So, to organize your paper files, you use file folders: one for sales reports; another for complaint letters; another for canceled checks.

In Windows, **folders** help you organize your computer files in much the same way. When you first look inside a drive, you see the **root folder**, a special folder that uses only a backslash (\) as its name—C:\, for example. Inside that folder, you can create other folders (and subfolders within those folders) to store groups of files. Most people have a folder called WINDOWS, for example, where all the operating system files are stored. If you used the default installation, your Office files wound up in a folder called MSOFFICE, which in turn contains subfolders for the individual pieces of Office.

 Plain English, please!

How is a **folder** different from a **directory**? It's not, really. If you've used DOS and Windows for a while, and you've gotten used to storing your files in directories, you'll find that folders work much the same way.

Like files, folders have names and creation dates. On my computer, I've created a folder called DATA, and inside that folder I've created a bunch of subfolders, like BOOKS and LETTERS and TRAVEL—one for each project or group of related files I'm working on.

Most of the time, you'll open and save files by browsing through folders until you find the right one, then clicking the file's name. But you can also use the full name of a file, including all the folders it's contained in, by typing backslashes to separate the folder names from one another. If you're the sort of person who likes to sort your socks by color, you can put folders inside of folders inside of still more folders until you wind up with a long file name that looks like this:

```
C:\DATA\LETTERS\COMPLAINTS FROM CUSTOMERS\1995\AUGUST\LETTER
FROM BOB SMITH.DOC
```

 TIP **If the full name of the file you want to open or save (including the** list of folders in its path) contains a space, you may have to enclose the entire name in quotation marks. If you don't, Windows and Office can get confused over where the name begins and ends.

Why should I care?

Organizing your working files probably doesn't seem like such a big deal now. But just wait till a year from now, when you've created a few hundred (or a few thousand!) working files with the Office programs. Even a basic filing system will make it a lot easier for you to sort through all those letters and reports later.

How do I create a new file?

If you use the Office Shortcut Bar, you can create a new document without even starting a program. Just click the Start a New Document button (the same command is also available at the top of your Start menu; just click the Start button and choose New Office Document). The next step is to choose one of the templates from the tabbed dialog box that appears (see fig. 4.1.) To begin work on a newsletter, for example, follow this series of steps:

Fig. 4.1
It doesn't matter what kind of document you want to create. Click the Start a New Document button on the Office Shortcut Bar to choose from this complete collection.

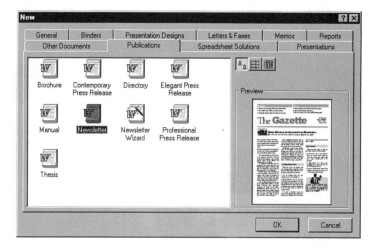

1 Click on the Publications tab to see which templates are available.

2 Click the Newsletter icon and check the Preview window at right to see what it looks like.

3 Click OK to create the new document, and open the program (Word, in this case) that you'll use to work with it.

Of course, that's not the only way to get to work on a new project. Whenever you start one of the Office programs, you begin with a brand new, squeaky-clean document (or spreadsheet or presentation). You don't need to do anything else to start working. You don't even need to worry about what to call it—Office gives it a generic name like Book1 or Document1 until you get around to giving it a more meaningful name.

 After you've started an Office program, it's easy to create more new documents. Just click on the top choice in the File menu: New. Or click the New button (the one that looks like a blank sheet of paper).

 TIP **If you're in too much of a hurry to reach for the mouse, you can** always press Ctrl+N to open a new document. This keyboard shortcut works the same in Word, Excel, and PowerPoint, and it's easy to remember: "N is for new."

What should I call my file?

Eventually, you'll want to save your file, usually on the hard disk inside your PC. To do so, you'll need to pick a file name. If you've used previous versions of DOS, Windows, and Office, you probably learned all the restrictions for naming files, and your hard disk is probably stuffed full of files with names like COMP0824.LTR and IMPTMEMO.DOC. Those files were limited to eight characters, plus a three-character extension, and there were all sorts of characters you couldn't use in a name, including periods and commas.

The good news about Windows 95 is that it allows you to create file names that are up to 250 characters long (although it's a good idea to keep them much shorter than that). So go ahead and call your new Word document My really important, highly confidential memo if you'd like. The rules for file naming are greatly relaxed, but there are still rules. If you break one, you'll see an error message like the one in figure 4.2.

Fig. 4.2
If you type a file name that breaks one of the Windows rules, you'll see an error message like this one.

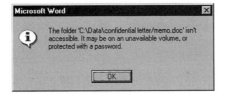

How do I know if my file name is legal?

A legal file name has to follow these rules:

- It can be as long as 250 characters —or it can be much shorter. You can create a one-character file name if you'd like.

- Every file name can also have an **extension**, usually three characters in length. The extension is whatever appears after the last period in a file name. Common extensions for Word documents, for example are DOC (short for *document*) and TXT (for *text*). Office programs create these extensions automatically, and Windows hides them from view most of the time.

- File names may use any of the letters from A to Z and numbers from 0 to 9.

- The following special characters are allowed in a file name: $ % ' - _ @ ~ ` ! ( ) ^ # & + , ; =.

- You can use brackets ([]), curly braces ({}), single quotation marks, apostrophes, and parentheses as parts of the name.

- You may *not* use a slash (/),backslash (\), colon (:), asterisk (*), question mark (?), or angle brackets (< >) as part of a file name.

- You *can* use periods within a file name. Windows will treat the last period in the name as the border between the file name and its extension.

Why should I worry about file extensions?

File extensions may seem a little silly—what can you do with three characters, after all?—but they actually serve a purpose. Windows uses a file's extension to create an **association** between your file and the program that created it. When you use these associations, you can automatically start up your program *and* load a document just by double-clicking on the file's name in a folder window or the Windows Explorer.

 TIP **If you just type the file name, without adding a period or an** extension, the Office programs will automatically add the right extension for you.

Enough already! I just want to save this file!

Once you've chosen a legal file name, the only remaining task is to tell Office to give that name to whatever you're working on right now.

Pull down the File menu and choose Save. You'll see a dialog box like the one in figure 4.3.

Choose the folder where you want the file to be stored.

Fig. 4.3

Whenever you want to save your work, you'll use a dialog box like this one.

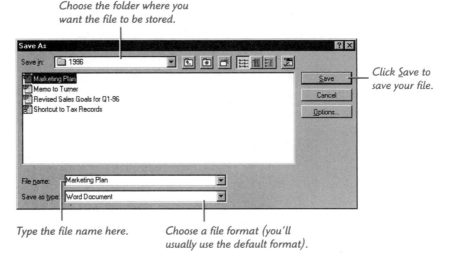

Click Save to save your file.

Type the file name here.

Choose a file format (you'll usually use the default format).

What are all those options for?

Whenever you save a file in Word or Excel, the dialog box includes a button called Options. Click that button, and you'll see *another* dialog box, like the one shown in figure 4.4.

These options let you do three useful things:

- If there's something important in your original file that you might want to look at again, use the **Always Create Backup** option to make a copy of the original version every time you open a file.

- Instead of tying a string around your finger, use the **Automatic Save** option to tell Word (but not Excel) to save your work every so often, because you tend to forget. Until you tell Word to stop, it will automatically save every document you work on, at whatever interval you choose.

Fig. 4.4

More decisions! If you press the <u>O</u>ptions button when you try to save a file in Word (top) or Excel (bottom), you can ask Office to handle your document with a little extra care.

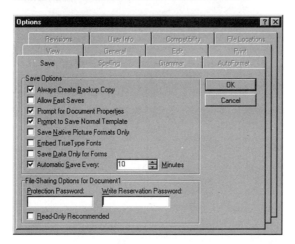

- Use the **Protection Password** option to lock up your document or worksheet tighter than James Bond's little black book. Unless someone else knows the secret word, he or she can't look at your Top Secret words or numbers.

CAUTION **If you forget your password, you can kiss your data goodbye.**
There's no way to figure out the password except by trying every possible combination of letters and numbers—and that would take hundreds of years! If your data's important, write down the password and put it in a safe place, like your wallet.

Should I add summary information to my files?

Summary information helps you figure out what's really inside a file. In the days of eight-character file names, it was essential: Draft presentation for Super Bowl promotion means a lot more than SBPROMO1.PPT, wouldn't you say?

Summary information is saved along with a document's properties. For some simple documents, you may choose not to use the Summary dialog boxes (see fig. 4.5), since a descriptive file name can tell you everything you need to know about the document. But for more complicated documents, the extra information found here—including keywords and categories—can help you track down a useful data file months or years after you last worked with it. And, of course, the Comments box can help other users understand what you were trying to do with a given document.

To see and edit the Summary information for a document, choose File, Properties. The remaining four tabs in the Properties dialog box let you see information about the file itself, its contents, statistics (like the number of slides in a presentation), and even custom fields you can create to track your own information. These dialog boxes work exactly the same in every Office program. Best of all, you can use these extra details—like keywords and comments—to search for a lost file later.

Fig. 4.5

What's inside that file? The Properties dialog box lets you add keywords and comments to your documents, presentations, and worksheets.

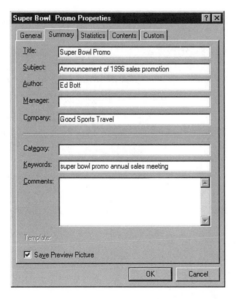

I want to work with a file I saved earlier

Opening a file is easy. Just pull down the File menu and choose Open, then pick the name of the file from the list in the File Open dialog box. If you can't find the file, you may need to switch to a different folder or choose a different file type.

Where did that file go?

Imagine how tired you'd get if every time you wanted to put a folder in a file cabinet, you had to go down to the lobby, switch to another elevator and travel up two floors, then walk all the way down a long hall. So Office tries to make things a little easier when you want to open or save a file. When you first installed Office, it created a folder called My Documents, on the same drive where your Office program files are stored. By default, whenever you use the File Open or File Save dialog boxes, Office highlights this folder.

Using the My Documents folder is a good idea: you'll be much more productive if you keep your files in a clean, well-organized place that you can get to in one or two steps. If you'd rather store your files elsewhere, it's relatively easy to set up the Office programs so they always take you to the folder in which you prefer to save your data files (and look for them again). If you use

How to be a highly effective Office user

Everyone has a junk drawer—that one catch-all drawer where you plop things that are too valuable to throw out.

If your entire work area is one big junk drawer, this section's not for you. But if you're even slightly organized, these tips can help you keep important items from landing in your computer's junk drawer.

- It's a bad idea to store your data files in the same place as your program files. Use the default My Documents folder if you'd like, or create a new folder and store all your working files there. You can name the folder Data, Documents, Files, Work, Projects, or whatever works for you.

- Use subfolders to keep groups of related documents organized. Inside your

Documents folder, for example, you might create subfolders for LETTERS and MEMOS. Or you might create separate folders for each person who uses the computer.

- Use a consistent file-naming strategy. It doesn't matter what you do, as long as it makes sense to you. For example, you might use the word Letter to start every file name that refers to a letter, so that Letter to Bob Smith, 8-24-95, sorts into a neat group with all your other letters.

- Begin a new document with its title. Word and Excel pick up the first line of your document and plop it into the Title section of the Summary box for you.

lots of subfolders to stay highly organized, you may need to move down the list of folders to find the right one, but at least you start in nearly the right place.

How do you tell each program where you prefer to store your data files? Unfortunately, this is one area where the three big Office programs definitely do not work alike.

Plain English, please!

When you first set up Office, it makes all sorts of assumptions about where you want to store files and how you want each program to look. These assumptions are called **defaults**. The default program folder, for example, is Msoffice, and the default size for the buttons on the Office Shortcut Bar is tiny. If you don't like one of these assumptions, change it. Whose default is it, anyway?

Setting up default file locations

Setting default file locations for Word, Excel, and PowerPoint involves three slightly different sets of steps to get the job done.

To tell **Word** where you prefer to store your data files, choose Tools, Options, and click on the File Locations tab. Click on the first line (the one that begins with the word Documents), and click on the Modify button (see fig. 4.6). Type in a folder name, or browse through the list of folders until you find the right one, then click OK.

Fig. 4.6

Use the Options dialog box to tell Word where you want it to take you first whenever you open or save a file.

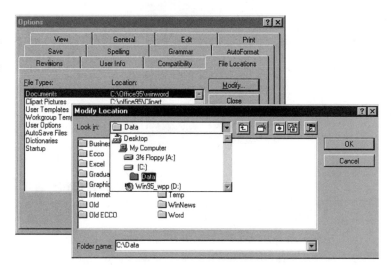

With **Excel**, you also click Tools, Options, but then you choose the General tab, as shown in figure 4.7. In the box labeled Default File Location, type the full DOS-style path of the folder where you want your data files. No browsing allowed, unfortunately.

Fig. 4.7

To set up a default file location for your Excel workbooks, you have to know the exact DOS-style name and path, complete with colons and slashes. Yeccch!

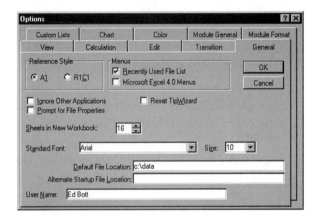

For **PowerPoint,** choose Tools, Options, and click on the Advanced tab; then enter the default location, as seen in figure 4.8. As you did in Excel, you'll have to enter the full path name—slashes, colons, and all—without browsing.

Fig. 4.8

To start in the same place whenever you open or save your PowerPoint files, you'll have to use this technical-looking dialog box.

How do I move or rename a file after I've created it?

Most of the Office programs have some simple (or not so simple) ways to work with files, but the easiest way is to open a folder window or the

Windows Explorer. From there, you can move a file, copy it, create a folder, rename a file, or erase it without any fuss.

I can't find a file! Where do I look?

All this fuss over saving and naming files has one goal: to help you find those files later, when you need to work with them again. A good filing and naming system can help you find most files, especially when you know exactly what you called the file and in which folder you stored it.

But what happens when your memory gets fuzzy? You know the file is on your hard disk, but it could be in any of a hundred folders. And even if you're lucky enough to find the right folder you still might have to sort through dozens of files to track down the right one. That's why all the Office applications include a set of file-finding tools that work like a quick, tireless, and thoroughly efficient file clerk.

How Office finds files

Whenever you want to open a file—even if you're not sure where the file is stored—you'll start with a File Open dialog box, like the one in figure 4.9. If you've used other Windows programs, you'll recognize this dialog box, but you'll also notice a few file-finding features found exclusively in Office programs.

Fig. 4.9

The File Open dialog box also helps you find files. In this example, Office will search for matching files no matter where they're stored on the hard disk.

When you first choose File, Open, you'll see a list of all the document files stored in the current folder. What happens if the file you're looking for isn't in that list? Well, you could begin clicking and scrolling through all the folders on your hard disk until you find it. But there's an easier way: give Office a few scraps of information to search for—part of the name, a date, or even a phrase you remember using—and let it look in one or more folders at the same time. After it's finished searching, it will display a complete list of all the files that match.

Using the Find feature is a four-step process:

1   **Tell Office what you're looking for.** Enter some part of the name you're looking for in the box labeled File name. You don't have to know the full name—if you type **Fin**, for example, the list will include files named Final report, 1996 financial projections, and Letter to Scott Finley. If you can't remember any of the name, click in the box labeled Text or property, and enter a word or phrase that you think may be in the document. If you know you last saved the document yesterday or last week, you can make a choice from the Last modified box as well.

 CAUTION   **When you ask Office to search for a file, it takes all the clues** together. So if you enter part of the name, *and* a word or phrase, *and* a date, Office will find only those files that match every single one of those criteria.

2   **Tell Office where to look.** See the Look in list in the upper left corner of the dialog box? That's the folder where Office will begin looking. To choose another folder or your entire hard disk, click the arrow at the right, and select the drive or folder from the drop-down list. By default, Office will search only in that location, but you can widen the search to include all the folders inside that folder. Just click the Commands and Settings button, then choose Search subfolders.

3   **Narrow the list, if necessary.** If you're sure you created the file using an Office program, make sure the appropriate document type (Word documents, Presentations, and so on) is selected in the box labeled Files of type. To expand the search, click the arrow at the right of this box and choose All Files from the drop-down list.

4 Tell Office to start searching. Click the button labeled Find Now, and Office will begin the search. You can monitor its progress in the status bar along the bottom of the dialog box. When it's finished, it will tell you in bold letters how many matching files it found, and all the matching files will appear in the Name box.

TIP **Before you click the Find Now button, look at what you're asking for.** If you give Office too little information, you won't get meaningful results. Asking it to find every file that contains the letters "the", for example, will probably turn up every file you've ever created. But avoid giving too much information as well: If you enter the word **finance**, for example, you won't find files that contain "financial." When a search doesn't work right, sometimes adding or subtracting a letter will work wonders.

OK, I found a bunch of files. Now what?

When Office has finished searching, it fills the Name box with all the files that match the settings you entered. You can open a document, peek at its contents or properties, give it a new name, even move or delete it—all from right inside the File Open dialog box.

- **To open one or more files,** select the entry or entries in the list, and click Open.

- **To see what's inside a file without opening it,** use the Preview pane. Click the Preview button, and select a file. As you move from file to file in the list, a thumbnail version of the document will appear to the right of its entry.

- **To see summary information about a file,** click the Properties button. Then, as you select different entries in the list at left, the document properties will appear in the Preview pane.

- **To manage files,** select the file name and right-click. The shortcut menus here work just as they do anywhere in Windows: you can inspect the file's name, size, and other properties. You can also move, copy, delete, or rename a file using this menu.

Fig. 4.10

Don't just stick with plain old List and Details view. The File Open dialog box lets you see what's inside a document as well.

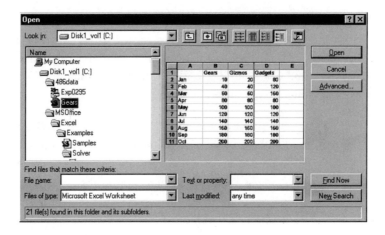

What does the Advanced button do?

The Find Now button is perfect for simple searches, and most of the time that will return the file you're looking for. If you want to become an Office expert, you can put together much more complicated searches with the help of the buttons and lists in the Advanced Find dialog box.

In a big department, for example, a sales manager can look on the network file server for all presentations created by her employees in the past week that contain the words "Super Bowl." Or, if hard disk space is tight and you're looking for files to clear off, you can look for Word documents that were created more than 6 months ago, or ones that are larger than 1M in size. Best of all, you can save these complicated searches and reuse them later.

When you click the Advanced button, you enter a territory that separates experts from casual Office users. For most of us, it isn't worth the hassle.

5

The Office Shortcut Bar Saves You Time

● In this chapter:

- **How to use the Office Shortcut Bar**

- **Start Office programs the easy way!**

- **How do I switch between programs?**

- **You can even start a document without wondering which program to open**

- **Add extra buttons to the Office Shortcut Bar**

There's a full-service information kiosk in the lobby of our Office building. The Office Shortcut Bar offers quick help when you need it . . . .

In the lobby of my office building, there's a security guard on duty 24 hours a day. Most of the time, people just walk right past his station; he might as well be invisible. So, is he useless? Not on your life.

That guard eyes everyone who walks in and out of the building. Whenever anyone asks, he gives directions. And even though the building directory is never up-to-date, he knows exactly where to find any person, place, or business in the whole building.

Microsoft Office has an equally unobtrusive caretaker that you'll see every time you start your computer. It's called the **Office Shortcut Bar**, and most of the time it sits quietly on the title bar of whatever program you're running right now. You may never use the Office Shortcut Bar. But its nice to know that it's there when you need it.

Q&A *The Office Shortcut Bar doesn't start when I start Windows. Can't I just load it automatically?*

Sure. The Office installation program should have done this, but something must have happened on your computer. Click the Start button and choose Settings, Taskbar. In the Taskbar Properties dialog box, click the Start Menu Programs tab and click Add. You could type directly into the Command line box, but there's a more foolproof way: Click the Browse button, then double-click the MSOffice folder, and then on the Office folder. Select the Msoffice icon and choose Open. Click Next. In the folder list, select Startup and click Next again. Give the shortcut a new name, if you'd like. Click the Finish button and you're done. The next time you start Windows, the Shortcut Bar should load automatically.

What is the Office Shortcut Bar?

If you've learned how to get around in Windows 95, you already know how to use the Start menu and Taskbar to start programs and switch from one window to another. The Office Shortcut Bar serves a slightly different function, with a selection of buttons that let you create new documents or open existing ones, add information to Schedule+, and get quick answers when you can't figure out how Office works. You can also add icons and folders to the Office Shortcut Bar, so that you can start programs, open windows, and switch between applications just by using these buttons.

You can arrange the Office Shortcut Bar to suit your style: By default, the shortcut bar tucks neatly into the title bar of any window that's maximized. You can make the buttons bigger, if you prefer, and line them up along any edge of the screen. Regardless of which configuration you choose, the row of buttons works just like the buttons in an elevator, taking you directly to the program you want to use next.

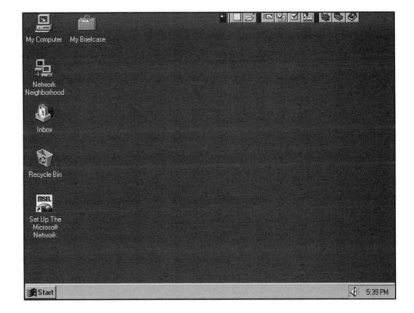

The following table shows the names of the various buttons.

Button	Name
	The Office Shortcut Bar Control Menu
	Start a New Document
	Open a Document
	Send a Message

continues

continued

Button	Name
	Make an Appointment
	Add a Task
	Add a Contact
	Getting Results Book
	Office Compatible
	Answer Wizard

By default, the Shortcut Bar sits right on the title bar of all your maximized applications. The buttons are exactly the same height as a typical title bar, so they blend right in, as you can see in figure 5.1. (If your program isn't maximized, the toolbar just sits in the upper right corner of the screen.)

Fig. 5.1

Don't worry if your toolbar doesn't look exactly like the one shown here. As we'll see later, it's easy to add buttons and move them around.

Tiny, aren't they?

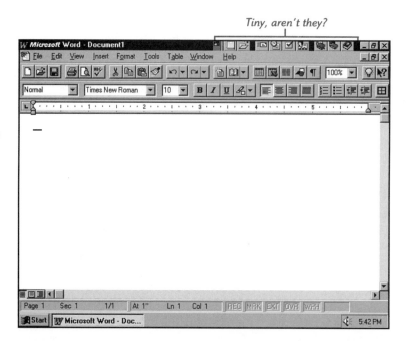

Get directions

The Office Answer Wizard offers everything from quick explanations of technical terms to detailed instructions on how to get the different tenants (Word, Excel, and PowerPoint, in particular) to work together better.

You can add buttons to the Office Shortcut Bar to help you start programs like Word and Excel, but we'll cover that later. First, let's go over the buttons Microsoft supplies for you.

With one exception, all these buttons work exactly as you would expect them to work. The one that's different? Look at the far left, where you should see a four-color square surrounded by gray. It looks like a button, but this is actually the title bar for the Office Shortcut Bar. Click the colorful part and the Microsoft Office Control menu appears; click in the gray and you can drag the toolbar around the screen. (The menu should look like the one in fig. 5.2.)

Fig. 5.2

Click the tiny four-color square at the far left of the Office Shortcut Bar to pull down this menu of Office services.

Ask the Answer Wizard

Anytime Office has you stumped, this should be the first place you turn. Click the Answer Wizard button on the far right of the toolbar to ask Office a question, like "How do I paste an Excel spreadsheet into a Word document?" No, the Answer Wizard can't tell you where your assistant hid your extra copy of that report, unless it's on your computer! For more details about what's inside Office Help, look in Chapter 3.

Get great results with the Getting Results Book

If you have a question about what Office can do rather than how to perform a specific task, the Office Shortcut Bar has another button that might help. The Getting Results Book (shown in fig. 5.3) offers help on a larger scale, with suggestions on how to use Office applications to create budgets, bids, and legal briefs. There's even a chapter on how to use this software in a home office. To use the Getting Results Book, you have to have your Office CD handy.

Fig. 5.3

Do you need specific advice for a law office? A home office? The Getting Results Book not only tells you how, it shows you how.

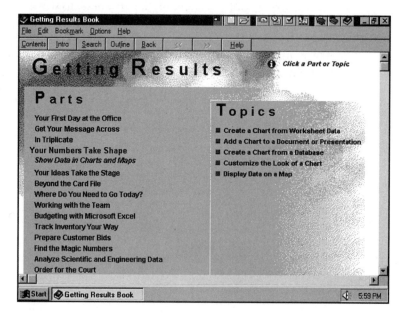

Office Compatible? What's that?

Advertising, pure and simple. Click the Office Compatible button and you can scroll through a list of programs designed to look like and work with your Office programs. You can read a description or see a demonstration. Here, too, you must have your Office CD handy to run the demos.

I want to get right to work...

Why go through the bother of opening a program and then starting a new document? Just click the Open a Document button to work on a document you've already saved in any Office program. Or click the Start a New Document button to see the dialog box in figure 5.4. It works just like its equivalents in Word, Excel, and PowerPoint.

 TIP **You'll also find the Open Office Document and New Office** Document buttons at the top of the Start menu.

Fig. 5.4
Click the Start a New Document button to pull up this consolidated dialog box that contains all the templates from all your Office programs.

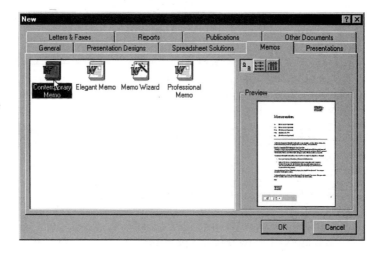

Choose a document type by clicking one of the tabs, then select any template and click OK. Office starts the program you need (or switches to its window if the program is already running), and presents you with a new document based on the template you selected.

If you need to open a specific document, you can do that directly from the Office Shortcut Bar as well. Just click the Open a Document button to see a dialog box like the one in figure 5.5. When you select a file and click Open, Office starts the program you need (or switches to it, if it's already running).

Will you use these buttons? If you spend your entire day in one program, probably not. A confirmed Word user, for example, would probably be more comfortable using Word's File Open dialog box. But if you shuffle data between all three of the big Office applications, you may appreciate the all-in-one-place nature of this collection.

Fig. 5.5
Think of it as a 3-in-1 dialog box. When you click the Open a Document button, Office prepares a list of all your data files, regardless of which program created them.

Click the Preview button if you want to see what's inside that document before you open it

Building your own Shortcut Bar

Like just about everything in Windows, the Office Shortcut Bar can be customized. If it doesn't work quite the way you want, you can change it with a few mouse clicks.

I can't read those tiny buttons!

For someone with the eyesight of a hawk, those little buttons are probably just fine. But if you find yourself squinting to see which icon is which, it's easy to make the buttons bigger.

Just choose <u>C</u>ustomize from the Office Control menu, and click the index tab labeled View. Pick <u>L</u>arge Buttons to make the buttons roughly twice as large. At that point, they won't fit very well in the title bar, so turn off the Auto <u>F</u>it into Title Bar area option; the toolbar readjusts to fill the entire top of the screen.

 TIP   If you choose <u>L</u>arge Buttons, the Office Shortcut Bar toolbar won't fit in your Windows title bars any more. When the toolbar is anchored to the edge of the screen, though, it uses up precious working space. To make the Office Shortcut Bar duck out of sight when you're not using it, open the Customize dialog box and deselect Auto H<u>i</u>de between uses check box. To make it reappear, slide the mouse up to the edge of the screen where the Shortcut Bar lives; slide the mouse back down to the document area and the toolbar disappears again.

Want more buttons? Here's how you get 'em

Would you rather skip the Start menu and use the Office Shortcut Bar to quickly open Office programs and switch between them? You can easily add buttons for Excel, Word, PowerPoint, Schedule+, and for other applications you regularly use. While you're at it, why not remove buttons you rarely use, like the Office Compatible demos? To change the toolbar, pull down the Office Control menu and choose <u>C</u>ustomize, then click the Buttons tab on the dialog box shown in figure 5.6.

Fig. 5.6
Keep an eye on the
Office Shortcut Bar as
you select and deselect
these boxes. You can
see the results (and
undo them, if needed)
as you work.

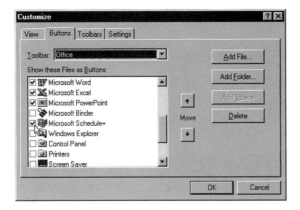

You can use any or all of these options to customize the Office toolbar.
When you're finished, the results might look like the toolbar shown in figure
5.7.

- **Add a Microsoft program...** Find the program's name in the scrolling
  list, then select the check box next to it.

- **Add a File...** Click the Add File button to add a new program or
  document to the toolbar. Browse through the dialog box, select a file,
  and choose Add.

- **Add a Folder...** Click the Add Folder button. Browse through the
  dialog box, select a folder, and choose Add.

- **Remove a button from the toolbar...** To make a button invisible
  without deleting it, just deselect the box to the left of the button's name;
  it remains on the list in case you decide to use it again.

- **Delete a button...** You can delete any button from the list by selecting
  it and clicking the Delete button. Deleting one of these shortcut buttons
  doesn't delete the file it's associated with.

Fig. 5.7
The Office Shortcut
Bar, after adding a few
buttons and removing
others.

I want to rearrange the buttons

Want to move a button to a new position on the toolbar? Just click the up and down arrows (above and below the word Move) on the Buttons tab of the Customize dialog box. To move the Answer Wizard button to the far left, for example, just click its name in the list, and then press the up arrow until its name is above the entry for Start a New Document.

Using the Shortcut Bar to move around

For some people, clicking the Start menu and searching through the cascading Programs menu is a colossal hassle. If that's you, try clicking the Shortcut Bar buttons instead—they're never more than a click away.

 TIP   **If you're not sure what a button does, let the mouse pointer sit on** top of the button for a few seconds. A ToolTip with the buttons full name will pop up.

- **To start an Office program...** Just click the button with the program's icon on it.

- **To switch from one program to another...** Click the same button you use to start the program. Office is smart enough to know that the program is already running, so it just switches you there.

- **To see the Microsoft Office menu...** Click the button at the far left of the toolbar.

Too many buttons? Add another toolbar

As I said at the beginning of this chapter, some people will never use the Office Shortcut Bar at all. But if you like the idea of one-button access to all your programs and data, you can organize all your files and folders on toolbars, turning this feature into a full-fledged control center for all of Windows. Here are your options:

- **Use the ready-made toolbars.** Right-click any empty space on the Shortcut Bar and select one or more of the predefined toolbars. There's one that contains all your non-Office programs, for example, and another that contains every icon on your desktop. Switch to another toolbar by clicking the icon next to its name.

- **Create new toolbars.** If that's not enough, you can also turn any folder into a toolbar, or create a new toolbar and fill it with shortcuts to your own files and folders. Pop up the Customize dialog box, switch to the Toolbars tab, and click <u>A</u>dd Toolbar.

Part II: Using Word

Creating a New Document

Word can't make you smarter or more creative, but it's filled with all sorts of clever tricks that can at least get you started . . . .

Any writer will tell you the hardest part of his job is coming up with that first sentence. Staring at a blank screen can be the most frustrating experience on earth—especially when the clock is ticking and the deadline is approaching.

Word can't make you smarter, or more creative, or more clever. After all, it's just a word processor. But it's filled with all sorts of clever tricks that can at least get you started. If you're really lucky, you'll run into one of the Word wizards, who can do part of your work for you.

And once you've broken through the creative logjam, Word can make your documents look downright irresistible, with colorful graphics, bold type, and eye-catching layouts that say, "Read me!"

We'll get to the business of making your words look good a little later. And eventually, you'll see how to use Word with the other Office programs to make powerful documents filled with facts and figures. But first, let's figure out how to get that first sentence onto the screen.

Where do I begin?

Ready, fire, aim! Oops—that's not the right order, is it? But some people are so anxious to get results that they forget the most important part of the writing process: What am I trying to say? Who's my audience?

Before you pick a paper size and start pounding on the keys, ask those two big questions first. Then answer these little questions:

- How formal do I need to be?

- Is there a wizard or a template that can get me started?

- Do I need to use any graphics or tables?

OK, I'm ready to start writing

Word assumes you want to get straight to work, but it has no idea what you want to do. So when you first start the program, it hands you the computer equivalent of a blank sheet of paper, as if to say, "Get to work!"

What's in a Word window?

The Word screen may look crowded, but everything you see is there for a reason—to help you turn words and pictures into great-looking, easy-to-read documents.

Standard toolbar
One-click buttons for the things you do all the time with Word, like open a file, save your work, or undo something you accidentally (oops!) did.

Title bar
The name of the program; if you've maximized your document, its name will show up here, too.

Office Shortcut Bar
Use these buttons to start up other Office programs (or jump to them, if they're already running).

Menu bar
All your options are lined up underneath these nine menu choices. Anytime you're not sure how to do something, look here.

Formatting toolbar
More buttons. This set lets you change the appearance of the words in your document.

Rulers
Help you see where your words and pictures will land on the printed page. If you find them distracting, you can always hide them.

Status bar
Look here for information about the current document ("What page is this?") and your computer ("What time does my computer think it is?").

Other toolbars (hidden)
Word has lots more toolbars, but they only pop up when you need them. Right-click any toolbar to see the list of available toolbars.

Document window
Every letter, memo, report, and brochure you work on gets its own window. You can open as many windows as you like. If the document is not maximized, it gets its own title bar, showing its file name.

Scroll bar
Use these sliders and arrows to see the parts of your document that don't fit in the window you're looking at now.

Now, that's fine if you just want to scribble out a bunch of notes. But most of the time, you're going to be producing some kind of familiar business document. A letter, maybe a memo, or even (if you're feeling particularly ambitious) a newsletter to send to all your customers or coworkers.

You'd be a lot more productive if you didn't have to start every one of those jobs from scratch, right? Well, you don't have to. Word includes more than 25 ready-made documents to get you started. They're called **templates**, and if you use them regularly, you can save a few minutes—or even a few hours—on each document you create.

Do-it-yourself with templates

Have you ever tried to create a work of art using a paint-by-the-numbers kit? You smear a little blue in the spots labeled "B," some red in the spots marked with an "R," and before you know it, you're looking at a pleasant little seascape.

Word templates work the same way. Instead of starting with a blank sheet of paper, Word creates each new document by copying a blueprint that contains text and graphics, lines and boxes, fancy fonts, and maybe even colors. As you replace the template's text and graphics with your own words and pictures, your letter or report begins to take shape—a lot faster than if you had to do it all.

To see what templates are available, choose File, New from the main menu. Word displays the New dialog box. Click a tab to look at the templates available in that category. For example, fig. 6.1 displays the templates under the Other Document tab.

Fig. 6.1

Pick a template, any template. When you choose File, New, Word pops up a dialog box displaying predefined templates so you can get a running start with your new document.

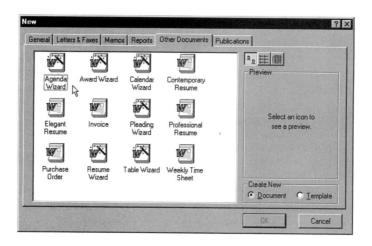

 **CAUTION**   **Templates are stored in special files, not the standard Word-type** files. Be extremely careful with these files! If you open the original template file by mistake (instead of creating a new document based on it), any changes you make will be saved in the template. From then on, every document you create using that template will include all those changes, whether you want them or not.

Chances are, there's a Word template for most of the documents you produce every day. You can make your own templates, too, by tinkering with one of the built-in templates or by starting from scratch.

Here are some of the most useful built-in templates:

- **Take care of business.** Use the Weekly Time Sheet or Purchase Order templates under the Other Documents tab.

- **Write letters and memos.** Take your choice of several different formats for each (Contemporary Memo, Elegant Memo, and Professional Memo, for example). These templates are under the Letters and Faxes tab.

- **Spread the news.** Try the Contemporary Press Release or Newsletter templates under the Publications tab.

 TIP   **Press Ctrl+N (or click the New button) to create a new** document based on the Normal template, which looks just like a blank sheet of paper. Choose File, New from the pull-down menus if you want to use a different template. Choosing the Blank Document template under the General tab is the same as pressing Ctrl+N.

Let Word do the work with wizards

For some jobs, even filling in the blanks on a paint-by-the-numbers canvas is too much work. You'll get better results if you hire a professional painter to do the work for you. Word has a few of those experts for hire: they're called **wizards**.

The concept behind a wizard is simple. He asks you some questions, and then, based on your answers, he does all the work, leaving you with a filled-in document. The first time you use a wizard, he might ask a lot of questions, filling in things like your name and address. Most wizards have a good memory, though, and the next time you use them they'll skip those questions and just ask those that pertain to the job at hand.

Here's just a sampling of what Word's wizards can do for you:

- **Letter Wizard.** Gets you started with business and personal letters, and even includes 15 "canned" letters you can use in various situations, like one you can use to demand payment for a bounced check.

- **Memo Wizard.** Helps you put together a complete interoffice memo using one of three different looks and including any information you specify.

- **Newsletter Wizard.** Helps you make like William Randolph Hearst, turning out professional-looking publishing projects with almost no work (see fig. 6.2).

Fig. 6.2
Wizards, like this one for making professional-looking newsletters, ask you a bunch of questions and then do your work for you. (Don't you wish there was a Do the Laundry Wizard?)

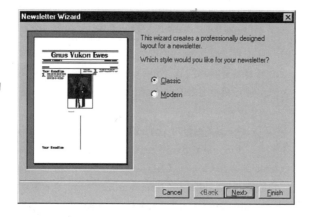

I just want to start writing

Enough already! After all, the whole point of a word processor is to help you write. So let's start writing.

On a fresh document

Most of the time, you'll want to pick an appropriate spot on your document to start working. If you used the Blank Document (Normal) template, you don't have a choice: you just start at the top. If you used another template, click where you want your words to appear, and then start typing.

TIP   *Don't* hit the Enter key when you come to the end of a line. Word knows you've run out of room and will wrap your words automatically to the next line. Press the Enter key only when you want to start a new paragraph.

Using a template

Some templates, like the Invoice template shown in figure 6.3, contain "generic" text that you have to replace before you can use the document. You don't want your customers making their checks payable to "Company Name," do you?

Fig. 6.3

Templates help you get started. Use the mouse to highlight the "generic" text—it will disappear as soon as you start typing.

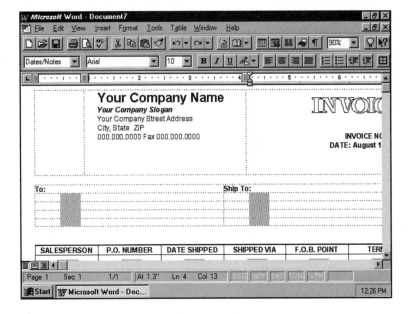

Fortunately, Word makes it easy to replace text. Just use the mouse to select the words you want to replace, and then start typing. As soon as you type the first letter, the template text will vanish and is replaced by your new, more relevant words.

If you try to select a word but don't seem to succeed (or even see a cursor), that's a sign that the document is **protected** so that you don't overwrite anything crucial by mistake. To unprotect the document, select Tools, Unprotect Document, and replace the generic text with your own information. When you're done, select Tools, Protect Document to lock your changes in place. Once you've customized your company name, address, and phone, re-save the template so you don't need to go through that anymore. To save a document as a template, select <u>F</u>ile, Save <u>A</u>s, click the down arrow next to Save as <u>T</u>ype, and select the option Document Template (DOT).

As for filling-in the blanks, Word supplies "Click Here" boxes, into which you type new information. After each entry, press the down arrow or the Tab key to "jump" to the next box.

CAUTION   **When you first start Word, you enter text in Insert mode—that is,** everything you type "pushes" the text that's already there out of the way. If you hit the Insert key by accident, you'll switch into Overtype mode, where every letter you type gobbles up the one to the right of the insertion point. (If the OVR indicator on the status bar is black instead of gray, you're in Overtype mode.)

If you press the Insert key by accident, click the Undo button on the Standard toolbar to get your old text back.

What happens when I get to the end of the page?

When you're writing, you probably won't even notice you've reached the end of a page. That's OK. Just as Word knows when you've come to the end of a line, it also knows when a page is full and a new page needs to begin. (We'll cover this topic in more detail in Chapter 8.)

Deleting text

OK, so maybe every word you write isn't deathless prose. If you want to get rid of some of those words you just typed, Word gives you lots of different ways to do it:

- (+Backspace) zaps the character to the left.
- (Del) zaps the character to the right.
- (Ctrl)+(+Backspace) cuts the word to the left.
- (Ctrl)+(Del) cuts the word to the right.
- (Ctrl)+(X) cuts whatever's highlighted and puts it on the Clipboard.

For more information about how the Windows Clipboard works, see Chapter 20.

Moving around in a document

Are you a fluid writer? Do you get caught up in the rhythm of it all and suddenly find yourself on page 20, with no idea what you wrote before page 5? Word has all sorts of shortcuts for moving around in a document.

What's normal?

Word makes a bunch of assumptions whenever you start a new document. For example, it assumes that you speak English, so it uses the U.S. version of the built-in dictionary and thesaurus (we'll get to them in Chapter 9). It also assumes that you use standard 8 1/2" × 11" paper most of the time, so every new document is formatted to go on plain old letter paper.

These built-in choices, taken together, make up the default document. They're stored in a special document template called Normal.

Here's what's inside Normal:

- A default typeface and size for the words in your document. Unless you change the default typeface, every Normal document you create starts out in 10 point Times New Roman.

- A default paper size and orientation. In the United States, you get letter-sized paper in portrait mode.

- Standard margins (1 1/4 inches on each side; one inch on the top and bottom) and single line spacing.

- All the toolbars, rulers, and styles you see on the screen. (Yes, you can change them, and when you do, the changes are stored in a template.)

- Special tricks like **macros** (miniature programs written in a special language called WordBasic) and custom menus.

Why does this stuff matter? Well, if you decide that you'd really like your Normal documents to start out in a larger typeface, or you want different top and bottom margins, you'll have to change the Normal template. Fortunately, that's pretty easy to do. The Format Font and File Page Setup dialog boxes both have buttons labeled Default. After you've reset the fonts and margins to your liking, push the Default button to tell Word that you want your preferences saved in Normal.

Now, whenever you start up a new document based on the Normal template, you'll get what *you* want.

The easy way, of course, is just to point the mouse at one of the scroll bars, and slide up or down until you hit the spot you want to see. But the keyboard shortcuts are more precise:

- Home and End move to the beginning and end of the line the insertion point is on right now.

- PgUp and PgDn move up and down one window.

- Ctrl+Home and Ctrl+End skip to the very top and very bottom of the document.

- ⬆Shift+F5 is one of the coolest Word shortcut keys of all. It remembers the last three places you did something, and jumps to those three places, one after another. This trick comes in very handy if you've scrolled through a long document and you want to jump back to where you started.

- **Go To** (Ctrl+G) lets you tell Word to hop to a specific page number or to other predefined areas in your document. You can also pop up the Go To dialog box shown in figure 6.4 by double-clicking the status bar.

Fig. 6.4

The fast way to jump around in a big document. Double-click the page numbers in the status bar to pop up this Go To box.

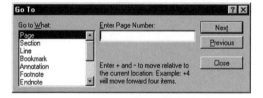

How do I adjust the margins?

You can leave extra room on either side, the top, or the bottom of your page, which is useful if you want to add comments in the right margin, for example. You can also trim the margins to pack more words on the page, although that option may sacrifice readability. You can't set the margins to zero, though, because every printer has an unprintable area that Windows won't let you use.

To adjust the margins, choose File, Page Setup, and then click the Margins tab (see fig. 6.5). You can set margins for all four edges, as well as the gutter—that's the inside of the page when you're printing on both sides of the paper. You can also change margins and even paper size in the middle of a document. Just pick This Point Forward from the drop-down list labeled Apply To.

Fig. 6.5

Click the Margins tab in the Page Setup dialog box to adjust the amount of white space around your pages.

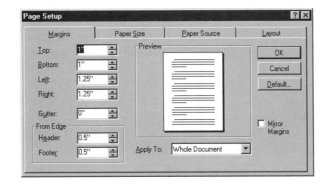

How do I change paper size?

Most of the time, you'll want to print your work on plain letter paper. But what happens when you want to use legal-size paper? Or when you want to work with your text going from side to side along the wide edge of the paper? That's where Word's Page Setup dialog box comes in handy.

Choose File, Page Setup to pop up the dialog box, then choose the Paper Size tab, as shown in figure 6.6.

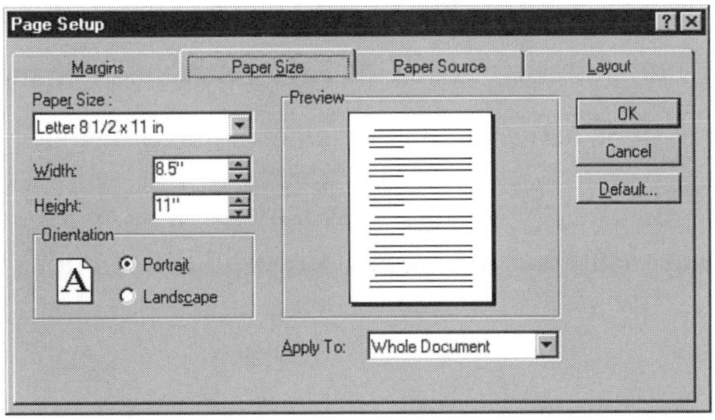

Fig. 6.6

Choose File, Page Setup to change paper sizes and switch from Portrait (tall) to Landscape (wide) orientation.

Using the Page Setup dialog box, you can do just about anything that has to do with your paper:

- Under the <u>M</u>argins tab, change the amount of white space (the **margins**) on the top, bottom, left, and right edges of the paper.

- Under the Paper <u>S</u>ize tab, switch to legal-size paper or the European-standard A4 format, or set up Word to use a special paper size. (You want to print on Christmas card stock, 5" × 8"? Word can handle it.)

- Under the <u>P</u>aper Source tab, tell Word to use a different tray in your laser printer. This comes in handy if you have letterhead in one tray and plain paper in another.

Saving a new document

If you've been writing for more than 20 minutes, it's time to take a break. For one thing, it'll keep your shoulders from cramping up and your wrists from developing repetitive-stress disorders. For another, it'll give you a chance to save the work you've done so far.

 CAUTION **Make it a habit to save your work regularly. There's no feeling** quite as sickening as the one you get when the power fails and your PC dies after you've been working for hours without saving. Remember: until you use the <u>S</u>ave command, your work can disappear at a moment's notice!

Saving your Word document is a simple, two-step process:

1 Press Ctrl+S (or click the Save button on the standard toolbar).

2 Enter a name in the File <u>N</u>ame text box, and click OK.

For extra security, you can instruct Word to save your file for you automatically at an interval you specify. Choose <u>T</u>ools, <u>O</u>ptions from the main menu and click the Save tab. Choose Automatic Save Every: and type a number in the Minutes box. Five to ten minutes is a good interval; anything less than that and Word's slight delay as it saves will become annoying.

Automatic save places your document in a temporary file. Changes you make to the document don't become permanent until you actually save it to its file name.

 TIP **Word saves the file in the My Documents folder by default, but** you can specify any folder you want to keep your documents together. Just select Tools, Options, and click the File Locations tab. Now click the Documents line and click the Modify button to find another folder in which to put your documents. This setting will now become your default.

Summary info

When you save a document, you can also include summary information such as the title, subject, author, and category. You can even add keywords and comments. This information will help you later identify what's in the document, and it will also help you find the document two years from now when you've forgotten its name and where it is on your hard drive.

To fill out the summary information, choose File, Properties from the main menu and choose the Summary tab in the Document Properties dialog box (see fig. 6.7). Enter as much information as you want and choose the OK button.

You can instruct Word to display the Summary box automatically when you save a file. Choose Tools, Options from the main menu and click the Save tab in the Options dialog box. Choose the Prompt for Document Properties check box under the Save Options heading.

Fig. 6.7
Don't forget to fill
in this Summary box.
It might seem like a
hassle now, but you'll
thank yourself later,
when you're trying to
pull this one document
out of the hundreds on
your hard drive.

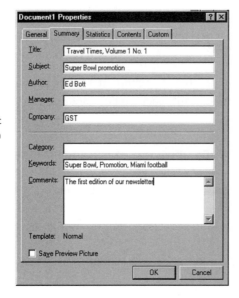

There. You're done. That wasn't so hard, was it?

7

Opening and Editing Documents

● In this chapter:

● **What's the best way to open a document?**

● **What's the best view for writing? For editing? For organizing my thoughts?**

● **How to move text from one place to another without hassle**

● **Using Word to replace one word with another**

● **Oops! Undoing mistakes**

Word makes it easy to add a new thought, change a word, replace one phrase with another, and move sentences around by dragging them with the mouse .... ➤

Great works of art take time. First, you sketch out the big picture with broad strokes. Then you take a finer brush and fill in the details. Finally, you go over the entire canvas with a magnifying glass, touching up those tiny flaws and making every square inch as close to perfect as you can get it.

If that sounds like a lot of work, you're right. Hey—do you think Rembrandt painted his masterpieces in an afternoon?

Really great writing takes time, too. If you've worked on a big report, you know that nothing ever gets done in one easy session. A paint-by-the-numbers Word template can get you started fast, but then you'll need all your concentration to find just the right thoughts and just the right words. And you'll probably want to move those words around so your message hits its audience with as much impact as possible.

There's no Writer's Block Wizard yet. Word can't do much to help you get your first thoughts on the screen. But once you've gotten started, Word makes it easy to add a new thought, change a word, replace one phrase with another, and move sentences and paragraphs around just by dragging them with the mouse.

Opening a document

What do you do when you want to pick up where you left off yesterday? (Or, for that matter, last month?) First, you have to find the file you were working on. Um, you *did* save it, didn't you?

I want to pick up where I left off yesterday

When you leave the office every night, you probably straighten up your desk. (Well, just a little, right?) At the very least, you take the papers you didn't finish today and stack them up in a neat pile so you can get right to work when you get in tomorrow morning.

You can do the same with the Word files you work on every day. Just look at the bottom of Word's File menu for a list of the files you worked on most recently (see fig. 7.1 for an example). To open any of the files on the list, just click the file's name.

Fig. 7.1

This one's a real time-saver: Word keeps track of the files you worked on most recently. You can reopen any of one just by clicking its name in the menu or typing the corresponding number.

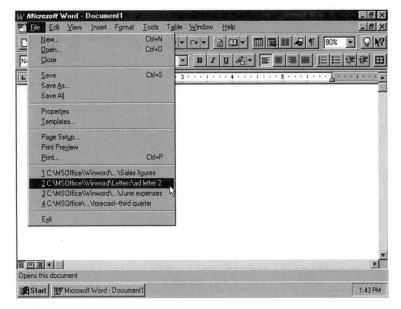

TIP By default, Word keeps track of the four files you worked on most recently, but you can boost that number to as many as nine. Choose Tools, Options, and click the General tab. Make sure there's a check mark in the box to the left of the Recently Used Files List entry, and use the little arrows to adjust the number in the box to the right. Or type a new number (up to 9) over it.

I know the file's out there *somewhere*

You say your boss *finally* got around to reviewing the first draft you wrote two weeks ago, and now you have to make a lot of little changes and a few big ones? No problem. As long as you can remember roughly what you named your document and where you stored it, it's easy to find it again. Word's document files are usually stored in the My Documents folder. You may have created additional folders or saved your files elsewhere. To find and open a file, just follow these steps:

1 Choose File, Open (or click the Open button) to display the Open dialog box shown in figure 7.2.

Fig. 7.2
The Open dialog box lets you choose the file you want to work with, no matter where it's located.

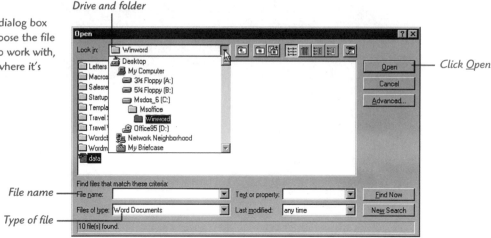

Drive and folder

File name

Type of file

Click Open

2 Tell Word which **drive** you want to look on. Most of the time, this will be drive C (the default). To look on your network drive or a floppy disk, click the little arrow beside the Look In box, and choose from the drop-down list.

3 Tell Word which **folder** to look in by double-clicking the folder icon. If you can't find the right folder, double-click the folder icon at the top of the list, and work your way down, one level at a time.

4 Tell Word what **type of file** to look for. Most of the time, it assumes you'll want to look for files that are Word documents. If your file is of another type, choose All Files from the Files of Type list.

5 Select a file name. You have plenty of ways to do this step, depending on whether you prefer typing or clicking. You can enter the **file name** in the File Name text box and press the Enter key, or select the icon and click Open, or double-click the file name or its icon in the list of files.

Word will open the file, and you're ready to start working.

I can't remember what that file's called

If you haven't the foggiest notion what you named a file or where you stashed it on your computer's hard disk, don't worry. Just give Word some scraps of information about the file and let it go to work. It can sniff through your PC with as much determination as a bloodhound and bring back everything that matches.

Hang onto the bloodhound's leash and follow these steps to find your missing file:

1 Choose File, Open. In the toolbar of the Open dialog box, click the Preview button, as shown in figure 7.3.

Fig. 7.3

Use Word's preview feature to look at a document before you open it. You can peek inside Word, Excel, and other types of files from here.

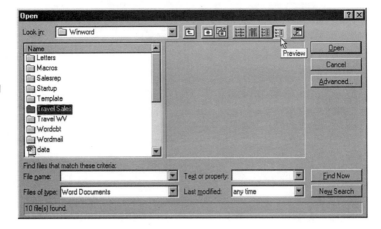

2 Select the folder and document you want to view. Word displays the beginning of the document in the preview window on the right, as shown in figure 7.4. You can scroll through the document to see more.

Fig. 7.4

Look at the contents of the document before you open the file.

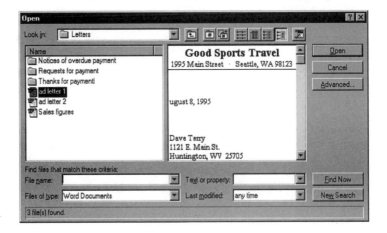

3 Still can't find the file? You can use the Find feature in the Open dialog box if you know a phrase or word specific to the file, such as a name or place. In the Te**x**t or Property text box, enter the name or phrase. Choose **F**ind Now. Word searches for the file and displays all files containing the text, as shown in figure 7.5.

Fig. 7.5

As long as you can remember a distinctive phrase or name in your document, Word can find it for you.

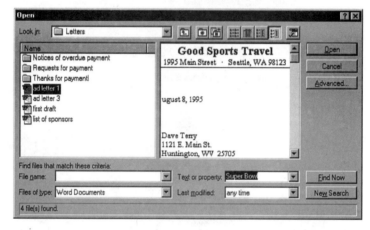

4 When you finally track down the document you've been searching for, open it by double-clicking the file name.

I use Word, but my boss uses WordPerfect

Word uses its own special language to store details about your document. WordPerfect (the other popular word processor in many offices) uses a completely different language. Fortunately, Word has a crew of translators on hand to make sure your WordPerfect documents will look OK. If Word recognizes the WordPerfect document, it will just open it.

Q&A *Sometimes my Word documents lose a few details in the translation to WordPerfect. What can I do?*

If you regularly exchange documents with a colleague who uses WordPerfect, choose **F**ile, Save **A**s, and pick WordPerfect from the Save As Type list. Make sure the version of WordPerfect you choose matches the version your colleague uses.

Finding the right point of view

Every great artist knows how to get the ideal perspective on a landscape. Just hold out your thumb at arm's length, then close one eye, squint, and look real serious. Fortunately, it's a lot easier to find the right point of view when you're working with Word. It all depends on what you're trying to do. Are you writing? Trying to make your document look great? Organizing your thoughts? Word has a special view for each step in the writing process, as described in the following sections.

TIP All the viewing options in Word are available on the Yiew menu. You can also switch between Normal, Page Layout, and Outline views using the three buttons on the status bar (found in the lower left corner of the screen).

I just want to type

Normal view is perfect for those times when you just want to get the words out of your head and you aren't ready to think about how they'll look when they're printed. Figure 7.6 shows this plain-Jane version of the Word screen.

Fig. 7.6
Normal view is the one people use most of the time. You get to see all the words and use the entire screen without any wasted space. Perfect for quickly typing a first draft.

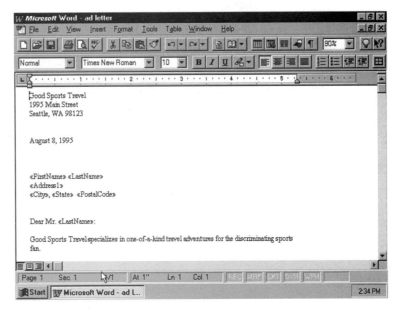

I want to see *exactly* what each page will look like

That's what **Page Layout view** is for. You can see how much space you have on each side of the page. As you scroll through your document, you can even see the edges at the top and bottom of each page. If you've put page numbers or a title on the page, those pieces will show up here, too. This view is particularly good for ensuring that you have everything on the page—headers, footers, and all—in exactly the right spot, *before* you print it (see fig. 7.7).

Fig. 7.7

Use Page Layout view to see exactly what your final printed pages will look like. You can see the edges of the "paper," and you get an extra vertical ruler to help you find your place on the page.

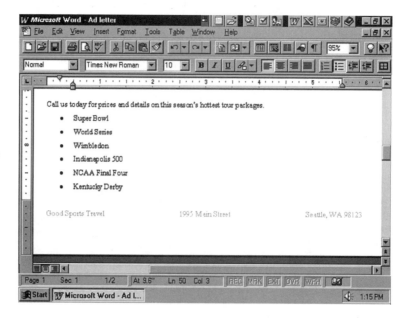

I need to organize my thoughts first

Outline view is perfect for making sure your thoughts are well organized. Use this view to shrink your document to just its main points and to see details under each main heading, then switch to Normal or Page Layout view to write and edit. The Outlining toolbar helps you collapse and expand each section (see fig. 7.8).

Fig. 7.8

Outline view lets you look at how your document is put together. Use the Outlining toolbar to collapse and expand each chunk of heading-and-text with just one click.

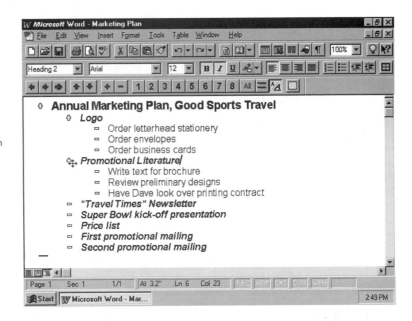

 TIP It's incredibly easy to edit your work in Outline view. Want to move a section, along with all of its subsections? Just touch the little box in front of the section with your pointer until the pointer changes to a four-headed arrow. Click and hold down the mouse button to select the section, then drag the section to its new location. For example, in figure 7.8, dragging the cross in front of Promotional Literature to the end of the outline moves the three subsections as well.

Arrrgghh! This screen is too cluttered!

For anyone who finds all those toolbars and rulers too distracting, there's Full Screen view, which you activate by selecting View, Full Screen (see fig. 7.9). In this view, all you typically see is the page and one lonely icon that you click to switch back to the regular Word screen. If you've displayed the MS Office toolbar, it too will remain on-screen.

 TIP What happens to the menus when you're in Full Screen view? Nothing. They're still there, hidden just above the upper edge of the screen. You can still use them, as long as you know the first letter of the menu you want to use. So if you want to print the page you're working on, you can press Alt+F to bring down the File menu. Once it's visible, use the arrow keys to move left and right and see all the other menus, too.

Fig. 7.9

Bye-bye, menus and
toolbars. Choose Full
Screen view if you
want to work with as
few distractions as
possible.

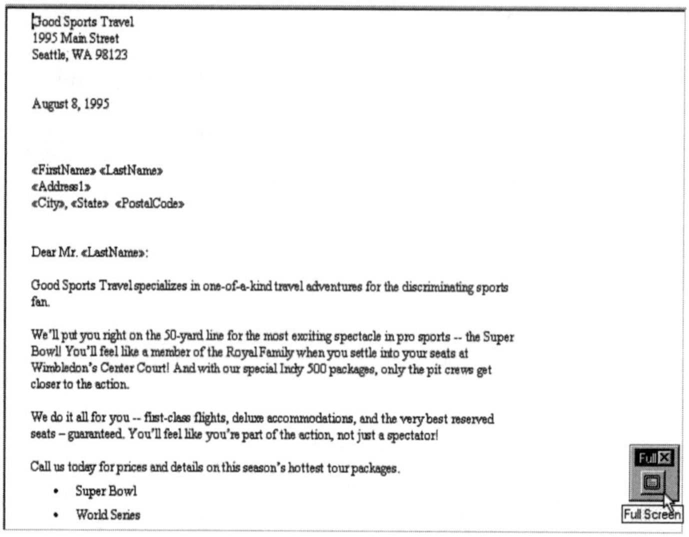

Good Sports Travel
1995 Main Street
Seattle, WA 98123

August 8, 1995

«FirstName» «LastName»
«Address1»
«City», «State» «PostalCode»

Dear Mr. «LastName»:

Good Sports Travel specializes in one-of-a-kind travel adventures for the discriminating sports
fan.

We'll put you right on the 50-yard line for the most exciting spectacle in pro sports -- the Super
Bowl! You'll feel like a member of the Royal Family when you settle into your seats at
Wimbledon's Center Court! And with our special Indy 500 packages, only the pit crews get
closer to the action.

We do it all for you -- first-class flights, deluxe accommodations, and the very best reserved
seats -- guaranteed. You'll feel like you're part of the action, not just a spectator!

Call us today for prices and details on this season's hottest tour packages.

- Super Bowl
- World Series

What about Master Document view?

If you have a bunch of small documents that you want to tie into one large
one, you might be tempted to try Master Document view, by selecting View,
Master Document. It looks similar to Outline view but with an extra toolbar
you can use to create, insert, and remove subdocuments. Master Document
view is very complicated to get the hang of and it doesn't always work the
way it's supposed to; don't use it unless you have a lot of time to figure it
out.

If you must use it, be sure you have backup copies of all your work. And
don't say I didn't warn you…

I want to make the text look a little bigger

What do you do if the words on the screen are a little too small to read
easily? Just get a little closer. If you've ever used a camera with a zoom lens,
you know exactly how Word's **Zoom** feature works. Choose View, Zoom to
display the Zoom dialog box shown in figure 7.10.

Click 200% for an extreme close-up. Try Whole Page to fit the entire page on
the screen. You can click the little arrows next to the Percent box, or type a
number in the box, to try out any zoom level between 10 and 200 percent.
Watch the preview screen to get an idea of how your selection affects the

view. Choose <u>P</u>age Width to expand the text so it's as large as possible without running off the edge of the screen.

Fig. 7.10
Zoom! Choose <u>V</u>iew, <u>Z</u>oom to get a closer look at your work.

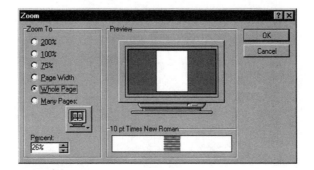

TIP **The Zoom control on the Standard toolbar lets you** quickly switch among different magnification levels.

Selecting text

The hardest part of editing your work is just moving words around. Before you can rearrange your text, you usually have to **select** it. It's easiest to use the mouse, but if you're comfortable with the keyboard, there are some shortcuts there, too.

With the mouse

Word has built-in mouse shortcuts that let you select chunks of text with simple mouse movements.

To select...	Do this...
A word	Point to the word and double-click.
A sentence	Hold down the Ctrl key, point to the sentence, and click.
A paragraph	Move the mouse pointer to the left margin until it turns into an arrow, position it alongside the paragraph, and double-click.
A whole document	Move the mouse pointer to the left margin until it turns into an arrow, and then triple-click.

Bugs! (It's not you, it's the program!)

"2+2=5?"

Fifty years ago, at the dawn of the Information Age, a computer that could barely add 2+2 took up more space than a two-bedroom house. The transistor hadn't even been invented yet, much less the integrated circuit, so this computer was filled with vacuum tubes (remember them?) and huge metal switches. To program it, a team of scientists literally crawled through the room flipping switches on and off.

This massive electronic calculator worked flawlessly, churning out numbers onto paper tape, day after day after day. Until one day, that is, when it decided that 2+2 actually equaled 5 (or maybe 22—the exact details are a little sketchy today). The puzzled scientists crawled through the room, checking every switch, and finally discovered that a cockroach had lodged itself inside one of the switches, causing it to short-circuit. The cockroach died, but it gave its name to a new term for computer users: the **bug**.

Today, computer users still have to live with bugs. And they're a lot harder to find than that original bug, because you can't see them.

Word, like all the programs in Microsoft Office, is a marvelous piece of work. But that doesn't mean it's perfect. Yes, Word has bugs. So do Excel and PowerPoint, and Windows itself, for that matter.

Sometimes you follow the instructions to the letter, and whatever you were trying to do just plain doesn't happen. You try it again, and again it doesn't work. You double-check the steps and try it again, and still the program doesn't do what you expect it to do. Have you found a bug? Probably.

What should you do when you think you've found a bug?

- First, call Microsoft (or send a fax or e-mail), describe the problem in detail, and ask whether you've found a bug.

- If you have, ask whether there's a new version of Word (or whatever program caused the problem). Sometimes the bug has been fixed, and Microsoft can send you a disk to solve the problem.

- If there's no easy fix, ask the technical-support representative if there's a **workaround**. Sometimes they can suggest a procedure that will do what you want to do while sidestepping that nasty bug.

And count your blessings. After all, to track down computer bugs in the 1990s, you don't have to crawl around on your hands and knees searching for cockroaches.

Q&A *I try to select part of a word by dragging the pointer over it, but as I move on to select the next word, Word insists on selecting the entire first word. What am I doing wrong?*

Word is trying to read your mind. It thinks you want to select the entire word, so it does that for you. That's actually a very handy shortcut, because you can be as sloppy with the mouse as you want, but your selection will still be perfect. Sometimes, though, that selection isn't what you've intended. To show Word that you mean business, and when you say *partial* you don't mean *whole*, select Tools, Options, click the Edit tab, and click next to Automatic Word Selection to turn it off.

With the keyboard

If you're a touch typist, it's aggravating to have to take your fingers off the keyboard, find the mouse, click to select a block, then move back to the keys. For you, there's a special keyboard technique that lets you select a word, a sentence, a paragraph, or the whole document. Just put the cursor where you want it and press the F8 key or double-click the EXT box on the status bar to turn on **extension mode**. That's a fancy term for a simple effect.

Once you've pressed F8, you can press any key to extend the selection. If you press the period key, for example, Word will extend the selection to the next period, which is usually the end of the sentence.

Keep pressing F8 to extend the selection more. Press it twice to select a whole word, three times for a sentence, four times for a paragraph, and five times to select the whole document. If you need to exit extension mode, press the Esc key. To "unselect" your selection, move any of the cursor keys. And here are a few keyboard tricks for selecting parts of your text:

To select...	Do this...
A word	Place the cursor at the beginning of the word, and press Ctrl+Shift+right arrow
One or more characters	Press Shift+right arrow; repeat pressing the arrow until you've selected everything you want
To the end of the line	Press Shift+End

continues

continued

To select...	Do this...
To the end of the paragraph	Press Ctrl+Shift+down arrow
To the end of the document	Press Ctrl+Shift+End
The whole document	Press Ctrl+A

CAUTION **Be careful when you have a block of text selected! If you inad-**
vertently hit any character on the keyboard or the space bar, whatever you
type will replace whatever you selected. You can bring it back with Undo,
but it's alarming to see everything disappear unexpectedly.

Moving words around

OK, the boss says the report you've been working on for three weeks is
nearly perfect. All you have to do is take that paragraph at the end of page 2
and put it at the top of page 4, then move a few sentences around on page 6.
"That's easy for him to say," you say. It's even easier for you to do. Depending on how far you want to move the text, you have two choices: you can
use the Windows Clipboard, or you can use the drag-and-drop feature.

Using the Windows Clipboard

The **Clipboard** is the best way to cut text from one place and move it to
another when you can't see both locations on a single screen. To move a
paragraph from one page to another, follow these steps:

1 Select the text and press Ctrl+X, or click the Cut button on the Standard
toolbar (the little scissors). Or (yes, there's a third way), right-click the
selected text and select Cut.

2 Use the scroll bars or the arrow keys to find the place where you want
to move the text. Click the exact spot where you want the beginning of
the text to appear.

3 Press Ctrl+V, or click the Paste button on the Standard toolbar.
Or...yes, you've guessed it, right-click the cursor and select Paste.

Dragging-and-dropping

For simple moves, like shifting a word from one end of a sentence to the other, or transposing two sentences in the same paragraph, the easiest way is just to **drag** the text from the old spot to the new one. The technique is simple: select the chunk of text you want to move, and then hold down the left mouse key as you drag it to its new home. It's easy to tell when you're about to move something, because the pointer changes shape, as shown in figure 7.11.

Fig. 7.11

The easy way to drag a word or a sentence a short distance: just drag it from its old site and drop it in the new one.

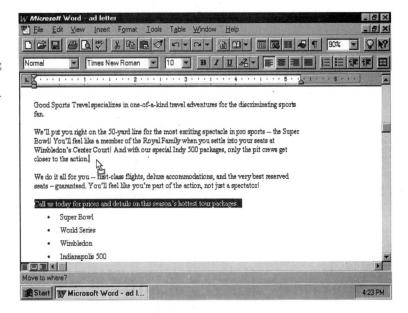

Don't worry about being too precise when you **drop** the text. Word uses a trick called **Smart Copy and Paste** that puts the right number of spaces on either side of a word or a sentence. It isn't perfect, but most of the time it does just what it's supposed to.

 TIP You can also use drag-and-drop to make a *copy* of a chunk of text. Highlight the text you want to copy, then hold down the Ctrl key as you drag the text. You'll know you're about to copy instead of move, because a tiny plus sign will appear alongside the pointer.

Where's that word?

Finding your way around a one-page memo is easy, but when you're editing a 50-page report, finding the exact spot you're looking for can give you a bad case of eyestrain. You'll get a headache and sore wrists to match if you have to edit a phrase that appears 20 or 30 times throughout your report. Fortunately, Word has an easier way.

Finding text

To find a chunk of text anywhere in your document, just press Ctrl+F (or choose Edit, Find) to pop up the dialog box shown in figure 7.12. Type the text to search for, and click the Find Next button. Keep clicking that button to find every place in the document where the text you're looking for appears.

Fig. 7.12

The Find dialog box lets you search for a word or phrase anywhere in your document. If you're not sure of your spelling, give it your best shot and then select the Sounds Like box.

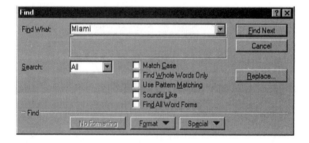

Q&A *I tried finding a word I know is in the document, but all I get is a message telling me the word wasn't found! What's happening here?*

Was any of your text selected before you started your search? If so, Word will look for the word only in the selected text. Click the document (you don't need to close the Find dialog box), deselect the text, and try again.

The other possibility is that you have the Match Case option turned on. Make sure the check box next to Match Case in the Find dialog box is blank.

Replacing text

It's one thing to search for a piece of text; it's quite another to do something with it. Let's say you've written a 50-page report covering everything you could possibly want to know about Acme Corp. Then you discover the company's actual name is Acme Industries, Inc. You can search through your document and painstakingly retype the name each time it appears. Or you can pop up the Replace dialog box and let Word do the work.

If the Find dialog box is on the screen, just click the Replace button. Or, to start from scratch, choose Edit, Replace, or press Ctrl+H. When you see the dialog box shown in figure 7.13, type the text to search for in the top box and the text to replace it with in the second box.

Fig. 7.13
Use the Replace dialog box to automatically substitute one word or phrase for another. You can even include formatting in the Find or Replace portion, as in this example.

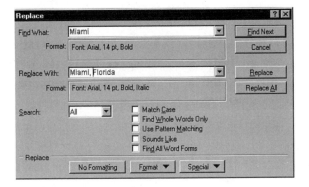

Choose one of these options, depending on how you want to make the replacements:

- To make the replacement in the current spot, click the Replace button.

- To skip this occurrence and find the next one, click the Find Next button.

- To have Word automatically change every occurrence, click Replace All.

CAUTION **Word is smart, but it's not *that* smart. When you tell it to replace** one thing with another, it simply looks for the sequence of letters you specified. So if you tell Word to replace *the* with *a*, it'll turn *thermometer* into *armometer* and *bother* into *boar*, because both those words have those three letters in them. To make sure Word finds only entire words, select the Find Whole Words Only box on the Replace dialog box. And keep both eyes open while Word works!

TIP   **If the words you want to replace are confined to one portion of** your document, you can save time by selecting that portion. Word searches and replaces only in the selected text.

Finding (and replacing) special features

Two of the buttons at the bottom of both the Find and Replace dialog boxes let you search for things other than text or numbers. You can use these buttons to search for **formatting** (like fonts and styles) or **special characters** (like tabs and paragraph marks).

CAUTION   **If your find doesn't work, check to see whether you've acciden-** tally specified some formatting (the information will appear in the gray area underneath the Find or Replace box). If that happens, click the No Formatting button and try again.

Oops! I didn't mean to do that!

Don't you just love Thanksgiving dinner? You slice, grind, mix, chop, cook, bake, clean, and decorate for twelve hours straight, then the guests show up and gobble up the turkey in two seconds flat. Computers are that way, too. No matter how careful you are, sooner or later your finger will slip and you'll zap a chunk of text that you've been working on for hours.

Relax. Word's coolest feature of all is the **Undo button**, that little counter-clockwise arrow smack in the middle of the Standard toolbar. Click it once to undo what you just did. Keep clicking, and it will keep undoing everything you've done, rolling everything back as much as 100 steps. If you know you want to undo a lengthy sequence of actions, click the little arrow at the right of the Undo button, then scroll through a list of the steps Word can undo for you (see fig. 7.14). If you click the fifth step in the list, for example, Word will automatically undo the last five actions in one swift motion.

Fig. 7.14

Don't panic! Word's miraculous Undo key can reverse the effects of one, 50, or even 100 keystrokes and mouse clicks. Now, when you make a mistake, it doesn't have to be permanent.

If you've never used Word's Undo button, you'll wonder what all the fuss is about. But the first time Undo saves half a day's worth of your work, you'll be ready to send a dozen roses and a big thank-you note to whoever it was at Microsoft who insisted that it had to be a part of Word.

Q&A *I deleted a paragraph a while ago and now I want to get it back, but I don't want to lose all the work I've done in the meantime. What do I do?*

Save your document under another name, then use the Undo button to roll your document back until you can see the lost paragraph. Copy it to the Clipboard and open the document you just saved. Paste the recovered text into the revised document.

Now for some housekeeping: close the original document (the one you rolled back), re-save the revised document to the original document's file name, and delete the revised file.

The Secrets of Great-Looking Documents

In this chapter:

- **How to make your words look more exciting**

- **What's the best way to arrange words on the page?**

- **Save your favorite styles and reuse them**

- **Adding special symbols to documents**

Word comes with a huge wardrobe of typographical accessories to help you dress your documents appropriately . . . . **>**

I can't even imagine what life would be like if my entire wardrobe consisted of nothing but gray flannel suits. I'd fit in just fine at the office, but I'd look hopelessly out of place at the company picnic. And I'd have a *really* hard time relaxing at the beach.

How you dress doesn't just define your comfort level. It also makes a statement about who you are. A gray flannel suit says, "I'm working. Take me seriously." On the other hand, faded jeans, running shoes, and a well-worn sweater say, "It's the weekend—let's have some fun!"

Your letters, memos, and reports make a statement about you, too. Think about it: should a memo to your boss share the same look as an invitation to a surprise birthday party? Of course not. Your new business plan needs a nice, conservative, dressed-for-success look; a flyer for next week's big sale demands a bold, attention-getting look.

Word can dress your documents for success, to get attention, or just for fun. In this chapter, we'll look at fonts, formats, and styles, the building blocks of great-looking documents.

 Plain English, please!

Styles are Word's shortcuts for dressing up text and paragraphs. Instead of picking every attribute off a list or a dialog box, styles save collections of these attributes in a simple name. So a heading style might be bold and centered in a large, easy-to-read typeface.

Making words look more interesting

Deep down inside, all the letters of the alphabet look pretty much alike—an A looks like an A, a Z is three slashes of Zorro's sword, and the numbers from 1 to 9 are familiar to anyone who's graduated from *Sesame Street.*

But something happens when you dress up those old familiar letters in a brand new font. Each character starts to acquire its own personality. The right font can help your words look strong and forceful, or light and delicate. You can even use a special font called **Wingdings** to put symbols right in the middle of your memo—like a big, bold ☎ to let everyone know about the new phone number.

What good are fonts?

If you stopped two strangers on the street—both roughly the same age and the same size—you might have trouble telling them apart. But put one in a police officer's uniform and the other in a tuxedo, and you'll have no trouble telling the two apart.

Fonts work the same way, as a kind of uniform that the characters on your page wear. When you dress up your text in Times New Roman, it looks like the words in your daily paper: serious and sober. Now change the same words into Britannic Bold: they look like headlines. It's hard to ignore those big, bold letters, isn't it? As you can see in table 8.1, there are big differences between fonts.

Table 8.1 A few typical fonts

What it's called	What it looks like	How it's used
Times	The quick brown fox	By far the most popular choice for letters and memos. Maybe *too* popular.
Helvetica	The quick brown fox	A good all-around typeface for headlines and text, especially in smaller chunks.
ITC Fenice Ultra	**The quick brown fox**	Big, bold typefaces like this one are best for headlines and labels.
Shelley-Allegro Script	*The quick brown fox*	This old-fashioned typeface is fine for a wedding invitation, but not for a memo.
Zapf Dingbats	✳❋✲ ❑◆✲❋✳ ❍❑❑◗■ ✷❑❙	You're not supposed to be able to read it. Use Wingdings and symbols for special occasions.

Windows gives you five TrueType fonts for starters. Office throws in as many as 36 more. Other programs come with fonts as well, and you can buy more fonts for literally a few dollars apiece. If you want to jazz up your documents, this is one of the best investments you can make.

TIP   **Windows uses several kinds of typefaces, but the most popular is** called **TrueType**. TrueType fonts are **scalable**, which means that Windows can stretch (**scale**) them like a piece of Silly Putty into the exact size you specify. **Printer fonts** and **screen fonts** usually come in a limited number of sizes, which means that Windows can only approximate what you ask for. (If you've ever worn a one-size-fits-all baseball cap, you know the problem.) When you want to add new fonts, be sure to choose the TrueType variety. They're guaranteed to work with Word and the other Office programs. TrueType fonts are the one preceded by a double T in the Fonts text box on the Formatting toolbar.

How to change the fonts in your documents

When you first start typing, your letters hit the screen in boring old gray flannel. That's fine, as long as you're just trying to capture those thoughts as they tumble out of your head and onto the screen. But eventually you'll switch gears and start thinking about your document's look and feel. How do you pick the look that's right for the occasion?

If you know exactly which typeface you want to use, the easy way is to use the **font list** on the Formatting toolbar (see fig. 8.1). (Actually, it should be called the **typeface list**, but if you want to know why, you'll have to read the sidebar later in this chapter.) Click the down arrow at the right side to pop the list into view, then scroll through the list and pick out the name of the typeface you're looking for. Those fonts you've already used in the document appear at the top of the list so they're easy to find; the rest of the fonts appear in alphabetical order. Use the **font size list** (just to the right of the font list) to make the font bigger or smaller.

Before you choose a font, you want to have some idea what it'll look like. What if you're not sure? You can cheat and let Word show you a preview before you make your font selection. Follow these steps to change the look of your text:

1 Select the text you want to change. Then choose F<u>o</u>rmat, <u>F</u>ont or right-click the selected text and choose Font from the shortcut menu. You'll see the Font dialog box shown in figure 8.2. (Before you can change a character's font, you have to select it. If you're not sure how to select text, look at Chapter 7.)

Fig. 8.1
Use the font and font size lists on the Formatting toolbar to change the typeface and size of the selected text.

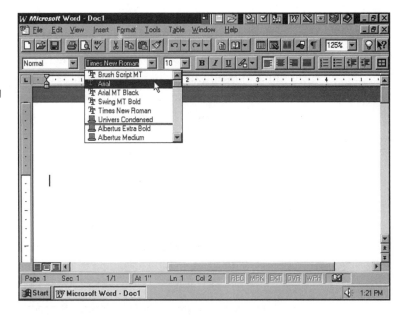

Fig. 8.2
When you're not sure which font you want, use this dialog box. The Preview panel lets you see what your text will look like before you actually change it.

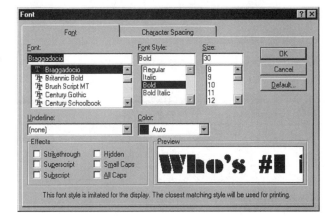

2 Choose a typeface from the Font list. For a preview of what your font will look like, see the panel at the bottom of the dialog box.

3 Pick a font **style**: Bold? Italic? Both? Neither? With most typefaces, you get one of these four options.

TIP **Use the buttons on the Formatting toolbar to make a selection** bold, underlined, or italic. You can always restore a chunk of text to boring old Normal style by selecting it, then pressing Ctrl+Spacebar.

4 Tell Word how big you want the letters to be. For most business documents, use 10 or 12 points for text. Headings can range from 14 points to 999 or more, depending on whether you're writing a memo or printing a poster (and whether your page is large enough to accommodate that mutation). Read the sidebar, "The most important words in desktop publishing," for more information on point sizes. Keep watching the Preview panel to see just how big (or small) your letters will appear.

5 Do you want to see the selection in color? Word gives you a choice of 16 colors. (Stay away from green and yellow, which are too bright for most people to read easily.)

 TIP **You can format text in bright, bold colors so it jumps off the** screen, but you'll need a color printer to see those same colors on paper.

6 Do you want to use any **special effects**? Select the Strikethrough box, for example, and your text will appear with a line through it: ~~like this~~.

7 Click OK to change the look of the selected text.

Here are some of the special effects you can use, and what you can use them for:

Use this effect	When you want
Strikethrough	a line through text; for example, to indicate text in a draft that you might want to delete ~~at a later date~~
Superscript	a small raised character; for example, in the mathematical formula $a^2+b^2=c^2$
Subscript	a small lowered character; for example, in the chemical formula H_2O
Small caps	lowercase letters capitalized, but slightly smaller than uppercase letters. A NICE EFFECT FOR HEADLINES AND HEADINGS.

Q&A *Someone sent me a document, and the fonts look horrible on my machine. What's wrong?*

The other person probably used some fonts that aren't installed on your computer. When that happens, Windows tries to substitute another font for the one your coworker used. Sometimes it works, but other times the substitution looks downright ugly. You have two choices: buy the same font and install it on your computer, or change the text formatting to another font that your PC can recognize.

Now arrange your words on the page

So far, we've talked about using fonts to make words and sentences stand out on the page. But all that attention doesn't do much good unless we also arrange the words so they fall in the right place on the paper. (When your words are all dressed up, give them someplace to go.)

Wouldn't that big 36-point headline look better if it were centered between the left and right sides of the page? And how about that important summary on page 4 of your report? If you leave a little space on the right and left, it will stand out from the rest of the text on that page, as surely as if you'd hung a sign on it that says, "Read me, please!"

Word's Format menu does much more than just let you adjust fonts. It also lets you set off text with extra spacing, stack your words up neatly on top of each other, draw precise lines, and center words on the page.

Adjusting the line spacing

Most of the time, you'll use single spacing for your documents. Some kinds of documents, though, are more readable when there's extra space between each line. Double-spacing is especially useful if you expect someone to add comments and corrections to your work. To adjust line spacing, choose Format, Paragraph; or right-click anywhere within a paragraph and select Paragraph from the shortcut menu. In the Paragraph dialog box, click the Indents and Spacing tab, then select an option from the Line Spacing drop-down list.

You'll notice several other options in the Line Spacing drop-down list:

- If you have large type or graphics mixed with small type, use At Least to tell Word what the minimum line space should be. Type the minimum spacing in the At box.

The most important words in desktop publishing

"I'll take Typographic Trivia for a thousand dollars, Alex."

Quick—hand me the remote control! My eyes glaze over when I hear all the technobabble that goes along with desktop publishing. Do you really have to know all these trivial details to put together a brochure or a company newsletter?

Of course not. Desktop publishing is actually quite simple. In fact, you can forget all about the jargon once you master some basic terms.

Let's start with typefaces and fonts. There's a difference between the two, but most people (including the people who designed Word) confuse the terms most of the time.

To understand the difference, imagine how you'd describe the way I'm dressed right now. (Hey, I said you'd have to use your imagination.) You could say I'm wearing a sweatshirt, but you'd paint a much more detailed picture if you described it as a long-sleeved blue sweatshirt, size 40 regular, with a hood.

That difference in detail is precisely the difference between a typeface and a font.

A **typeface** describes the overall look for a group of letters and numbers and punctuation marks. The **font** name is a much more detailed description of the same chunk of text. It includes not just the typeface, but also its **size**, **weight** (regular or bold), and **style** (such as italic).

Typefaces come in all levels of complexity, but they can generally be divided into two broad categories: serif and sans serif. **Serifs** are the little decorative flourishes at the end of some characters in some typefaces. *Sans* is French for *without*, so a **sans serif** face has none of these decorations. Look at the tips of the capital T in the type samples below to see the difference clearly.

This is a SERIF typeface.

This is a SANS SERIF typeface.

Most designers agree that serif typefaces are the best choice for big blocks of text because they're easier to read, while sans serif typefaces are better for headlines and short paragraphs.

And what's all this talk about **points**? Well, for more than 500 years, printers have used this standard unit for measuring the size of a typeface. There are 72 points to an inch, so a 12-point type is 1/6 of an inch in height, and a 72-point character is one-inch tall.

OK, class, let's see who's been paying attention. How tall is a 36-point character? A 144-point one? If you said half an inch and two inches, give yourself an A (and make it 200 points—you've earned it!).

At 1/72 of an inch, a point doesn't sound like much, but adding just one or two extra points of spacing after each line can make your text a lot easier to read.

- If you want to set the line spacing to something other than what Word offers (triple space, for example), choose Exactly in the Line Spacing box and enter the spacing in the At box (3 for triple-spacing, for example). Word does not adjust the spacing for larger type or graphics.

- Use Multiple to increase or decrease the line spacing by a percentage. For example, entering 1.25 in the At box increases the spacing by 25 percent.

 TIP **Some people like to press the Enter key twice at the end of each** paragraph. Don't! There's a better way to put space between paragraphs. See the Before and After boxes in the Spacing area of the Paragraph dialog box? If you're using a 12-point font and you want to add half a line at the end of each paragraph, for example, enter 6 points in the box labeled After.

Alignment

For every paragraph, you can also choose how it lines up on the page. When should you use the different choices of alignment?

- **Left.** People read from left to right, so this is the most popular choice for text. Every line starts at the same place on the left edge and ends at a different place on the right, depending on how many characters are in the line.

- **Centered.** Use centered text for headlines and very short blocks of text. Don't use it for lengthy passages.

- **Right.** As you type, the text begins at the right edge and each new letter pushes its neighbors to the left so everything lines up perfectly on the right edge. Use this choice only for short captions alongside pictures or boxes or to get a different look for a headline on a flyer or newsletter.

- **Justified.** When you choose this option, Word sprinkles a little extra space between the words in each line so that every line of your text begins and ends at the same place on the right and left. It's a good choice for text that's arranged into formatted columns, as in a newsletter, but don't use it in memos, because it will make them harder to read.

 TIP **The four alignment buttons on the Formatting toolbar let you** change a paragraph's alignment with a single click. Because this setting applies to the entire paragraph, all you have to do is click anywhere in the paragraph, then click whichever button you prefer.

I want to start a new page now

When you want to end the current page and force Word to start a new one—for example, to put a table in a report on a separate page—you'll need to add a manual page break. It's easy to do: just press Ctrl+Enter. You also can choose Insert, Break from the main menu and select Page Break in the Break dialog box. In Normal and Outline views, you'll see a dotted line, complete with the words `Page Break`, where you added this material.

What you need to know about paragraph marks

¶ See that button that looks like a backward P? It's called the **Show/Hide ¶ button**. The symbol on it (¶) is a **paragraph mark**. Click this button and you'll see a matching symbol everywhere you've pressed the Enter key. You'll also see marks for tabs, spaces, and other formatting characters.

There's nothing complex about a paragraph. Your high school English teacher would tell you a paragraph is a complete thought, but as far as Word is concerned a paragraph is everything that appears in between the two paragraph marks.

A paragraph can be as short as one word, or it can go on for page after page after page (like the average insurance form). How long (or short) *should* a paragraph be? The best writers use a mix—a few short, a few long. If all your paragraphs are exactly the same length, you'll put your audience to sleep just as surely as if you'd lectured them in a monotone.

When you use Word, there's one more important reason to pay attention to paragraph marks. That's where all your **paragraph formatting** is stored. If you tell Word you want this paragraph to use the Blippo Bold typeface with triple-line spacing, Word dutifully saves your instructions inside that paragraph mark.

Why does this matter? Because if you copy or move that paragraph mark, you'll also move the styles that go with it. And when you paste it into the middle of another paragraph, you almost always change the original styles that belonged with that paragraph.

If you're planning to move big chunks of text around, click the Show/Hide button to see all your paragraph marks. And then make sure you only move a paragraph mark if you also want to move the formatting that goes with it.

Using the ruler

The Word ruler sits just above your document, and takes all the guesswork out of adjusting margins, tab stops, and other pieces of your printed pages. You can skip a lot of formatting dialog boxes if you learn how to drag the little markers around on the ruler.

The ruler takes up a lot of room on the screen, so you'll probably want to keep it hidden until you need it. To make the ruler visible, choose View, Ruler. Use the same menu to hide it again.

Remember, ruler settings apply to the entire paragraph where the insertion point is located. And when you press the Enter key, the ruler settings for the current paragraph continue in the next paragraph.

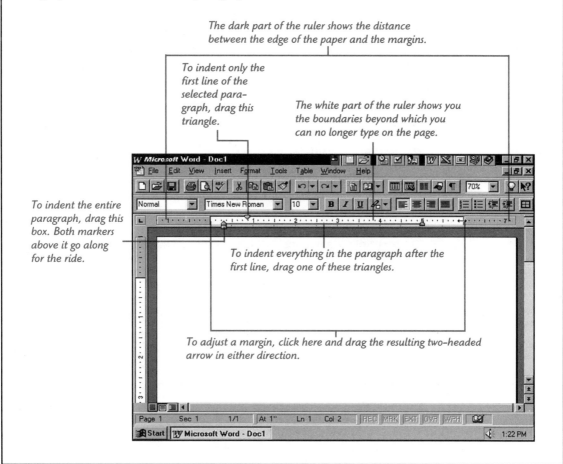

The dark part of the ruler shows the distance between the edge of the paper and the margins.

To indent only the first line of the selected paragraph, drag this triangle.

The white part of the ruler shows you the boundaries beyond which you can no longer type on the page.

To indent the entire paragraph, drag this box. Both markers above it go along for the ride.

To indent everything in the paragraph after the first line, drag one of these triangles.

To adjust a margin, click here and drag the resulting two-headed arrow in either direction.

Save your favorite formats and reuse them

Let's say you're a big-time producer and you're staging a remake of *Gone With the Wind*, with a cast of thousands.

Every time one of the extras playing a Confederate soldier checks in, you could scurry around to find him a gray uniform, a pair of boots, and a sword. But that would get pretty tiring after a while. Since you know you'll have hundreds of these characters, you can save time and hassle by putting together a special bundle with all the wardrobe pieces a Confederate soldier needs. Now, when each extra checks in, you hand him a big box labeled "Confederate Soldier." Easy, huh?

You can use the same principle to save time and energy with your Word documents. Your letters and memos and reports will use a lot of the same elements—body text, headings, signatures, address blocks, and so on. Instead of formatting each of these elements from scratch when you start a new document, you can use special labels, called **styles**, to keep track of your favorite formats. Now, when you highlight a character, word, or paragraph, all you have to do is tell Word which style to use and it will use all the formatting—fonts, colors, line spacing, everything—that you've assigned to that style.

Word uses two types of styles:

- **Character styles** store collections of information about individual characters—fonts and colors, for example.

- **Paragraph styles** let you collect all the formatting that has to do with paragraphs—alignments, line spacing, tab settings, and so on.

Define a style from scratch

If you're really brave, you can define a style from the ground up. Choose Format, Style to pop up the Style dialog box shown in figure 8.3. OK, now click the New button, type a name for your style, select a style to base your new style on, click the Format button, then select Font off the list, and… Hey, wait a minute! This is way too much work. Isn't there an easier way?

Redefine a style on the run

Of course, there's an easier way. If you've dressed up some text exactly the way you want it to appear, it's simple to assign that formatting to a style of your own creation.

Fig. 8.3

Creating a style from scratch the hard way. The Style dialog box makes you click button after button after button.

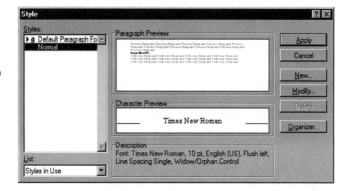

At the far left of the Formatting toolbar is a pull-down list of available styles (including Normal, Heading 1, Heading 2, and so on). Put the cursor somewhere in the paragraph that has the formatting the way you want it (or select the text with that formatting). Then click in the Style list box, type a name for the new style, and press Enter. In figure 8.4, for example, the name of the new style is Super Head. Word creates the new style for you, based on that formatting. (Note: If you already have a style by that name, Word applies the original style to the text. That's not what you had in mind.) The next time you want to use a style you've created, put your cursor in the paragraph, and choose the style from the Style list box.

Fig. 8.4

The easy way. To create a style by example, click in the Style list box, type a style name, and press Enter.

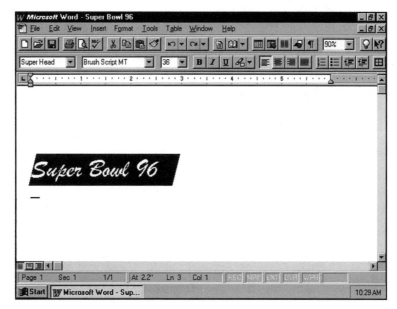

Paint formats by the numbers

Styles are the most powerful way to copy formatting from one place to another, but there's a quick-and-dirty way, too. Just use the Format Painter button. It's a simple, three-step process:

1 Highlight the text whose format you want to copy.

2 Click the Format Painter button on the Standard toolbar. The mouse pointer will change to a small paintbrush, as shown in figure 8.5.

3 Use the paintbrush to sweep the new format across the text you want to reformat.

Fig. 8.5

Use the Format Painter to copy formatting from one place and paint it onto another block of text.

Here's that special pointer

Choose a style from the Style Gallery

Word comes with a built-in collection of **templates**, each of which is chock-full of predefined styles. How can you tell what these styles are and how to use them? Simple—just choose Format, Style Gallery to see a close-up view of every template on your system. The three different views in the Style Gallery's Preview window allow you to:

• See examples of how the styles within each template work, so you can modify them to meet your own needs. (Figure 8.6 shows one such example.)

- See each style in a single, alphabetical list.

- Preview what *your* document would look like if you used that style.

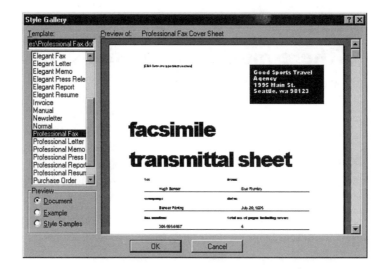

How do I add special symbols to my documents?

Anything that isn't a letter of the alphabet, a number, or a punctuation mark is called a **symbol**. When you realize how many symbols Word can produce, you'll use them a lot. Choose Insert, Symbol to pop up the dialog box you see in figure 8.7.

To add a symbol to your document, highlight it in the Symbols box, then click the Insert button. You can add a bunch of symbols at one time if you want. After you've inserted a symbol, the Cancel button turns to a Close button. Click it to make the box go away or close it by clicking the X (close) button on the title bar.

There must be an easier way to insert a copyright symbol!

Some special symbols can be entered directly from the keyboard, thanks to the AutoCorrect feature (see Chapter 9 for information on AutoCorrect). The folks who wrote Word were kind enough to make some of the most common symbols available in a way that's much easier than going through the Symbol dialog box. Those characters include copyright and trademark symbols, smileys, "frownies," and "who cares" faces, as well as some arrows. To insert these symbols at the cursor position, just type the corresponding characters from the following table:

Type this	To get this
(r)	®
(tm)	™
(c)	©
:)	☺
:(	☹
:|	☺
-->	→
<--	←
<==	⇐
==>	⇒

Pop in a character from a foreign language

If you have to type a word in French or Spanish, where do you get the accents and diacritical marks? ¡No problema! Open the Symbols box, choose (normal text) as the font, and look for your character.

TIP   **There's an even easier way to insert accented characters in Word.** Just press Ctrl and the accent character you want to add, then press the letter you want accented. To create an a with an acute accent (á, for example), press Ctrl+', and then press A. For an n with a tilde above it (ñ), press Ctrl+~,N. Use Ctrl+: for the umlaut symbol found in German words. (Don't forget to press Shift to get the tilde and the colon.)

Add some nifty graphics

If you like cool pictures, you'll love using the Symbols box with the Wingdings font. Take your choice of happy faces, bombs, the peace symbol, and a whole lot more.

These quotation marks don't look right!

There are two kinds of **quotation marks**. The normal kind (called **primes** and **double primes**) are straight up and down and look the same at the beginning and the end of a quotation. But slick, professionally published documents use **curly quotes** (like the ones in fig. 8.8), and you can, too. This feature is called **smart quotes**. By default, Word uses curly quotes in place of straight quotes; you can turn this option off. Choose <u>T</u>ools, <u>O</u>ptions, click the AutoFormat tab, and deselect the option Straight <u>Q</u>uotes with 'Smart Quotes.'

Q&A   *I like the curly quotes, but sometimes I need straight ones—like when I'm indicating feet (') and inches (") in a document. How do I keep Word from changing the straight quotes I want to keep to curly ones?*

If you want the curly quotes most of the time, you're in luck because that's the default setting. When you need to type a straight quote, just use this workaround: Immediately after you type the curly quote, click the Undo button on the formatting toolbar or press Ctrl+Z. This reverses the reformatting of the straight quote to a curly quote.

Fig. 8.8

Smart quotes just plain look better than ordinary quotation marks.

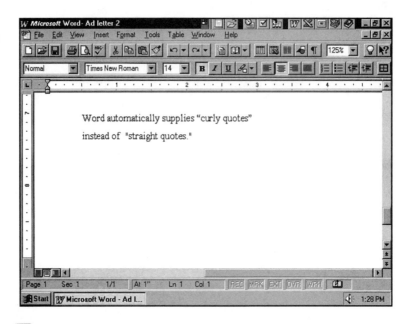

Word automatically supplies "curly quotes"

instead of "straight quotes."

CAUTION **If you use Smart Quotes in a document, then copy the text and** paste it into an e-mail message using the Clipboard, you're running the risk of losing your apostrophes and quotations marks because these fancy "Smart" types just don't survive outside of Word. So if you end up with an e-mail message that says, "Im one of the best typists youve got here. Thats why I deserve a promotion," you can kiss that promotion goodbye.

Exchange handles Smart Quotes just fine. But if you often copy text from Word to another e-mail program, turn off the Smart Quotes feature.

9

Let Word Do Your Work for You

Think of Word as your very own staff of hard-working special-ists. They take shorthand, they're perfect spellers, they've got a rich vocabulary, and they might even give your writing a little extra zip . . . . ⊳

n every office I've worked in, there's been at least one indispensable person. It's hardly ever the boss, of course. Most of the time it's not even a manager. The truly indispensable coworkers are the folks who do one thing so well that you can't imagine how you'd get through the day if they went away.

You know a few of these heroes. The amazing administrative assistant who can turn a page of shorthand into a complete set of minutes for a meeting. Or the mailroom guy, the only person in the whole building who knows how to unjam the copy machine.

Word has a few indispensable coworkers of its own. They're hard-working specialists, for the most part, who pop up just when they're needed, then vanish. They take shorthand, they're perfect spellers, they've got a rich vocabulary, and they might be able to give your writing a little extra zip.

Let Word do the typing and clicking for you

Why is Word like a pharmacist?

When you've got the sniffles you go see the doctor, who scribbles a few letters ("TID. PDQ.") on a prescription, which you take to the pharmacy. It's a miracle that the pharmacist can even decipher that chicken-scratching, much less translate it into plain English for you ("Take this three times a day, starting right now"). But that's what pharmacists are paid to do.

In the Microsoft Office, Word does something surprisingly similar, thanks to two special features: AutoText and AutoCorrect. You type in a few characters, press a key, and—boom!—Word looks up your shorthand on a list, then furiously types in whatever the two of you agreed on earlier.

Why would you want to use AutoText or AutoCorrect? Because you can save a lot of time and energy by using these shortcuts to insert chunks of text and graphics you use all the time. Here are some examples:

- Expand a set of initials into a **signature**, complete with "Sincerely yours."

- Create shortcuts for **lists of names** you use in memos and reports.

- Insert **boilerplate text**, especially the sort of gobbledygook that lawyers say has to be typed in exactly the right way.

- Spell out **technical terms,** and automatically add accents to **foreign words** such as *mañana*.

- Automatically correct frequently misspelled words.

AutoText and AutoCorrect solve the same problems, but in slightly different ways.

Using AutoCorrect: just start typing

As the name suggests, Word's AutoCorrect automatically corrects many mistakes as you type. When you first install Word, it includes entries for some commonly misspelled words. When you type **teh** and then press the space bar (or a period or comma, for that matter), Word checks its list, sees that you meant to type **the**, and changes the text for you. AutoCorrect names can be up to 31 characters long and can't include spaces; however, making the entry short is easier for you to use and to remember.

Is there a word you always mistype? Mine is Recycle, which I always type as Recyble. Don't ask me why, I just do. It's as if my fingers have a mind of their own. So I've instructed AutoCorrect to replace `Recyble` with `Recycle`, and the replacement happens as I type. I don't have to worry about it any more.

AutoCorrect is also good for creating shortcuts for common words and phrases you type regularly. For example, if you're a sports writer and you're tired of typing **quarterback**, tell AutoCorrect to replace every instance of `qb` with `quarterback`, as you go (or, as it's known in computer circles, on the fly).

Here's how to use AutoCorrect:

- To **add** an AutoCorrect entry, first highlight the text and/or graphics you want to reuse. Choose <u>T</u>ools, <u>A</u>utoCorrect to display the AutoCorrect dialog box shown in figure 9.1, and then type a shortcut phrase or the commonly misspelled version of the word in the text box labeled R<u>e</u>place. The selected text may include formatting, such as font and alignment information.

If you want to include the formatting with the entry, click next to Formatted Text. Another way to insert an entry is to type it in this dialog box. Type the shortcut on the left and the entry on the right, and click $\underline{A}$dd. You can add a bunch of entries at a time, but these entries won't be formatted.

- To **insert** an AutoCorrect entry in your document, just type the short-cut combination. Word will replace the text as soon as you press the space bar or a punctuation key, such as a period or comma.

- To **delete** an AutoCorrect entry, open the AutoCorrect dialog box, choose it from the scrolling list, then click the Delete button.

Fig. 9.1
After you highlight the text or graphics you want to reuse, type the misspelled word or shortcut name in the text box at the left. The scroll list shown here includes some common examples.

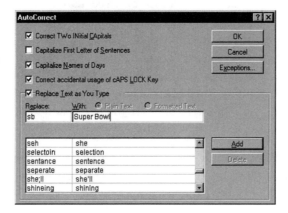

 CAUTION Don't use a real word as the name for an AutoCorrect entry, or you'll be unpleasantly surprised to see the results. For example, when you're working on next year's marketing plan, you might be tempted to redefine the letters **MR** to expand into **Market Research**. You'll change it fast the first time you try to type a letter salutation and accidentally turn "Dear Mr. President" into "Dear Market Research. President!"

However, if you insist on keeping that AutoCorrect entry, you can still type **Mr.** and get **Mr.** by pressing the Undo button as soon as Word replaces the word with its AutoCorrection.

Q&A *AutoCorrect isn't working. Where do I look?*

Maybe it's turned off. Choose Tools, AutoCorrect, and make sure that there's a check mark in the box labeled Replace Text as You Type.

Using AutoText: just press F3 and go

What's the difference between AutoCorrect and AutoText? AutoCorrect replaces your text automatically as soon as you hit the space bar. AutoText, on the other hand, doesn't go to work until you specifically request it by pressing the F3 key. AutoText entries can have up to 32 characters, including spaces, in their names. Oh, and one more tiny difference: AutoCorrect can be found under the Tools menu, and AutoText is under Edit.

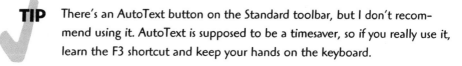

found under Tools, Auto correct

Here's how you use AutoText:

- To **add** an entry to the AutoText list, highlight the text and/or graphics, then choose Edit, AutoText to display the AutoText dialog box shown in figure 9.2. Give the entry a name, and press the Add button. (If your entry is a paragraph, make sure you include the entire paragraph in your highlighted selection!)

- To **insert** an AutoText entry into your document, click at the point where you want to add the text, type the name of the AutoText entry (make sure it's at the end of a paragraph or is followed by a space), then press the F3 key. Word looks down its list of AutoText shortcuts until it finds the one you asked for, then pastes it in.

TIP There's an AutoText button on the Standard toolbar, but I don't recommend using it. AutoText is supposed to be a timesaver, so if you really use it, learn the F3 shortcut and keep your hands on the keyboard.

- To **change** an AutoText entry, highlight the new text and/or graphics and choose Edit, AutoText. Highlight the right name on the list, click Add, and answer Yes when Word asks if you want to redefine the entry.

- To **delete** an AutoText entry, just highlight its name and press the Del key.

Fig. 9.2
You decide when to expand an AutoText shortcut into a chunk of formatted text. Just type the name (from the list at the top), press F3, and stand back while Word does the rest.

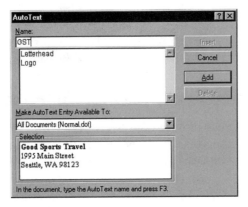

Let Word do the formatting

I call AutoFormat the "Make It Look Good" button. Here's how it's supposed to work.

You type like crazy, not worrying about formatting or other details. When you're done, you toss your file at Word and say, in essence, "Here—clean this up and make it look good."

Sounds great, doesn't it? Too bad it doesn't always work the way you expect it to.

What does AutoFormat do?

When you use AutoFormat, Word works its way through your document from top to bottom, replacing straight quotes with smart quotes, taking out extra spaces and unnecessary paragraph marks, and so on. (See Chapter 9 for more information on smart quotes and symbols.)

AutoFormat also tries to guess which style is best for each block of text. You can tell Word to skip one or more of these steps by choosing Tools, Options and clicking the AutoFormat tab in the Options dialog box. Just deselect the appropriate items under the Replace As You Type heading (see fig. 9.3).

Fig. 9.3
AutoFormat tries to make your document look extra-sharp. You can tell Word to skip any of the options on this list.

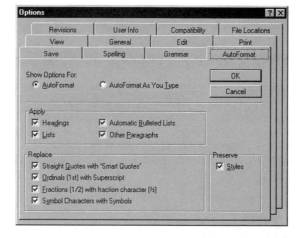

Fig. 9.4
Don't think—just type! All the words are there in this example, but it doesn't look too impressive, does it?

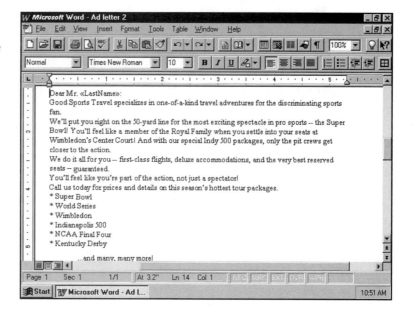

Fig. 9.5
After clicking the
AutoFormat button,
our document looks
better, but it's not
perfect. AutoFormat
added bullets to the
list of events, but
decided one paragraph
was a bold heading (it
took a stab at it
because the short
paragraph seemed like
a heading).

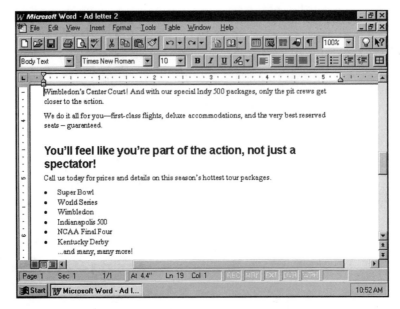

How do I use AutoFormat?

There's a fast way and a thorough way to use AutoFormat:

- Click the AutoFormat button on the Standard toolbar and shazam!
  Word sails through your document, makes all its changes, and puts the
  results on your screen.

TIP If you don't like what you see after clicking the AutoFormat button, use
Undo to put things back the way they were. Then try using the menu to run
the one-step-at-a-time version of AutoFormat.

- When you use the menu (Format, AutoFormat), Word formats the
  document, and then asks if you want to accept, reject, or review the
  changes. Figures 9.6 through 9.8 take you through the process.

Fig. 9.6
Click OK to begin
AutoFormatting.

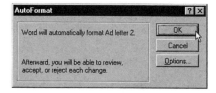

*1. **On your mark...** Word tells you what it's about to do.*

Fig. 9.7
When you choose
Review Changes, Word
lets you say yes or no
at every step of the
process.

*2. **Get set...** Word analyzes your document and prepares its list of changes.*

Fig. 9.8
Choose Find to locate
the first change; accept
the change by
choosing Find or reject
the change by
choosing Reject. The
final step is to accept
or reject all changes.

*3. **Go!** You go through each suggestion, one at a time, and decide
which ones to accept and which to reject.*

Helping AutoFormat work better

The bigger the document, the more likely AutoFormat is to make some
mistakes. The most common one is to apply the wrong style tag, turning
body text into lists, for example. AutoFormat works best on short documents. It also works well on blocks of text, such as numbered lists and
addresses.

Can't Word just format for me as I go?

Just like the AutoCorrect picks up after you and tidies up your mess,
AutoFormat examine your document as you type it, and applies different
formatting as it sees fit. But first, you need to decide which features you
want to AutoFormat on the fly.

Select Tools, Options, and click the AutoFormat tab. Now click next to AutoFormat As You Type, and check out all your options. Do you want numbered lists to be replaced by Word's own numbering feature? When you start a paragraph with an asterisk (*) or a hyphen, do you want Word to replace that character with a bullet? Oh, and when you type a line of hyphens or underscores, do you want Word to replace it with a perfect line that goes margin-to-margin? Select each option in this dialog box until you're happy. (Note that the long-line feature is called Borders.)

TIP What if you *want* five hyphens in a row, and Word replaces them with a line because that's what you told it to do? No problem. Tell Word to bring back your five hyphens by pressing the Undo button.

Let Word check your spelling

Whoever came up with the idea for a spelling checker deserves a medal. Think about it. All the Office programs share a complete dictionary, and whenever you push the right button, Word (and Excel and PowerPoint) zips through your document searching for embarrassing typographical errors and misspellings. Even if you're the type who can spell *antidisestablishmentarianism* backward and forward, Word's spelling checker will often come in handy (especially when you've been working for eighteen hours straight, and you've run out of coffee, and your *typeing gets realy slopppy...*).

What the spelling checker can—and can't—do

Word's spelling checker will only alert you when you use a word that isn't in its dictionary. It can't tell you when you've used the wrong word. So if you type **Supper Bowl** instead of **Super Bowl**, Word will think you meant it. The moral? Spelling checkers are useful, but the old human brain is still your best tool. So don't forget to read your document carefully before you pass it around.

How to check your spelling

There are two kinds of cooks. One washes every spoon, pot, and pan as he or she prepares a meal, so that by the time the meal is ready, the sink is sparkling clean and there's nary a crumb on the counter. The second type leaves a mountain of dishes in the sink, grease all over the stove, and unidentified foodstuff on the counter. As you've already seen in this chapter, Word also gives you two options for cleaning up after yourself: during or after. The first method marks mistyped words as you go with a red squiggly line under them. This option is turned on by default.

SuperBowl 96 will take
place in suny Miami,
Floridda. We hope
you have a grate time!

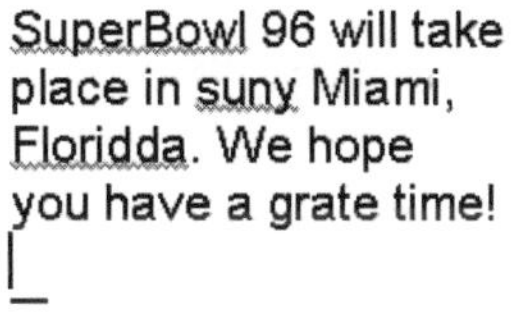

Fig. 9.9
Grate time? Are we talking about parmesan cheese or football? Word doesn't recognize the typo because it's a regular English word.

To correct a typo, right-click the marked word, and make a selection from the pop-up menu you see in figure 9.10, as follows:

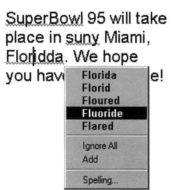

SuperBowl 95 will take
place in suny Miami,
Floridda. We hope
you hav
e!
Florida
Florid
Floured
Fluoride
Flared
Ignore All
Add
Spelling...

Fig. 9.10
Errr... Nine out of ten dentists prefer Super Bowl 95?

- **Use one of the suggestions.** Word takes its best shot at guessing what you tried to type. Most of the time, the correct spelling will be right there in that bold-faced list.

- **Tell Word the spelling is fine.** It may be a foreign word or name, and it's not in Word's dictionary. Just select Ignore All, and all occurrences of that word in the document will lose the red squigglies. And, yes, Word tried to tell me that *squigglies* wasn't a proper English word, but I told it to mind its own business, because I'd made up that word and I happen to like it.

- **Add the word to the dictionary.** Is your name Kozlowski? How much do you want to bet that Word thinks its just a typo instead of a reminder of your family's proud heritage? But you know it's the right spelling, so select Add and Word will never argue with you again.

What if I don't want Word to highlight my errors as I go?

Though the AutoFormat As You Type feature is a terrific tool, to some people it's the equivalent of the hypercritical in-law sitting in the back seat of your car while you drive (*Why did you take Main Street? Center Avenue would have been a shorter route!*)

If you want to run the spelling checker only when you're done typing, select Tools, Options, and click the Spelling tab. Click next to Automatic Spell Checking to turn it off, and click OK to exit.

You're the driver now. The in-law is taking a nap in the back, and you can decide when and how much of your document to check. You can use the spelling checker to look up a word, check a paragraph, or go through your entire document:

- To check the spelling of **one word,** double-click to select the word, then click the Spelling button on the Standard toolbar. If the word is misspelled, a list of suggested alternatives will pop up. If it's correctly spelled, you'll see the message shown in figure 9.11. Um, didn't Word forget to mention that the highlighted word is spelled correctly?

Fig. 9.11
Believe it or not, this message means the word you wanted to check is spelled correctly.

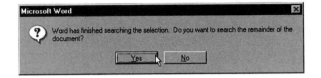

- To check the spelling of **a paragraph or part of a document,** select the text to check, then follow the same procedure.

- To check the spelling of **the whole document,** make sure that no text is selected, then click the Spelling button. When Word finds a word it doesn't recognize, it pops up a dialog box like the one shown in figure 9.12.

Click Change to fix the typo instantly.

Fig. 9.12
When Word finds a word it doesn't recognize, you can change it, ignore it, or add it to your own dictionary.

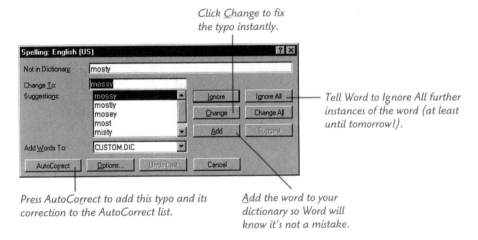

Tell Word to Ignore All further instances of the word (at least until tomorrow!).

Press AutoCorrect to add this typo and its correction to the AutoCorrect list.

Add the word to your dictionary so Word will know it's not a mistake.

Q&A

Word's spelling checker keeps finding the same mistakes. Can't it just fix them all?

The best you can do is add the misspellings to your AutoCorrect list. If you press the AutoCorrect button from the Spelling dialog box, you'll automatically tell Word to substitute the correct spelling when you use this incorrect spelling again.

Let Word suggest the right word

Suppose you're typing a long proposal regarding the Super Bowl 96 advertising budget. After using the term **advertising campaign** fifteen times on the first two pages, you know you're in trouble. You need a new phrase to liven up the document. You scratch your head. What's another word for *advertising*? What's a good synonym for *campaign*? You need a good synonym book. You need a thesaurus. And, not surprisingly, Word has one.

 Plain English, please!

A **synonym** is a word or phrase that means almost the same as another word or phrase. Car and automobile. Dog and canine. Joe Montana and Super Bowl.

Then there are **antonyms**, which are opposites. Like east and west, black and white, George and Gracie. 99

How to use the thesaurus

To use the thesaurus, click the word you want to look up (you don't need to select the whole word), then choose Tools, Thesaurus. You'll see a screen like the one in figure 9.13.

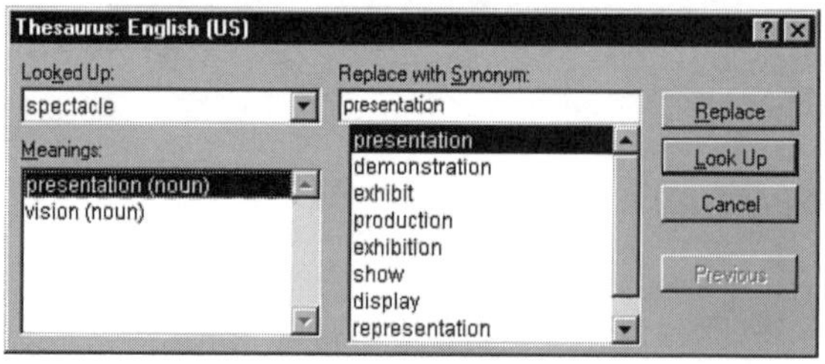

Fig. 9.13
Use Word's thesaurus to search for a more appropriate word.

Thesaurus: English (US)	? ✕
Looked Up:	Replace with Synonym:
spectacle	presentation
Meanings:	presentation — Replace
presentation (noun)	demonstration — Look Up
vision (noun)	exhibit — Cancel
	production
	exhibition
	show — Previous
	display
	representation

Here's how you use the thesaurus options:

- **To replace the original word,** pick a word from the Replace with Synonym list, and press the Replace button.

- **To look for more options,** click a word, and press the Look Up button.

- **To exit without making any change,** just click the Cancel button or press Esc.

Word can help make you a better writer. (Really?)

Can Word really make you a better writer? Well, that depends. If you sailed through high-school English with A's and B's, probably not. But if you think that a split infinitive needs whipped cream, nuts, and a cherry on top, keep reading.

What the grammar checker does

There's nothing magical about the **grammar checker**. It checks your document against more than 40 different rules of grammar and style (see fig. 9.14 for a partial listing), and suggests words you might want to change. You can turn off some or all of its rules, thank goodness, so that Word won't continually harass you about an "error" that you consider an irreplaceable part of your personal style.

Making your own dictionary

Using a spelling checker can be as maddening as listening to a leaky faucet. Word is constantly telling you that it's found a word that's not listed in its dictionary. The trouble is, you'll regularly use all sorts of words that aren't in Word's dictionary:

- Proper names, including your name and your company's name.

- Technical terms and jargon unique to your business.

- Slang words and foreign words not found in the standard Office dictionary.

- Words like *I'm* and *you're,* which contain "smart apostrophes."

Drip, drip, drip, drip. Arrrrrghhhh! It's no fun telling Word to ignore all those words, especially in a long document.

The solution? Create your own custom dictionary and use it to give Word an even richer vocabulary. If you look in the directory where Word stores its dictionary and thesaurus (usually `C:\Program Files\Common Programs\Proof`), you'll find a file called `CUSTOM.DIC`. It's easy to guess that that's Word's custom dictionary.

To add a bunch of words to `CUSTOM.DIC`, you can open the file directly in Word and just type new words into the list, one per line. To add words to the dictionary one at a time, press the Add button anytime Word tells you it can't find the word in its standard dictionary.

Fig. 9.14

Word's grammar checker analyzes your writing against more than 40 separate rules of grammar and style. You decide which rules to follow and which to ignore.

How does the grammar checker work?

Choose <u>T</u>ools, <u>G</u>rammar to start analyzing your document. The grammar checker jumps to the top of the document and works its way down. As it goes, it checks both spelling and grammar simultaneously, one paragraph at a time. Every time it has a question, it stops and offers a suggestion like the one in figure 9.15.

Fig. 9.15

Using Word's grammar checker is like having Mrs. Grundy, your high school English teacher, in your computer. (Sit up straight!)

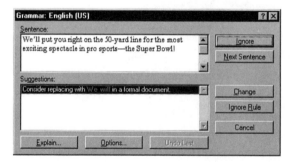

Here's how you use the grammar checker options:

- For each **grammar suggestion**, the grammar checker shows you the sentence and the corresponding rule.

- For a **detailed explanation** of the rule, push the <u>E</u>xplain button.

- To **ignore the suggestion** and move on, press the <u>N</u>ext Sentence button.

- To **ignore the rule** ("I like to begin sentences with And!"), push the Ignore <u>R</u>ule button.

- If the Change button is visible, you can press to **have Word make the change for you**. Otherwise, just click in the text and start editing. There's no need to close your dialog box until you're all through.

 TIP The grammar checker window is like the spelling checker window. You can leave it up on the screen while you add a new sentence or make another change. When you're done, press the <u>S</u>tart button to resume your grammar (or spelling) check.

Readability? What's that all about?

When you first learn how to read, you struggle over every word. With practice, though, most people get better at it, and most people with a high school education can handle long, complicated sentences with big words.

Word's grammar checker counts up the length of your sentences and the size of your words, and then crunches the data through a couple of special formulas. Eventually, it comes up with a laundry list of statistics like the one in figure 9.16.

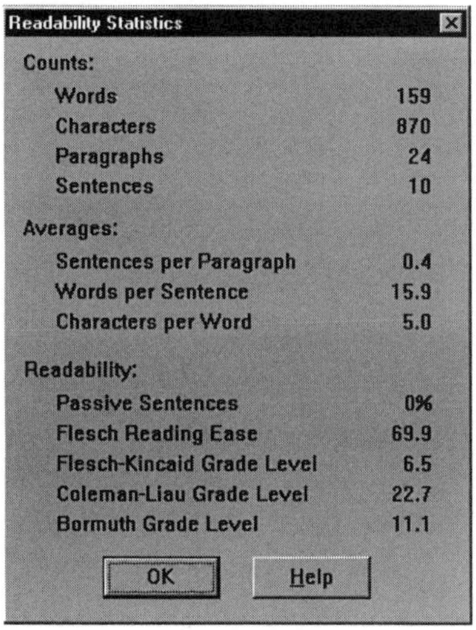

Fig. 9.16

When it's through checking your document, Word's grammar checker tells you more than you wanted to know.

Readability Statistics	
Counts:	
Words	159
Characters	870
Paragraphs	24
Sentences	10
Averages:	
Sentences per Paragraph	0.4
Words per Sentence	15.9
Characters per Word	5.0
Readability:	
Passive Sentences	0%
Flesch Reading Ease	69.9
Flesch-Kincaid Grade Level	6.5
Coleman-Liau Grade Level	22.7
Bormuth Grade Level	11.1

OK   Help

What should you do with all this information? Mostly, I just ignore it. If you must know how your writing rates, look at the Flesch-Kincaid Grade Level, which rates readability along a scale that uses the school grades we all know too well. In the previous example, the writing should be understandable by anyone with at least a sixth-grade reading level.

Readability statistics help only if you know your audience. If you're writing for rocket scientists, your reading level naturally will be higher because you have to use technical terms that make words and sentences longer. But for an advertisement that's designed to be read by average people, shoot for a sixth-grade reading level, so that anyone can read and understand your message quickly.

TIP   How many words have you written? There's an easy way to count the words in your entire document. From the main menu, choose <u>T</u>ools, <u>W</u>ord Count. If you have a block of text selected, this choice will tell you how many words are in the selection.

10

Lists and Tables

● In this chapter:

- ● **I want to put bold bullets in front of this list**

- ● **Can Word number this list automatically?**

- ● **What can I do with a table?**

- ● **How do I create a table?**

- ● **How do I enter data in a table?**

- ● **How do I change the column widths? Delete rows? Add columns?**

- ● **How can I make my tables look great?**

Set off a list with big, bold, bullets, and it practically jumps off the page. Or give each item its own row, break the details into separate columns, and you wind up with an easy-to-read, information-packed table . . . . ❯

Everyone uses lists. You don't believe me? Just look around. To-do lists. Packing lists. Laundry lists and grocery lists. The A list. Mr. Blackwell's Best-Dressed List. David Letterman's Top Ten List. The Ten Commandments.

Quite a list, huh?

When you need to communicate with other people, lists are among your most powerful tools. When it's set off from the rest of the text with bold bullet characters, a list practically jumps off the page. And the steady progression of examples adds authority to your arguments. Each new item on the list helps hammer your point home—by the time you reach the end, your conclusion is nearly irresistible.

After a list picks up enough details, though, it becomes too big and complex to be handled by a few bullets. Give each item its own row, break the details into separate columns, and you wind up with an easy-to-read, information-packed table. No matter which format you choose—list or table—Word can handle it for you.

Simple lists: bullets and numbers

Turning plain text into a list is one of the easiest things you can do using Word.

I want to use a bulleted list

To create a bulleted list on the fly as you type, just click the Bullets button (found on the Formatting toolbar). Type the first item in your list, then press Enter to add another bulleted item. The items in a list can be anything—numbers, words, phrases, whole paragraphs, even graphics. To stop adding bullets and return to normal paragraph style, click the Bullets button again.

To add bullets to a list you've already typed, first select the text. Then click the Bullets button to add a simple black dot in front of each item.

TIP   **Remember typewriters? Those big, loud machines that didn't read** your mind? If you used one for years, you'll know what I mean when I say that some habits are hard to get rid of. For example, if you've been using asterisks (*) or hyphens as your bullet characters, you're likely to continue using these, even though you now have a fancy word processor that can use any character imaginable for bullets. See Chapter 9 for information on AutoFormat As You Type, which converts your typewriter characters to state-of-the-art bullets.

I want more interesting bullets

When you first create a bulleted list, Word sets off each item with a big, bold, boring dot. Ho-hum. I prefer more visually interesting bullets. In the Bullets and Numbering dialog box, Word gives you a choice of six pre-defined bullet types. You can also use practically any symbol as a bullet.

Here's how to use a more interesting symbol to set off each item in a list:

1 Highlight the entire list, then right-click the highlighted list to open a shortcut menu. Select Bullets and Numbering to pop up the Bullets and Numbering dialog box (see fig. 10.1). You *could* click one of these choices, but we don't want to settle for anything so mundane. So let's click the <u>M</u>odify button.

Fig. 10.1
When you choose Bullets and Numbering from the shortcut menu, Word offers you these six bullets. Not that interesting, are they?

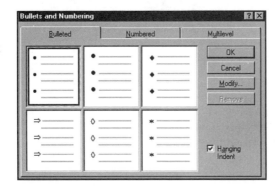

2 In the Modify Bulleted List dialog box that appears (see fig. 10.2), click the button labeled <u>B</u>ullet.

Fig. 10.2
Don't settle for boring old bullets! Choose any symbol you want, and even modify the size, color, and position.

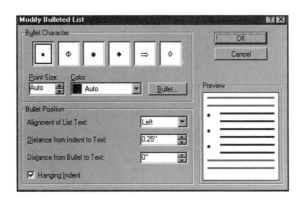

3 Pick a character from the Symbol dialog box. (Change fonts if necessary—this check mark is from the bottom row of the Wingdings font.)

4 Adjust the size, color, and position of the bullet, if necessary. The Preview window shows you how each change will affect the look of your list.

5 When you're satisfied, click OK to change the bullets in your list.

If you do every step correctly, you'll be rewarded with a bulleted list like the one in figure 10.3.

Fig. 10.3

The check marks make effective lead-ins for each item in a bulleted list. Note that we're poised to add another item to the list unless we click the Bullets button again.

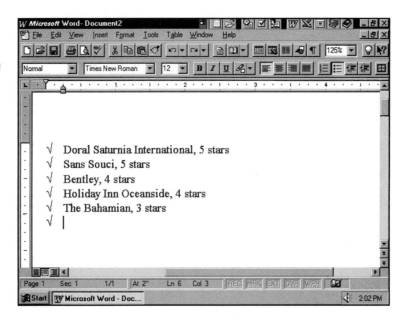

I want to use a numbered list

Bullets signify that the items on the list are of equal importance. When you want to indicate some items as more important than others, or when you're writing step-by-step instructions, you'll want each item to be numbered.

When you choose the numbering option for your list, Word adds a number to each item. If you add a new item or move items around, Word automatically renumbers the list to keep each item in the proper order.

To start a numbered list, type **1**, or **1)**, or **a.**, or **a)**, or whatever style you want to use. Type a space, followed by the text you want for that item. When you press Enter, Word will automatically convert the paragraphs (the one you just typed and the one you're about to type) to a numbered list, adding the right number or letter in your desired style as you keep pressing Enter. This option is AutoFormat As You Type (see Chapter 9 for more information), which is turned on by default.

To change the number format, select the entire numbered list, click the right mouse button, choose Bullets and Numbering, and then click the ~~Modify~~ *customize* button to display the dialog box shown in figure 10.4. Now we can add some more descriptive text to the bare numbers. If you're writing a list of instructions, for example, you can add the word **Step** before each number and a colon afterward, so your readers see Step 1:, Step 2:, and so on, in front of each item. Type the word followed by a space in the Text Before text box.

Fig. 10.4

Replace Word's dull numbering schemes with your own formats. Word will take care of the naming and numbering automatically.

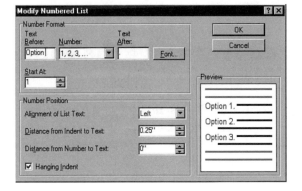

After just a few seconds' worth of fiddling with dialog boxes, you can turn the simple text list into one that outlines options for your readers, as in figure 10.5.

 TIP **When you add a word in the Text Before box of the Modify**
Numbered List dialog box, make sure you follow it with a space. Otherwise, the word will press up against the numbers in the list.

No text box, write text to number format.

Fig. 10.5
Word automatically
adds the word Option
and a space before
each list entry, then
numbers the whole list.
If you move an item or
add a new one, the
numbering adjusts
automatically.

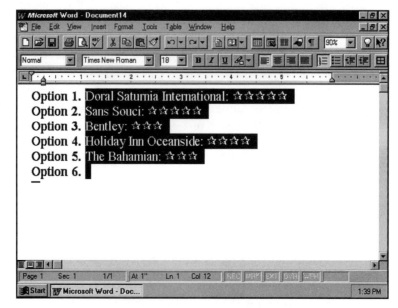

How do I rearrange the entries in my list?

Here's where Word really earns its keep:

- **To reorder list items,** first select the entire item, including the paragraph mark (¶). Then use cut and paste, or just drag the item to its new spot.

- **To add a new list item,** move the insertion point to the very end of the last row in the list, and press Enter.

- **To insert a new item,** click where you want the new item to be added, and press Enter. Word will create a correctly numbered blank entry, and all you have to do is type something in.

- **To skip or stop numbering,** click the right mouse button, and choose Skip Numbering or Stop Numbering from the shortcut menu.

- **To restore a list to plain text format,** select the list, and press the Numbering button or the Bullets button.

Q&A *I tried to move one item in my numbered list, but it didn't work right. The text moved, but the number stayed where it was. What did I do wrong?*

To move a bulleted or numbered item properly, you must make sure you've selected the paragraph mark (¶) at the end of the item. (Press the Show/Hide button on the Standard toolbar to make the job easier.) If you don't select the paragraph mark, the bullet formatting stays where it is, and only the text moves.

What can I do with a table?

Word's built-in list formats work great when the lists are simple enough. Apples, peaches, pears, pineapples—no problem. But what happens when you start to add more detail, like a price? Apples, 49¢ a pound; peaches, $1.49...although it's starting to get more complicated, our list can probably still handle it. But what if we add pictures and a description of where each type of fruit is found? Now we've strained our list past the breaking point.

It's time to organize all that information into neat rows and columns. And Word tables are the perfect tool for the job. With the help of tables, you can:

- Align words and numbers into precise columns (with or without borders).
- Put text and graphics together with a minimum of fuss.
- Arrange paragraphs of text side by side.
- Create professional-looking forms.

Word supplies faint grid lines that help you see the outlines of the rows and columns when you're entering text. If you want, you can add borders, shading, and fancy type to make your tables look ultra-sophisticated. And if you've ever struggled to line up columns using tabs, you'll marvel at how much easier it is to work with tables!

How do I add a table?

You can put together a table from scratch, but it's much easier to use one of Word's many wizards to do the job.

Tables made easy: ask the Wizard

Word has a wizard that automates the process of creating a table. Choose File, New and select the Table Wizard in the Other Documents tab. If you're already in a document, you can choose Table, Insert Table, and select Wizard from the dialog box.

Word will open a new document for you and begin asking a series of questions specific to your table (see fig. 10.6). If you tell Word you want 13 columns, for example, it will offer to automatically add the months of the year as column headings.

Fig. 10.6
Let the Table Wizard build a perfectly formatted table for you. As with all the Word wizards, you answer a series of questions, and Word does the work for you.

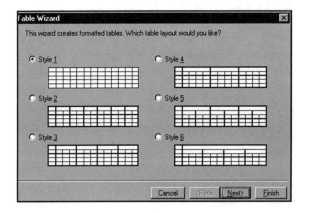

 After the Table Wizard has worked its magic, you're offered the chance to choose a look for your table from Word's built-in list of automatic formats. (We'll talk about Table AutoFormat in more detail later in this chapter.)

Quick tables

Use the Insert Table button on the Standard toolbar to quickly add an unformatted table to your document. When you click the button, a table grid (like the one in fig. 10.7) drops down from the toolbar. Drag the pointer down and to the right to tell Word how many rows and columns you want in your table.

If you just want to add a few rows and columns to your document, this technique works OK. But for anything complex, use the Table Wizard.

Word tables at a glance

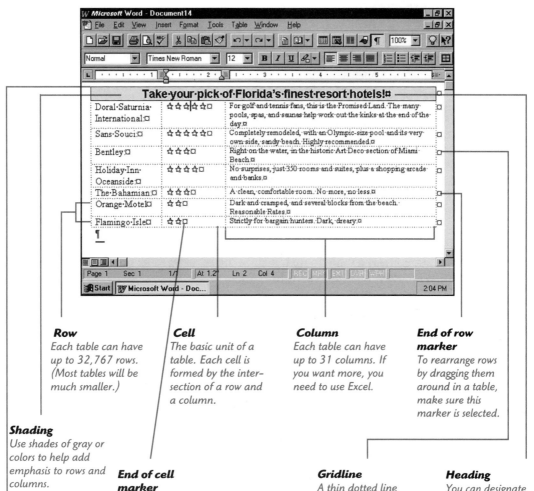

Row
Each table can have up to 32,767 rows. (Most tables will be much smaller.)

Cell
The basic unit of a table. Each cell is formed by the intersection of a row and a column.

Column
Each table can have up to 31 columns. If you want more, you need to use Excel.

End of row marker
To rearrange rows by dragging them around in a table, make sure this marker is selected.

Shading
Use shades of gray or colors to help add emphasis to rows and columns.

End of cell marker
Cell formatting (such as text alignment) is stored here. To move a cell and its formatting, be sure to select this marker.

Gridline
A thin dotted line shows you the edges of each cell while you work. It doesn't show up when you print, and you can turn it off if you want.

Heading
You can designate one or more rows to be labels for the columns below. These headings will then appear at the top of every page.

Border
These lines do show up when you print. You can adjust their thickness and location.

Fig. 10.7
Insert an unformatted
table with one click
and a little dragging.
Be forewarned,
though: you'll have
plenty of formatting
work to do afterward.

Converting text to a table

Let's say you're scanning through a document and you see a block of text
that you just know would work better as a table. No problem—select the
entire block and click the Insert Table button on the Standard toolbar to
instantly surround the text with a table. If the one-button approach doesn't
work (the columns are too wide, or there aren't enough rows, for example),
click Edit, Undo and try again using the menus: Table, Convert Text to
Table. The pull-down menus give you more control over your options.

To convert a table to text, just do the reverse: Select the entire table and
choose Table, Convert Table to Text.

TIP   You can save a table as an AutoText entry, complete with formatting
and headings, then insert it into your documents that way. See Chapter 9
for more about the AutoText feature.

How do I work with a table?

Once your information is neatly stashed in a table, you can rearrange it to
your heart's content. You can move cells, rows, or columns. You can change
the height of a row or the width of a column with a few mouse clicks. You
can even have Word reformat your entire table automatically.

Picking out the pieces of the table

Before you can rearrange, resize, or reformat a part of a table, you have to
select it. Use the techniques in table 10.1.

Table 10.1 Picking out the pieces of a table

	To select this part of a table...	Do this...
	Cell Contents	Drag the mouse pointer over the text you want to select.
	Cell	Aim the mouse pointer just to the inside left edge of the cell, and click.
	Row	Aim the mouse pointer just to the outside left edge of the first cell in the row, and click.
	Column	Aim the mouse pointer at the grid line at the top of the column (until it turns into a small down-pointing arrow), and click.
	Multiple rows or columns	Select row or column as detailed previously; hold the mouse button or columns down while dragging to select additional rows or columns.
	Whole table	Choose Table, Select Table.

What can I put in a cell?

Anything you can put in a Word document can also go into a table: text, numbers, symbols, or graphics, for example. You can even add automatic numbering to the items in a row or column of a table; as you move items around, they stay in the right sequence. A table can also be a mini-spreadsheet, performing Excel-like calculations.

Entering and editing data

To begin entering data into a table, just put the insertion point anywhere in the cell and start typing. Don't press Enter unless you want to start a new paragraph within the cell—if Word runs out of room, it will wrap the text within the cell. To move to the next cell, press Tab. To move to the previous cell, press Shift+Tab. Use the arrow keys to move up or down, one row at a time.

Q&A *I know I entered text in this cell, but I can't see it all. What's wrong?*

You've run out of room in a row that has been formatted to be an exact size. To fix the problem, choose Table, Cell Height and Width, then reset the row height to Auto. Now, all the rows in your table will adjust in height to accommodate what you type.

Changing column widths and row heights

One way to make a table more readable is to adjust its column widths so that each column takes up just enough room to accommodate the information in it.

The easiest way is to simply use the **mouse** to change the width of a column or the height of a row.

What about the **ruler**? Well, all those little rectangles and triangles and symbols can be dragged around, but it's really hard to remember what they do. If you want to memorize those techniques, be my guest—but I prefer just to drag the edges of the column directly, as shown in figure 10.8.

Fig. 10.8

To make a column wider or narrower, just grab its sides with the mouse pointer until the pointer changes to this shape. You can also use the ruler to rework columns, but the rules are quite complicated.

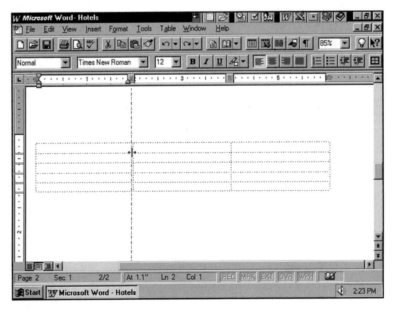

Word includes an option, called **AutoFit,** which automatically adjusts the width of your columns according to what you've already typed in them. If you want to use AutoFit for the entire table, make sure to select the entire table. Then choose Table, Cell Height and Width to display the dialog box shown in figure 10.9. Click the AutoFit button in the Column tab.

Fig. 10.9
Use the AutoFit button to let Word automatically adjust its columns and rows to the right size.

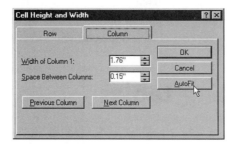

Adding and deleting rows and columns

It's easy to **insert a row** in your table. To add a new row at the bottom of the table, move the insertion point to the end of the last row and press Tab. To insert a row elsewhere, click in the row below the place where you want to insert a new row, click the right mouse button, and choose Insert Rows from the shortcut menu. To insert another row in the same place, just press F4 (Word's do-it-again key).

To **insert a column**, you first have to select a column. Move the mouse pointer to the top of a column until it turns to a small, down-pointing arrow. Click to select the entire column, then right-click and select Insert Columns. Your new column will appear to the left of the one you selected. What if you want to add a column at the right side of the table? You'll have to select the new column and drag it to the end of the table. (Sorry.)

It's a bit tougher to **delete a row or column**. Pressing the Del key clears the contents of the cell, but the cell itself sticks around like a bad cold. The only way to get rid of the cell is to select the entire row or column it sits in, then click the right mouse button and choose Delete Rows (or Delete Columns).

Q&A *I'm trying to delete some rows from my column, but I can't find the right choices on the menu. Where are they?*

All the Word menus—the ones you pull down and the right-mouse-button shortcut variety—can drive you crazy. Why? Because the menus actually change, depending on what you're pointing to. If you want to delete a row or a column, your pointer needs to be inside the table, and you need to select the row or column; otherwise, you'll never see the menu choices!

Making great-looking tables

Every table starts out as just a collection of cells, rows, and columns, and nothing stands out from the rest of the table. If you had a talented graphic artist and plenty of time, you could add bold headings, decorative borders, and background shadings to make your table easy to read.

Or you can use Word's built-in design smarts to automatically reorganize your table. This feature, called Table AutoFormat, works so well that even a graphic artist might use it to get started.

Let Word do the work with AutoFormat

Every time you use the Table Wizard, Word offers to reformat your table with one of more than 30 predefined formats. But you don't have to use the Table Wizard to use this feature; you can choose Table, Table AutoFormat from the pull-down menus any time. Just make sure the insertion point is somewhere in the table you want to reformat.

When you use Table AutoFormat, the results are remarkable. They're also much more reliable than the AutoFormat button that Word uses for general documents. Why? Because information is contained in neat rows and columns, so it's much easier for Word to figure out how to treat rows, columns, and headings. Look at the following before and after pictures to see what a difference it can make.

Figure 10.10 shows a basic table, with a few symbols and some bold-faced headings, but otherwise minus any pizzazz.

Fig. 10.10

There's nothing wrong with this table, but it's not very interesting or readable, is it?

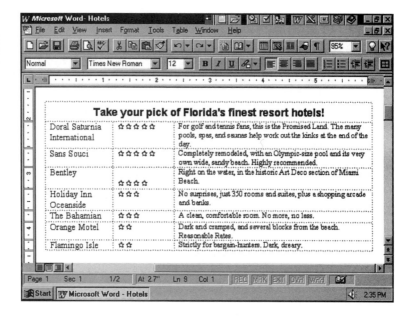

OK, now position the insertion point in the table and choose Table, Table AutoFormat. Take your pick of more than 30 prebuilt designs (see fig. 10.11). Different formats are appropriate for different types of data; for example, there are AutoFormats that work perfectly with lists and others that give you your choice of grids. We'll choose one of the Colorful options.

Fig. 10.11

The Table AutoFormat feature gives you more than 30 different "looks" for your table.

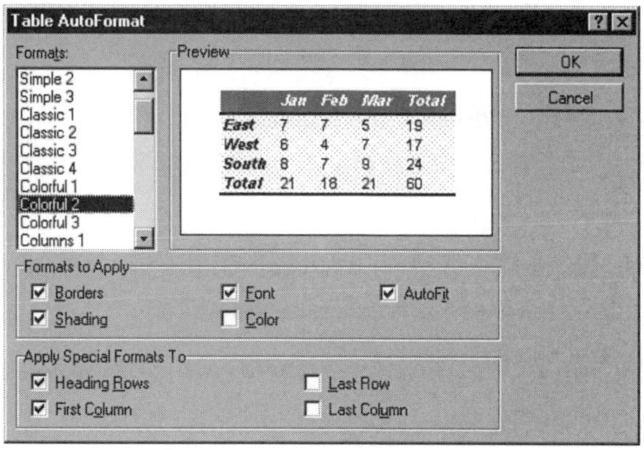

After using Table AutoFormat, we eventually got the look we were after (see fig. 10.12). Because the column widths and fonts were generally OK, we told Table AutoFormat to leave them alone. It added colors, shading, and borders, though, in one smooth motion.

Fig. 10.12

After Table AutoFormat. Our ho-hum table has some life, thanks to shading, borders, and the judicious use of color. (That's a soft yellow in the body and a bright red in the heading.)

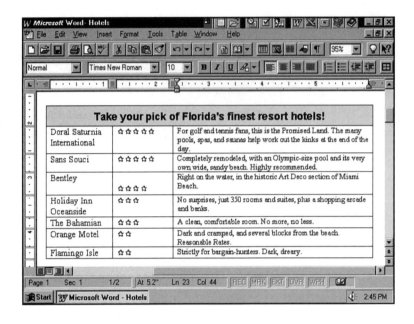

Here are a few tips for using Table AutoFormat effectively:

- Don't be afraid to experiment! If the Table AutoFormat feature doesn't work the first time, choose <u>E</u>dit, <u>U</u>ndo AutoFormat (or just press Ctrl+Z), and start over again with different options.

- Text formatting, such as fonts and alignment, can be applied to individual cells, rows, or the entire table. If you're happy with the fonts you've used, deselect the <u>F</u>ont box.

- If your table doesn't have labels in the first column or headings in the first row, remove the check mark from the boxes under Apply Special Formats To.

- If your table doesn't have totals in the last row and the last column, make sure those boxes are deselected.

- The AutoFit feature doesn't work properly if you've merged cells to form a single cell in one row. Deselect this option if you have trouble.

How do I make rows and columns stand out?

Use lines and shading to help your readers follow along as they read items in the same row or column. This is especially important when you have wide rows and long columns filled with detail. And column headings should be formatted in bold, easy-to-read fonts so they stand out.

Adding borders

Adding **borders** to a table is simple. First, select the cells, rows, or columns where you want to add borders. If nothing is selected, Word assumes that you want to add borders to the entire table. Choose F_ormat, _Borders and Shading to pop up the dialog box shown in figure 10.13.

Fig. 10.13

Use the _Borders tab of the Table Borders and Shading dialog box to set border types, add grid lines, and pick line styles and colors.

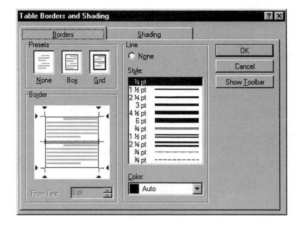

This is the place to turn to when you want to draw thick lines around the outside of the table, thin lines between rows and columns, and colored lines wherever you want them.

1 Choose one of the preset border types. **Bo_x** puts lines around the outside of the selection; **_Grid** adds lines around every cell in the selection.

2 Choose a **Line St_yle** and **_Color** for your borders.

3 To adjust the look of one border (or to remove it completely) click the line in the box labeled **Bor_der**. If you've done it right, you'll see an arrow at either end of the line you've selected, and all the others will go away.

4 Choose a new **Line St_yle** (or select **N_one**) from the list in the middle of the box. For example, to change the border underneath a row to a thin double line, click the 3/4 point double border.

5 Click **OK** to see your changes. If you don't like it, use Undo and try again.

CAUTION Don't confuse table borders with the grid lines you see around your table on the screen. Borders don't print unless you specifically add them by using one of the many table-formatting options!

Adding shading

Adding **shading** is a simple process. Make sure you have first selected the cells, rows, or columns you want to change, then choose F<u>o</u>rmat, <u>B</u>orders and Shading. Click the <u>S</u>hading tab to bring up the dialog box shown in figure 10.14.

Fig. 10.14

Use the <u>S</u>hading folder of the Borders and Shading dialog box to add foreground and background colors and shading to your tables.

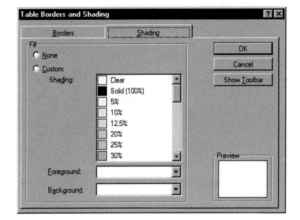

Come here when you want to add a dark background behind bold headings, a light background behind rows and columns, or no background at all for keep-it-simple tables.

1 Pick a **Foreground color** from the drop-down list. This is the color you want to add to your selection.

2 Leave the **Ba̲ckground color** box set to Auto unless you want your table to get really ugly, really fast.

3 Choose the amount of **S̲hading** you want to apply. For rows and columns where you expect people to be able to read text, start with a value of 10%, or at most, 20%.

4 To remove shading, select the **N̲one** box.

5 Click **OK** to apply your changes to the table.

TIP To quickly add lines and some shading options, try clicking the Borders button on the Formatting toolbar. This displays the Borders toolbar, which gives you one-click access to boxes and grids.

I need bigger headings!

Most of your table will consist of identical arrangements of cells, but sometimes you'll want to make one row a little bit different. You might want your table heading to stretch across the entire first row in big, bold type, for example. Or you might want to add a footnote, in little tiny type, in the last row of a table.

To merge two or more cells into a single cell, first select the cells you want to merge. Then select Table, Merge Cells from the pull-down menu. In figure 10.15, for example, we selected the three cells above Jan, Feb, and Mar, then used this feature to combine them in one centered label, Q1.

Fig. 10.15
The top row of this formatted table once contained 13 cells. Using the Merge Cells option, we've created four larger cells, one for each three-month period.

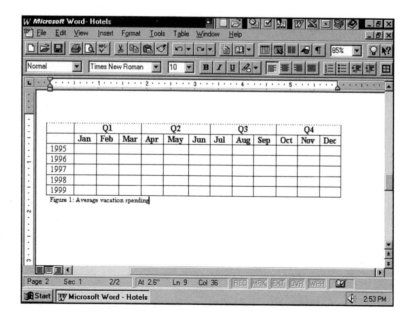

Can I use tables to create a form?

Every business uses forms, whether they want to or not. Purchase orders and invoices. W-2s, W-4s, and 1040s (yikes!). Sign-up sheets and petitions. Every form has two common elements:

- **Label text**, to tell whoever's filling in the form what they're supposed to fill in.

- **Lines and boxes**, so the information goes where it's supposed to go.

Most people create forms using a felt-tipped pen and a ruler. Those who've mastered the art of setting tab stops can probably create a good-looking form that way, although it can take hours of trial-and-error work.

But the best way, by far, to create a form is with the help of Word tables. The weekly time sheet in figure 10.16, for example, looks like it was professionally printed. In reality, though, it consists of four simple Word tables.

Fig. 10.16

This form wasn't printed at Kinko's—it actually consists of four simple Word tables and some clever formatting.

The **header** at the top of the page is actually a one-row table consisting of three columns. Because there are no borders, it looks like these three elements (a WordArt logo, some text, and a Word picture) are floating on the page.

The **name block** is also a table, consisting of three rows and two columns. Borders underneath each row help the user fill in the information correctly.

The **time and date block** looks more like a table, doesn't it? In fact, it consists of 9 rows and 6 columns, with borders everywhere except in the lower left corner, where three cells have been merged into one to form an easy-to-spot label. Note the thick border above the section that helps anchor it on the page.

Finally, the **signature block** at the bottom of the page is really a two-row, two-column table with borders underneath each row.

TIP   **Want to fill in the form on your screen, not on paper? Let Word** calculate totals, multiplications, and so on. Click the cell in which you want to enter a formula, select T̲able, F̲ormula, and type your formula (friendly advice: you'll need some Excel experience first). Note that the formula won't get recalculated as you type numbers into the table. Instead, you'll need to right-click that cell and select Update Field.

11

Letters by the Dozen

● **In this chapter:**

- **I need to send the same letter to a bunch of people**

- **How do I manage my mailing lists?**

- **Word can print envelopes and mailing labels, too?**

Send personalized copies of your letter to all the people on your mailing list. Or to just a select few. Word even prints the envelopes for you! . . . . ➤

magine that you are Ed McMahon. You need to send a letter to everyone in the country, telling them all that they may have just won $10,000,000. Of course, each one needs to be addressed personally, so they know you took the time to give their letters individual attention. How long do you think it will take you to write all 250 million or so letters?

And since you are Ed McMahon, think about all the people you know! Friends and family, Star Search contestants, magazine subscribers, Dick Clark, Johnny Carson, and other celebrities. Now think about all the trivial bits of information you know about each of these people, like addresses and phone numbers, golf handicaps, favorite foods, and birthdays.

If computers didn't exist, you'd probably be buried under 3x5 index cards, trying to keep track of all this data. But because you have a PC and Microsoft Office, you have no trouble keeping track of all that information.

In fact, you can use a Word feature called **Mail Merge** to write one sweep-stakes letter and then send personalized copies of it to all the people on your list. If you had to do all those letters by hand, you'd wear out your copying machine—and get a bad case of writer's cramp! Word does it in seconds. No writer's cramp, no index cards. And it even prints the envelopes for you!

I have a *lot* of letters to write

Okay, so you're not Ed McMahon, but you still do need to do a lot of mass mailings. Let's say you want to send a promotional mailing to some of your best customers. Without a computer, you'd put on a pot of coffee, haul out your little metal box full of index cards, and start copying names and addresses, one by one, into the blank spaces on each copy of your letter. When you were done, you'd have a stack of invitations, each a little different from the others in the stack.

Word does exactly the same thing automatically, using an original letter you compose, plus a table full of names and addresses. And it can do hundreds of letters in the time it would take you or me to do two or three.

Word's Mail Merge Helper isn't called a wizard, but it acts just like one. It does everything but load the paper for you when you want to send a person-alized copy of a standard letter to everyone in your address book.

Mail Merge in a nutshell

Here's basically what you do (we'll get into specific procedures in a minute):

1 Create your main document (a form letter).

2 Create a data source document.

3 Tell Word to merge your source document into your main document.

Although Microsoft promises that merging is as simple as 1-2-3, that promise is a little misleading. Merging really is a simple process, but you have to backtrack to step 1 before you can go on to step 3. Don't worry! We'll walk you through it.

What's Mail Merge, and how does it work?

Start with two pieces: a fill-in-the-blanks form letter and a list of names, addresses, and other information. Wind up with a big stack of letters, each personally addressed to one of the people on your list.

I'm ready to start

Before you fire up the Mail Merge Helper, take a few minutes to think about what type of information you need in your form letter. Most often, you'll need to insert names and addresses into the letter, but you also might want to add special information, like a price, a local phone number, or an E-mail address, that will be different for different people in your list. Jot down your list on a scrap of paper, the margin of this book, or your napkin. Keep it handy—you'll need it a bit later.

Got your list? Let's get started!

1 Close any open documents. Choose File, New, click the General tab in the New dialog box, choose the Blank Document template, and click OK.

2 To start the Mail Merge Helper, choose Tools, Mail Merge. You'll see a dialog box like the one in figure 11.1.

Fig. 11.1

This is the first screen you see when you start Word's Mail Merge Helper.

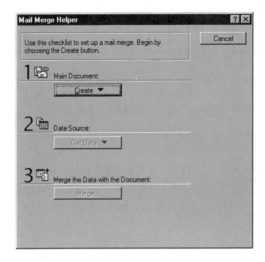

3 In the Mail Merge Helper dialog box, click the Create button under number 1 (Main Document,) then choose Form Letters from the list, as you see in figure 11.2.

Fig. 11.2

We'll create a form letter now, and look at labels and envelopes a little later.

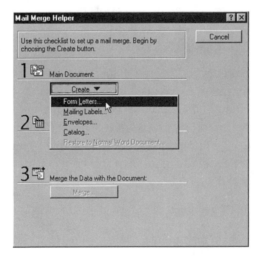

4 In the next dialog box, Word tells you it can work with the document you have open, or it can start a new one. Since we want to create a new form letter in the current blank screen, go ahead and click Active Window. Word then does some background work and returns you to the Mail Merge Helper. If you don't want to use the document you have open right now, click New Main Document.

TIP   **The text boxes in most of the Mail Merge Helper dialog boxes**
coach you about what to do next. If you get lost, look there first for help.
If you're still stuck, ask for help! Choose Help, Examples and Demos, then
press the button next to Mail Merge. Word's built-in demonstration of how
mail merge works is seriously useful stuff.

Get out that list you jotted down earlier

Now that Word knows which document it will be using as the "blanks" part
of the form letter, it's time to create the "fillers" for those blanks:

1 Under number 2, Data Source, click the Get Data button, and choose
Create Data Source. Word opens the Create Data Source dialog box
(see fig. 11.3).

Fig. 11.3

This is where you
create the fields for
your form lettter that
will be filled in the
individual letters.

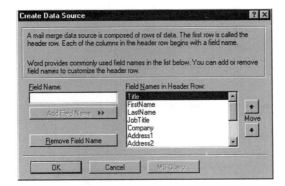

2 The long list at the bottom of the dialog box includes some common
fields that Word thinks you might want to use, such as Title (like Mr.,
Ms., Dr., and so on). If you don't want to keep a field in this list, click it,
then click the Remove Field Name button. If your list is intended to
keep track of people interested in vacationing in Florida, for example,
you probably don't need to store JobTitle and Company.

3 If you want to add your own field (like the ones you wrote down on that
napkin), type it in the Field Name box, then click the Add Field Name
button right below it. Depending on what you plan to do with your list,
you might choose to track golf handicaps, credit ratings, birthdays, or
customer referrals.

CAUTION   **You can't use spaces to name a field in a data source file. So** Referred By won't be accepted. Either run the words together or separate them with the underscore character. Both ReferredBy and Referred_By are acceptable names for data fields.

4 The order of the fields doesn't affect the merge, but it can make it easier for you to enter data. (It's easier for your brain to think "Ms., Beth, Lucas, Indianapolis, IN, Scorpio" than "Lucas, Indianapolis, Scorpio, Beth, IN, Ms.") Click the field you want to move, then click the up or down Move arrows to the right of the list. Word moves the selected field up or down on the list, as you indicate.

5 When you're happy with the list, click OK. Word asks you to give the data source a name. Do it, and click OK again.

6 If the Document Properties dialog box appears, enter summary information, if you want, and choose OK. A message box appears, telling you that your data source contains no data. No problem—that's what we're getting ready to do next. Click Edit Data Source, and read on.

Plugging in your people

When you first create a new data source document, it starts out empty, just like a stack of blank index cards. Once you fill in the blanks on the "cards," you can use your information over and over again.

After you press the Edit Data Source button, Word displays an easy-to-use data form that works just like an index card. The form should look like the one in figure 11.4. Use the form to add new **records** (cards) or change the information in records you've already entered:

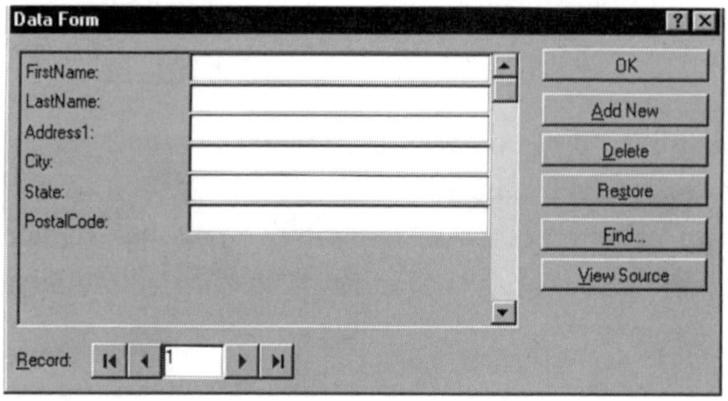

Fig. 11.4

To add new records or edit existing ones, use Word's data form.

- **To add another record to your data source document**, just press the Add New button, and start typing in the blank data form.

- **To move from one field to another**, use the Tab key. Use Shift+Tab to move to the previous field.

- **To move from one record to another** in your data source document, use the VCR-style controls at the bottom of the data form.

- **To change information in your data source document**, simply move to the record, click the field you want to change, and make the correction.

- **To undo changes you've made** to a record, click the Restore button.

- **To delete a record**, click the Delete button.

CAUTION The Restore button works only if you catch your mistake before you've moved to a new record. Clicking this button won't bring back a record you've deleted, either. Yikes!

When you're finished adding all your people and their info, click OK.

Form letters 'R' us

Word switches back to the blank document and adds the Mail Merge toolbar to your workspace (shown in fig. 11.5). You'll learn more about the buttons on this toolbar shortly.

Fig. 11.5
Use the Mail Merge toolbar to insert merge instructions into a form letter.

Start typing your letter like you would any other letter. When you come to a place where you want to insert a merge field, follow these steps:

1 Make sure the insertion point is in the place you want the merge field to appear.

2 Click the Insert Merge Field button on the Mail Merge toolbar to drop down a list containing all the merge fields in your data source document.

3 Click the name of the merge field you want to insert in your letter, as we're doing in figure 11.6.

CAUTION **Those funny << and >> characters on either side of each merge** field are called **chevrons**. They're special codes that Word uses to recognize merge fields.

You wouldn't try to use tape to attach sergeant's stripes to your sleeve—you have to sew them on so they become an integral part of the uniform. Similarly, you can't type or insert the chevrons around the names of your merge fields. You *must* use the Insert Merge Field button, or Word will ignore your instructions and treat your intended field as just another part of the letter.

Fig. 11.6

This field will insert the name of the customer.

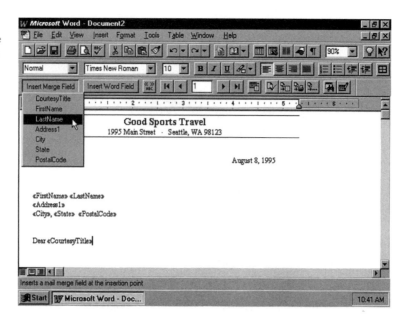

4 Continue typing the rest of your letter, repeating these steps for each additional merge field. When you're done, save the letter. It will look something like figure 11.7.

TIP **Remember to add spaces and punctuation between merge fields** when necessary; for instance, you'll usually want to add a space between first and last names, and a comma and a space between the city and the state. Otherwise, everyone who gets your merge letter will see their names all squished together like this:

```
MrDavidJones
```

Fig. 11.7

If these potential customers knew how little individual attention you're putting into these advertising letters, they might think twice about answering you. But they'll never know!

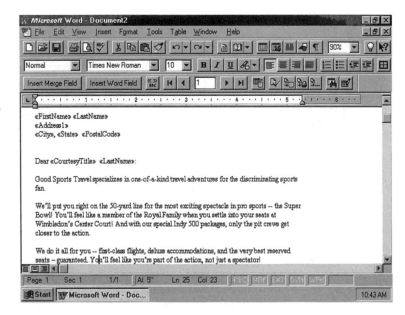

I want to see what my letter and data will look like together

What if you want a sneak preview of what the finished product will look like? Like the "index cards" in your data source, you can flip through your data source document when you're working with the main document, thanks to Word's Mail Merge toolbar. To switch between the field view and the preview, click the View Merged Data button on the Mail Merge toolbar. Remember, this is just a preview—the merge hasn't actually happened yet.

Use the following buttons on the Mail Merge toolbar to control your view of the data:

View Merged Data switches between viewing merge fields and showing you what the final letters will look like.

The **Go To Record** buttons let you flip through your data source document to see what your merged letters will look like. (You'll have to push the View Merged Data button to see the results.) If you know exactly which record you want to see, click in the box between the buttons, and type in the record number, and press Enter.

The **Mail Merge Helper** button takes you back to the Mail Merge Helper dialog box.

 Check for Errors in your main document or data source document. (See <u>H</u>elp for details on this function. You won't use it very often.)

   These buttons allow you to **Merge to New Document**, **Merge to Printer**, or display the Merge dialog box for additional options.

 Find Record locates a specific record in your data source document.

 Edit Data Source displays the data form so you can add a new record or change an existing one.

 Q&A *I'm seeing all this gibberish about Merge Fields in my main document. What happened?*

Somehow you've turned on the View Field Codes option, and Word is showing you the normally hidden codes it uses to track your merge information. If you have the Show Field Codes option turned on for some reason, then you'll see {MERGEFIELD FirstName} instead of <<FirstName>>. To shoo those bizarre codes back into hiding where they belong, press Alt+F9.

Merging east and west

Okay, you've got your letter and you've got your data. You have a basic idea of how the finished letters will look. The hard part is done! Just a few housekeeping issues, and you're home free.

To get the merge started, make sure you have your main document open, then choose <u>T</u>ools, Mail Me<u>r</u>ge again and choose <u>M</u>erge in the Mail Merge Helper dialog box. The Merge dialog box opens on your screen, as in figure 11.8.

Fig. 11.8

Almost there!

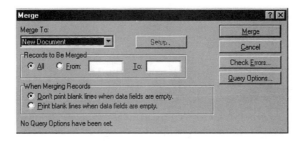

But I don't want to mail my letters to *everyone*

You might have hundreds or even thousands of names and addresses in your data source document. When you merge the data source document into a form letter, Word lets you specify a set of conditions to use. For example, you can select only customers who have made purchases in the last 60 days, who live in New York , who *don't* live in Florida, or whose last names begin with H.

To filter out only the records you want, click the Query Options button in the Mail Merge Helper dialog box. You'll get a dialog box that has two tabs: Filter Records and Sort Records. Click Filter Records to bring it to the front (see fig. 11.9). Here you can tell Word what you want to include or exclude in your merge. If you only want to send letters to people who live in Florida, you'd do this:

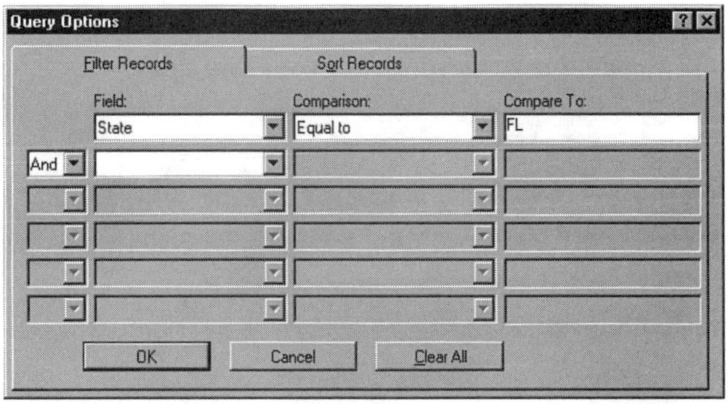

Fig. 11.9

Press the Query Options button on the Mail Merge Helper, then tell Word which records you want to include in your mail merge.

1 Select State from the Field list.

2 Select the Comparison criteria. These are your typical "equal to," "not equal to," "greater than," and so on. To find an exact match for our example, choose Equal to.

TIP For details on each of these comparison operators, click **Help** or press F1.

3 In the Compare To box, enter what you want to find—in this case, enter **FL.**

4 If you need even more specific search criteria, choose And or Or, and fill in the next row of blanks.

5 When you click OK, Word will take you back to the Mail Merge Helper dialog box.

Are we there yet?

At last, the time has arrived to put it all together. You should be back at the Mail Merge Helper dialog box; in number 3, choose <u>M</u>erge. In the Merge dialog box, click the Me<u>r</u>ge To drop-down list, you get three choices (see fig. 11.10):

- **New Document.** Word will put the merged letter into a file, so you can check the results before you print them. This file is huge, so don't save it unless you really think you'll need to print it again.

- **Printer.** Be careful about printing big merges straight to the printer. If something goes wrong, you have to start it again. This is handy, however, if your hard drive is almost full and you need to run a bunch of letters.

- **Electronic Mail.** You have to have an E-mail system installed to use this feature. For more help, choose this option, then press F1.

Fig. 11.10

Most of the time, you'll choose New Document.

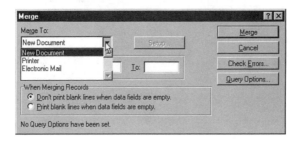

What about these 500 matching envelopes?

It's sad but true: in most American offices, there's a typewriter next to the laser printer. What's it there for? Well, the letter may be perfectly printed, but most people don't know how to make their word processor and their laser printer work with envelopes. So they type the envelopes—or worse, address them by hand.

Fortunately, Word lets you create envelopes and mailing labels automatically. Best of all, it works just as easily with one letter as it does with a hundred. It might take a few tries to get it right the first time, but once you learn Word's envelope secrets, you'll send that old Selectric to the scrap heap.

I want to make mailing labels

Sometimes it's more practical to use a mailing label—I don't know of many printers that will address *boxes*, for example! Word can print out sheets of labels to match any of 56 styles of standard Avery mailing labels.

 TIP   **If you want to create labels for a mass mailing, you'll need to go** through the Mail Merge Helper. Go on to the next section.

To create a single label, choose <u>T</u>ools, <u>E</u>nvelopes and Labels, then click the <u>L</u>abels tab (see fig. 11.11). To choose a label format, click the <u>O</u>ptions button, and select the kind you need from the scrolling list. When you're ready, put the label sheet in the printer, then click <u>P</u>rint.

Fig. 11.11

Don't waste them! To print a single label on a sheet that has some labels missing, choose Si<u>n</u>gle Label, and enter the Ro<u>w</u> and <u>C</u>olumn numbers of the label you want Word to hit.

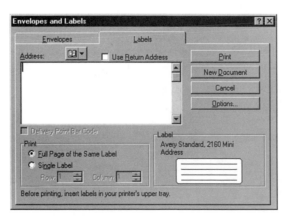

CAUTION **Always be wary of what you try to feed your printer. Some printers** don't digest used label sheets very well. Some don't even like envelopes. If you're not sure about your printer's recommended diet, check its user manual.

I want to address envelopes for my whole mailing list

Word uses the same tools to address envelopes and labels, whether you're doing one or a hundred. Setting up a data source document to print envelopes is no more difficult than building a form letter.

TIP **To address a single envelope using your printer, position the** insertion point anywhere in your letter, and choose <u>T</u>ools, <u>E</u>nvelopes and Labels to display the Envelopes and Labels dialog box. If necessary, correct the <u>D</u>elivery Address, and then set up the <u>R</u>eturn Address. Use the Feed icon to change the way Word feeds envelopes into the printer.

Just as with a form letter, you'll use the Mail Merge Helper to handle envelopes. Click the <u>C</u>reate button in the Main Document section, then choose <u>E</u>nvelopes from the drop-down list.

TIP **The procedure for setting up mass-mailing labels is identical,** except that you choose <u>M</u>ailing Labels.

Create your data source like last time, then in the Mail Merge Helper dialog box, choose <u>S</u>etup in step number 1. Set the envelope size and other options and choose OK. Next comes the heart of the envelope-addressing routine: the dialog box shown in figure 11.12.

Fig. 11.12
Use your Word data source document to print matching envelopes for every one of your form letters.

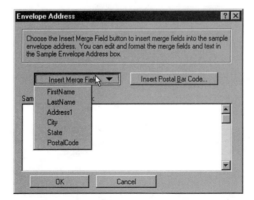

TIP **If you're using a previously saved data source, open that source in** step 2 of the Helper, then choose <u>S</u>et Up Main Document, <u>S</u>et your Envelope Options, such as size and font, and choose OK.

Use the In<u>s</u>ert Merge Field button to add information to the Envelope Address, then click OK to return to the Mail Merge Helper. From this point on, your merge document will work just like a form letter.

TIP **How do you change fonts in a mail merge envelope? In the Mail** Merge Helper, choose <u>E</u>dit in step 1 and select Envelope. Word displays the envelope with the field names and your return address on-screen. Select and format any of the text in the envelope as you normally would. You also can edit your return address, if necessary.

Q&A *Our mail service prints our labels out by ZIP code. Can I do this, too, so the letters and labels are in the same order?*

Sure! If the order in which the letters are printed is important, you can sort the records before you do the merge. In the Query Options dialog box, click the S<u>o</u>rt Records tab to bring that page to the front. You can base the sort on up to three fields. For example, start with the ZIP code. In the <u>S</u>ort By list, choose the PostalCode field. Then choose <u>A</u>scending, so that 00000 is first and 99999 is last.

12

Fancy Word Tricks

In this chapter:

- **How to keep from getting lost in a long document**

- **Add the date and time to your document**

- **What do I need to know to use Word for desktop publishing?**

- **Tricks to help you move graphics around**

- **Put a paragraph in a box so it really stands out**

- **How can I break my document into columns?**

For casual writing, you don't need to dress up your documents. But when you really want to impress your audience, dress your documents in formal wear—the equivalent of a tuxedo or an evening gown . . . . >

There are documents, and then there are DOCUMENTS. Most of the time, you'll use Word for everyday documents, like letters and memos. You don't need to dress up for this kind of casual writing—for you and your documents, blue jeans and sneakers will suffice.

But every so often you have to produce something that really matters. A report that's going all the way to the board of directors, say, or a brochure you plan to mail to 500 top customers. When the stakes are that high, it's time to dress your documents in the best available outfits.

In this chapter, we'll cover maneuvers most people never try with Word: desktop publishing, for example, and tricks that help you keep your place, even in a 50-page document.

I'm lost in this long document

Suppose you dropped this book as you were reading the hundred-and-sixty-third page. Now suppose the page numbers weren't printed on the pages. How would you find your place again?

Publishers add page numbers, chapter numbers, section names, and so on to help readers find their way around the book. When this information is at the top of the page, it's called a **header**; at the bottom of the page, it's a **footer**.

You might not be publishing 450-page books, but headers and footers can make it easier for your audience to find their way around your reports. Word has some pretty simple but sophisticated methods for adding them to your documents.

You can put just about anything in a header or footer, but most often you'll use these spaces for things like titles, page numbers, dates, and labels (like "Confidential" or "Draft").

Create headers and footers

There's no need to *insert* a header or footer into your document, because both are already there, just waiting for you to fill them in. To add text to a header or footer, you first have to make them visible. Switch to Page Layout view, then choose View, Header and Footer (see fig. 12.1).

Fig. 12.1

In Page Layout view, the text of your document appears in gray while you work with the header and footer.

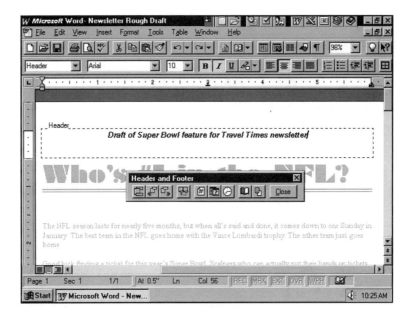

You can type anything you want in a header or footer box. You can also change typefaces and sizes, realign the text, and adjust the space between the header or footer and your text.

While you work, the Header and Footer toolbar floats nearby with all the buttons you need to get around. Here's what the buttons are for:

Button	What it does
	Switches between header and footer
	Finds the previous header or footer
	Finds the next header or footer
	Creates the same header/footer as the previous section

continues

continued

Button	What it does
	Inserts the page number
	Inserts the date
	Inserts the time
	Shows the Layout tab of the Page Setup dialog box
	Shows or hides the document text

How to move a header or footer around

Headers are always at the top of the page; footers are always at the bottom. You can't change those facts, but you *can* change the space between where the header ends and where your document begins—if, for example, you want to get more lines of text on each page. You can also add space between the end of the text on each page and the beginning of the footer.

To reposition and resize headers and footers, use the vertical ruler to the left of either element, as follows:

1 If you can't see the ruler, it's just hiding. Choose View, Ruler to bring it back. Then use the Header and Footer toolbar to switch to the header or footer you want to change.

2 Place your pointer on the top or bottom of the white part of the vertical ruler (called the **margin boundary**) until the pointer changes to a two-headed arrow, as shown in figure 12.2.

3 As you drag the margin boundary up and down, the header or footer will grow or shrink to match.

4 Use the buttons on the Formatting toolbar to change the alignment of your header or footer (centering the text, for example). Two tabs are set up in a header or footer, by default: a center-aligned tab and a right-aligned tab.

Fig. 12.2

Use the vertical ruler to change the size and position of a header or footer.

Click here —
Or here —

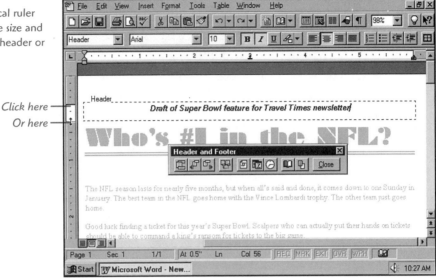

Extra-special header and footer tricks

Do you want the exact same header and footer on every page? Maybe not. If you have a fancy title page, you probably won't want to mess it up with a label at the top and bottom of the page. And if you're planning to use both sides of the paper for your printouts, you can set up different headers and footers on left and right pages. If the title of your report is on the right page header, for example, maybe you don't need it on the left page.

Word lets you handle both instances with ease. To pop up the Page Setup dialog box (shown in fig. 12.3), just click the Page Setup button on the Header and Footer toolbar.

In the dialog box, you can:

- Select the box labeled Different Odd and Even to use different headers or footers on left and right pages.

- Select the box labeled Different First Page to set up a different header or footer for the first page of a document or section.

Use the Header and Footer toolbar to jump back and forth between different headers and footers. Double-click the header or footer area to activate it at any time and double-click anywhere on the page (outside of the header or footer area) to return to the text of your document.

Fig. 12.3
The Page Setup dialog box lets you tell Word where you want your headers and footers to appear.

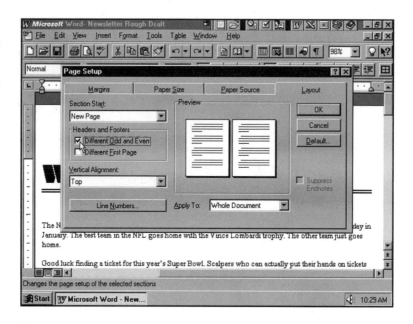

Q&A   *I added the date in a footer, but now I don't want it any more. How do I get rid of it?*

To zap any part of a header or footer, choose View, Header and Footer. If you're not already in Page Layout view, Word will switch for you. Select (highlight) the date code (and anything else in the footer that you don't want any more), and press Del. Voilá! It's gone.

But I just want some page numbers

You don't have to hassle with headers or fuss with footers if all you want to do is slap some numbers on your pages. Word has a special shortcut for that job. When you choose Insert, Page Numbers, Word creates a footer (or a header, if you prefer) in your document, then plops a page number into it. It just takes a few clicks in the dialog boxes shown in figure 12.4.

TIP   **You'll only see page numbers in Page Layout view or Print Preview.** In Normal and Outline views, headers and footers are hidden.

Fig. 12.4
Choose Insert, Page Numbers to quickly add page numbers to your document.

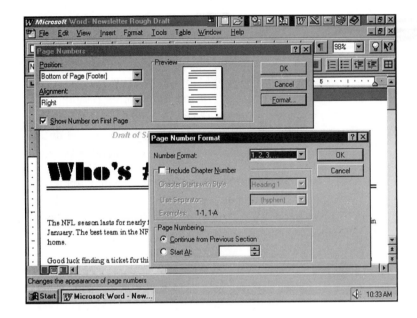

Here's how to tell Word that you want to include page numbers:

1 In the Page Numbers dialog box, tell Word where you want numbers to appear: on the top or bottom of the page.

2 Left? Right? Centered on the page? Tell Word how to align the page numbers. The Preview box will show you where your choice will appear.

3 Click the Format button to display the Page Number Format dialog box, and pick a numeric format. If you're happy with a simple 1, 2, 3, skip this step. Click OK to return to the Page Numbers dialog box.

4 Do you want a number to appear on your first page? (If you have a fancy title page, you probably don't.) Deselect the Show Number on First Page box to hide the first page number.

5 OK? Then click OK.

Q&A   *I'm trying to add a page number, but the command on the Insert menu is gray. What's wrong?*

Try it again, and this time look in the status bar at the bottom of the screen for an error message from Word. You're probably working in Outline view. The command you want doesn't work unless you're in Normal or Page Layout View.

Add today's date

Let's say you've been polishing the same report for three weeks straight. Every day you print out at least one new version of your work-in-progress, either to read yourself or to send to other people for their comments. How can you tell yesterday's version from today's? One easy way is to add a footer to your document, then insert a code that automatically displays the current date and time every time you open the document.

To add today's date to your document—in a header, in a footer, or just in regular text—choose Insert, Date and Time. You'll see a dialog box like the one in figure 12.5. Pick a format, click OK, and Word will type today's date wherever you've placed the insertion point.

CAUTION   **Word uses the date and time settings from the computer's system** clock. If your system clock isn't set correctly, you'll get inaccurate results in Word. To change the clock settings (which include both date and time), right-click the clock at the right end of the Windows 95 Taskbar. A shortcut menu pops up; choose Adjust Date/Time. Then change the settings as necessary and close the dialog box.

Fig. 12.5
Add today's date and time in any format you like.

That's not exactly what we want, though, is it? If we simply insert today's date, it will never change, and we won't be able to tell one version from another. What we really want is to insert a secret code that tells Word to look up today's date and put that in our footer every time we open the document. This secret code is called a **field**, and it's easy to insert a **date field**—just select the box labeled Update Automatically (Insert as Field).

Q&A *I just printed my report, and the date in my footer is wrong. What do I do?*

Make sure your footer contains a date field, and not just text. To check, point to the date and click the right mouse button. Choose Toggle Field Codes from the shortcut menu to see the hidden code; if that menu choice isn't available, try replacing the date with a date field. Highlight the date; choose <u>I</u>nsert, Date and <u>T</u>ime; and make sure the <u>U</u>pdate Automatically (Insert as Field) box is selected.

I want my document to look its best

No, this isn't the Twilight Zone, but we definitely *have* left the comfortable boundaries of Word, the word processor. Now we're heading straight for the heart of Word, the desktop publisher. When you discover this side of Word, you learn that there's a lot more to your documents than just words, numbers, and the occasional table.

Word, the desktop publisher, lets you dress up your memos, reports, and newsletters with pictures, charts, fancy logos, and colorful backgrounds. With the help of special boxes called **frames**, you can pin graphics down on your pages exactly where you want them. Without frames, you might as well try to pound nails through Jell-O.

To use Word for even the simplest desktop publishing chores, you absolutely, positively need to know about frames.

What are frames? And why should I care?

Just as the name implies, **frames** surround objects, such as charts and pictures, in your documents. Frames make objects easy to resize, move around, and position exactly where you want them on the page. And frames help separate objects from document text, by clearly indicating the space those objects occupy. When Word sees the frame, it knows that that space is reserved, and it rearranges the words and numbers around the outside of the frame.

TIP **You can put anything in a frame, including tables and text.**
If you're having trouble positioning a headline on the page, consider putting it in a frame.

Here's what you need to know about frames:

- Whatever you put inside a frame stays inside the frame, no matter where you move it.

- When you add text or another picture inside a frame, it expands to make room for the new stuff.

- You can move a frame anywhere on the page, even outside the margins.

- Text "flows" around objects when they're inside a frame.

- You can spot a selected frame by the thick dashed line around the outside (see fig. 12.6 for an example).

Fig. 12.6

The thick dashed line around the outside of the picture means it is inside a frame. Grab the dark squares to resize the frame, or drag the whole thing to a new position.

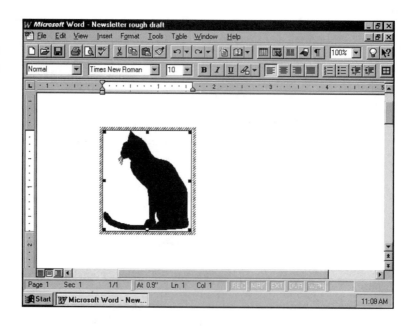

frames are not listed in Word 97

How to put something in a frame

The easiest way to create a frame is to wrap it around an object that's already sitting on your page. To put a frame around a picture, for example, first select the picture, then choose Insert, Frame. The frame wraps around the picture as snug as a sheet of cling-wrap.

If you don't have a picture in your document, you can put one there in a flash. To insert a picture, choose Insert, Picture. Office provides many clip art files in the MsOffice, Clipart folder. Double-click the picture file and it inserts into your document at the insertion point, as explained in the next section.

You can also create an empty frame and then fill it with a picture, text, table, or other graphic. Choose Insert, Frame and the mouse cursor changes to a cross. Move the cross to the place you want to put the frame and hold the left mouse button and drag the cross. As you drag, a dashed rectangle defines the frame. When you release the mouse button, the frame appears, exactly where you placed it.

Now put the frame where you want it

It's easy to move a frame or change its size, but first you have to be able to see the frame. You can only see a frame when it's selected. To select the frame, click anywhere inside the framed area. A gray hashed border around the outside will appear. Position the mouse on the gray border and the pointer will change to a four-headed cross, as shown in figure 12.7. Drag the mouse and the frame to its new position.

Fig. 12.7

When the pointer changes shape, you can move the frame.

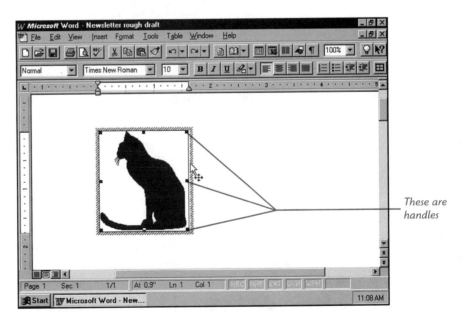

These are handles

To resize a frame, select it so the gray hashed border shows. If small boxes do not appear in the corners and on the sides of the frame, click the gray border. These small boxes are called **handles**. Position the mouse over a handle so that the pointer changes to a double-headed arrow. Drag the arrow towards the center of the frame to reduce the size, or away from the center of the frame to enlarge the size of the frame.

I want my picture perfectly positioned

That's easy. Select the frame. Choose F<u>o</u>rmat, Fra<u>m</u>e to display the Frame dialog box, shown in figure 12.8. Then check out the ways that Word can help rearrange your text and frames for you.

Fig. 12.8

The Frame dialog box lets you position graphics precisely—and automatically—on the page.

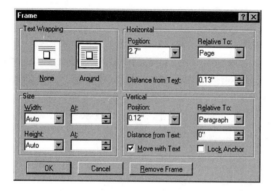

From the Frame dialog box, position the elements on your page as follows:

- Click in the Text Wrapping box to tell Word whether or not you want text to flow around the edges of your framed object.

- Choose a Horizontal and Vertical position for your frame. If you drag the frame to a position, Word will record the exact measurements. If you want Word to do the work, choose a relative position. To center a frame horizontally, for example, choose Center in the Horizontal Po<u>s</u>ition list box.

- Leave both the <u>W</u>idth and Height set to Auto; that way Word will always make sure that the frame fits perfectly, no matter what's inside.

How do I get rid of a frame?

To remove the frame without losing whatever's inside it, switch to Page Layout view, select the frame, and choose F<u>o</u>rmat, Fra<u>m</u>e. Then click the <u>R</u>emove Frame button.

To zap the frame and everything inside it, you also have to be in Page Layout view. Select the frame so that the handles are showing, and press Delete.

TIP **If you accidentally delete a frame or a graphic, don't worry.** Just click the Undo button and it will return.

I want to put a picture inside this report

To add a picture to a Word document, you have two choices: you can take a picture that's already been created in a graphics program and paste it into your document. Or you can draw your own pictures, using Word's built-in tools.

To insert a picture, follow these steps:

1 Choose Insert, Picture from the pull-down menus. You'll see a dialog box like the one in figure 12.9.

Just choose the Preview button

Fig. 12.9
Word lets you sneak a peek at a picture before you insert it into your document.

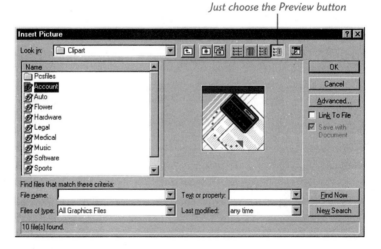

2 Change directories, if necessary, to find the place where your picture files are stored. (Usually these files are stored in c:\MsOffice\Clipart.)

3 Scroll through the list of graphics files until you find the one you want.

4 Select the Preview button if you want to take a sneak peek at each picture as you select its name.

5 Select Link to File, and deselect the Save Picture in Document box if you don't want to save the picture in a separate file. Leave the Link to File box blank to add the entire picture to your Word file.

6 Click OK to insert the picture into your document.

TIP **Don't forget to add a frame around each picture as soon as you've** added it to your document!

Q&A *I have a picture that I can see in another program, but Word says it doesn't understand the file format. What do I do?*

Use the Windows Clipboard to put it in your document. Open the picture using your graphics program. Select it, and press Ctrl+C to copy it to the Clipboard. Now switch back to Word, put the insertion point in the space where you want to add the picture, and press Ctrl+V. Windows will translate the picture into a format that Word can understand, then paste it into the current document.

You can draw your own pictures. Really!

If you're an accomplished artist, you'll take to Word's drawing feature like the proverbial duck to water. But even if you think you can't draw anything more complicated than a stick figure, you should give Word the chance to bring out the artist in you. It's fun, and you might be surprised at how even a modest graphic of your own creation can spice a letter or report.

To switch into the Microsoft drawing program, choose Insert, Object, then choose Microsoft Word Picture from the list. To actually start drawing, use the Drawing toolbar (see fig. 12.10).

You can add charts, pictures, and other graphic items from other programs—including built-in Office programs like ClipArt Gallery and Microsoft Graph. We'll cover this topic in more detail in Chapter 26.

Fig. 12.10
The Microsoft drawing program starts out with a blank canvas. The Drawing toolbar lets you add basic shapes, lines, and chunks of text.

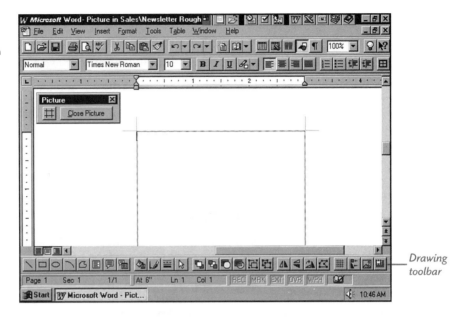

Drawing toolbar

How can I make part of my document really stand out?

You can add borders and shading around any object, whether it's in a frame or not. To add a box around pictures, text, or tables, just choose Format, Borders and Shading. These options are identical to the ones you use with tables.

Let's say you're producing a promotional mailing, and you know that your reader will spend, oh, three or four seconds looking at your letter, if you're lucky. If you put the most important paragraph in a box, then add a colorful tint over it, the reader can't help noticing it. (See fig. 12.11 for an example.)

Here are a few things to remember when using borders and shading to highlight text:

- Borders are applied to the entire paragraph. You can't put a box around a word within a paragraph.

- To display the Borders toolbar, click the Borders button at the far end of the Formatting toolbar. Use the Outside Border button to draw a box automatically. The No Border button removes all lines.

- Use the Line Style box to adjust the line thickness to the size you want.

- When you indent a boxed paragraph, the box automatically resizes to fit.

- Use the Bottom Border button alone to underline the entire paragraph.

- When you select a shading, it fills the entire box.

Fig. 12.11

Use borders and shading to make a paragraph leap off the page. In this example, we've also made the text bigger and bolder, centered the text in the box, and indented it all for emphasis.

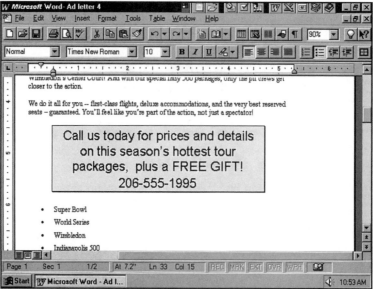

Making a long document easier to read

When you type a memo, you'll most often let your text run from one side of the page to the other in an unbroken line. For short documents, that works just fine. But long documents are much more readable if you use two or three narrow columns instead of one extremely wide page. The smaller your type, the more columns you can use; for example, use three columns with 10-point type and two columns with 12-point type.

The quickest way to get columns is to click the Columns button on the Standard toolbar. A drop-down box with four miniature columns appears. Click the column that represents the number of columns you want—for example, the third column if you want three columns.

You can apply columns to selected text or to text you're about to type.

In Normal view, your text will look like it's in one long column running down the left-hand side of the page. To see what the document looks like in actual columnar format, choose View, Page Layout.

You also can break your text into columns using the Columns dialog box. It's a bit slower, but you have more options. Follow these steps:

1 Position the insertion point where you want the columns to begin. Choose Format, Columns. You'll see a dialog box like the one in figure 12.12.

Fig. 12.12

Just point and click to turn your text into newspaper-style columns.

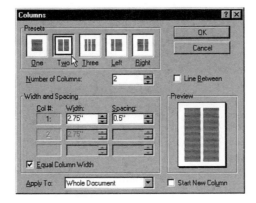

2 Choose one of the preset column layouts—two or three equal columns, or two unequal columns.

3 If you want to draw a line between the columns, select the box labeled Line Between. Preview your page layout in the box at the lower right.

4 To reformat just a section of your document into columns, change Whole Document to This Section or This Point Forward in the Apply To box. Choose OK to insert the columns.

 TIP Use the Newsletter Wizard to create a blank document already set up for two, three, or four columns. If you don't want the fancy logo or graphics, just delete the first page, and use the second page to start composing your document, one column at a time.

13

Putting It
on Paper

● In this chapter:

- **How can I see what I'm about to print?**

- **How can I cancel a print job in a hurry?**

- **My letter's one line too long. Can I shrink it just a bit?**

- **My printer isn't working. What can I do?**

When you're in a foreign country and you want to communicate with the natives, you pull out your Berlitz phrase book, right? Windows lets you do the same thing. . . . . ▷

If you knew how complicated the process of printing a page really is, you'd swear it couldn't be done.

You type words, insert pictures, arrange numbers into neat rows and columns, and slide boxes around on the imaginary piece of paper sitting on your computer's screen. Word turns your brilliant thoughts into a few million little dots, which it sends off to Windows' Print Manager, which in turn sends them across a wire to your printer, which clanks and whirs and buzzes and spits out something that looks like what you see on the screen.

When it works, it's magical. When it doesn't, it's a Maalox moment. Let's put the magic back in printing, OK?

Before you print, preview!

Some people like surprises. Not me. I especially hate that surprised feeling you get when you pull a 48-page report out of the printer and discover that you forgot to add that chart on page 3. Oops! See you in half an hour.

Some people just print and pray. Not me. I always, always, always click the Print Preview button before I send those pages to the printer. You should, too. With a single click, you get to see *exactly* what you'll pull out of the printer.

When you flip into the Print Preview screen, everything changes (see fig. 13.1). The Standard and Formatting toolbars vanish, and the tiny Print Preview toolbar appears. The whole idea is to show you your pages—one at a time or all at once—just the way they'd look if you were to lay them out on your desk.

You can preview one page or an entire document. You can zoom in for a quick look at the details, then step back to see a bunch of pages at once. If there's a mistake, or you just don't like the way one of your pages looks, you can fix it right there. And you have complete control over your document, thanks to the Print Preview toolbar.

Who needs menus? The Print Preview toolbar lets you move around, zoom in, even edit your document in Print Preview mode:

Print Preview toolbar

Fig. 13.1
Use Print Preview to
see exactly what your
document will look
like before you send it
to the printer.

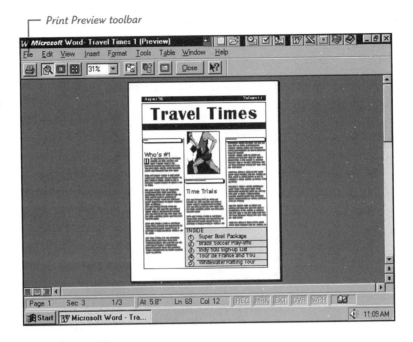

Print tells your printer to spit out one copy of the document you're looking at—no questions asked.

When you click the **Magnifier** button, the pointer changes to a magnifying glass. Click on a spot you want to see up close. Click anywhere on the page to return to full page (or multiple-page) view. Click the Magnifier button again to change the pointer back to a normal insertion point.

The **One Page** button fills the window, from top to bottom, with just the page you're looking at right now. Use the Page Up and Page Down keys to move around in the document.

Tell Word you want to see **Multiple Pages** side-by-side in the preview window. A great view for seeing the big picture, but not for reading text.

Zoom Control is nearly useless; you'll use the buttons to the left much more often.

View Ruler hides the ruler when you're not using it, and brings it back again when you need it.

The **Shrink to Fit** button has nothing to do with Levi's. Use it when your report is running two or three lines long and you want to squeeze everything into one page less.

Click the **Full Screen** button to clear nearly everything off the screen except this toolbar and the document you're previewing. (Press it again to get back where you started from.)

Close sends you back to a normal editing screen.

When you click this **Help** button, the pointer changes to a matching shape. Point to a part of the screen, click once, and Word will pop up instant Help or a box filled with formatting information.

How many pages can you preview at one time? The answer depends on your computer's hardware, especially the video card and monitor. If you have a Hulk Hogan-size monitor, you might be able to set things up so you can see 50 pages at once. On the average screen, though, you'll only be able to see 18 at one time. And even then, you'll feel like you're looking the wrong way through a telescope (see fig. 13.2).

Fig. 13.2
Click the Multiple Pages button, and drag to select the number of pages you want to preview at once.

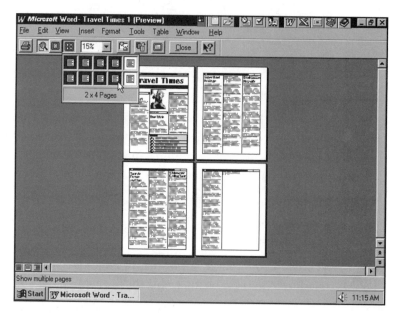

You mean I can edit here?

Yes, you can edit your text here. You can move whole chunks of text, reformat characters or paragraphs, adjust margins, or even insert a graphic. But only if you can actually see what you're doing, which is rarely true when you're using Print Preview.

The only time I use Print Preview's editing mode is when I want to fix a mistake in a big headline or move a graphic from one page to another. To change a word or a sentence, I switch back to Normal or Page Layout view.

Can I get a quick close-up of my page?

When you spread all the pages of your document out on the screen, you get a great sense of the big picture—where graphics are placed and where headlines fall, for example. But what if you want to quickly look at some picky little detail, like what that headline *really* says? There's an easy way to zoom in for a quick look, then pull back to see the big picture again.

 Click the Magnifier button, then click anywhere on a previewed page. The pointer changes to one of the two magnifying glasses you see in figure 13.3.

Fig. 13.3
When the pointer turns to either of these magnifying glasses, you can click (with either button) to zoom in and then back out again.

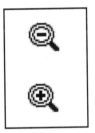

It *almost* fits. Now what?

 Use the Shrink To Fit button. But don't expect miracles, especially if your document is heavily formatted or filled with graphics. Shrink To Fit works best on simple memos and letters, when you want Word to make things just a teeny bit smaller so that last line will tuck itself in on the previous page.

If you don't like what Word does when you push the Shrink To Fit button, just use Undo to put everything back the way it was.

Enough already! I just want to print

 All systems go? Then click the Print button. Just like the Print button on the Standard toolbar, this one doesn't stop to ask questions. You get one copy of your entire document using whatever paper type your printer is set to use right now.

If you want to print an extra copy, or print just a few pages, skip the toolbar and head for the menus. When you choose File, Print, the Print dialog box, shown in figure 13.4, displays.

Check the printer. Is that the printer you really want to use? (If it isn't, click the Name box drop-down arrow, and pick another from the list.)

Fig. 13.4
Don't touch that button! Choose File, Print if you want to print extra copies or set other printing options.

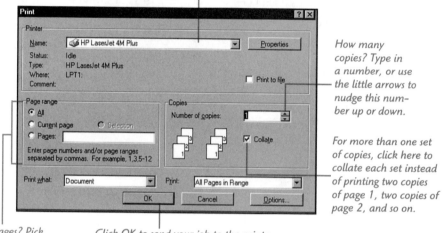

How many copies? Type in a number, or use the little arrows to nudge this number up or down.

For more than one set of copies, click here to collate each set instead of printing two copies of page 1, two copies of page 2, and so on.

Which pages? Pick just the current page, a list of pages, or the whole document.

Click OK to send your job to the printer.

Q&A *My pages come out in the wrong order every time I print, with the last page on top and the first page on the bottom. Is this a bug?*

It's not a bug, it's just the way your printer works. Fortunately, Word can work with your printer by sending pages to the printer in reverse order. Choose File, Print, and click the Options button. Make sure there's a check in the box labeled Reverse Print Order. Click OK and try it again.

What is Print Manager, and what does it do?

Windows is like a big corporation filled with middle managers. There's an Explorer, and a taskbar, and *this* guy, who handles all the print jobs that come from Word and all the other Office programs.

When you send a document to the printer, you're actually sending it to the Windows Print Manager, which will send it off to the printer as quickly as the printer can handle it. Because your programs can send stuff to the printer faster than the printer can print, it's possible for a bunch of print jobs to stack up at your printer like airplanes circling O'Hare Airport.

If you want to see what's happening to a Word document after you sent it to the printer, look in the Printers folder (Start, Settings, Printers). Double-click your printer's icon and poke through the list of documents waiting to be printed. As long as you're here, you can delete a job before it gets to the printer. You can also pause and resume different print jobs from here.

 CAUTION **Don't close Print Manager until it's handled all the print jobs in its list.** When you close Print Manager, it automatically deletes all the documents that are waiting in line. If you want to put the Print Manager out of the way, use the Minimize button instead.

 TIP **Did you just send a bunch of pages to the printer and realize you'd made a mistake?** Quick! Double-click the Printer icon on the taskbar at the botttom of the screen. If you're fast enough, you might be able to stop the job before it reaches the printer.

It's not working!

Printers have to be way, way up there on the list of Things That Cause Ulcers And High Blood Pressure. The average laser printer is a big, complicated machine, filled with gears and belts and sticky black powders and an *actual laser*. There's an entire volume in the Murphy's Law series dedicated exclusively to printers. So there's no way we can cover every possible thing that can go wrong when you try to print a Word document. But this list covers the most common problems.

I push the Print button and nothing happens

I once spent more than an hour cursing at a laser printer before I noticed that it was, well, uh... OK, it wasn't plugged in. I remember that embarrassing moment vividly every time I run through the following checklist of Incredibly Obvious Printer Boo-Boos:

- Is the printer connected to your PC? (Check the plugs on either end of the connection, just to be sure.)

- Is the printer plugged in and turned on?

- Does Windows know about your printer? Before Word can work with a printer, you have to install a **printer driver**—a small program that lets Windows communicate with your printer. When you use Word's File, Print command, press the Properties button to make sure your printer is set up as the default printer.

- Is the printer out of paper? Is there a paper jam?

- Are there any error messages on the printer's front panel? If there are, try turning the printer on and off to clear its memory and reset it, then try again.

It takes too long to print

Is that really the problem? Or are you frustrated by how long it takes before you can use your computer again? If your pages take too long to come out of the printer, you might just need a faster printer. But if you want to get back to work more quickly, the problem could be Word, which sometimes acts like it can't walk and chew gum at the same time.

When you push the Print button, Word puts all its energy into printing your documents. If you have a lot of pages, you can find yourself waiting a long time. To tell Word you want it to go into walk-and-chew-gum mode, choose

File, Print, and click the Options button. Put a check mark in the box next to the Background Printing option. From now on, Word will print a little more slowly so that it can continue to pay attention as you work with the next document.

My printouts don't look right

You'll have to be more specific. You mean that what you see doesn't match what you get? The problem might be fonts. Check the font-formatting in your document at the point where it starts looking out-of-kilter. If your printer doesn't support those fonts, you'll have to change the text to another font that your printer can cope with.

Q&A *How can I tell which fonts are OK to use?*

When you select a font from the Font List, look for a TT symbol or a tiny printer icon alongside the name. Those two labels point out TrueType fonts and fonts that are built into your printer. If there's no symbol next to the font name, it's a screen font only, and your printer might not print it the way it appears on the screen.

The Print menu is grayed out!

Windows doesn't know enough about your printer. Word (sensibly) won't allow you to waste time trying to print to a printer until it's properly set up. If you know how to use the Windows Control Panel, you can fix this problem yourself by double-clicking on the Printers icon and adding your printer to the list. If you have no idea what I'm talking about, you'll have to find your local Windows expert and ask for help.

When it works, it's magical. When it doesn't, it's a Maalox moment. Let's put the magic back in printing!

Printing in color

No doubt about it—Word is a colorful program. You can format any piece of text in a color, and throw shades and color patterns behind tables and charts. All that clip art is in color. Even the toolbars are filled with colorful icons.

So what happens when you take your colorful image and send it to the printer? If you're using a standard laser or dot-matrix printer, it's like heading into a '50s sitcom: all black and white.

Today, you have plenty of choices if you want a color printer, with prices that are competitive with those plain black-and-white models. The hottest models these days are called **inkjet printers;** they use a bunch of tiny tubes that splatter drops of colored ink on your paper in precise little patterns.

Should you get a color printer? If all you print out are letters and memos, probably not. Color printers are slow, and each page costs more than an equivalent page from a black-and-white printer.

If you use lots of charts and graphs, then color is a must. When you don't have a color printer, everything gets translated into different shades of gray, and no one will be able to tell the difference between the bars on your graph or the slices in your pie chart.

If you use PowerPoint a lot, I don't need to tell you that color counts. Go ahead—put together a presentation and prove conclusively that you need a new color printer *now*.

Part III: Using Excel

14

Creating a New Worksheet

● **In this chapter:**

- **What's the difference between a workbook and a worksheet?**

- **The Excel screen is pretty easy to figure out**

- **How to move around in the worksheet**

- **What's a range?**

- **Doing calculations**

- **Okay, I'm done now. How do I save my work?**

Excel can race through millions of calculations—literally!
—while you're still trying to find your desktop calculator's
ON switch . . . . ●

Excel can add, subtract, multiply, and divide, and a whole lot more. It has the memory of an elephant, the level-headed logic of Mr. Spock, and the specialized knowledge you'd expect from a banker, broker, mathematician, and all-around financial wizard, all rolled into one.

Excel lets you raise a number here or lower a number there to see exactly what would happen under different circumstances. This is called "What if?" analysis, and it's the real reason why a spreadsheet is a million times more powerful than a calculator. What if sales go up 10%? What if we cut the price of potatoes by 20 cents a pound? What if I refinance my mortgage? What if my boss gives me a $10,000 raise next year? What if I win the lottery? (Hey, it could happen...)

Starting out with Excel

When you start up Excel by clicking the Start button and choosing Programs, Microsoft Excel, you automatically open a new, blank Excel workbook. Excel gives this workbook the temporary name Book1. (Nobody expects you to use this generic name, of course; you'll get a chance to give your workbook a more meaningful name later.)

 TIP **If you start up Excel and immediately open a workbook you've** already created and saved, Excel closes the blank Book1 workbook automatically.

What's a workbook?

If you've ever used an accordion file folder, you'll understand how Excel workbooks work. Inside that accordion folder, individual compartments keep all your important papers separated from one another. An Excel workbook starts out with 16 similar compartments, each designed to hold one **worksheet**. Just like the expandable folder, you can make room in a workbook for a lot of worksheets or just a few (any number between 1 and 255).

The Excel workspace at a glance

This file, GST 1995 Expenses, is an Excel **workbook**. Like an accordion file folder, it can hold up to 255 separate worksheets, each in its own separate compartment.

Formatting toolbar
Lets you change the font, alignment, and number format with a single click.

Standard toolbar
Looks a lot like its counterparts in Word and PowerPoint, doesn't it? Open files, save files, cut/copy/paste—all the most-used Excel features are here.

Formula bar
One of two places where you can enter or edit a cell's contents. (You can also edit directly in the cell.)

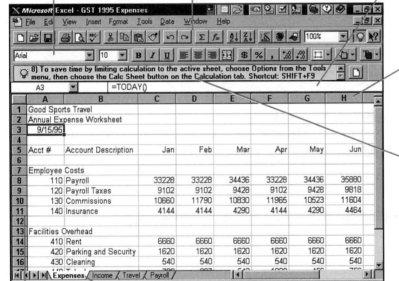

Column headings
Column headings are usually letters.

TipWizard box
This smart built-in trainer gives you advice about whatever you're currently doing.

Row headings
Row headings are usually numbers.

Worksheet tabs
Help you find individual worksheets easily. You can give plain-English names to worksheets, but you can't use spaces.

Status Bar
Watch it for hints on what's going on with your spreadsheet (like maybe the Caps Lock is on and that's why your words LOOK LIKE THIS).

Index **tabs** separate the individual worksheets; you can put plain-English labels on each tab (electronically—we'll show you how in a minute) and then rifle through them quickly to find exactly the worksheet you want. You start out in Sheet1, and if you look down at the bottom of the window, you'll see tabs for Sheet2, Sheet3, and so on. We'll talk more about those other worksheets later. For now, let's concentrate on the wide-open worksheet in front of us.

Plain English, please!

The terms **worksheet** and **spreadsheet** mean basically the same thing in Excel, but differ a little in the computer industry. *Spreadsheet* is generally used to describe the type of program Excel is: a **spreadsheet program**. The term for the files used by a spreadsheet program varies a lot: worksheet, workbook, page, sheet, and notebook are all common. The term *worksheet* in Excel is often abbreviated to just **sheet**.

OK, what's a worksheet?

A worksheet is a grid of **columns** and **rows** (columns go top to bottom and rows go left to right). There are 256 columns and 16,384 rows in each worksheet. At an intersection of any column with any row you get a **cell**. What does that give you? A whopping 4,194,304 cells per worksheet (more than enough for anybody's needs, really).

Columns are labeled by letters, and rows by numbers. I know what you're thinking: *but there are only 26 letters in the alphabet!* Excel solves that limitation by starting with A–Z, then double-parking, as follows: AA, AB, AC, and so on, to AZ. Next, there's BA, BB, BC, and… you get the idea. The last column is IV, which looks like the Roman numeral 4, but it's the column that follows IU, which follows IT, which comes after IS, and so on…

Cells are identified by an **address**, which is the marriage of the column's letter and the row's number. So the very first cell, at the top left corner, is A1 (see figure 14.1). The last cell in any worksheet is IV16384.

Fig. 14.1
Rows, columns, cells.
Welcome to the
incredibly orderly Excel
neighborhood.

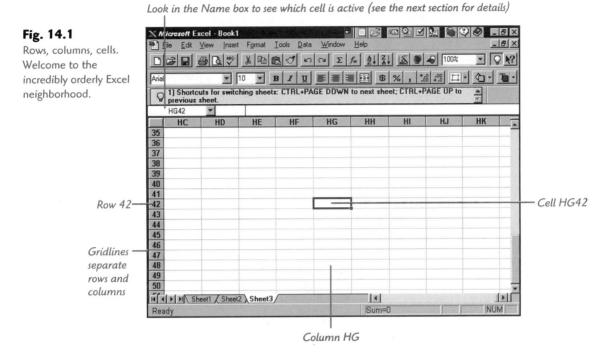

Look in the Name box to see which cell is active (see the next section for details)

Row 42 ——— Cell HG42

Gridlines
separate
rows and
columns

Column HG

Moving around in a worksheet

Whether an Excel worksheet is empty or full, you should have no trouble
finding your way around. If you start from cell A1 and move one cell to the
right, you land in cell B1. In this neighborhood, getting or giving directions is
easy: "F124? Sure, just keep going one block past Avenue E, then hang a
right and go 123 blocks. You can't miss it."

In a new worksheet, you automatically start in cell A1. The cell where you're
currently working at any time is said to be **active** or **selected**, so A1 is
active by default in a new worksheet. As you move around in the worksheet,
the active cell changes, but you can always tell which cell is active by the
dark box that encloses the cell, and by the matching address in the Name
box. If you jump back to figure 14.1 for a second, you'll notice that cell HG42
is active. Moving one cell to the right would make HH42 the active cell;
moving one cell down instead would make HG43 the active cell.

Moving from cell to cell

As long as your worksheet is just a few rows and columns, it's easy enough to get around by just pointing and clicking or tapping the arrow keys—it's like moving around in a Word document or a text file. The arrow keys and scroll bars work pretty much the same way. Sooner or later, though, your worksheet will get so big that it won't fit in a single window. When that happens, refer to table 14.1 to learn how to get around by using just the keyboard.

Table 14.1 Getting around with the keyboard

To do this...	Press this
Move to beginning of row	Home
Move up/down one window	Page Up/Page Down
Go to the top left corner of the worksheet	Ctrl+Home
Move to the lower right corner of your worksheet	Ctrl+End
Jump to the next worksheet	Ctrl+Page Up
Jump to the previous worksheet	Ctrl+Page Down
Move to a specific cell or area of the worksheet	F5 or Ctrl+G (GoTo); type the cell address
Move from left to right or top to bottom in a selected area	Tab
Move the opposite direction in a selected area	Shift+Tab

Q&A *I pressed the End key, but I didn't go to the end of the row the way I expected. What does this key do, anyway?*

When you press the End key, you turn on End mode. What happens next depends on which key you press next. If you press an arrow key, you'll jump in the direction of that arrow to the last cell in that row or column that has data or formatting in it and is next to an empty cell. Whew. Did you follow that?

End Home goes to the last cell in the current worksheet (the one in the bottom right corner). Press End Enter to move to the last cell in the current row. End mode is handy when you're jumping back and forth between two adjacent blocks of cells, but it's fairly confusing to use. The best method is just to practice jumping around with End mode until you get the hang of it.

Selecting cells

If you want to do something with a single cell, you start by selecting it. Use these techniques:

- To select the cell, point and click or use the arrow keys to get there.

- To position the insertion point in the cell, point to the position in the cell contents where you want the insertion point, and double-click.

- To select characters in the cell, double-click in the cell, then drag through the characters you want to select.

- To select a word in the cell, select the cell, then double-click the word. (This also works with cell addresses and other things that aren't, strictly speaking, words.)

How to build a worksheet

Before you begin to enter data, think about what you want to do with your worksheet. Do you want to analyze last year's expenses, category-by-category and month-by-month? Then you'll need 12 columns, one for each month of the year, plus one row for each category. Most worksheets start out with a simple arrangement of rows and columns. The easiest way to get started is to enter descriptive titles for rows and columns. With that task out of the way, you can then enter your data and analyze it.

There's no need to worry too much about the structure of your worksheet at this point. It's easy to move things around and add more rows and columns later.

Just start typing

Once you've formed a mental picture of the basic layout of your worksheet, it's time to start filling in the titles and the data. Typing in a cell is easy: move to the cell with the mouse or the arrow keys, and then start typing.

Whatever you type shows up in two places: in the cell and in the **formula bar**, just above the A-B-C headings over your columns. Think of the formula bar as a scratch pad, where you can type anything you like; your characters don't actually go into the cell until you explicitly tell Excel to put them there.

As soon as you begin typing, three small boxes appear to the left of the formula bar (see fig. 14.2).

Fig. 14.2
The **cursor** flashes on and off just like in Word to show the **insertion point**—the place where you're currently entering data.

Click the Cancel box to tell Excel, "Oops! Never mind." Excel restores whatever was in the cell before you started typing.

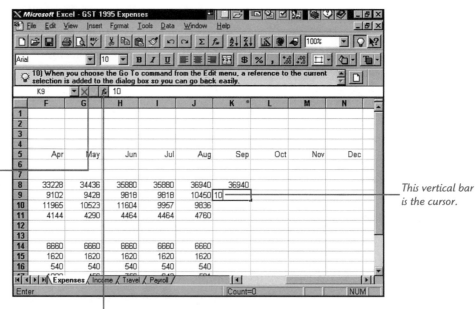

This vertical bar is the cursor.

Click the Function Wizard button to pop up a fill-in-the–blanks form that builds Excel formulas automatically.

If you hit the wrong key while you're typing, press Backspace to fix your mistake. To cancel the entire entry, press Esc. Entering a bunch of data in a column? Press Enter instead of clicking the Enter box. This trick puts the data in the cell *and* moves down to the next cell in that column. Going across a row? Press the right-arrow key when you're done typing the cell entry. That parks the entry in the cell and moves you one cell to the right.

TIP **Want to type the same cell entry in more than one place? Select** the cells you want, type the entry, and press Ctrl+Enter.

Q&A *The cursor doesn't move when I press Enter.*

Somebody's been playing with your system settings. Choose Tools, Options, click on the Edit tab, and click next to Move Selection after Enter. Then click on the drop-down arrow and specify whether you want to progress up, down, or sideways.

Oops—that's *not* what I meant to type!

There are a few easy ways to fix mistakes you've already entered:

- If you just need to fix one or two characters, select the cell. The cell contents appear in the formula bar; click at the place in the text where you want to make a change.

- Rather edit in the cell? Press the F2 key while the cell is selected, or double-click the cell. Then use the mouse to select the portion you want to replace. When you start typing, the highlighted text will be replaced by whatever you type.

- To clear (erase) the contents of a cell, select the cell and then press the Del key on your keyboard.

  Don't use the space bar to "empty" the contents of a cell. You've just replaced the existing contents with a space, and Excel might miscalculate averages or counts. And don't choose Edit, Delete to clear a cell, either. That menu choice actually removes the entire cell and readjusts the cells on your worksheet like pieces in a jigsaw puzzle.

- To replace all the contents of a cell with something new, select the cell, type the new stuff, and hit Enter.

Q&A   *I just erased the contents of a cell, and I didn't mean to! Now what do I do?*

Relax. Press Ctrl+Z or click the Undo button. Most of the time, this will bring back the data you accidentally wiped out—as long as it's the last thing you've done.

BUT—Excel has a really lousy memory, so be careful. After you've used Word for a while, you might get used to fiddling around recklessly with documents, knowing that you can always click Undo (and keep clicking it) to put things back the way they were. But Excel's Undo button only keeps track of the very last thing you did. If you delete a row, then reformat another cell, you can undo the formatting, but not the deletion.

I typed a number, but all I see is ######.

Your number is too long to fit in the cell. If you only saw a few digits of the number, you could get horribly confused. So Excel puts a bunch of number signs (####) in the cell to tell you there's something there, but you can't see it. You'll have to make the column wider before you can see the number.

If you type a really big number (like 1000000000), you might get the scientific version: 1E+09. That's discussed in the Chapter 15, and Chapter 16 shows you how to format column widths so you can see everything appropriately.

TIP   **Negative numbers usually are shown in parentheses on your** worksheet (and in red if you have a color monitor).

What if the text is sticking out of the cell?

Text that doesn't fit in one cell will spill over into the next cell if that cell is empty. If there's something there, your text will cut off at the border between the two cells. To see all the information in the cell, select it and look in the formula bar. Better yet, make the cell wider. (Look in Chapter 16 for more details on adjusting column widths.)

Can't figure out where you are?
Try these tricks

Sometimes as you're entering a lot of data you sort of lose track of which column you're in. Help yourself out with one of the methods in the following sections.

Zoom out to see the whole worksheet

Use the Zoom Control button on the Standard toolbar to step back and see the "big picture" of your worksheet. Click on the drop-down arrow and then click on Selection. Now you'll see your entire worksheet (although if your worksheet is big enough, you may not be able to read it!). To return to normal view, click Zoom Control again and select your normal zoom mode (100% or 90% or whatever you prefer).

Keep the headings from sliding off-screen

If your column or row headings have moved off the screen, it's easy to type stuff in the wrong cells by accident. But you can freeze the headings in place and let the rest of the worksheet move past them. It's like folding the headings over on a piece of paper so they line up with whatever you're writing—but it doesn't hurt your worksheet a bit.

In figure 14.3, notice that you can see the row titles at the left, *and* the columns for August, September, and so on at the right. Normally, you wouldn't be able to see both on-screen at the same time.

To freeze the window, select the cell to the right of the column(s) you want to freeze, and/or below the row(s) you want to freeze. Then choose Window, Freeze Panes. To unfreeze, choose Window, Unfreeze Panes.

Fig. 14.3
To get to the frozen areas, click the cell you want.

Notice that some column letters are missing—they've "slid past" the frozen columns

The dark lines indicate frozen panes

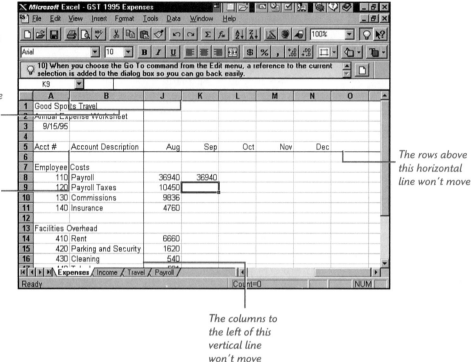

The rows above this horizontal line won't move

The columns to the left of this vertical line won't move

>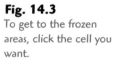
>
> **TIP** **If a worksheet occasionally won't let you move to the upper left** corner of the worksheet, check to see if the panes are frozen. You can tell by opening the Window menu. If you see Unfreeze Panes on the menu, the panes are frozen.

Split the window into pieces

If you grab one of the **split boxes** (shown in fig. 14.4) and drag it down or to the left, Excel splits the window into two **panes**, horizontally or vertically— or four panes if you split it both ways. Each pane has its own scroll bars for moving around. **Split bars** divide the panes visually. To get rid of a split bar, double-click it or drag it off the window.

Fig. 14.4

If you drag the split bars instead of the split boxes, the split bars line up on the spreadsheet's gridlines, which is handy.

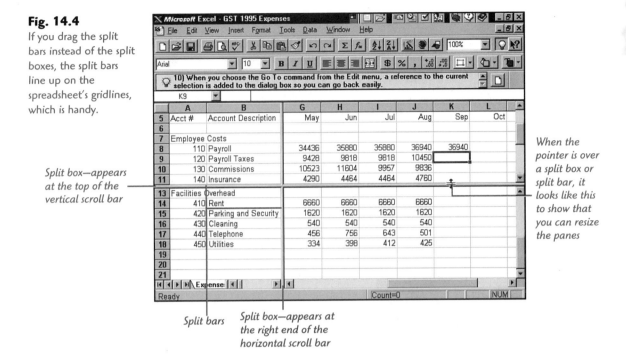

Split box—appears at the top of the vertical scroll bar

When the pointer is over a split box or split bar, it looks like this to show that you can resize the panes

Split bars

Split box—appears at the right end of the horizontal scroll bar

Working with more than one cell at a time

When you drive along the streets and avenues in your town, you pass one house after another. Each one's different, but you can still think of all those houses in logical groups—like that row of brownstones on A Street, or all the addresses in ZIP code 90210, or every house that has a big barking dog.

As you cruise up and down Excel's rows and columns, you can arrange cells into a group, called a **range**. And working with ranges instead of dealing with one cell at a time can cut hours off your work day. Anything you can do with one cell, you can do with a range. You can, for example, **format** a range of cells all at once. If you highlight a range and click the Bold button, for example, all the characters in the range will turn to bold-face type. You can even give a range a plain-English name so it's easier to refer to later.

Ranges are usually rectangular. The smallest range is a single cell—which, you'll notice, is rectangular. If a range is three cells deep and four cells wide, that rectangle contains 12 cells. But the ranges don't have to be rectangular—you can even select a range containing cells that are scattered around the worksheet. Figure 14.5 shows a variety of ranges.

Plain English, please!

When cells in a range are next to each other, they're called **contiguous** (kuhn-TIG-you-us). When they're not next to each other, of course, they're **noncontiguous**.

Excel uses two addresses to identify a range, beginning with the cell in the upper left corner and ending with the cell in the lower right corner of the selection. A colon (:) separates the two addresses that identify the range.

Fig. 14.5

The active cell in a range is not high-lighted when the range is selected, but is outlined in bold—and a different color if the range contains a colored background.

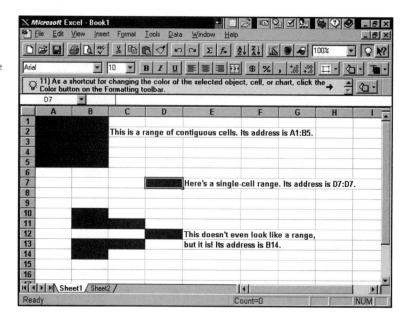

Selecting ranges

Selecting a range is really pretty easy:

- To select a contiguous range, click in the cell at one corner of the range and drag the mouse pointer to the opposite corner.

- To select a noncontiguous range, select the first cell or group of cells, hold down the Ctrl key, and select the next cell or group of cells. Continue holding the Ctrl key down until you've selected all the cells you want.

- To select an entire row or column, click on the letter or number in its heading (see fig. 14.6).

- To select multiple rows or columns, select the first row or column, and hold down the mouse button while dragging through the rest.

Fig. 14.6
Notice how the heading labels (HG and 42, in this example) change shading to show they've been selected.

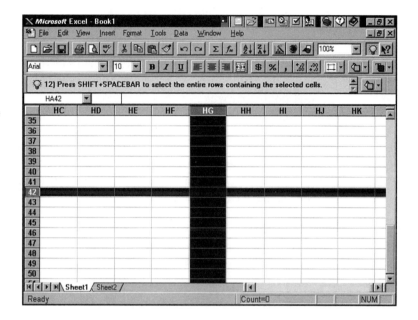

How to move around in a range

To restrict your data entry to a specific range, select it first. After you've selected a range, the Enter key still moves you down to the next cell, but only within the range. When you reach the bottom row of the range, Excel moves the active cell to the top of the next column to the right in the selection. When you get to the lower right corner of the range, pressing Enter moves you back to the upper left corner. To move within the range from right to left, one row at a time, use Tab; Shift+Enter and Shift+Tab move in the opposite direction.

Best part of Excel: formulas

If all you wanted to do was type columns of numbers, you could do that in Word. Word's table feature can even do some basic calculations with the numbers. So why do you need Excel? What's the point of using a spreadsheet program, anyway? Spreadsheets can perform extremely complex calculations with the information you enter. Better yet, a spreadsheet program can do something even more interesting—it can update your information *for* you.

Suppose you're balancing your checkbook at home one evening. You start with the ending balance shown on the bank statement, add in any deposits not shown on the statement, subtract any outstanding checks and fees, and you're supposed to get the total shown in your checkbook. No? You probably typed something wrong, and now you have to start over. Your calculator can't remember what you typed, so you have to type the whole thing again.

But not in Excel. It doesn't matter how huge the worksheet is, or how complex the calculations are. Once you spot your mistake and correct the cell entry, Excel can automatically recalculate everything for you. And it's virtually instantaneous!

This magic trick occurs because of Excel's **formulas**. A formula is just a calculation that you create in a cell. It can be as simple as "2+2," or as complex as "1995 revenues, minus expenses, multiplied by projected sales increase percentage for 1996…" you get the idea.

How to type a formula

Most of what you type in your spreadsheet will be data—text and numbers—dates, column headings, account numbers, sales figures, etc. When you type the data, you're sending a message to the selected cell in the worksheet: "Put this information right here." When you enter words or numbers, Excel assumes you're entering a **value**, and simply takes your message and stuffs it into the appropriate cell. If you start your message with an equal sign, though, Excel knows you're typing a formula, and handles it differently. When you type **=950-21**, you're telling Excel, "Please subtract 21 from 950, and show the result in the cell."

Pay attention to that *result*. This is a little confusing about Excel at first. When you enter a formula in a cell, Excel keeps track of the formula, but displays the result of the formula in the cell. So, if you type **=2+2** in a cell, Excel displays 4, of course. But if you select the cell, you'll see the formula, =2+2, displayed in the formula bar. Check out figure 14.7 to see what I mean.

Fig. 14.7

For every formula you enter in your worksheet, Excel displays the result in the cell, but remembers the original formula. You can edit the formula any time you want.

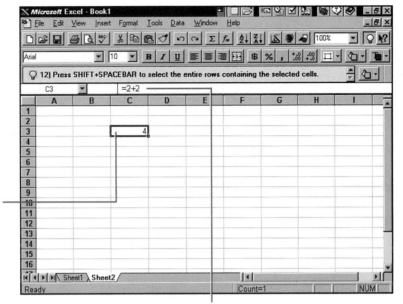

Here's the result displayed in the cell

Here's the formula I typed

Q&A ***One of my cells has*** #DIV/0! ***in it. What's that all about?***

Any time you see a cell that begins with the number sign (#), that's Excel telling you that it can't handle your formula. In this case, Excel is scolding you like a high school math teacher, telling you that you can't divide by 0. The formula you entered is still under there; you'll have to fix the problem before Excel will take away the error message.

Rules for using formulas

A formula can combine values, cell references, mathematical signs, **functions** (special built-in Excel formulas), and even other formulas.

When you enter a formula, you have to follow Excel's rules:

- A formula always begins with an equal sign.

- You can use any of these mathematical **operators** as part of a formula: add (+), subtract (-), multiply (*), divide (/), calculate percentage (%), or increase exponentially (^).

- To control the order of calculation, use parentheses. Excel does multiplication and division before addition and subtraction, so =3+4*5 is 23, while =(3+4)*5 is 35.

Q&A ***My calculation didn't work! The cell just says 2+2 instead of showing 4. What did I do wrong?***

You left out the equal sign. Excel is maddeningly consistent about this sort of thing. Without the equal sign, Excel treats your formula as simple text.

Excel can usually figure out what you're typing

Excel is pretty smart. If you type something that looks like a date, say **10/15/95**, Excel decides it's a date and displays it that way. Is it a number? Excel not only displays it as a number, but aligns it at the right side of the cell. Plain old text? Aligned at the left. When Excel can't figure out what to do with something you type, like a formula that you didn't get quite right, it fills in the cell with #NAME? or #REF? or something equally confusing. That's Excel's way of saying, "Huh?"

Table 14.2 gives some examples of stuff you might type into an Excel cell, and tells what Excel does with it. Weird-looking formulas like those in the last rows of the table are discussed in the next chapter.

Table 14.2 What you type and what Excel does with it

Enter these...	Examples...	Excel treats it as...
Numbers only, in any format	42 $999.95 34.8%	Number
Letters and numbers	Travel Expenses 12 #10 envelopes 5% Discount	Text
Anything that looks like a date or time	12/20/95 3:30 AM September 15	Date/Time
Anything beginning with an equal sign	=2+2 =F124*.0825 =SUM(D4:D15)	Formula

Saving the Workbook

As you build the basic structure of your worksheet and enter data, it's always a good idea to save the workbook periodically, using a descriptive name. If you get interrupted, you can always close the file and come back to it later, and your work is protected if the power goes out. Click the Save button, choose the proper folder, and give your workbook file a descriptive file name. (You don't have to type the .XLS extension. Excel will automatically add that for you.)

For more details on how to save and name files, see Chapter 4.

Opening another new workbook

To create another new workbook, press Ctrl+N, or click the New Workbook button. Excel doesn't even try to be imaginative with names—each new workbook gets another generic name, like Book2, Book3, and so on. After the new workbook is open, you're ready to start working again!

TIP **You can also create new workbooks by right-clicking on the** Windows Desktop or within an Explorer window, then selecting New, Microsoft Excel Worksheet. Once that blank worksheet has been created, type a new name, then double-click on its icon to launch Excel and start typing into the new worksheet.

15

Get the Most Out of Your Worksheets

● In this chapter:

- **Typed the wrong thing in a cell? Edit it!**

- **How do I move things from one place to another?**

- **Hate typing lists? Excel can do it for you**

- **I forgot a column**

- **Work smarter with more than one worksheet**

When you move, you have to learn new shortcuts to get you where you want to go by the quickest route. This chapter shows you the shortcuts for Excel. . . . . ➤

Whenever I move to a new neighborhood, the first thing I do is drive around. I learn where the good Chinese restaurants are hidden, how late the grocery store stays open, and which houses have big barking dogs.

When you first look at an Excel worksheet, you might figure it's a pretty boring place. Rows, columns, cells—what's so complicated about that? Actually, there's a complex world inside that worksheet, and once you learn some simple techniques, you'll discover ways to do everyday work faster. You'll also find that Excel lets you look at data—words and numbers—in ways you've never considered before.

In this chapter, you learn how to take a simple worksheet design and adjust all the pieces so they match the work you want to do. Once you learn your way around, maybe this neighborhood isn't so dull after all.

Opening a saved workbook

Good morning! It's another working day, time for you and Excel to pick up where you left off yesterday.

To open a file you've already created and saved, pull down the File menu first. Excel automatically keeps track of the four files you used most recently, in a list at the bottom of the File menu. If the file's not there, click the Open option and hunt through your data folders until you find it.

Substitute names for addresses

When you mail a letter, what's the most important piece of information on the envelope? To the post office, the address is everything. But as far as you're concerned, it's the name that matters most.

Like the post office, Excel is most concerned about addresses (cell references) because its job is to make sure that all your data ends up in the right cells. So, Excel is content to know that the formula that totals up all your annual expenses is located in cell G24. But that connection isn't so obvious to you or me, unless we want to puzzle out what each formula means. Wouldn't it be more convenient if you could simply assign that cell a name like TotalExpenses?

You can. Excel lets you give any cell or range a plain-English name. The effect is just like nailing up a sign that says "The Wilsons" on the mailbox outside G24. Your postman knows where the Wilsons live, just as Excel knows how to track down your cell named TotalExpenses. Now you can use either the boring, Excel-style rows-and-columns address or the plain-English version. If the Wilsons move, they take the sign with them; likewise, if you move TotalExpenses from G24 to F13, the cell name moves with it.

Naming your cells and ranges

Every important cell on your worksheet—especially the ones where you plan to change data to test different "What if?" scenarios—should have a name, not just a number. On an invoice worksheet, for example, you can name one cell SalesTaxRate and another InvoiceTotal. Then, in the TotalAmount cell, you can replace those confusing cell addresses with the easy-to-understand formula **=InvoiceTotal*SalesTaxRate**.

Here are some very good reasons why you should use range names:

- You're less likely to make mistakes as you move cells around, because Excel automatically keeps track of named cells and ranges.

- Names make it easier for you to understand how your worksheet works, especially when you want to reuse a worksheet you created long ago. After all, which of the following formulas is easier to figure out? The first has a lot more letters, but at least you can tell what's going on without having to jump to a cell address to see what's in there.

    =InvoiceTotal*SalesTaxRate-Coupon_or_Discount

    =HG42*HI57-HJ411

- When you make mistakes, it's easier to find them, because your formulas are written in plain English.

- It's easier to get around because you can jump to different cells or ranges by choosing their names from a list.

What kind of names can I use?

Excel is picky about what you can and can't enter when naming a cell or a range. (Just to make things extra confusing, the rules are completely different from the ones for naming a file or a worksheet tab.) Here are the rules:

- You can use a total of up to 255 characters (but it's better to keep them simple).

- The first character must be a letter or the underline character. You can't name a cell 1stQuarterSales, but Q1Sales is OK.

- The remaining characters can be letters, numbers, periods, or the underline character. No other punctuation marks are allowed.

- Spaces are forbidden. If you try to name a cell Sales Tax Rate, Excel will just beep at you, but Sales_Tax_Rate is OK.

- A cell or range name cannot look like a cell reference or a value, so you can't rename a cell Q1 or W2, for example, or a single letter or number.

How to name a range

The easiest way to name a cell or a range is to use the Name box, located just to the left of the Formula bar (see fig. 15.1). Here's how you do it:

1 Select the cell or range you want to name.

2 Click in the Name box to highlight the entire cell address.

3 Type a legal name for the cell or range (remember, you can't start with a number).

4 Press Enter to add the name to the list in your worksheet.

Fig. 15.1
Click the down-arrow button; then use the drop-down list of range names to jump to named ranges in a worksheet.

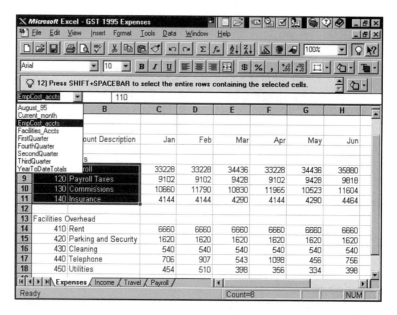

Once you've created a range name, you can select the entire range with a couple of mouse clicks. Just choose the range name from the drop-down list, and Excel will instantly jump there.

 TIP **Use the drop-down list of range names to fill in formulas, as well.** Instead of typing in the range name, just point to the name in the list and click. Excel will paste the name directly into your formula.

Moving stuff from one place to another

What happens when you move something from one place to another? Let's say you tell Excel, "Pick up whatever's in G24, and move it to F13." What happens next?

- If there's anything in the destination cell, F13, it'll be wiped out just as surely as if you'd hit the Del key. Zap! Gone.

- If there's a formula in G24, it may adjust itself to reflect the new location. (See the sidebar, "Understanding cell references," for an explanation.)

- Because you moved the contents of G24 to F13, G24 is now empty. If you had *copied* G24 instead of *moving* it, the contents would have remained unchanged.

Can I just drag something from one place to another?

If you just want to move a cell a short distance, the easiest way to do it is just to drag the cell (or an entire range, for that matter), and drop it on the new location. Well, it's easy once you get the hang of it. Excel doesn't give you an obvious clue that you've actually grabbed a cell, the way that Word does, but you can watch the status bar. You'll just have to practice until you get it.

When you point at various parts of a cell, you'll see several Excel pointers that are designed to do different things. The trick is learning how to tell these pointers apart (see table 15.1). You may see other pointers in Excel periodically; these are the most common.

Table 15.1 Excel's pointers

When you do this...	You'll see this pointer...	And then you can...
Point anywhere in a cell	⊕	Select a cell or a range
Select a cell or range, then point at its border	↖	Move a cell or range by dragging and dropping it
Make a selection, hold down the Ctrl key, then point at the border of the selection	↖+	Copy a cell or range by dragging and dropping it
Select a cell or range, then aim at the fill handle in the selection's lower right corner	+	Automatically fill in a series of data (see AutoFill, later in this chapter)
Make a selection, hold down the Ctrl key, then aim at the fill handle	+⁺	Automatically fill in a changing series of data

When you point to the thick border on the edge of a selection, the pointer changes to an arrow. When that happens, you can drag the selection and drop it in a new location. As you drag, you'll see a ghostly reflection of the cell's borders follow the mouse pointer around.

If you hold down the Ctrl key while you drag the selection, the mouse pointer changes to an arrow with a plus sign beside it; that's your only cue that you're about to copy rather than move the contents of the selection.

Frankly, I find this Ctrl+key rigmarole hopelessly confusing, which is why I use the *right* mouse button when I want to drag something from one place to another on a worksheet. When you right-drag a selection and drop it in a new location, a shortcut menu pops up, giving you a chance to tell Excel exactly what you want it to do (see fig. 15.2).

CAUTION **Be careful where you right-click. The mouse pointer should be in** the arrow shape, or you'll get a menu with different options. (See the next section for details on how to use that menu.)

Fig. 15.2
Use the right mouse
button to drag a
selection from one
place to another, and
this shortcut menu will
pop up at your
destination.

Understanding cell references: it's all relative (except when it's absolute)

The first time you move or copy a formula, you might be surprised to see that Excel automatically changes any cell references in your formula. Is this a bug? Not at all—it's an example of how Excel uses **relative references** to help you build powerful worksheets without a lot of typing.

What's a relative reference, and why should you care? Imagine you're lost in a strange neighborhood. You stop a passer-by and ask for help in getting to the train station. He might give you directions that relate to where you are right now: "Go three blocks straight ahead, then turn right and go five more blocks." Or he might use an **absolute reference**: "It's at the corner of Avenue D and 24th Street."

When you copy or move a formula, Excel automatically adjusts cell references to reflect their relative position. If you move the formula three rows down and five columns to the right, it adds 3 to each row number and counts five letters higher in the alphabet for each cell address in the new formula. So a reference to D5 changes to I8.

But what happens when you store a scrap of crucial information, like the current interest rate, in one cell? You want your Excel formulas to look in that one cell whenever they need to make an interest-related calculation. In that case, use dollar signs to order Excel to use the cell's absolute address. When you type **$A$4**, Excel treats that as an absolute address, and doesn't adjust it when you move or copy a formula. No matter where the formula ends up, that part of the formula always refers specifically to cell A4.

You can mix and match relative and absolute addresses in a formula, or even in the same address. For example, $A4 tells Excel to leave the column address at A any time you move or copy the formula, but adjust the row address relative to the new location.

When you enter a cell address in the formula bar, you can quickly cycle through relative, mixed, and absolute addresses. Just point anywhere in the address, and press F4 to cycle through all four variations.

TIP **When you copy one cell to a range, it fills that whole range. This** is an extremely useful technique when you're adding formulas to a highly structured worksheet. To total every column in a budget worksheet, for example, just create the SUM formula under the first column, then copy the formula below all the other columns and Excel will adjust each formula so it totals the cells above it.

When to cut, copy, and paste

To move or copy a selection outside of the current window, your best bet is to click the right mouse button and pop up Excel's shortcut menu (see fig. 15.3). Don't bother dragging and dropping. It's too easy to overshoot your target.

Fig. 15.3
Don't like to drag-and-drop? Click the right mouse button, then use the shortcut menu to quickly cut or copy a range from one place...

...and paste it in another.

Follow these steps to cut or copy, and then paste a range:

1 Point at the selected range, right-click, and choose Cut or Copy from the shortcut menu.

As soon as you click the menu choice, the border around the selection begins to move, like a line of marching ants. (You don't believe me? Just look...)

2 Point to the cell where you want to paste the selection and right-click.

3 Choose Paste to insert the selection. (Or press Esc if you change your mind.)

CAUTION **The Excel version of cut and paste doesn't work like other**
Windows programs. When you cut something in Excel, you get to paste it
somewhere else, and then the Windows Clipboard empties out. Other
programs (including Word) leave the stuff you cut in the Clipboard so you
can use it again if you want.

Moral: If you want to reuse the same range, use Copy instead of Cut, then
delete the original.

Excel's amazing mind-reading tricks: AutoFill, AutoComplete, and AutoCorrect

Excel can count from 1 to several gazillion. It knows the days of the week
and the months of the year, and it knows that Q2 comes after Q1 and before
Q3. That's not exactly rocket science. But you can take advantage of Excel's
skills with lists to fill in the rest of the months after you type **January**.

This feature is called **AutoFill**, and you can use it to fill in standard lists,
series of numbers and dates, or even custom lists (as long as you don't mind
teaching Excel what to do the first time). It's a simple mind-reading trick,
really, but it'll save you a minute here, and 20 seconds there.

Fill in a list automatically

First, you need to learn to recognize Excel's **fill handle**. Select a cell or a
range; you'll see a thick border around the entire selection. Look in the
lower right corner for a small black square. That's the fill handle. When you
aim the mouse pointer at the fill handle, it turns to a thin black cross; at that
point you can drag in any direction to start filling in values.

This is the fill handle

TIP **If there's no fill handle on your selected cell range, you'll need to**
activate it. Select Tools, Options, click on the Edit tab, and click next to
Allow Cell Drag and Drop to turn the handle on.

Using AutoFill is like refilling an ice cube tray in your freezer. As you drag
(pour the water), the selection gets bigger and includes more cells. When
you release the mouse button, Excel fills every cell in the selection with

values, as shown in figure 15.4. Which values? That depends on what's in the first cell. There are several such predefined AutoFill lists in Excel:

- Q1–Q4 or any other variation of that (2nd QTR 1995, 3rd QTR 1995, and so on)

- Jan–Dec (or January–December)

- Sun–Saturday (or Sunday–Saturday)

Fig. 15.4
Filling in a series automatically.

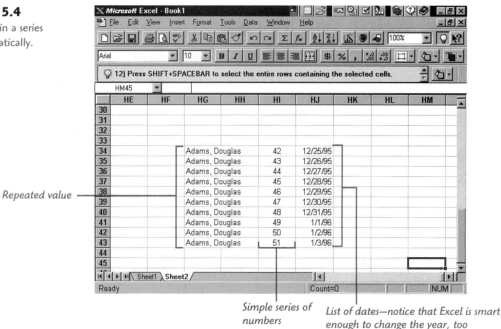

Repeated value —

Simple series of numbers

List of dates—notice that Excel is smart enough to change the year, too

Here's how you insert the various kinds of automatic lists:

- To **repeat a value**, type it in the first cell, then grab the fill handle and drag. Your value, the words Due Date, the number 42—whatever—will be repeated in the AutoFill selection.

- To **create a simple series of numbers**, type in a starting number, grab the fill handle, hold down the Ctrl key, and drag the AutoFill pointer. Your list starts with the original number, and increases by one throughout the AutoFill selection.

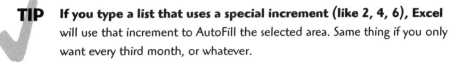

TIP If you type a list that uses a special increment (like 2, 4, 6), Excel will use that increment to AutoFill the selected area. Same thing if you only want every third month, or whatever.

- To **fill in a list of months or days**, type the first entry in the list, in full or abbreviated, and drag the AutoFill handle.

- To **extend a list of dates**, type the first date, in any format, and drag the AutoFill selection.

Create your own AutoFill list

Once you get used to using AutoFill, it'll be one of your most valuable data entry tools. Use it for any repetitive list—names of your employees, your products, your divisions, and so on. So rather than typing Super Bowl, Rose Bowl, World Series, and the rest of the major sporting events on your list every time you create a new spreadsheet, you can create a custom list, so that whenever you type Super Bowl in a cell and drag the AutoFill handle, the rest of the events will fill in like magic. To do so, follow these steps:

1 Select Tools, Options, and click on the Custom Lists tab.

2 In the List Entries box, type your list, pressing Enter after each entry.

3 Click on Add.

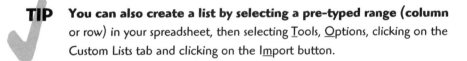

TIP You can also create a list by selecting a pre-typed range (column or row) in your spreadsheet, then selecting Tools, Options, clicking on the Custom Lists tab and clicking on the Import button.

AutoComplete and AutoCorrect

Court stenographers, newspapers reporters, and college students have to be very efficient when they take notes. You just can't write at your regular pace, dotting each i with a circle or heart, when somebody's talking a mile a minute. That's why the shorthand system has been invented, where one tiny symbol stands for a whole word or phrase. Because Excel can be pretty heavy on the data-entry side, it offers two life-saving (or wrist-saving) shorthand tools: AutoComplete and AutoCorrect.

- **AutoComplete** is really spooky. It truly reads your mind. Type one or two characters, and Excel takes its best shot at guessing what you're about to type, based on other entries in the column. So if you've typed **Adams, Douglas** several rows before and now start typing **Ad**, the rest of the name gets typed in for you. Just hit Enter or down arrow, and it's inserted in the cell. If you don't want to accept it (because you really meant to type **Addams Family** this time), just continue typing, and Excel will remove its suggestion from the cell. Note that AutoComplete doesn't apply to numbers, only text.

TIP   **Too lazy to type even one or two characters? You can also select** from a list of all the previous entries in the column by right-clicking on the cell you want to type into, and selecting Pick from List.

- **AutoCorrect** works exactly the same way it does in Word. Assign abbreviations (shorthand symbols) to text you often have to type, so that when you type **SB96**, you'll get Super Bowl 1996. You can even create new AutoCorrect entries.

Adding (and deleting) cells, rows, and columns

When you first set up a worksheet, you probably won't get the arrangement of rows and columns just right. That's OK—you can always insert or delete a cell, a row, or a column.

Whenever you insert or delete cells in a worksheet, Excel shuffles everything around to make room. If you delete Row 12, for example, Row 13 moves up into Row 12; the folks in 14 move to 13, and so on.

The best way to insert or delete anything is with the right-mouse-button shortcut menus. Make a selection, then pop up the shortcut menu and choose Insert or Delete. Excel will display a dialog box like the one in figure 15.5, asking you how you want the worksheet rearranged.

TIP   **If you work with the Tables feature in Word, you'll recognize** this dialog box. It works the same way in Excel as in Word.

Fig. 15.5
When you select a cell and choose Delete, Excel asks how to rearrange the worksheet.

 Q&A *I deleted a column, and now some of my formulas don't work any more.*

When you delete a cell, Excel removes every trace of it. If formulas elsewhere in the worksheet referred to that cell, Excel will get hopelessly confused and say something like #REF! It means Excel has lost track of a reference and can't display the value for the formula. You'll have to put the formula back in with corrected references.

Working smarter with worksheets

Some people just stuff papers into file folders and leave it at that. If your approach to organizing information is that casual, skip this section. Otherwise, read on for instructions on keeping the worksheets in each workbook neatly arranged and clearly labeled.

Renaming a worksheet

How would you like it if you went in search of important information in a file cabinet, and found that all the folders were labeled Folder1, Folder2, and so forth? How could you possibly know that your January expense report was in Folder143?

The default labels on Excel worksheet tabs are nearly that useless. Sheet1, Sheet2? How uninformative. You'll get more work done if your sheets have plain-English names like Sales Forecasts, Departmental Expenses, or Golf Scores, right?

To rename a worksheet, just double-click on the tab for that sheet, type in a new name, and click OK. Or, if you're as fond of the right mouse-click as I am, right-click on the tab and select Rename.

Of course, there are a few rules for naming your worksheets:

- You get 31 characters for each tab.

- Spaces are allowed.

- Brackets ([ ]) are allowed as long as they aren't the first character (but parentheses are OK anywhere).

- You can't use / \ ? * : (slash, backslash, question mark, asterisk, or colon). Other punctuation marks, including commas and exclamation points, are allowed.

How do I switch to another worksheet?

Workbooks let you keep all your similar worksheets in one place, where you can get to them in a hurry. To move from one worksheet to another, just click on the index tab of the sheet you want to work with. If you can't see all the tabs, click on the arrows to the left of the tabs to riffle through the sheet tabs you can't see.

TIP **I usually don't need more than one or two worksheets in my workbook, so I lowered the number of blank sheets that Excel puts in a new workbook from 16 to 4 (you can set it to any number between 1 and 255). This also makes your files smaller and saves disk space. To change the setting, choose Tools, Options, click the General tab, and fill in a number in the box labeled Sheets in New Workbook.**

Move, copy, insert, or delete worksheets

Go ahead and treat worksheets in your workbook as though they're sheets of paper in a three-ring binder. If you need a new one, add it. If you've made a mess of a worksheet and want to start over, tear it out and throw it away. You can also rearrange sheets in any order by dragging them around:

- To **insert a new worksheet**, select any sheet tab and right-click. From the shortcut menu, choose Insert, and pick Worksheet in the dialog box of options that appears. The new sheet will be added to the left of the selected sheet—but with a higher sheet number, if you're using the default sheet numbers. (Weird, eh?)

- To **delete a worksheet**, select its tab and right-click; then choose Delete from the shortcut menu. Choose OK when Excel asks you to verify the deletion.

- To **move a worksheet**, select its tab and hold down the left mouse button until the mouse pointer turns into an arrow with a sheet of paper (look in the margin next to this paragraph). Slide the pointer along the sheet tabs until the small black arrow is pointing to the place you want to move your worksheet and release the mouse button.

- To **copy a worksheet in the same workbook**, hold down the Ctrl key, and drag the sheet tab to the left or the right. The pointer will change to an arrow with a sheet of paper containing a plus sign (as shown in the margin). If your old worksheet was named Sheet1, your new sheet will be called Sheet1 (2).

- To **copy a worksheet to another workbook**, use the right-mouse-button shortcut menus to copy the sheet and paste it in the new workbook.

Adding it all up automatically

The one Excel function that you'll use more than any other is SUM. Using this function is just like hitting the Total button on your desktop calculator. In fact, there's even a button on the Standard toolbar that adds up a column or row of numbers automatically. To use the AutoSum button, just select a blank cell beneath a column of numbers (or at the end of a row of numbers), then click the AutoSum button on the toolbar (although it looks like a stylized E, it's actually a Greek sigma). Excel will insert the SUM function with the argument already filled in (see fig. 15.6). Click the Enter box in the formula bar or press Enter to make it official.

Fig. 15.6
Click the AutoSum
button to have Excel
automatically add up
the numbers in the
column above.

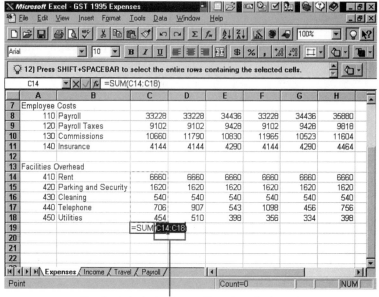

*Excel only includes these cells in the calculation
because the cell above C14 is blank*

Can I use Excel as a calculator?

While you'd normally want to keep the results of your calculations within
the spreadsheet, sometimes you just need to calculate something quickly for
your own information, and not for inclusion in the spreadsheet. You can
easily do that, providing that the Excel status bar is active. To activate the
status bar, select Tools, Options, and click on the View tab. Click next to
Status Bar, then click OK to exit. No dramatic changes yet, right? But look at
the bottom of the screen—there's a new grey bar under the workbook tabs.
Now select a group of cells which contain numbers, and the message Sum=
appears on the status bar, displaying the total amount of the selected cells.

When you select a range, keep your eyes on the status bar; the amount
changes as you drag your mouse pointer across the screen, constantly
calculating as you increase or reduce the range.

But what if you want to calculate the *average* amount within the selected
range? Just right-click on the status bar and select Average from the pop-up
menu. From now on, any range you select will yield the average amount on
the status bar. The calculations you can display on the status bar are:

- Sum

- Average

- Count (counts all the non-empty cells in the selected range)

- Count Nums (counts only those cells that contain numbers and formulas)

- Max (displays the largest number in the range)

- Min (displays the smallest number in the range)

Calculations too complicated? Try a function instead

Asking Excel to do only simple addition or multiplication is like hiring a Harvard MBA to balance your checkbook. Sure, Excel can add up a column of numbers, but its biggest asset is its repertoire of mathematical, financial, statistical, and logical **functions**. If you've got a stack of numbers, Excel can crunch them in more than 300 ways, from simple averages to complex trigonometric formulas. An Excel function is simply a specialized formula that Excel has memorized. Every function includes two parts: the **function name** (such as AVERAGE) and any required **arguments.**

 Plain English, please!

Arguments are the various items Excel needs to know to produce the right result. An argument might be a word, a number, or the name of another cell. Arguments always appear to the right of the function name, inside parentheses.

The formula =AVERAGE(number1,number2,…), for example, needs at least two numbers to be calculated. You'll need to replace number1, number2, and so on, with something else. Thus, the formula =AVER-AGE(5,10) gives you a result of 7.5.

The ellipsis (…) means you can have an unlimited number of arguments in the formula.

Some functions are so simple they don't need any arguments. If you type **=TODAY( )** in a cell (complete with the empty parentheses), Excel will display today's date in the cell. You're probably saying, "Big deal! I could have typed **4/8/96** and it would have been less hassle!" But the beauty of this function is that whenever you open a worksheet with this function in it, the date in that cell will be updated (by pulling from your computer's clock/calendar).

The most complicated functions demand that you fill in just the right information. To calculate the monthly payment on a loan, for example, you use the function PMT(rate,nper,pv,fv,type). You have to fill in (in this order) the interest rate, the number of payments, the present value (whatever that is), the future value (whatever *that* is), and the type of loan. But you don't have to memorize these complicated formulas, at least!

What good are functions?

Remember this golden rule: if you're typing a long, complex formula or doing anything else in Excel that takes too long, you're working too hard. There are so many wonderful time-saving shortcuts in this program that you shouldn't have to sit there and re-invent the wheel. Among some of the functions you get with Excel, you'll find the following (this is just a sampling; there are hundreds of Excel functions; some are pretty esoteric, highly-specialized for specific professions, and others are just too complex and require a separate book):

Function	What's it do?
SUM(number1, number2...)	Calculates the total of all the values in the parentheses
AVERAGE(number1, number2...)	Calculates the average of the values in the parentheses
COUNT(value1, value2...)	Counts the number of cells which contain numeric values
MAX(number1, number2...)	Finds the highest value within the list in the parentheses
MIN(number1, number2...)	Finds the lowest value within the list in the parentheses
TODAY()	Displays today's date in this cell
NOW()	Displays the correct date and time

Here are a few examples of using these functions:

=SUM(C4:C24)	Calculates the total of all the numbers in cells C4 through C24
=SUM(67,21,95,54)	Calculates the sum of all the numbers in the parentheses
=AVERAGE(B7:E20)	Finds the average of all the numbers in cells B7 through E20
=AVERAGE(68,46,40)	Calculates the average of these three amounts
=COUNT(F4:F54)	Counts how many cells from F4 to F54 contain numbers or formulas (not text)

Let the Wizard handle tricky calculations

Sure, you can type in functions yourself, but there are just too many and they're pretty confusing. Don't worry, you don't need to memorize all kinds of weird and cryptic functions—there's a **Function Wizard** whose job is to hold your hand when you type a function.

Let's say you want to know whether you can afford the mortgage payments on a new house. You could call your local bank and throw a whole bunch of "What if?" questions at your loan agent: "What if I put up a bigger down payment? What if I find a more expensive house? What if interest rates go up next month?" You'll spend the entire afternoon on the phone, and at the end of the day you'll have a piece of paper full of scribbled numbers that won't make any sense when you look at them next week.

Formulas and functions

Some of the most useful functions are the **logical functions**. There are countless practical uses for Excel's simplest logical function, called IF.

Let's say you've created an Excel worksheet that automatically calculates monthly invoice statements for your customers. You'd like to reward your best customers with an extra 10-percent discount, and you'd like Excel to apply the discount automatically.

Normally, you'd use the SUM function in the cell where you display the grand total. If you use the IF function instead, you can ask Excel a simple yes-or-no question: did this customer spend more than $1000 this month? Then you provide two sets of instructions—one for Excel to use if the answer is yes, the other if the answer is no.

The IF function uses three arguments: the logical test, the value if true, and the value if false. In our invoice example, assuming that the subtotal was in cell D24, we'd fill in the following formula: =IF(D24>1000,D24*90%,D24). It looks a bit intimidating, but Excel will have no trouble figuring out what to do.

Each of the three arguments is separated from the others by a comma. The first argument, the logical test, asks Excel to look in cell D24 and see whether the number in the cell is greater than 1000 (we could also use <, the less-than symbol; =, an equal sign; or <>, the not-equal sign). If Excel says, "Yes, it's greater than 1000," it uses the second argument and calculates 90% of the subtotal, effectively passing along a 10% discount. Otherwise, it uses the third argument and simply picks up the subtotal from cell D24.

As you become more experienced with Excel functions, you'll find plenty of uses for the IF function.

Or you could use Excel to build a worksheet and ask it all the "What if?" questions. Excel, the mortgage analyst, is open 24 hours a day and never gets tired of answering questions. It might take a few minutes to set up your worksheet, but once that job's done, you can save your work and reuse it any time.

 Click on the Function Wizard button on the toolbar; then follow the steps in the dialog boxes just as you do with the other Microsoft Office wizards. Most of the functions you'll want to create are easy to build and self-explanatory with the Function Wizard. If you start getting into really complex functions, you'll need much more information than this book can provide. Try Que's *Special Edition Using Excel for Windows 95* when you get to that point.

 TIP **Any time you are working with menu options or wizards, you're** likely to get dialog boxes that hide the part of the screen you need to see. In most cases, you can click the title bar of the dialog box and just drag it out of the way.

16

Making Great-Looking Worksheets

● In this chapter:

- **I want my worksheets to look nice**

- **Can I just skip the formatting?**

- **Reuse your favorite formats**

- **How to resize rows and columns**

- **Let Excel do the formatting for you—automatically!**

When each section of your worksheet is clearly marked off with lines, boxes, and special fonts, it's easier to see the big picture . . . .

How important is organization and clear labeling? For an instant object lesson, take a trip to your local supermarket.

If you're a really good shopper, you can get in and out of the grocery store in ten minutes. A quick raid on the produce section, a quart of milk from the dairy cabinet, and a fast pass down the frozen-food aisle on your way to the checkout stand. You find your way around fast because someone organized the store that way. Every section is clearly marked, all similar products are organized together, and when you can't find something, you just look at the signs over each aisle.

That's the way to organize an Excel worksheet, too. It doesn't matter whether you're preparing a financial analysis for yourself or crunching numbers for a big presentation to the boss. When key information is enhanced with colors, shading, and distinctive typography, the most important information—like the bottom line—jumps off the page.

This worksheet looks boring

When you enter a value in a cell, Excel doesn't always display exactly what you typed. Instead, the program looks in the workbook to see whether you've left instructions about how to display the contents of that cell. If Excel can't find any instructions from you, it looks at the data and tries to figure out how you probably want to see it. Whatever Excel does with the characters in the cell is called **formatting**.

You use formatting instructions to tell Excel precisely how to display the characters in a cell or a range. **Make this sentence bold**. Put these three words in a different font. Put the bottom line in color, please: (**$38,592**).

True, there are shortcut buttons on the Formatting toolbar. But the best assortment of Excel formatting options pops up when you make a selection, click the right mouse button, and choose Format Cells. Then click a tab in the dialog box shown in figure 16.1 to adjust one of these six choices.

Fig. 16.1
Use the Format Cells dialog box to adjust the look of any cell or range.

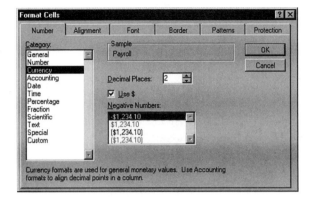

Here's the scoop on each of the tabs in the dialog box:

- **Number** formatting tells Excel how many decimal points you want to see for each number in a given cell, whether there's a dollar sign or a percentage, whether the number is a date, and so on.

- **Alignment** tells Excel where you want your cells to line up. Usually, numbers press against the right edge of the cell, text leans to the left, and labels are centered. You can even set the text to print up or down instead of across, or wrap paragraphs within a cell, like Word does with table cells.

- **Font** defines the size, shape, and thickness of each character in the cell. Fonts are measured in **points**—more points mean bigger letters. The default Excel font, 10-point Arial, is a good choice for most worksheets.

- **Lines and boxes** (controlled by the Border tab) allow you to draw a literal "bottom line" to set off your total beneath a column of numbers. You can also use borders to put parts of a worksheet into their own boxes.

- **Color and shading** (controlled by the Patterns tab) let you draw attention to a section of the worksheet, such as titles and totals. Remember, though, you can only see color on paper if you have a color printer!

- **Protection** lets you add a **lock** that prevents you or anyone else from accidentally changing the contents of a cell.

Selecting cells for formatting

To apply formats, you select the cells you want to be affected. (Selecting methods are covered in Chapter 14.) To select the entire worksheet, click in the tiny, unmarked gray button at the top-left corner of the worksheet window. (It's just above the row heading for 1 and to the left of the heading for column A.) When you select the entire worksheet, any formatting options you choose will apply to the entire worksheet. To deselect, click any cell in the worksheet.

 TIP If you want to format multiple cells, drag across them if they're next to each other. If the cells are scattered around the worksheet, hold down Ctrl and click each cell.

How to prevent (apparent) rounding errors

When does 2+2=5? When you've entered **2.3** into two cells, added the two cells with a formula, and formatted the three cells to show no decimal places. When Excel uses those values in a calculation, it uses the *actual* amount stored in the cell, not the clipped-off version you see. But it displays the cell contents in whatever way you formatted the cell. If the total comes out to 4.6, the no-decimal format will display that number as 5.

 CAUTION If you use rounded numbers in your worksheets, indicate that fact on charts and reports that will be presented to other people. Rounding causes apparent mistakes—and viewers make judgments about your accuracy based on what they see.

Make your worksheets more readable

How do you turn the wallflower worksheet from figure 16.2 into the slick, easy-to-read worksheet shown in figure 16.3? All it takes is a few clicks.

Fig. 16.2

Worksheets don't get much duller than this. If you just type, Excel puts every word and number into this normal font.

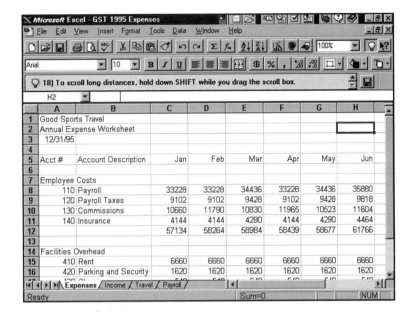

Fig. 16.3

A worksheet make-over. Select the right cells and click a few buttons to make this easy-to-read worksheet.

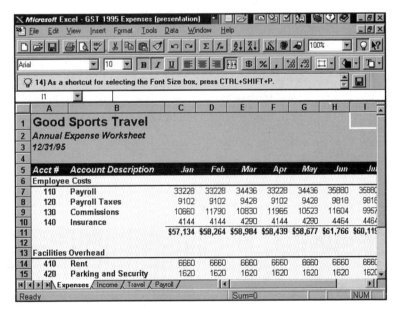

Here's how to give the worksheet example a make-over:

1 Reformat every number, and make sure all the columns align properly.

2 Make worksheet and column titles bigger and bolder, so they clearly define each column. Use a dark background and bold, italic, white type to make the titles impossible to ignore.

3 To really make the bottom line pop off the page, use the Borders button to add an emphatic double underline beneath the month columns. Add a thinner border under the subtitles.

4 Use soft yellow shading throughout the data section. This shading is easier on the eyes than the standard harsh white.

5 Turn off the normal Excel gridlines. You'll be amazed at how uncluttered the worksheet suddenly looks.

You can format a cell (or a group of cells) even if the cells are empty.

The numbers have to look right

When you get right down to it, spreadsheets are all about numbers, so it stands to reason that there are lots and lots of ways in Excel to display those numbers. When you type a number and press Enter, how should Excel display it? You have dozens of choices; fortunately, Excel keeps them neatly organized into categories. In the Number tab of the Format Cells dialog box, pick a category from the list on the left, select a format from the list on the right, and look at the sample at the top of the dialog box to see what will appear in the cell if you click OK.

Table 16.1 gives you a summary of the most popular choices for displaying numbers.

Table 16.1   Popular display options

Kind of numbers you want to enter	Choose a format from this group	Numbers end up like this
Don't know yet; could be anything.	General format	-34.7 34 34731
Adding numbers to a profit-and-loss report	Number or Accounting	34,731 (34,731) $34,731.92 [in red]

Kind of numbers you want to enter	Choose a format ___ from this group	Numbers end up like this
Working with dollars and cents	Currency	$34,731 $34,731.00 $34,731 [in red]
Playing with percentages	Percentage	34% 34.7% 34.731%
Dealing with dates and times	Date or Time	2/1/96 01–Feb–96 10:05:43 PM

TIP   **If you choose Number format, and you want a comma to separate** hundreds and thousands, select the Use 1000 Separator (,) option.

These are just a few of the many, many format options available. Chances are, if you need it, you can find it. (If not, you can create your own!) And now, a couple of notes to keep in mind when you're using special number formats:

- Be careful how you enter percentages into your worksheet. If you use one of the Percentage formats, and then enter a number like **7**, it will appear as 700% (and your calculations will be off by miles). To enter percentages into a worksheet, remember to use the percent sign (**7%**) or the proper decimal point (**.07**).

- To automatically convert a fraction to its decimal equivalent, enter a **0** and a space first. If you don't, Excel will convert some fractions to dates (5/8, for example, would become May 8) and others to text labels. But when you enter **0 5/8** into a cell, Excel correctly stores the number as 0.625, and displays the fraction you entered, unless the cell has a decimal format.

How to use the Formatting toolbar

Font, Font Size
The two drop-down lists at the left of the Formatting toolbar let you apply various fonts and sizes to different characters.

Currency Style, Percent Style, Comma Style
These three buttons let you apply preset styles with one click.

Bold, Italic, Underline
*Use these buttons to make text or numbers **bold**, italic, or underlined. You can also use the keyboard shortcuts Ctrl+B, Ctrl+I, and Ctrl+U.*

Increase Decimal, Decrease Decimal
These two buttons let you increase or decrease the number of displayed decimal places.

Alignment
Use the Align Left, Center, and Align Right buttons to line up entries as the names suggest. The fourth button, Center Across Columns, is perfect for setting up worksheet titles. (Select the cells across which you want to center, then click the button.) If you don't like the results, click the button again to return to the previous format.

Borders, Color, Font Color
Click any of these three down-arrows to take your pick of borders, background colors, and text colors. Or click the buttons themselves to apply the most recent selections (which show on the faces of the buttons).

Q&A *My cell says 1.03E+08—but that's not what I typed. What's going on?*

You must have slept through that part of your high school algebra class (just like me). That's **scientific notation**, and Excel uses it when you type a number with more digits than it can display in the General number format. Take the number before the E and move the decimal eight places to the right (if that were a minus sign, you'd move the decimal to the left). So your number is actually 103,000,000.

How can I emphasize words and numbers?

The manager at my local supermarket is no dummy. He puts the Snickers bars and the *National Enquirer* at eye level, right next to the checkout stand. By the time I get to the front of the line, half the candy bar is gone, there are chocolate fingerprints all over the newspaper, and I'm probably going to pay for both.

You can make parts of your worksheet nearly as irresistible. How? By using bigger, bolder fonts, of course. The default font is fine for endless rows and columns of numbers, but titles and totals can always stand a little punching up. Here's how to do it:

- To use a new font for a cell or range, just select the cell(s), and choose a font from the drop-down Font list on the Formatting toolbar. Use the Font Size drop-down list to make it bigger, and click the Bold button to add some oomph to those labels.

- If you want, you can apply different fonts and sizes to different characters in the same cell. Maybe your lawyers want you to add a copyright symbol, ©, but you'd prefer that it not be *too* obvious. Click in the formula bar, select the character you want to reformat, then use the Formatting toolbar to adjust fonts and sizes.

When should you use the Font section of the Format Cells dialog box instead of the Font button on the Formatting toolbar? Whenever you're not sure what a given font looks like, you'll welcome the preview window shown in figure 16.4. This dialog box also offers some formats not found on the toolbar, like strikethrough and double underline.

Fig. 16.4
Use the Font tab when
you want to see what
your change will look
like before you click OK.

Pick a font, a font style, a size, and a color

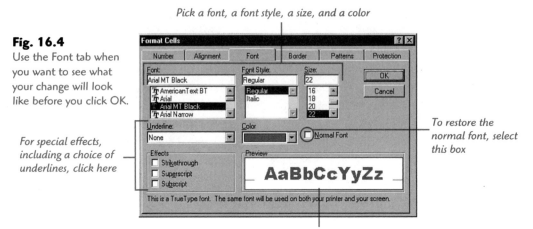

*For special effects,
including a choice of
underlines, click here*

*To restore the
normal font, select
this box*

Preview a sample of your selection in this window

How can I type a pound symbol (£)?

If your worksheets track the stock market, monetary funds, etc. you may
sometimes need to insert special characters that don't appear on your
keyboard—like a trademark (™) or yen (¥) symbol. Excel offers several
methods for inserting those characters.

The AutoCorrect feature can pop in the copyright, registration, or trademark
symbol in an instant. Type the characters shown in the following table and
press Enter. That's it!

Type this...	Get this...
(c)	©
(r)	®
(tm)	™

If you need more interesting symbols, the simplest method is to use the
Character Map accessory program that comes with Windows. Open the
Start menu and choose Programs, Accessories, Character Map (see fig. 16.5).

Fig. 16.5
Hold down the mouse button and scroll around in the window; Windows enlarges each symbol or character as you touch it.

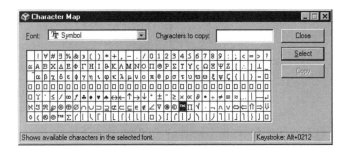

It's 34731.9583—do you know where your kids are?

When you type a simple date or time into a cell, you set off a complicated chain of events. Consider dates. In Excel's world, you see, every date is actually just a number, and the world began in 1900. Confused? Here's what's really going on.

When you enter **2/1/96** into a cell, Excel examines it carefully: "Hmmm, looks like a date." Instead of plunking that date into the cell, though, Excel grabs its built-in Franklin Planner, and counts the number of days that have passed since January 1, 1900. (The answer, in this example: 35,096.)

Of course, this all happens in a few millionths of a second, and Excel continues to display the date you entered, so you're not even aware anything happened. If you added the time to your date, **2/1/96 11:00:00 PM**, Excel would simply figure what percent of the day had passed and tack that fraction onto the end of the number.

So figure it's 35096.9583, with a few more decimal points thrown in for good measure.

The obvious question is, "Why?"—why does Excel go through this weird, convoluted process in order to display dates? The answer may surprise you. Dates are values which can be used in calculations. Say you need to calculate how many days are left until the grand opening of the new plant, or how many months since an employee was hired—plug the date value in a formula, and Excel will do the rest. Try this now. Let's find out how many shopping days are left 'til Christmas: In any blank cell, type **=DATE(95,12,25)- TODAY()**—substitute the right year for 95 if necessary. So what, you ask? Every time you bring up this worksheet, the number of days remaining to Christmas will be updated automatically. How does Excel do it? It subtracts today's value from that of Christmas day, based on how many days have passed since January 1, 1900.

Want to know more? Sorry, it's .7083333, and I'm knocking off for the day.

To insert a special character, follow these steps:

1 Open the Font list in the Character Map window, and select the font you want to use. Most of the time, the Symbol font will have everything you need, but you might find the character in the font that you're using in the worksheet. (Makes for a better match.)

TIP   **Just for fun, try the Wingdings font sometime.**

2 Double-click the character or symbol you want. It appears in the Characters to Copy box.

3 Click any additional characters you want.

4 Click the Copy button to copy the character(s) to the Windows Clipboard.

5 Close the Character Map window, return to the worksheet, and position the cursor where you want to insert the character(s).

6 Choose Edit, Paste or press Ctrl+V.

7 At this point, you'll probably see something that's not even close to what you thought you copied, unless your worksheet happens to use the Symbol font by default (not likely). Select the character(s) and choose the same font you selected in the Character Map window.

Add text wrap (or other interesting alignments)

If you have a long line of text that doesn't fit in a cell, have Excel wrap it to a second or third line. Pop up the Format Cells dialog box, click the Alignment tab, and select the Wrap Text box. Now, instead of running out of sight when they hit the edge of the cell, your words will begin filling up a second line in the same cell.

Format Cells also includes a few other options that come in handy:

* Center Across Selection lets you enter text into one cell and center it across a range of cells in one row. This is great for worksheet titles, grouped columns, and so on.

* Try changing the vertical alignment of a headline to Center; that way, it will seem to float in space instead of sitting on the bottom of the cell.

- Excel also lets you change the orientation and stack a cell on its side so it can act as an ultra-slim column title. Just click the version you like in the Orientation section of the dialog box.

How to make sections stand out

There's no mistaking the produce section down at the local supermarket. It's got wider aisles, different lighting, and those little spritzers that keep the lettuce from wilting until it gets to your refrigerator.

You can create the same sort of distinctive identity for sections of a worksheet by using boxes and colors. Excel lets you use thin lines, thick lines, and double lines to add borders to cells and ranges.

You can also add colorful backgrounds (and change the type to complementary colors): dark backgrounds and white type to create powerful worksheet titles; soft, light backgrounds to make columns of numbers more readable; alternating colors or shading to make it easy to tell one row from another in a wide worksheet.

Pop up the Format Cells dialog box and choose the Border tab (see fig. 16.6) to draw a box around a selection. With the dialog box displayed, follow these steps:

1 Where do you want the lines? Outline draws a box around the selection, Bottom underlines it, etc.

2 Choose a line style—thick, thin, doubled, dotted, or dashed.

3 Choose a different color for the border, if you like.

4 Click OK to add the borders to your worksheet.

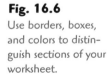

Fig. 16.6

Use borders, boxes, and colors to distinguish sections of your worksheet.

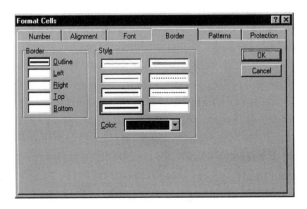

Recycle the best formats

You may tinker for an hour trying to find the just-exactly-perfect formatting for one section (or even one cell) on your worksheet. That's OK this time, but if you do that every time, your computer isn't exactly a labor-saving device, is it? Fortunately, Excel has a solution when you find a format that works.

Just like Word, Excel lets you collect favorite combinations of formats and store them in reusable **styles.** Instead of clicking in six different dialog boxes, you choose Format, Style to display the dialog box shown in figure 16.7. Then you choose a name from the drop-down list, and click OK. Here's how to work with styles:

- To create a style, select a cell with the formatting you want to save (such as Arial 24, bold, and underlined), then choose Format, Style. Type a name in the Style Name box and click OK.

- Styles only apply to the workbook you designed them in. But don't worry—you can cheat! To copy styles from another workbook, first open the workbook containing the styles you want to copy. Then go back to the workbook that's missing the styles. Choose Format, Style to open the Style dialog box, and click the Merge button. In the Merge Styles dialog box, pick the name of the workbook containing the styles. After you click OK, your styles will be available in the current workbook, too.

Fig. 16.7
Create a masterpiece of a cell format? Save it using Excel's styles, then reuse it in another worksheet or even another workbook.

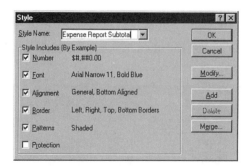

Can I copy formatting from one place to another?

When you don't particularly care about saving your format for posterity, there's a quicker way to copy formats from one cell to another. The **Format Painter** works just like the paintbrush pictured on its button. You dip the brush in one cell, and it picks up all the formatting in that cell. Swipe the brush across another cell, or a whole range of cells, to "paint" the identical format into the new location. Here are the steps:

1 Select the cell whose format you want to copy.

2 Click the Format Painter button. (If you plan to copy the format to more than one place, double-click the button to lock the Format Painter in place.) When you move the pointer back over the worksheet, you'll see that there's now a paintbrush alongside the regular Excel pointer:

3 Click the cell where you want to copy the formatting. To "paint" the formats across a range of cells, hold down the mouse button and drag the paintbrush across the entire range.

4 If you locked the Format Painter on, press Escape or click the button again to return the pointer to normal.

I need to resize rows and columns

When you first begin working with a worksheet, every row is the same height, and every column is the same width. It soon becomes obvious that that state of affairs can't last. A column that contains only two-digit numbers doesn't need to be as wide as one that's filled with descriptive labels. And rows need to get bigger when the fonts inside them get bigger.

Fortunately, Excel takes care of that last problem for you. Rows automatically adjust in height when you change the font size of the text within the cells. If you want to adjust a column width, or make a row just a little taller, you'll have to master a simple adjustment technique.

- To drag a column or row to a new size, point to the thin line between the row or column headings until the pointer looks like this:

    ‡   Rows

    ⊹   Columns

    Hold down the mouse button, and drag the edge of the column or row until it's the size you want, then release the button.

- To let Excel resize a column or row to fit the size or length of text, make a selection, then choose Format, Row, AutoFit; or Format, Column, AutoFit Selection.

TIP **Double-click the right border of a column heading (or the bottom** border of a row heading) to automatically adjust column width or row height to fit the widest or tallest entry.

AutoFormats and templates: let Excel do it all for you

I don't know about you, but my favorite aisle in the grocery store is the microwave section. Popcorn in three minutes? Yes! Soup in 90 seconds? All right! And a perfectly formatted Excel worksheet with one mouse click? Sounds too good to be true.

AutoFormat makes a worksheet look great

AutoFormat, Excel's instant do-it-all formatting feature, works pretty much as advertised on most simple worksheets. It's a simple process, really:

1 Select a range. If you skip this step, Excel will try to guess how much of your worksheet you want to be automatically formatted.

2 Choose Format, AutoFormat to display the AutoFormat dialog box shown in figure 16.88.

Fig. 16.8
Most of the time, AutoFormat will make your worksheet look better, although you'll still want to polish the final product.

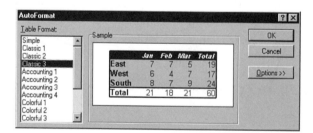

3 Pick one of the built-in formats. As you scroll through the list, you can see a sample in the preview window at the right.

4 Click the Options button, and make selections from the resulting check box to keep Excel from resizing columns, changing fonts, and so on.

5 Click OK to see the results.

If AutoFormat doesn't quite work out the way you expected, hit the Undo key right away to return to the previous worksheet formatting. Then try a smaller range or a different format.

Use Excel's templates—they're easy!

Too lazy to create a new spreadsheet from scratch and format it just right? Trying to create an invoice or an expense statement? Don't re-invent the wheel. Use the built-in templates that come with Excel. Select File, New, and click the Spreadsheet Solutions tab. These templates are ready-to-use spreadsheets, no need to add water, just plug in your data. If you need to tweak either of these templates, click the Customize button in the template, and make any changes you wish—it'll still be a lot less work than creating the spreadsheet from scratch.

17

Fancy Excel Tricks

● In this chapter:

- **Working with lists**

- **I need to search for data**

- **Oh no! I typed the wrong area code for all those names!**

- **How to link workbooks or worksheets**

- **Quick tricks to start work fast**

You can use Excel for many of your daily tasks, including those that have nothing to do with number-crunching. . . . . . . ▶

We haven't even begun to scratch the surface of what Excel can do for you and your business. The more you work with it, the more useful features you'll discover. And once you discover the power hidden within this program, you may find yourself using it for many of your daily tasks. In this chapter, we show you how to take your rows and columns of numbers beyond mere calculations.

Clear up the clutter with lists

Are you a collector? A friend of mine collects sports caps of all sports in all leagues—professional, college, even Junior League. They're all hanging on his office wall. Hundreds of them. I asked him once how many baseball caps he had. It took him 20 minutes to go around the room and count them, because they were spread out randomly all over the place. Next, I asked him how many caps came from California. I haven't heard from him since 1992.

Collecting data is important, but *managing* it is crucial. Just the fact that the data exists doesn't mean you can get to it quickly and make sense out of it. You need to be organized. You need a list-management system.

A **list** is Excel's term for a database. If you have the Professional Edition of Microsoft Office 95, you may be using Access 7.0, the database-management program. Even if you are, Excel lists are simpler to use because you run them from the familiar Excel program.

 Plain English, please!

A **database** is a collection of **records**. Your phone book has thousands and thousands of records. What's in a record? Here's one:

Smith, Mary, 234 Elm Street, Anytown, 555-2345

In this case, there's a last name, a first name, a street address, a city, and a phone number. Each of these categories is called a **field**. Fields make up the structure of the list or database. You can search on a field ("Is there anybody called Smith in Anytown?") or sort the list according to any field, name, city, and so on.

How to build a list

Excel lists are created in regular worksheets, but you must follow some rules:

- Field names must be in the top row of the list (Excel calls it the **header row**).

- Each record goes in a separate row.

- Avoid having blank rows between records, or between the header and the first record.

- Efficient lists break down the fields to the smallest element possible, so you can use the information more flexibly. For example, if you split a name field into Last Name and First Name, you can use the First Name by itself in the salutation of a letter.

Figure 17.1 shows an example of a list.

Fig. 17.1

You can only see part of the list at any time. This particular list includes several more fields off to the right, and hundreds more records below.

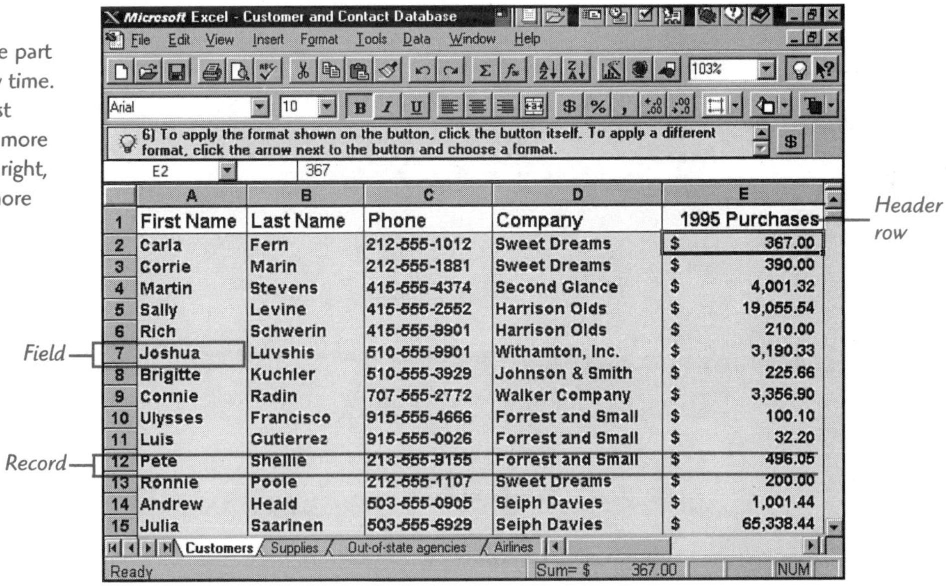

More info? Add data to your list with a form

You can jump around from cell to cell when entering data in a list, just like you do when building a worksheet. But there's a simpler way to do this data entry—using a **data form**. You can use the data form to add new records at any time. (New records are added to the end of the list.)

Once you've created the list—it just needs a header row and one record to get started—park the cursor in a cell somewhere in the list and then follow these steps:

1 Choose <u>D</u>ata, F<u>o</u>rm to display a dialog box like the one in figure 17.2.

Notice that the data form displays field names from the header row, and the information from the first row of the list, to show you what kind of information is currently in each field.

2 Click Ne<u>w</u> to enter a new record.

3 Type the data in the blank text boxes. Press the Tab key after each entry to go on to the next field.

4 Click C<u>l</u>ose when you're done entering data.

Fig. 17.2

How smart is this form? It knows which fields are in the list and how many records you already have; it even displays the list title.

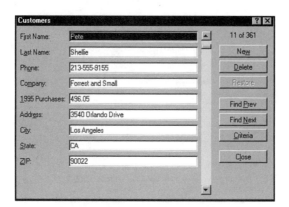

Sort your data the easy way

Just like your file folders, which are placed in alphabetical or some other order in your cabinet, a good list should be **sorted**. You can sort it by name, city, state, or whatever. Unlike using your file cabinet, though, you don't need to shuffle dozens of file folders when you want to sort or re-sort. Let's say you need to sort data by state, and within these, by city (so that California comes before Texas, and then San Francisco comes before Santa Rosa within the California set). Here's how you set up a sort:

1 Click any cell within the list.

2 Choose <u>D</u>ata, <u>S</u>ort. Excel identifies the list, selects it, and presents you with the Sort dialog box, shown in figure 17.3.

Fig. 17.3

If you don't have a header row, click next to No Header Row, and your sort options will be the mysterious Column A, Column B, and so on.

3 Click the drop-down arrow next to Sort By and select the major sort key. For this example, you would select State because that's the first breakdown we want in this list.

4 Select Ascending or Descending, depending on which direction you want this major group sorted. Ascending sorts A-Z and 0-9; descending sorts Z-A, 9-0, etc. In this case, we want the states in alphabetical order from A to Z, so we choose Ascending.

5 If you want a second sort order within the first, click the drop-down arrow next to Then By, and select the second sort field. Then choose ascending or descending order. For this example, we want to sort the cities within the state, so we would select City in ascending order.

6 If you want to sort the list even further, select a field name within the Then By list and choose a sort order for it. In figure 17.3, we're sorting by the amount of the customers' purchases during 1995, from $0 through $whatever.

By the way, if you change your mind after selecting a sort order, just open the list again and choose (none).

7 Click OK. Figure 17.4 shows the result of the sort on the example list. The cities are all nicely in alphabetical order within the alphabetized state list.

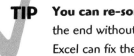 **TIP** **You can re-sort the list at any time, so feel free to add records at** the end without worrying about putting them in the appropriate order. Excel can fix the order with a quick sort!

Fig. 17.4

You can't see the purchases column in this figure, but the companies are in order within their cities, by how many $$$ they spent in 1995.

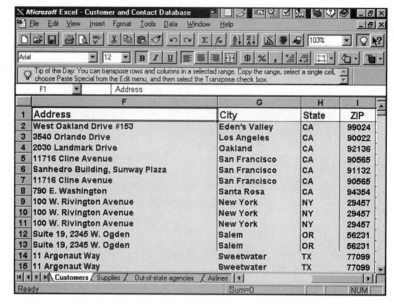

Microsoft Excel - Customer and Contact Database

	F	G	H	I
1	Address	City	State	ZIP
2	West Oakland Drive #153	Eden's Valley	CA	99024
3	3540 Orlando Drive	Los Angeles	CA	90022
4	2030 Landmark Drive	Oakland	CA	92136
5	11716 Cline Avenue	San Francisco	CA	90565
6	Sanhedro Building, Sunway Plaza	San Francisco	CA	91132
7	11716 Cline Avenue	San Francisco	CA	90565
8	790 E. Washington	Santa Rosa	CA	94354
9	100 W. Rivington Avenue	New York	NY	29457
10	100 W. Rivington Avenue	New York	NY	29457
11	100 W. Rivington Avenue	New York	NY	29457
12	Suite 19, 2345 W. Ogden	Salem	OR	56231
13	Suite 19, 2345 W. Ogden	Salem	OR	56231
14	11 Argonaut Way	Sweetwater	TX	77099
15	11 Argonaut Way	Sweetwater	TX	77099

Customers / Supplies / Out-of-state agencies / Airlines

Desperately searching for data

I have a terrific filing system. There's a folder labeled 1995, where all my letters, receipts, and invoices go. When I need to find one of them, I... well, I give up and hope the IRS didn't really mean business when it asked for those receipts.

If you only have a few documents to file, that system may make sense to you. And if there are only 20 records in your list, you can just glance at the screen and find the one you're looking for. But if you have hundreds or thousands of records, you can't take the time to scroll down the list until you find the customer you're looking for (with your luck, he will be record number 2198). You can use a form to quickly find the information you're looking for, based on your search criteria.

Plain English, please!

Criteria (cry-TEAR-ee-a) is the plural form of **criterion** (no, not the automobile). You specify criteria—or a single criterion—that you want Excel to use to find certain records in your list. Maybe you want a list of all the sales reps who sold above a certain dollar amount last quarter. Or you want to find out in which months the manatees you're tracking left Florida and went north. (I'm not kidding. I saw a scientist tracking this kind of information last night on TV.) 🙶🙶

To find records that match your search criteria, click the first record, and then:

1 Choose Data, Form.

2 Click Criteria. The form's contents are cleared.

3 Type your search criteria in the appropriate boxes. For example, if you're looking for contacts at Seiph Davies who made more than $50,000 in purchases last year, type **Seiph Davies** in the Company box and **>50000** in the 1995 Purchases box (see fig. 17.5). You can look for values that are greater than, less than, or different than your search criteria. Use the following symbols to designate these operators:

Symbol	Meaning	Example
>	Greater than	>10000
>=	Greater than or equal to	>=42
<	Less than	<10000
<=	Less than or equal to	<=42
<>	Different than	<>Cicely (you'll get anything other than Cicely in the result)

4 Press Enter to start the search.

5 You may have more than one match, so click Find Next to see the next record. Repeat the process until you hear a warning beep, telling you there are no more matches. (If you don't have sound, you'll just notice that nothing happens when you click Find Next in the last record.) You can also click Find Prev to go back. Only records that match the search criteria will be displayed.

6 Click Close to exit.

Fig. 17.5

Don't feel like typing out **Connecticut**? Is that client called Sanderson or Sandersen? Don't worry. You don't need to type it all in the Criteria form. Just type the first few characters, followed by an asterisk (*). For example, enter **Conn*** or **Sander***.

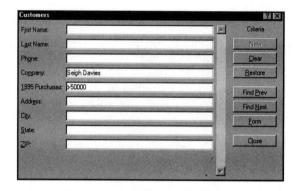

Filter out what you don't need

Forms are an acceptable search tool if your needs are simple, but the best search tools in your Excel list are **filters**, which display the list in the worksheet, but only show the data specified by the filter. The advantage of this method is that you can continue working with the worksheet as you're used to, but you don't clutter the screen with information you don't need to see. Let's say you only want to look at your San Francisco, California contacts. To activate a filter, follow these steps:

1 Click anywhere in the list.

2 Choose Data, Filter, AutoFilter.

3 Look at figure 17.6. Notice the drop-down arrows next to each field name? For this example, you would click the one next to State and select California. Then click the one next to City and select San Francisco. (If only one such city by that name exists in your list, like San Francisco, you can skip selecting the state.) Check out figure 17.7 to see the result.

TIP **Printing selected records is easy if you use filters. Just click** the Print button on the toolbar; only the visible records get printed.

Fig 17.6

Click these arrows to select a filter.

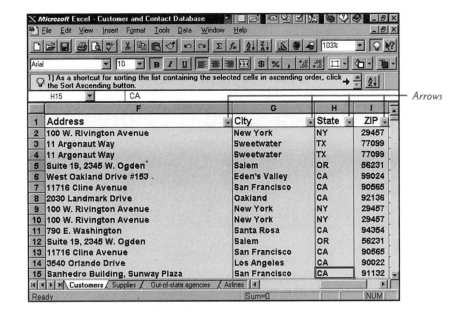

Fig. 17.7

Magically, the only records now on display are those that match these search criteria. To redisplay the whole list, open the filter(s) for the field(s) you choose and click (All).

These records match your criteria—the others are filtered out

Watch this area of the status bar—you won't always be able to see all the selected records in one screen

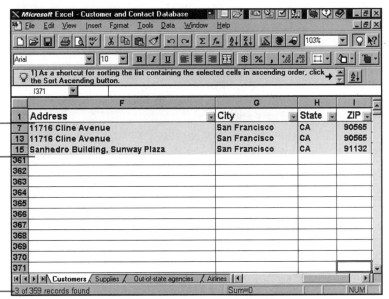

You can even filter the filter!

When you click a drop-down arrow in an autofiltered list, you get these special options, with which you can narrow your list even more:

- **Top 10:** A great way to display just the highest or lowest x number of records, according to the value in the field. (Note that this only works for fields containing numbers.) Click (Top 10). Excel displays a dialog box like that in figure 17.8.

  The Office developers took creative liberties with this option's name—you can specify that you want the top 100 or bottom twenty, or whatever—not just the top ten.

Fig. 17.8
Select Top or Bottom, then a number of records to display.

- **Custom:** Here you can combine two search criteria, using the AND and OR operators. For example, all the customers whose purchases were greater than $1,000 AND less than $10,000. Or maybe customers who are with Seiph Davies OR Sweet Dreams. Here's how you do these two examples with this list:

```
> 1000          = Seiph Davies
     And              Or
< 10000         = Sweet Dreams
```

- **Blank**: Display all the records that have blank cells in the current column. Use this option to find records where you didn't enter any information, maybe by accident, and now want to fill it in.

- **Non-blank**: Display only those records that don't have empty cells in the current column. Tracking the behavior of students in a scientific study? You could use this option to display only the folks who had lunch on Tuesday, and correlate that with your studies of academic performance. (Hey, you can use Excel for all kinds of things!)

- **All**: Reset to normal. Your row numbers and drop-down arrow will change back to gray and the list will be displayed in its original size.

Search-and-replace can save a lot of time

Suppose you get a postcard from the phone company, informing you that all the phone numbers that start with 555 are changing as of April 1. The new prefix is 111. This is a data entry nightmare. What do you do? Hire a temp?

Spend a week reentering numbers? Of course not. Just tell Excel to replace all instances of 555 with 111. Here's how:

1 Choose <u>E</u>dit, <u>R</u>eplace (or press Ctrl+H) to launch the dialog box you see in figure 17.9.

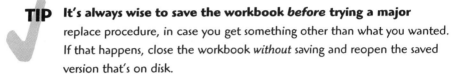

TIP **It's always wise to save the workbook *before* trying a major**
replace procedure, in case you get something other than what you wanted. If that happens, close the workbook *without* saving and reopen the saved version that's on disk.

2 Type **555** in the Fi<u>n</u>d What box (don't press Enter). Make sure that Find Entire Cells <u>O</u>nly is deselected. If you select this option, and you're looking for a phone number like 555-1234, Excel won't find it because it'll look for an exact match, while you're looking for a partial one. Press Tab to move to the Replace with box.

3 Type **111** in the Re<u>p</u>lace with box (still, no Enter).

4 Click Replace <u>A</u>ll.

5 Click Close to exit.

CAUTION **Sometimes your search doesn't go quite as expected. For example,**
if you have ZIP codes in your list, and you replace all instances of 555, some of your ZIP codes might be corrupted (because they contain 555). No problem. Immediately select the <u>E</u>dit menu, and choose <u>U</u>ndo Replace. If it's completely screwed up, go back to your saved version on disk.

Fig. 17.9
To replace in only part of your worksheet, select that area before you start.

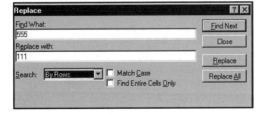

Linking data between workbooks or worksheets

You often need to consolidate data from different sources into one worksheet. For example, you may have a separate sales-tracking worksheet for each month, and one year-to-date worksheet. Or you might have one for each division in your company, and one for the entire company. One thing you want to avoid like the plague is repetition of data entry. As you may have guessed, Excel can help.

Establishing a link may seem a bit tedious, but you'll only do it once. After you establish the links, you'll never have to go through this again. Follow these steps:

1 Open all the related workbooks.

2 In the **source** worksheet (the one that has the info you want), select a cell you want to link to a master worksheet or workbook, and press Ctrl+C to copy it to the Clipboard. (See Chapter 20 for more about copying to the Clipboard.)

3 Go to the master worksheet or workbook (called the **target** or **destination**), and select the cell in which you want to insert that information.

4 Choose <u>E</u>dit, Paste <u>S</u>pecial.

5 From the Paste Special dialog box (see fig. 17.10), choose Paste <u>L</u>ink.

Fig. 17.10
When worksheets are linked, any change to the source worksheet is automatically reflected in the target worksheet.

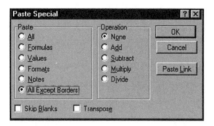

Speed up the file-open process

Don't you wish there were a few minutes every day when you could just kick back and check out the latest office gossip? Excel makes it easy, because while you wait for your workbooks to open, you can take a walk, make a phone call, go grocery shopping, and so on. The larger the files, the longer it takes to open them. But there are a few things you can do to automate the file-open process. Read on.

Open your files from the Documents list

You may not have noticed, but Windows keeps track of the last bunch of documents you've had open—from Word, Excel, WordPad, or anywhere else. Click the Start button and choose Documents. Is your file there? If so, click it. Windows launches Excel (or whatever) and opens that document. Easy!

Add a shortcut

If you continually use the same workbook (or document, or whatever), you can create a shortcut for it on the Windows desktop. Open Explorer and click the Restore button to shrink the Explorer window a bit. Drag the window around until you can see the area where you want to place the shortcut. Find the document you want in the Explorer window, click it, and drag it onto the desktop. The next time you want to open that document, just go to the desktop and double-click the shortcut icon.

Quick start

You're a person of habit. Every morning you launch Excel, open the Budget file, then the Payroll file, then the Sales Tracking spreadsheet, and while you wait for your files to wake up, yawn and stretch, you go out for espresso and a bagel. Excel makes that process simpler for you. If you always open the same workbooks, tell Excel to open them at the same time it launches. Just save each of these files into the XLStart folder on your hard disk (use Explorer to find the folder and files), and each time you open Excel, these files will open by themselves.

Create a workspace (if it's Tuesday, it must be payroll)

You may have specific tasks you work on at different times. Sometimes you need to open all the payroll-related files, and other days you need to work with all the budget-type files. Luckily, you can save groups of files as one **workspace** file, which is an umbrella file containing several related workbooks. To create a workspace file, make sure all the files you want in it are open, then choose File, Save Workspace, and give it a name. Excel will add the extension XLW to that name. To open that workspace, just choose File, Open and choose the file from the list, or create a shortcut for it on the desktop and do the double-click trick.

➤

18

Chart Your Progress, Map Your Future

● In this chapter:

● View your numbers as a chart or a map

● How do I change the type of chart I've made?

● Dress up a chart with a legend, titles, color, and more!

● Now it's done. How do I print it?

● Add a map to your worksheet

Excel makes it easy (and fun) to create charts out of your data. A handy ChartWizard is always at your disposal . . . . ●

There are two ways you can look at your Excel data: in worksheet form or as charts. (Excel calls them *charts*; other people call them *graphs*. Same thing.) While worksheets are necessary for plugging in the data and performing calculations, it's very difficult (practically impossible) to analyze the information just by staring at row after row after row of numbers. Which division sold the most last year? Did the earthquake have an effect on sales?

We could use the yellow highlighter to make that information stand out. Better yet, let's plot those numbers. Did sales drop after the earthquake? When you look at a line chart, if it's shaped like the Grand Canyon, and the lowest point is around the date of the earthquake, the answer is immediately apparent. Or let's create a map out of our numbers, so we can tell at a glance which state consumes the most of what.

Navigating your way around charts

When you look for an address on a map, you usually consult the index. Suppose the street you're looking for is marked M7. This reference means that the street is located within the M7 square: M is the horizontal axis, and 7 is the vertical axis. Somewhere within the area where they cross, you'll find the street you're looking for. This system makes it easy to find information.

Charts work much the same way. Without **axes** (pronounce it AKS-eez— more than one **axis**) as points of reference, you'd be looking at meaningless piles of numbers and words. Some people say that the Y axis is the vertical one and the X axis is the horizontal one. But they're wrong. The *direction* is not the point, only what's *plotted* on it. Here's how you can tell your axes apart:

- X axis: **categories**
- Y axis: **values**

For example, look at figure 18.1: the names are on the X axis, while the numbers are on the Y axis. Figure 18.2 shows the same information, but the axes are "flipped" for effect.

Fig. 18.1
This is the traditional way of looking at charts: the Y axis is on the left, and the X axis is on the bottom.

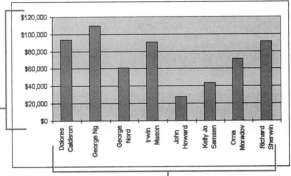

These are the numbers (or **values**) we're plotting

This is the **category** axis (in this case, the category is people)

Fig. 18.2
What's wrong with this picture? Nothing. This "sideways" chart is perfectly legitimate.

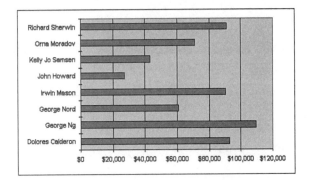

The ChartWizard—just add water

Creating a chart in Excel is as easy as pointing to the data and starting the ChartWizard. The wizard does most of the preliminary work for you, and all that's left is some customizing and minor tweaking. Just like everywhere else in Office, this wizard takes you through a series of questions, then builds the chart according to your specifications.

Drag and plot

Look at the worksheet in figure 18.3. This is a sales-tracking worksheet, where each salesperson's figures are logged. Let's say we want to look at the overall sales picture for January, and put the information into a chart. Start by selecting a range: in this example, we're using A5:B14, which includes the salespeople's names and their figures for the month.

Now click the ChartWizard button on the toolbar. Your cursor changes to resemble a tiny column chart. Click where you want to place the upper left corner of the chart, or click-and-drag an approximate size for the chart. You can just guess as to how big you'll want it—resizing it later is a snap.

Fig. 18.3
When you're charting the data, don't include totals, like those in column E and row 15 of this example, or you'll skew your results.

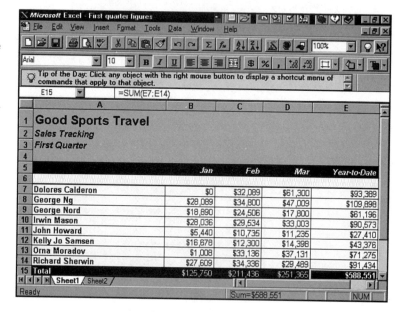

 TIP I find it's easier to jump between the data and the chart if I put the chart in a separate worksheet within the workbook.

Now show the ChartWizard where the data is

As you see in figure 18.4, the wizard starts asking you questions. The first one is about the range you want to plot. Although you've preselected it, you can change it here, if you like. Simply highlight the range in the Range box, type a new range, accept it, and go on to the next step. If you don't remember the addresses or don't want to type them, click the title bar and drag the dialog box out of the way, then select the cells you want.

 TIP You can include more than one value series in most charts. In this example, to chart the sales figures for January, February, and March, you would select columns B, C, and D.

Fig. 18.4

Even though you preselected the range, you can still override it; just type a new name here or select a new range with your mouse.

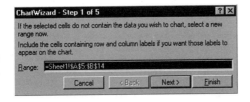

Pick the kind of chart you want

Now you get to choose the chart type. The ChartWizard offers several chart types, as shown in figure 18.5. Excel suggests a column chart for this data, but we want to show more clearly the percentage of the total sales for the month. Three formats that might make sense are pie charts, 3-D pie charts, and doughnut charts. The differences between them are really cosmetic. 3-D pies look more professional than the flat 2-D variety, and a doughnut is another appetizing prospect. Click one of them, then click Next.

CAUTION Pie charts can depict only one value series at a time, regardless of the number of value series you select before you start the ChartWizard. The wizard will only act on the value series that's furthest to the left in the worksheet.

Any customizing you want to do?

The ChartWizard next gives you some options for customizing the chart. For this example, I'll select option 7, which will label each slice with the sales-person's name and the percentage that is his or her contribution to January's total sales amount. Choose the options you want, and then click Next.

Now you get a preview of the actual chart you're creating (see fig. 18.6). The Wizard is clever enough to discern that the values you want to plot (that is, the Y axis) are placed in a column, not a row. What happens if we select Rows under Data Series in? One pie, no slices. No good. Quickly, click next to Columns to restore the chart, and then click Next.

 Plain English, please!

A **data series** is just the information that you're charting. In this example, the data is in two single columns: A—the salesperson's name, and B—the sales figure for January for each person.

Fig. 18.5
Don't worry if you make the wrong selection here. You can always go back and change it.

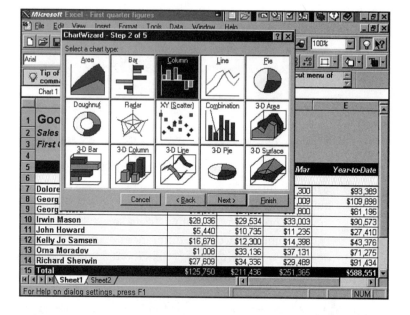

Fig. 18.6
Now is the time to evaluate. Is this the look you're after? If not, click Back and try another one.

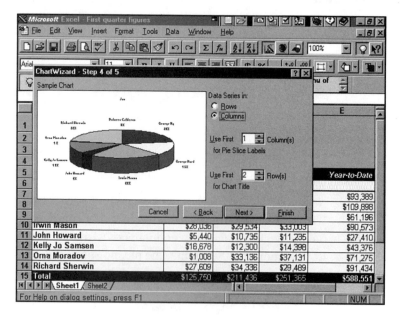

Doughnut or pie... Which chart do I use?

Even if you slept through this class in high school, don't let charts intimidate you. All a chart does is give you a clearer idea of how your numbers look. Would you rather look at row after row of numbers, or a color picture that tells the same story? (You only get one guess.)

But which chart do you use? One size doesn't fit all. For some types of information you need pie charts, and for others, a line chart is more

appropriate. Ever seen the Dow Jones chart on the evening news as a pie chart? Of course not.

When you want to portray a trend over a period of time, you use a line chart. If, on the other hand, you want to look at your portfolio and see what portion of your money is invested in junk bonds, use a pie chart.

Here's a breakdown of all the Excel charts and what they're good for:

Chart type	How it looks	What it's for
Bar/Column		Comparison between values in one or more series. For example, you can show how much money each of your salespeople generated over a period of three months.
Pie/Doughnut/Radar		The relationship between the parts and the whole; for example, the ethnic background of your state. Only one series can be plotted.
Line		A trend, or the relationship between the values and a time period (so that the X axis is the time). Often used to depict stock activities, temperature changes, and so on.
Area/Surface		Illustrates cumulative values. You can use this chart for your sales figures, whereby each level adds to the total sales amount.
XY (Scatter)		Shows the correlation between several value series (for example, between weather data and sales figures).
Combination		A combination chart, like a combination pizza, gives you more than one thing layered on top of another. You can combine a column chart with an area chart to show how trends in two areas are related (for example, how the trend toward two pizzas for the price of one affects the consumption of pizza).

Almost there—add a title

In the last ChartWizard dialog box (Step 5 of 5), you can add a chart **title**, a legend, and axes titles (more on those last items in a bit). Although you don't have to give your chart a title, it's a good idea to help the viewer figure out what exactly he or she is looking at. Click the box under Chart Title, and type a title, such as **January Sales**. Click Finish; the chart is placed in the worksheet and the Chart toolbar appears nearby.

This chart isn't exactly what I had in mind...

As you can see from figure 18.7, you don't usually get perfect results from the ChartWizard. You'll have to tinker with the chart to get it to look just the way you want, but that's pretty easy, too.

Fig. 18.7
In this example, I let the ChartWizard choose the chart size, and everything ran together.

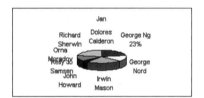

To resize the chart, click once anywhere on the chart and notice the **frame** that appears around the chart. It has small black **handles** that you can use to resize the chart. Drag any of the handles in or out to reduce or enlarge the size of the chart, then click outside the frame to deselect it.

I want to move the chart

If you just want to move the chart within the current worksheet, click it once, then drag the entire frame to a new location. But if you want to move it to another worksheet, use the Clipboard to transport it, as follows:

1 Click once anywhere on the chart.

2 Press Ctrl+X to cut it and place it in the Clipboard.

3 Click the target worksheet's tab.

4 Move your cursor to where you want the chart pasted, click once, and press Ctrl+V to paste it. The cell you've selected is the upper left corner of the chart.

Can I change this chart to a bar chart?

Come to think of it, you may want that monthly sales chart to be a bar chart. Don't worry, you don't need to re-create the chart. Just click once anywhere within the frame around the chart, and notice the tiny Chart toolbar that pops up. (Or you may have to choose View, Toolbars, and click Chart to get the toolbar to appear.)

Click the drop-down arrow next to the Chart Type button, and select any of the bar charts you see in figure 18.8.

Fig. 18.8
You don't get as many choices here as in the ChartWizard, but make a selection anyway, and you can later fine-tune it to have all the bells and whistles you need.

 TIP If the new chart looks strange, you can clean it up by clicking the Default Chart button on the floating Chart toolbar. This may not be the chart you want, but in most cases, it's easier to customize from this point than if your chart has been previously bent out of shape.

Fancy formatting

Look at figure 18.9. The slice for Orna Moradov is so thin, it's practically hidden. What you need is to take that slice and slide it out, so that it's easier to see. Follow these steps:

1 Double-click somewhere in a wide pie slice to switch to the chart editor. The Excel menus change to reflect charting options, although it's not immediately evident. Choose Format or Insert, and you'll see options you've never seen there before.

2 Click the slice you want to slide out. Notice the handles around it. This sometimes requires practice, so if it doesn't work at first attempt, try again.

3 Gently drag the slice out as far as you want. Your pie should look like that shown in figure 18.10.

Fig. 18.9

You can see a dark line by Orna's name, but is that a slice or a hole? It's hard to tell.

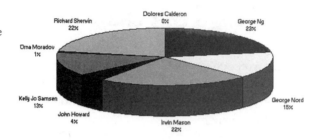

Fig. 18.10

Believe it or not, this is called exploding the slice.

Notice this heading—if your chart extends beyond the edges of the worksheet window, Excel shrinks it into this little window so you can see the whole thing

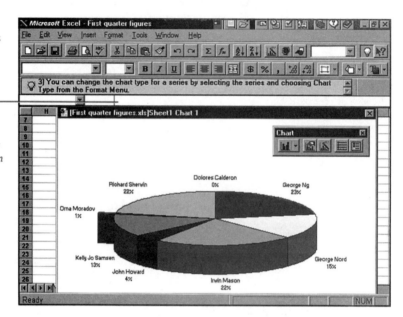

Which bar is which?

If you use a multiple-value series like the one in figure 18.11, where there is more than one value charted for each time period, it's hard to tell what each bar stands for. Each group of bars is identified on the X axis, but the individual bars are only identifiable by different colors.

What you need is a **legend**, which is a set of labels that indicate which colored or shaded series of data is which. In this case, the legend helps the reader determine that the blue columns are January, the red columns are February, and the pale yellow columns are March.

To add a legend, click the Legend button on the floating Chart toolbar. A **legend box** similar to the one in figure 18.12 is inserted next to your chart. You can move the legend box somewhere else within the chart frame, if you wish, or enlarge it by dragging the handles.

Fig. 18.11
This overcrowded bar chart is too confusing.

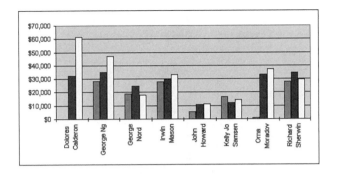

Fig. 18.12
Without the legend, you would have no idea what each of the columns is about.

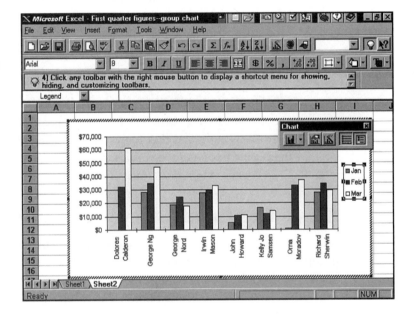

What's the exact amount of that column?

Legends are great for identifying what the different pieces of a chart represent. But they're not enough. Exactly how much money does that red bar represent? To label the different parts of your chart with their actual values, follow these steps:

1 Double-click the chart.

2 Right-click any of the value elements (bar, line, and so on). You'll get a shortcut menu with several options. One of them is Insert Data Labels—click it.

3 Select Show Value and click OK. As you can see in figure 18.13, the actual amounts are inserted as labels.

Fig. 18.13
Reading specific values for chart elements becomes a breeze when you place data labels on them.

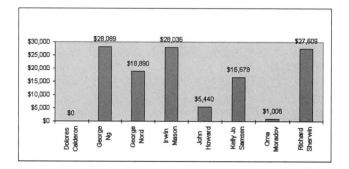

Q&A *My legend is confusing. Can't I label the slices of my pie chart, so that I don't need the legend?*

No problem. Double-click the chart, then right-click anywhere. Select Insert Data Labels, and click Show Label and Percent. You'll notice that the Legend box is still there, so click the Legend button in the floating Chart toolbar, and it disappears.

Move the labels somewhere else

Data labels can be placed above or below the bars in a chart (in all charts except pies), and you can even choose between vertical and horizontal alignment. Double-click the chart, move the pointer to any of the labels, and right-click. Select Format Data Labels. The resulting dialog box, shown in figure 18.14, probably looks pretty familiar from formatting cells.

To change the alignment of your data labels, click the Alignment tab and indicate whether you want the text centered above its column, stretched from one edge of a bar to the next (Justify), etc. In the Orientation section, click the box with the word Text going the direction you want it. You may need to experiment with this tab a bit until you get the labels positioned exactly as you want them.

These labels are boring

You don't have to put up with the default font and color that Excel picks for your labels. Just right-click any of the labels, and select Format Data Labels. Let's say you want to use red Arial, 14-point fonts. Just follow these steps:

1 Click the Font tab.

2 Select Arial from the Font list box.

3 Select the color.

4 Select the size, and choose OK to accept the changes.

Fig. 18.14
For a nice effect, select vertical orientation to place labels inside bars.

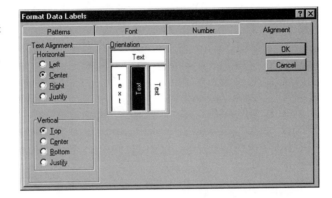

The X axis is too crowded

Look at figure 18.15. The X-axis labels are incomplete because of the limited space.

You can either try a smaller font or change the text alignment so that the words are written vertically. Double-click the chart, and right-click any of the X-axis labels. From the shortcut menu, select Format Axis, and click the Alignment tab. Select a vertical alignment, and your chart will look much better.

Fig. 18.15
When your chart looks like this, it's time to rearrange the text.

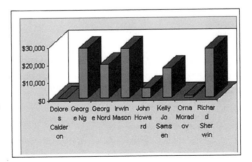

Add a title

Your chart is meaningless unless you identify it with a title. As you saw earlier, you can specify a title in Step 5, the final step of the ChartWizard. But if you skipped that step or need to change the title, it's not too late:

- **Create a new title.** Right-click anywhere within the chart, and select Edit Object. Right-click again anywhere within the chart box, but not on the chart itself, and select Insert Titles. From the Titles dialog box, select Chart Title, and click OK. Type the title, and press Enter.

- **Modify an existing title.** Double-click the title, and make your changes.

- **Modify the title's format.** To select a different font or color, right-click anywhere within the title, and select Edit Object. Right-click within the title again, and select Format Chart Title. Click the Font tab, and make your selections.

- **Move a title.** Double-click the title, then drag it to its new location.

Change the scale

One of the decisions the ChartWizard makes on your behalf is which values to place on the Y axis. A typical setting is to show values from 0 to whatever, with different value points at increments of 10,000.

There is a problem with this setup: a column representing a value like 24,500 is pretty hard to spot. As you saw earlier in figure 18.13, you can add data labels that show the specific amounts of each data series, but they may clutter the display. A better way is to change the **incremental value** to something smaller than 10,000.

 Plain English, please!

The increment is the amounts by which Excel chops up the axes. You can divide by thousandths of a point, millions of dollars, or whatever makes the most sense for the data you're charting.

The scale is the beginning and end points of the axis. You know, as in "On a scale from 1 to 10, I give it an 8."

To control the minimum or maximum amount on the axis, or change the increment value, follow these steps:

1 Double-click the chart.

2 Right-click any of the Y-axis labels.

3 Select Format Axis.

4 Click the Scale tab.

5 Excel displays the current values it's using to scale the axis. To change any of them, double-click the value box, and type a new value. Double-clicking the value box and entering a new value turns off the automatic mode (or you can turn it off by deselecting the Auto box).

These bright colors are a bit much

Just as you'd expect, you don't have to put up with the default chart color schemes. You can easily apply your own colors. The technique for changing colors differs from chart type to chart type, so read on.

Much as you'd like to, you can't change all the colors in a pie chart, line chart, or a multiple-series bar chart in one fell swoop. You need to deal with each element individually, as follows:

1 Double-click the chart.

2 Right-click the line, bar, or slice you want to modify.

3 Select Format Data Series, and you get the Format Data Series dialog box shown in figure 18.16.

4 From the color chart in the middle of the dialog box, select any color you want.

5 Click OK.

TIP **Single-series bar charts normally display all the bars in the same** color, so right-clicking any of the bars will apply to all of them. Right-clicking any bar or column in a group will apply the color changes to all of its matching series (for example, everybody's column for March will change to green or orange or whatever).

Fig. 18.16
Although these colors
may look fine on your
monitor, if your printer
is of the black-ink
variety, try playing with
different patterns
instead of colors.

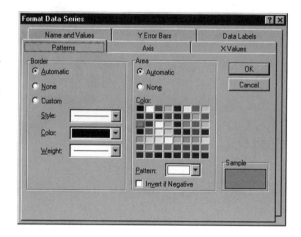

Q&A *I modified my worksheet, but I don't see any changes.*

If you have Excel configured for automatic recalculation, the changes to
your worksheet are automatically reflected in your chart. If not, you'll need
to press F9 to refresh the chart, or choose <u>T</u>ools, <u>O</u>ptions, click the
Calculation tab, and select <u>A</u>utomatic.

Printing your chart

When it's time to print your chart, you have two options: you can print the
chart as part of the worksheet or on a page by itself. Your CPA may need
to do some serious analysis, which requires the worksheet data, but your
employees need only see the motivational charts you want to show. Also, if
you prepare overhead transparencies for a presentation, you'll need to print
the chart as a full page.

 TIP **Although your screen may be able to display your chart in color,**
you may have a black-ink printer. Always preview your selection before you
print it—the preview screen shows the colors translated to shades of gray.
You may want to replace some colors or play with patterns to make the
chart more legible.

 To print the chart alongside the worksheet, select the print area, then click
the Print Preview button on the toolbar to make sure that it all fits nicely. If
you don't like the layout, and want to move the chart a bit or resize some of
the text, click Close, make your changes, and then return to Print Preview.

When you need to print the chart on a page by itself, double-click the chart and select Print Preview. Happy? Click the Print button.

Mapping a worksheet

One great new feature in Microsoft Office for Windows 95 is **Data Map**, a program that can create maps based on information you supply. Mapping can be helpful when trying to analyze data. For example, you can map:

- Where major universities are located around the world (from an address list)

- Hot spots for potential sales (from demographic data)

- Which regions produce the highest revenue for your business (from a sales worksheet)

Figure 18.17 shows a typical U.S. map, indicating areas where customers are clustered.

Fig. 18.17
It looks better in color, of course.

You work with the map in a different window— notice that the toolbars and menus have changed

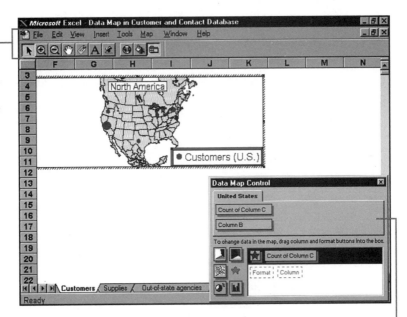

The Data Map Control window lets you change the map after you draw it—add charts, change colors or formatting, etc.

TIP   **The Data Map program was created by MapInfo Corporation,**
based in Troy, New York. For detailed mapping, you can order additional
maps and demographic information from them. Check out the MapInfo
forum on The Microsoft Network, or call 1-800-488-3552.

How to create a map

To map the data in a worksheet, keep in mind that you need at least one
column of information with geographic locations specified. Then follow
these steps:

1 Select the data you want to map.

2 Choose Insert, Map.

3 Click in the worksheet where you want the upper left corner of the map
to appear.

TIP   **You can drag to define the area for the map to occupy, but it's**
easier to let Data Map define the size. Resize it later, if necessary.

4 Depending on the type of data you selected, you may see one or more
dialog boxes where you'll need to define what you want to see in the
map. Respond to the questions appropriately in each case, and click OK.

That's it. The map appears in the worksheet. Here are some basic ways you
can manipulate the map:

- To deselect the map and return to the worksheet, click outside the map
  frame.

- To move the map, click inside the map, and drag to where you want it.

- To resize the map, grab a handle and drag.

- To delete the map, click it and press Delete.

- ▨ To move the map in its frame (when you're working in the map
  window), click the Grabber button, click the map, and drag the
  map where you want it.

Editing the map

The first version of the map probably won't be exactly what you want. Double-click the map to open the map window, and edit it as you like. You can add titles, legends, labels for the geographic areas, text notes, and so on with the map window's menus and toolbar. Many of the mapping features work like the charting features discussed earlier in this chapter. Limited space prevents us from covering the many features of this program in this book, but we can hit the highlights.

Figure 18.18 shows the earlier map, now enhanced. This particular version has been converted to a pin map, with pins showing specific areas to target for sales.

Labels help you visualize where you are

Fig. 18.18
It takes only a few minutes of fiddling to produce a customized version of your map, like this.

The red push pins are easy to spot against the light green of the map

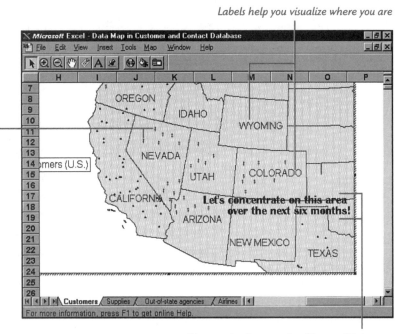

Text can be formatted to "jump off" the map

❝❝ *Plain English, please!*

If you like using maps with push pins to mark territories, sales, etc., you'll like the pin map feature. Click the Custom Pin Map button and then click where you want to place "pins." You can even add text to name or explain the pin location. Type away after placing the pin, and then click elsewhere. ❞❞

CAUTION **For each change you make in the map, Data Map reworks and** redisplays the map. This can take a few seconds or a few minutes, depending on the size of the map, speed of your computer, and so on.

Narrow (or expand) the geographic area

You can change the boundaries of the map by right-clicking it, and then selecting or deselecting items in the Map Features dialog box (see fig. 18.19). For example, if you start out with the full map of North America, but you really only need the U.S. West Coast, trim out the parts you don't want with a few quick clicks.

Fig. 18.19
Click the check boxes to turn areas on or off.

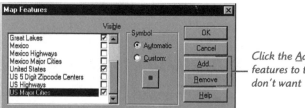

Click the Add or Remove button to add features to the map or remove ones you don't want

Where *are* we? Adding labels and text

Some of those rectangular states look a lot alike, don't they? Adding **labels** to the map can really help.

To use map labels, click the Map Labels button. A dialog box will appear, indicating the areas in the current map for which you can add labels. Choose an area, and click OK. Then slide the mouse pointer around the map. Labels will pop up as you cross territory boundaries (for example, from state to state). The labels move around with the pointer; click where you want to place the label. You can move it later. (See the next section on moving objects.)

Q&A *I accidentally put in two labels. How do I get rid of the extra one?*

Right-click the one you don't want, and choose Clear.

Some labels are abbreviated by default. To spell out the label, double-click it and then type your correction.

Putting text on the map can really help provide specific details. Maybe you want to comment on why test subjects are clustered in a particular area. Or you need to point out that a particular region has few sales because it's largely uninhabitable. To add text, click the Text button, and type the text you want. To change the default text size, right-click the text, choose Format Font, and select the font, size, etc.

Move or delete the object if it's in the way

 If you add labels, text, pins, or other objects to the map, you may find that areas are covered or you have too much junk in one spot. Click the Select Objects button, and then click and drag the object you want to move. To delete the object, right-click it, and choose Clear.

19

Printing Your Worksheets

● **In this chapter:**

- **The best way to print a worksheet**

- **How to select a printer**

- **You can even rearrange the pieces on the page**

- **How many pages will this worksheet need?**

- **Squeeze an entire worksheet onto one page**

Here's a common problem for Excel users. How do you fit big worksheets onto small pieces of paper? . . . . ➤

It's not easy to put together a map of a really big city like Los Angeles or Chicago. How do you squeeze 400 square miles onto one of those fold-out maps? Well, you shrink the streets and avenues into smaller sizes, you divide the big city into smaller neighborhoods, and print the neighborhood maps on the back. In other words, you use every trick in the book to make sure all the information fits on the paper.

Like cities, Excel worksheets come in all different sizes and shapes. The trouble is, you'll almost always want to print your worksheet on plain old 8 ½-by-11-inch letter paper. How? You use the same tricks the mapmakers use: You shrink rows and columns to a size that will fit on the page. You divide the worksheet into smaller sections, then give each of these "neighborhoods" its own page. Best of all, you don't have to worry for even an instant about folding your worksheet exactly the right way so you can stuff it into the glove compartment.

Can't I just click a button and print?

On Excel's Standard toolbar, there's a button you can click to print your worksheet automatically. If you want instant results, just click the Print button and wait for your pages to fly out of the printer. Be careful, though!

Here are just a few of the things that can go wrong when you click the Print button:

- Your worksheet doesn't quite fit on the page, so your column full of totals winds up lost and lonely on its own page.

- One or two columns aren't wide enough, so you see ###### instead of the numbers you expect.

- You've selected the wrong printer, so you have to wander through the halls like a bloodhound, trying to track down your hard copy.

TIP **Excel lets you know, ever so gently, when your data spills over the** margins. When you notice a very fine dotted line to the right of and below your allocated print area, you know that you'll print that spreadsheet on two or more pages, or that you'll need to tweak it to make it fit on one page.

OK, so what's the best way to print a worksheet?

There's one surefire way to get perfect printouts every single time. It's a simple three-step process:

1 Click the Print Preview button. Excel changes the display so you see exactly what your printout will look like on paper. See figure 19.1 for a typical example.

2 Use the Setup button on the Print Preview toolbar to make any necessary adjustments to the margins. Position the selection where you want it on the page, and add headers and footers if you want. You can even ask Excel to force your worksheet to print on a specific number of pages.

3 Now that your worksheet looks just right, it's OK to click the Print button.

Fig. 19.1

Look at the Preview screen's status bar: it says Page 1 of 3. Without the Preview, it's hard to estimate the size of the printed spreadsheet.

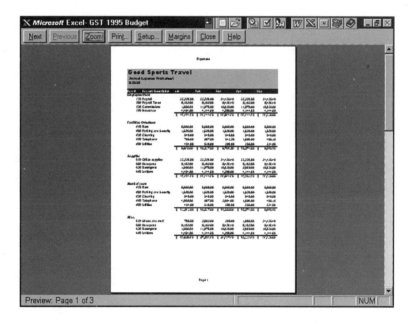

While you're previewing, these Print Preview tools can help you make adjustments:

- If there's anything not quite right with your worksheet, click the Setup button. The Setup dialog box lets you fine-tune the look of your printout without wasting paper.

- Click Zoom to switch between the big picture and a close-up view. The pointer changes to a magnifying glass—click the area where you want to zoom in. The pointer changes back to an arrow; click anywhere to go back to the full-page view.

- Use the Next and Previous buttons to skip between pages. Look at the bottom left corner of the screen to see how many pages Excel has used for your selection.

- Use the Margins button, and Excel will show thin dotted lines along the margins for the page, headers, and footers. You can drag the lines up and down, left and right, to adjust margins instantly. You can also adjust column widths.

- Print lets you send the job to the printer. (Just make sure you've selected the right one!)

- Close sends you back to the worksheet.

- Not sure what to do next? Click the Help button.

 TIP **If most of your worksheets are simple one-page jobs, use Print** Preview to confirm that everything fits. Quickly check that the Next and Previous buttons are grayed out. That way, you won't stand by helplessly (as I did once) while 60 pages of nearly blank printout pours out of the printer because you didn't set the print area correctly.

Secrets of printing great-looking worksheets

When you're building a worksheet, paper is the last thing on your mind. You're more concerned with making sure that the formulas are correct, that rows are the right height, that columns are wide enough to show the numbers inside, and that all your data shows up in the right bars on your charts.

That's OK, because once you switch into Print Preview mode, it's easy to rearrange nearly every aspect of the printout. Most often, you'll use the Page Setup dialog box, with its four tabs that let you control the way your printout looks.

Choose the pieces to print

Suppose you filled all 4,194,304 cells in a single worksheet. If you tried to print them all out, it would take more than two million sheets of paper, which means you'd probably have to buy your own acre of rain forest. Make it easy on Excel (and on the rain forest) by being specific about the section you want to print:

- **I've already selected the section I want to print.** You and Excel will get along just fine. When the Print dialog box pops up, choose Selection in the area labeled Print What.

- **I want to print the worksheet I'm working with now.** Then you don't need to do anything special. If you don't specifically set aside an area to be printed, Excel assumes that you want to print the current worksheet. In this case, the print area starts with cell A1 and extends to the edge of the area containing data or formatting.

CAUTION **Be careful when you ask Excel to print the entire worksheet,** especially if you've added formulas, supplementary tables, etc. below or to the right of the main worksheet. Excel considers everything you enter to be part of the worksheet, so you may need to define the print area more precisely.

- **I want to print the same area every time.** If you have a complex worksheet, with lots of detailed sections that you don't want to see on your printout, you'll get tired of selecting the same area every time you print the worksheet. So don't. Instead, tell Excel which section you want to use as the standard print area:

  1 Select the area you want to designate as print area.

  2 Select File, Print Area, Set Print Area.

When you define the print area, Excel adds it to the list of named ranges. If you need to select it (maybe to zoom in and double-check some figures?), click the down arrow next to the Name box (just to the left of the formula bar), and choose Print Area from the list. Voilá! The entire region is now highlighted.

CAUTION

Once you've defined a print area, Excel *always* prints that area— even if you've added other things to your worksheet (unless, of course, you redefine the print area to include your changes).

To temporarily override the defined print area, select the range you want to print, choose File, Print, and click Selection.

Extra items you can print (or not)

Before you send something to print, specify the little extras that you want to see in the printout—or that you want to avoid. Choose File, Page Setup, and click the Sheet tab in the Page Setup dialog box (see fig. 19.2). You can select the following options:

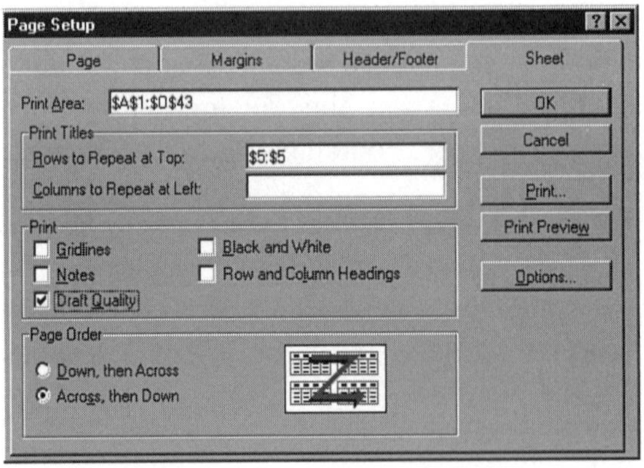

Fig. 19.2
Tell Excel how you want the printout to look.

[Page Setup dialog box screenshot showing tabs: Page, Margins, Header/Footer, Sheet. Print Area: $A$1:$O$43. Print Titles — Rows to Repeat at Top: $5:$5; Columns to Repeat at Left. Print — Gridlines, Notes, Draft Quality (checked), Black and White, Row and Column Headings. Page Order — Down, then Across; Across, then Down (selected). Buttons: OK, Cancel, Print..., Print Preview, Options...]

- **Gridlines**. The gridlines on your screen are just coordinates, to prevent you from being lost. They shouldn't print with every spreadsheet. On the other hand, sometimes they can be pretty handy to help you find your way around a complex printout. If you leave this item turned off, it's a pretty safe bet for most circumstances.

- **Notes**. Notes are pop-up messages embedded in cells (see Chapter 20 for more information on creating and using notes). As notes are invisible, they don't normally print, but here you can tell Excel to print them.

- **Draft Quality**. If your spreadsheet is heavily formatted, with plenty of fancy fonts, graphs, borders, and so on, printing can be a painfully long process. Especially on an inkjet printer. If you just need figures for a quick meeting, select Draft Quality, which will print all the text without any formatting, and thus take a fraction of the time.

- **Black and White**. All those colors look great on your monitor, but if you have a non-color printer, you may end up with a few surprises. If your printout is unsatisfactory (for example, there's little contrast between areas you need to separate), select this option and see if it corrects the problem. Also, just like the draft choice above, select this option if you want to speed up the print job.

- **Row and Column Headings**. On some rare occasions, you'll want to print out the spreadsheet with its reference points, those letter column headings and number row headings.

- **Print Titles**. If your printout spans across several pages, you're likely to lose your points of reference, such as the heading above columns of data. Identify the Rows you want to repeat at the top of each page or the Columns that'll go on the left of each page (depending on which direction your printing goes).

- **Page Order**. Why should you care whether a large spreadsheet gets printed sideways first, then down, or the other way around? Because the order you set here tells Excel how to number your pages.

Pick the right paper (and turn it the right direction)

Most printers hold regular letter-size paper: 8 $\frac{1}{2}$×11 inches. A few have trays that hold legal paper (14 inches long). Most printers can also handle special paper sizes, as long as you're willing to feed it in manually.

With Windows' help, Excel lets you choose the right size paper for your job. Then it asks you to make a more important decision: Portrait or Landscape?

- In **Portrait** mode, the page is oriented with the long side running from top to bottom. This is the way you typically see letters, and it's ideal when you're using Excel to print a list of three or four columns.

- In **Landscape** orientation, the page is turned on its side so that your rows read from left to right on the long edge of the paper. Choose this option when you have a lot of columns to show, as in a yearly budget.

To pick a paper size and orientation, choose File, Page Setup, and click the Page tab to display the dialog box shown in figure 19.3. Then set the options you want.

Fig. 19.3
If the naming clues aren't enough, Excel shows you a picture to remind you which is portrait mode and which is landscape mode.

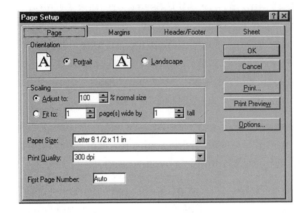

 TIP   **Here's one good reason *not* to use the Print button on the** Standard toolbar. If your printer is set for portrait orientation and your worksheet is designed for landscape mode, you'll get a printout with lots of white space along the bottom; meanwhile, your data will be distributed across two or three pages instead of being neatly arranged on one page.

Arrange your rows and columns

When you first create a workbook, Excel sets up common margins for every sheet in the book. These **margins**—which vary, depending on the kind of printer you're using—define how much white space will appear on each of the four edges around your worksheet. Think of the margins as being a fence around your worksheet. Inside that fence, you can move pieces of your worksheet around to your heart's content. But they can't leave the fenced-in area.

If you have a lot of data to show—as in a 15-month budget—you might want to push the fences out to give your data more room on the page. Or you can increase the margins on the right if you want to leave yourself room to make comments on the printout.

I need help setting the margins

There's a tab on the Page Setup dialog box that lets you set margins by typing in numbers. But there's an easier way that also allows you to see exactly what your new margins will look like. From the Print Preview screen, click the Margins button. You'll see a string of small black boxes ringing the worksheet, plus thin dotted lines that represent each margin (see fig. 19.4 for an example). The lines work much like the row and column headings in the worksheet: Click and drag either direction to give your worksheet more (or less) white space in the header, footer, and margins.

Fig. 19.4

Keep the limitations of your printer in mind when changing the margins. Many laser printers won't print within a half inch of the paper's edge.

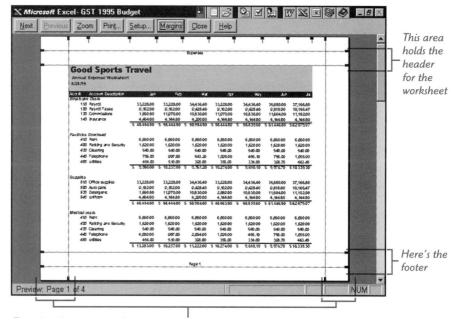

This area holds the header for the worksheet

Here's the footer

To widen the margins, drag toward the center of the worksheet; to narrow, drag out

I want my worksheet centered on the page

If you leave the printing up to Excel, your worksheet will be jammed into the upper-left corner of your page, like a shy teenager at a high school dance. For a big worksheet, you might not notice the difference, but if your worksheet is small, the effect is ugly and a little strange. Fortunately, you can order Excel to automatically center your worksheet between the margins. Choose File, Page Setup, click the Margins tab, and then select the boxes to center either horizontally or vertically (as shown in fig. 19.5). Select both boxes if you want the worksheet perfectly centered.

Fig. 19.5

If your worksheet doesn't fill the page, try using the Center on Page options to bring it out of its corner.

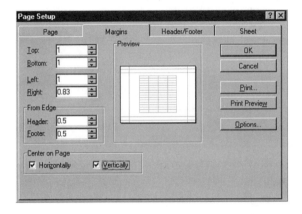

Use these guidelines for choosing your options:

- If the worksheet is relatively shallow—less than half a page deep—select only the box labeled Horizontally. This centers the sheet from side to side but starts it near the top of the page.

- For larger worksheets that fill up all or most of the page, select both Center on Page options.

Label the printout with a header, a footer, or both

Any document that spans more than one page should be labeled with a **header** or a **footer**, to identify the document, the date it was created, the author, and so on.

By default, Excel inserts the file name for your workbook in a header at the top of the page, and adds a page number along the bottom. Your boss probably doesn't care what the file name is, and that page number looks pretty silly on a one-page worksheet, doesn't it?

When you choose File, Page Setup and click the Header/Footer tab, you get access to all sorts of useful options for these labels (see fig. 19.6). Excel includes a set of preconfigured headers and footers that mix page numbers, worksheet names, dates, and your name. (How does Excel know your name? It's under Tools, Options, on the General tab, in the User Name box—Excel just uses the name you typed in when you installed Office.)

Fig. 19.6

You might try scrolling through the list before you give up and type something. Excel is pretty creative...

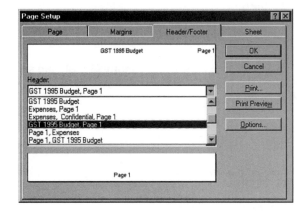

If you can't find a header or footer on the list that matches what you want to say, go ahead and create your own by clicking Custom Header or Custom Footer. You'll get a dialog box like that in figure 19.7. (The header and footer options work exactly the same way.)

Fig. 19.7

This custom header puts a warning on the left, the file name in the center, and the page number on the right.

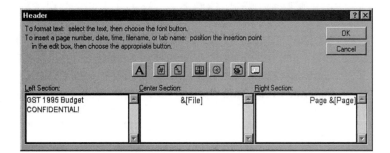

Type any text you want in the three text boxes. Everything in the middle box is centered on the page, while the left and right boxes are aligned against the margins.

To insert a code for the date, page number, time, and so on, position the insertion point, and click one of the buttons in the center of the dialog box. The ampersand (&) tells Excel, "Okay, the next thing coming up is a code, not actual text." In figure 19.7, for example, &[File] puts the file name in the center of the header. The code itself doesn't appear. Left to right, here's what the buttons do:

Accesses the Font dialog box so you can change the formatting

Inserts the page number

Inserts which page of how many (1 of 4, and so on)

Inserts the date

Inserts the time

Inserts the file name

Inserts the worksheet tab name(s)

To change the formatting of your header or footer, select the text you want to change, and click the button labeled with a large A. The dialog box works just like the one you use to format a cell.

I'm through tinkering; can I print now?

Thanks to Print Preview, you can get an almost perfect picture of what your pages will look like when they roll out of the printer. When you're ready to print, just click the Print button, set the number of copies (if you want more than one), and click OK.

How many pages will it take?

When you click the Print button, Excel automatically inserts **page breaks** in your worksheet to section the worksheet into 8 ½×11 pieces—or whatever size you specified. How does Excel know where to put the page breaks? It doesn't, really. It just looks to see how many rows and columns will fit on each page, then plops in a page break at regular intervals. It's easy to spot these breaks, which take the form of dashed vertical and horizontal lines, right in your worksheet, as shown in figure 19.8.

Fig. 19.8

Where the dashed lines cross is the end of one page. Columns to the right or rows below—depending on the direction you're printing—will print on the next page.

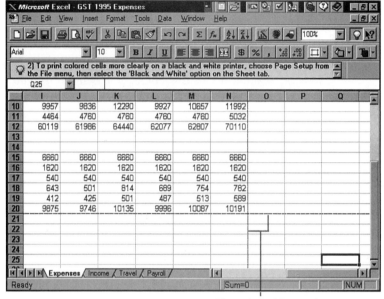

These dashed lines indicate the page break

I want the page to stop right here

The best way to make sure that Excel prints your worksheet the way you want is to insert page breaks precisely where you need them. Select the cell that's one row below and one column to the right of the place where you want the page to break. Then choose Insert, Page Break. Dashed page break lines appear above and to the left of the cell pointer.

To select a horizontal or vertical break only, select an entire row or column, and choose Insert, Page Break.

To remove a page break, position the pointer in the cell just below or to the right of the page break, then choose Insert, Remove Page Break.

Q&A *I can't get my worksheet to print right. All the pages break at the wrong places. What should I do?*

Remove all the manual page breaks and start over. First, select the entire worksheet (click the gray area just above the heading for row 1), then choose Insert, Remove Page Break. Now click the Print Preview button, and try it again.

Worksheet's a bit too big? Force it to fit

I saved this piece for last, because it's probably the coolest thing Excel does. When you choose File, Page Setup, look on the Page tab for the section labeled Scaling. With a few clicks, you can reduce your printout to as little as 10% or as much as 400% of its normal size. By changing the **scale**, you can squeeze more rows and columns onto each page, just the way you can fit more streets and avenues on a map by using a smaller scale.

But how do you know what values to put in the scaling box? You don't need to know. Just tell Excel to fit your worksheet in a specific number of pages. In our sample worksheet, for example, the final column doesn't fit on the first page. We could experiment with the scaling until we found the right setting, but it's easier to simply select the box labeled Fit to 1 page wide by 1 tall in the Page Setup dialog box.

With this box selected, as shown in figure 19.9, Excel automatically rescales the page to 87% of its normal size. The result is a perfect fit!

 TIP **If a worksheet that has always printed just fine starts printing funny**—too small, maybe, or with data sticking out of its column—check to see whether you selected the shrink-to-fit option by accident.

Fig. 19.9
If your worksheet goes on for several pages, don't put anything in the box for the number of pages tall.

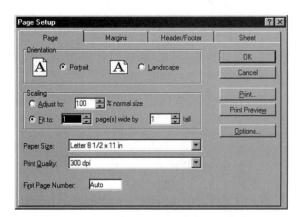

20

Using Word with Excel, and Vice Versa

● In this chapter:

- **Don't retype it—cut-and-paste it instead**

- **I need to do the same old report with different data**

- **How to move data between Word and Excel**

- **Will the numbers in my memo change when I change the spreadsheet numbers?**

- **Share a spreadsheet with a colleague**

Okay, maybe Word and Excel don't belong on the same list as Lennon and McCartney, but they make a great team just the same . . . . ▶

Great teams do great work together. If you don't believe me, just think of the most productive partnerships of our time. Laurel and Hardy. Ruth and Gehrig. Lennon and McCartney. Roseanne and Tom. Errrr…

With all due respect to PowerPoint and Schedule+, Excel and Word are the superstars of the Microsoft Office. For simple day-to-day documents that mix words and numbers in a convincing fashion, you can't beat this team. (For more complex jobs, you need to use the Binder—see Chapter 25 for more information.)

How can Word and Excel team up to work for you? In this chapter, we'll look at the simple ways you can move words into your worksheets and numbers into your memos and reports.

Plain English, please!

Word and Excel (and the other Office products) work well together because of two things: the Windows **Clipboard** and **OLE**. The Clipboard is discussed a little later in this chapter, but we saved the OLE details for Chapter 23. If you want a quick preview on OLE, hop over there, to the section called "I want to use a Word table."

I don't want to retype all this stuff

Your boss just sent you a piece of e-mail with a Word document attached. This memo (which looks a heckuva lot like the one in fig. 20.1) contains the names, birthdates, and departmental assignments of a group of new employees in your company. She wants you to transfer that information into an Excel worksheet, so you can add information about salaries, commissions, and accrued vacation time.

Count your blessings that the boss didn't print this memo on a piece of paper and leave it on your chair. If she had, you'd have to retype every word (and probably make a mistake or three along the way, if you're a two-fingered typist like me). Because it's in a Word file, though, you can automate the whole process. After you select the text from the Word document, copy it to the Windows Clipboard, and then paste it into your Excel worksheet.

Fig. 20.1

How do you move this list of names from a Word document into an Excel worksheet? The first step is to copy it to the Windows Clipboard, so you can paste it into a fresh, new worksheet.

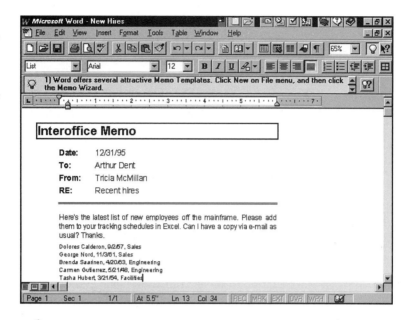

 TIP **Yes, you can drag stuff from one program and drop it in another** program window. But do you really want to do that? Drag-and-drop editing is fine for moving words and numbers around on the same screen, but it's just a gimmick (and it never seems to work right) when you're using two programs at once. Save yourself a headache. When you want to share data between programs, use <u>C</u>opy, Cu<u>t</u>, and <u>P</u>aste instead.

The Clipboard? What's that?

This may be the first time you use the Windows Clipboard, but it sure won't be the last. Whenever two Windows programs get together, you can bet that the Clipboard is going to play a part. How does it work? Well, cutting-and-pasting in Windows is just like the cutting-and-pasting we've all done since age four. If you've ever cut up a magazine and then pasted parts of it somewhere else (a photo montage, a découpage plaque, etc.), or copied something on the copier and posted it on your office door or refrigerator, you've got the idea. The only difference is that you're working with electronic information instead of something printed on paper.

Here's how you do it. Just select something—a block of text in a Word document, or a range in an Excel worksheet, or whatever—and then choose Cut or Copy from the shortcut menu.

TIP **In most Windows programs, you can press Ctrl+C to copy the** selection to the Clipboard. If you never use any other keyboard shortcuts, you should memorize this one and its companions: Ctrl+X to cut and Ctrl+V to paste.

When you capture this chunk of text, Windows stores it in the computer's electronic memory until you move the insertion point and paste in your clipping (see why they call it the Clipboard?). When you reach your destination—in the same program or a completely different program—choose Edit, Paste to plop whatever's on the Clipboard into the current document.

By the way, the Clipboard only holds one clipping at a time—so the next thing you cut or copy replaces the one that was just there. The old one is *gone* from memory.

TIP **Cutting and copying aren't the same thing. If you cut something** from a magazine and take off with it, it's not in the magazine any more, is it? (Ever been disgusted by finding a big hole in the next page, where somebody clipped an ad or a coupon? Now you'll *never* know how that story ends!)

If you use the Cut command, Windows cuts the selected text or picture or whatever completely, and places it in the Clipboard. So it's gone from the original program. Want to leave it in place? Copy, don't Cut.

Copy things from one place to another

Here's how to use the Clipboard to copy the list from Word into Excel:

1 In the Word document, select the text you want to copy.

2 Right-click the selection, then choose Copy from the shortcut menu.

3 Switch to Excel. Create a new workbook if necessary, then position the cursor in the cell where you want the pasted-in list to begin.

4 Click the right mouse button, and choose Paste from the shortcut menu. The text on the Clipboard appears in the first column, as shown in figure 20.2.

Well, that's not exactly what we had in mind, is it? Each line from the Word document landed in a single cell, even though there are three pieces of distinct information in each one. The trouble is, Windows indiscriminately pasted the whole chunk of text into the worksheet in one spot.

Fig. 20.2

When you paste a block of text into an Excel worksheet, each line lands in a single cell. Then you have to split each line into columns.

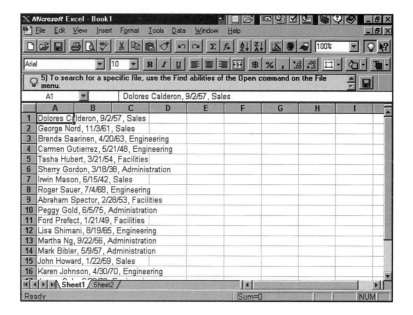

Fortunately, there's an Excel wizard that specializes in splitting text into separate cells. To call the **Text To Columns wizard**, choose Data, Text To Columns. You'll get a dialog box similar to figure 20.3. This Wizard takes three steps to work its spell:

1 In the first step, choose Delimited or Fixed Width, whichever describes your data. The employee list is delimited with commas (I'll explain that in a sec), so I choose Delimited and click Next.

2 In the next box, click the option for the **delimiter** (dee-LIM-it-er) you're using (see fig. 20.4). In other words, what separates the pieces of data from each other? For the employee list, the names are separated from the dates, and the dates from the departments, by a comma. So I click Comma and then click Next.

3 In the final box, you can click each column and indicate what kind of data is in that column. Then click Finish and you're done!

Fig. 20.3
The data is **fixed width** when all the items in the text are the same length. That doesn't apply to this example.

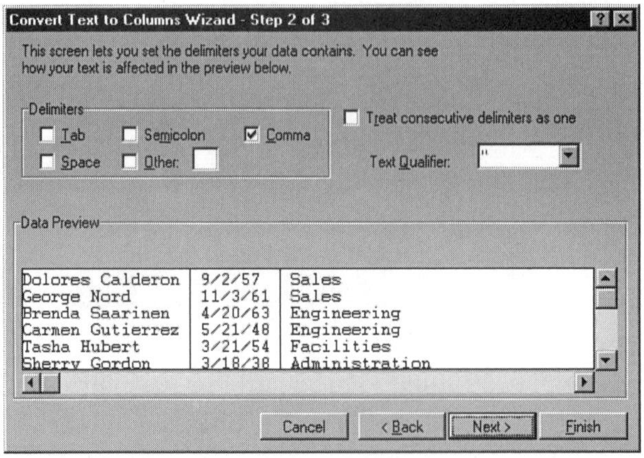

Fig. 20.4
Notice that the preview has changed. The commas tell Excel that I have three columns of data to be separated.

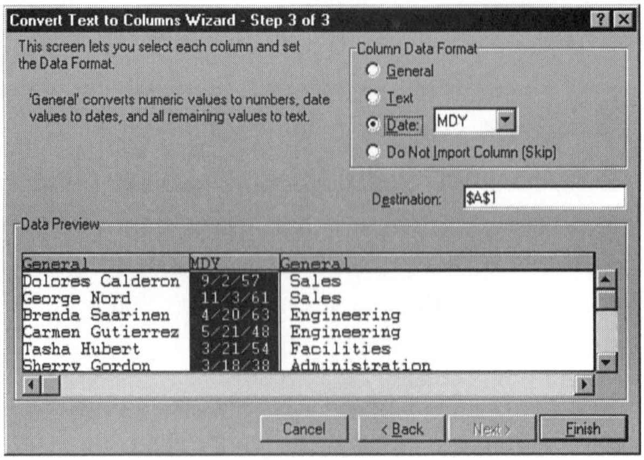

Fig. 20.5
To change the location of the formatted list in the worksheet, type a different address in the Destination box.

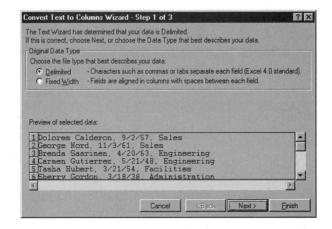

With a few touch-ups, the list from the memo makes a handsome worksheet. Add a row of bold column headings, resize the columns, sort the data if you like, splash some paint on the spreadsheet, and give it a name. The finished worksheet might look like the one in figure 20.6.

Fig. 20.6

It only took a few mouse clicks to move the list of names from a Word document into a well-formatted worksheet.

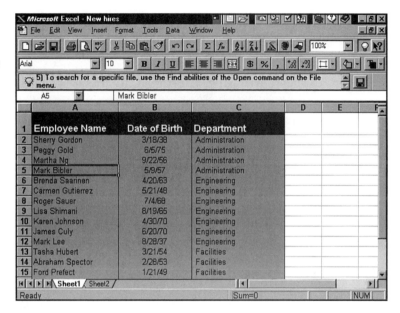

Q&A *I have several extra columns between chunks of my data. What happened?*

If you have data separated by several spaces, rather than a comma or tab, and you are using a space as your delimiter, you will get blank columns. Be sure to delete any extra blank spaces between the items in your data, or use a different delimiter.

There's more than one way to paste that text

You have a budget in an Excel worksheet. You have a Word document. What happens when you try to move the budget from Excel into Word? That depends on how you do it:

- **Paste with formatting.** In this option, the spreadsheet range becomes a Word table. Word tries to match fonts, colors, shading, and column widths, but some formatting glitches may creep in, like column headings disappearing.

- **Paste as text.** The numbers appear in the Word document just as if you'd typed them in directly. All of the Excel formatting is lost.

- **Paste as picture or bitmap.** An image of the selection appears in the Word document. Double-click to edit it as a picture, although the numbers themselves are no longer there.

- **Paste with link.** The spreadsheet range becomes a Word table. As long as the link is alive, any change in the worksheet causes a matching change in the Word table.

- **Embed as worksheet.** The entire workbook file is stuffed inside the Word document. Double-click to start up Excel and change the numbers.

I need to do the same old report next quarter

You've added up this quarter's sales results in an Excel worksheet. The numbers look great (check out fig. 20.7, if you don't believe me), so you want to pass them around, along with an inspirational note and a few congratulations.

You could simply copy the data from your worksheet, paste it into a memo in Word, and print out a sharp-looking memo on your company's letterhead. But if you simply cut and paste these numbers, you'll have to do it all over again when you get next quarter's sales results.

What's your alternative? Instead of just copying the data and pasting it into your document, create a link between the Excel spreadsheet and your Word document.

Creating a **link** is like focusing a remote-controlled security camera on the data you want to copy. When you create a link in your Word document, you're telling Word, "Please keep an eye on this worksheet. If the numbers in the worksheet change, make sure the numbers in this memo change, too."

The result will look as if you'd simply pasted in your data, but there's a big difference—next quarter, when you update the sales worksheet with the new figures, your memo will automatically be updated as well. Add a new set of comments, and your sales report is ready to distribute.

Fig. 20.7

When you want to create a permanent connection between numbers like these and a Word document, don't just cut and paste—use a link.

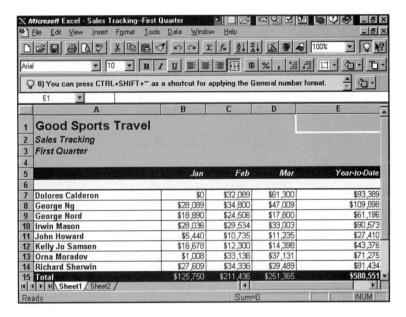

How to create a link

To create a link between a document and a worksheet, you start by copying data to the Windows Clipboard. Instead of using the Paste command, though, use a fancier version of this command: Paste Special:

1 In your Excel worksheet, highlight the range you want to copy.

2 Right-click the selection, and choose Copy from the shortcut menu.

3 Switch to Word. Create a new document if necessary.

4 Choose Edit, Paste Special. You'll see the Paste Special dialog box, shown in figure 20.8.

5 Choose Paste Link, and make sure that Microsoft Excel Spreadsheet Object is highlighted. Click OK. It will take a few seconds, but eventually you'll see the copied text in your document. It should look a lot like

the range from your worksheet. (Even though it looks like a Word table, it isn't. You can't do table operations on it.)

Fig. 20.8

The helpful text at the bottom of the box makes it easy to see what your choice will do.

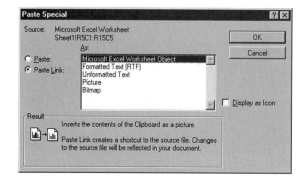

TIP   **If you're pasting stuff from a non-Office application, select the** RTF option in the Paste Special dialog box. **RTF** is short for **Rich Text Format**. It's a special set of instructions Windows uses to share formatted text between programs that otherwise don't have anything in common. Anytime you're not sure how to move data from one place to another, look for an RTF option.

Links are especially useful when you're working on a set of documents with other people in your company. Let's say that your sales-tracking worksheet is in a shared folder where your coworkers can see it as well as you. If Bob in Accounting finds a mistake in your figures, he can update the Excel file stored on the network. The next time you open your quarterly sales report memo, which is linked to that worksheet, Word will look at the data in the worksheet file and adjust the numbers in your memo. The two documents carry on their conversation without bothering you, and you're assured that the data in your memo is absolutely up-to-date.

Just minutes later, the Word memo (with the linked table) looks like the one in figure 20.9.

How to change a link

Word keeps track of links to other documents by hiding complicated formulas inside a document. If you need to change a link after you've set it up, choose Edit, Links. You'll see a dialog box like the one in figure 20.10.

Fig. 20.9
You can't tell by looking that the table in this Word memo is linked to an Excel worksheet. But if any of the numbers change there, the data in this memo will change, too.

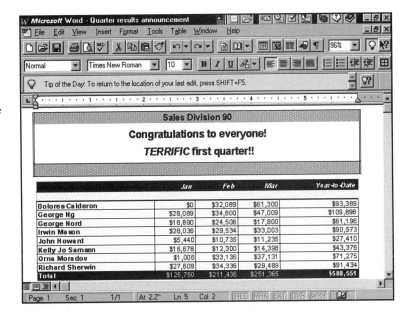

Fig. 20.10
Choose Edit, Links to break a link or change the source document.

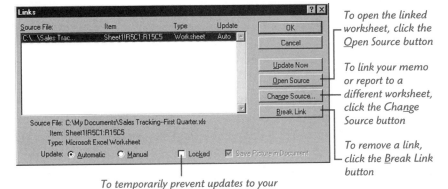

To open the linked worksheet, click the Open Source button

To link your memo or report to a different worksheet, click the Change Source button

To remove a link, click the Break Link button

To temporarily prevent updates to your document, check the Locked box

 Q&A

I updated my Excel worksheet, but the numbers in my Word document didn't change. What happened?

Maybe the link broke. That can happen if you rename the source document or move it to a different folder. Try choosing Edit, Links and click the Change Source button to re-establish the link. If that doesn't work, you'll have to delete the linked range and insert a fresh copy of your worksheet range.

I want to keep these files together

Links can be fragile, especially when you send them somewhere away from your computer or your network. If someone accidentally wipes out or moves the source document—the Excel worksheet with all your numbers—Word will get hopelessly confused, and your carefully constructed link won't work any more.

This possibility is worth worrying about if, for example, you want to make sure all your regional sales managers have a copy of the sales-tracking worksheet along with the accompanying memo.

You could copy both files to a bunch of floppy disks and mail them to all your managers, but you have no guarantee that the two files will end up in the right folders or even on the right computer. And if the two files get separated, the links don't work any more. How do you make sure the files stay as close as Siamese twins? **Embed** the Excel worksheet in your Word report.

How is embedding different from linking?

Instead of simply pasting a *picture* of the data in the second file, embedding packs your entire Excel worksheet into the computer equivalent of a cardboard box, and stuffs it inside your Word document. Now you can distribute a single file that contains all of your data. When you print out your Word memo, it still looks like you've pasted the worksheet data onto the page. But you have access to all the values, formulas, and formats of the original worksheet.

You don't have to worry about breaking links. You don't have to keep track of two different files. If you want to change the data in your sales-tracking worksheet, just double-click the table in your Word document, edit the Excel worksheet, then resave it.

Embedding a worksheet in a Word document

Just like a copy or link, the secret of successfully embedding a worksheet into a document is to use the Windows Clipboard. Do this:

1 In the Excel worksheet, highlight the range you want to embed.

2 Right-click the selection, and choose Copy from the shortcut menu.

3 Switch to Word. Create a new document if necessary.

4 Choose Edit, Paste Special.

5 Choose Microsoft Excel Worksheet Object from the list. Don't click the Paste Link button!

6 Click OK to embed the worksheet in your document.

At first glance, the names and numbers look like a Word table, but they actually behave very differently. For example, the status bar shows this message: Double-click to Edit Microsoft Excel Worksheet. To change the numbers, just double-click the object. Excel will start and load your embedded file.

Sharing Excel files with others

First-quarter sales were great, and your company is working on strategies for growth in new markets in the second quarter. That's when Excel gets an extra workout. Everybody's examining the numbers, trying to see what trends you should focus on, and whose performance could improve with extra incentive. The best way to do this is to pass around a copy of a spreadsheet, and let everybody comment on it.

I know! We'll use sticky notes!

One way to gather everybody's feedback is to let them scribble things in red ink all over a printout of the spreadsheet. Or do the nineties thing and clutter the paper with dozens of Post-It notes of any color imaginable. A much better way is to let them **annotate** the file. Excel has a feature called **Cell Note**, which lets you stick *electronic* Post-It notes anywhere. And, unlike their paper counterparts, these yellow sticky notes go into hiding when you don't need them, eliminating the annoying clutter. Here's how to embed a Cell Note:

1 Click a cell you wish to annotate, and select Insert, Note. A dialog box like the one in figure 20.11 pops up.

Fig. 20.11

The Cell Note feature is useful for embedding comments, or even for customized online-help. Your comments can be fairly lengthy.

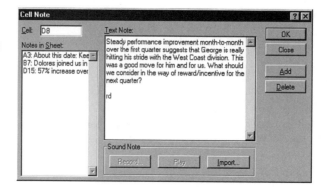

2 Click in the <u>T</u>ext Note box and start typing your comment or message. The first few words are important, because Excel puts them in the Notes in <u>S</u>heet box. So if all your notes start with ***IMPORTANT!!!***, you won't be able to tell them apart.

3 You can also embed sound files here. If you have a microphone, click the Record button, and as you can see in figure 20.12, you'll get a tiny sound-recorder. Click the button labeled with a dot, and start talking to the microphone. When you're done, click the Stop button (the one with the square) and save the file.

4 Click OK to exit.

Fig. 20.12

Sound files are notoriously large, so record your message only if you think that the typed note won't do your message justice.

Notice the tiny red square on the cell you've just annotated? That's how you can tell that there's a message there. Move your pointer over that cell, and, *pop* goes the message! See figure 20.13 for an example.

Move the pointer away, and the message disappears. If there's a sound file embedded in the note, you hear it when the pointer is over the cell. Move the pointer, and it goes quiet.

Sure this is all very useful and practical, but it's also great fun...

Fig. 20.13
The Cell Note's size depends on the amount of text you type into it.

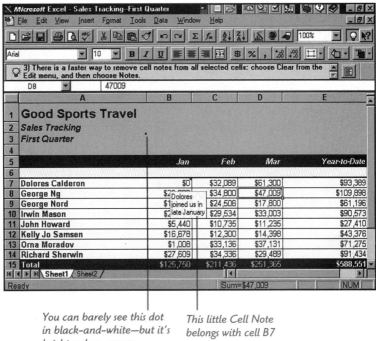

You can barely see this dot in black-and-white—but it's bright red on-screen

This little Cell Note belongs with cell B7

Can we all access the same file?

If your office computers are networked, you should be able to give other people in your workgroup access to this spreadsheet, so they can all update it, annotate it, and print reports from it simultaneously. To do so, select File, Shared Lists and click the Editing tab. In the resulting dialog box, click next to Allow Multi-User Editing, to give others access to the file, and—more importantly—to let them all use it at the same time. Then click OK. At any point, you can click the Status tab in this dialog box and get a list of all the users who are currently using this file.

CAUTION If you and other users plan to share important files, work out in advance who will make changes to the file, and when. It can be very frustrating to think you've got the latest version for a meeting, and then find that someone else's updates changed your totals after you were done printing!

TIP **Don't need to make changes in the file? When you open it,** choose the <u>R</u>ead Only option in the Open dialog box. You'll get a version you can read and print, but not save under that name. This trick is a little safer than actually sharing the file.

See Chapter 23 for information on using Excel and Word with PowerPoint, and Chapter 25 for combining work with Binders.

Part IV: Using PowerPoint

Creating a New Presentation

● In this chapter:

- **How to start building your presentation**

- **Adding words, pictures, and more to a slide**

- **PowerPoint can do the work for you**

- **Creating slides from scratch**

- **Is it ready? Viewing your presentation**

To create a presentation with PowerPoint, you don't need a degree in multimedia productions from the Spielberg School of Whiz-Bang . . . . ●>

How many times have you suffered through uninspired slide shows put together by friends? You didn't have the option to refuse the invitation to look at the world's dullest vacation photos. And you *did* stay awake, didn't you?

Slide shows don't have to be sleep-inducing. When used right, they're powerful tools for selling products and ideas. Done professionally with special effects, they can turn the most reluctant audience member into an attentive participant. In PowerPoint, you already have all the tools you need.

What's more, this program produces powerful results and is a breeze to use. Because so much of the work is done for you, you'll almost be embarrassed to accept your colleagues' compliments. But go ahead, take credit for these breathtaking sight-and-sound shows. After all, you were smart enough to let PowerPoint create them. Oh, and when you thank the Academy for giving you that award, don't forget to mention this book.

Where do I begin?

Start by planning ahead, and make sure that you run the show, not the other way around. Jot down some ideas on how you want the presentation to look, but leave some room for spontaneous changes, because PowerPoint is bound to give you a few brilliant ideas along the way.

When PowerPoint starts, it graciously presents you with some options for creating a new presentation or opening an existing one. Take a look at figure 21.1.

Fig. 21.1

The startup options: notice that there's something here for just about any working style.

One of the options features the very resourceful **wizard.** The other options involve a bit more work on your part, and you'll turn to them as you become more comfortable with this program.

PowerPoint and its tools

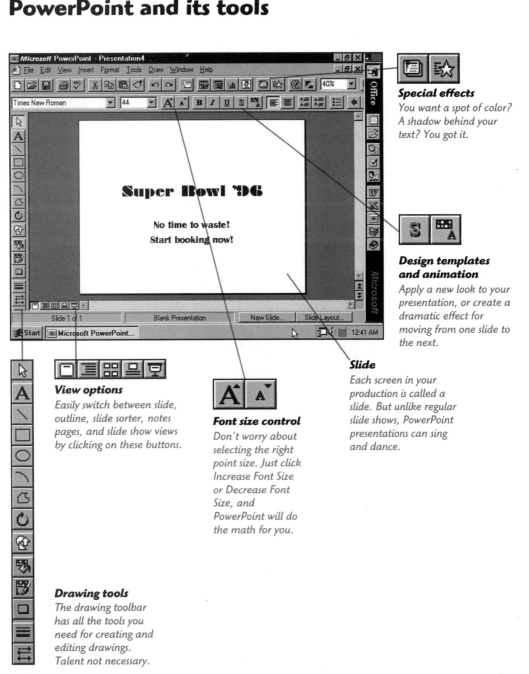

Special effects
You want a spot of color? A shadow behind your text? You got it.

Design templates and animation
Apply a new look to your presentation, or create a dramatic effect for moving from one slide to the next.

Slide
Each screen in your production is called a slide. But unlike regular slide shows, PowerPoint presentations can sing and dance.

View options
Easily switch between slide, outline, slide sorter, notes pages, and slide show views by clicking on these buttons.

Font size control
Don't worry about selecting the right point size. Just click Increase Font Size or Decrease Font Size, and PowerPoint will do the math for you.

Drawing tools
The drawing toolbar has all the tools you need for creating and editing drawings. Talent not necessary.

Sit back and let a wizard work for you

Let's talk about wizards: those wand-waving creatures whose sole purpose in life is to make *your* life easier by doing the grunt work for you. There's really nothing magical about what wizards do—they don't read your mind; they first interview you and then carry out your instructions. Who says it's hard to find good help anymore?

As the name implies, the AutoContent Wizard automatically guides you through the process of adding your ideas to a presentation. In this four-step interview process (see fig. 21.2), the Wizard finds out your name and your company's name, the purpose of the presentation (Are you selling a product or an idea? Is this part of a training program?), and creates a dummy presentation that you can customize by replacing text, changing colors, and applying special effects.

Fig. 21.2

The AutoContent Wizard creates a skeleton of a presentation, based on the information you provide. Change your mind? Just repeat the process, and the Wizard will apply your new input.

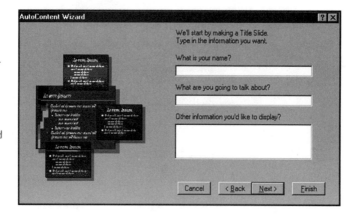

The AutoContent Wizard appears whenever you start up PowerPoint. To summon the Wizard after you've been working for a while, just choose File, New. Click the Presentations tab and choose AutoContent Wizard—it should be first on the list.

Starting without a wizard

Okay, so maybe you're the hands-on type. No wizards, no coaches, no training wheels. You want to do everything on your own. Go ahead and bypass the wizards completely. PowerPoint offers a couple of other ways to get started.

Templates

Remember stencils? You used them in school, and, if you're at home in a wood-working shop or sewing room, you probably still use them. In wood or fabric, the cut-out design guarantees that each new project will have the right shape. PowerPoint **templates** accomplish the same end for your presentations. These electronic stencils let you start with the skeleton of a document, inserting your own text and graphics in place of dummy place-holders.

Where the AutoContent Wizard makes it easy to plug your ideas into a predesigned structure, Design Templates, like those shown in figure 21.3, focus almost exclusively on look and feel. If you choose the Template option when PowerPoint starts up, you can choose from 32 different designs, then build your presentation one slide at a time around that look. You can also apply a new design template to a presentation at any time, as well see in the following chapter.

Fig. 21.3

Check the Presentation Designs tab for a preview of what your presentation will look like.

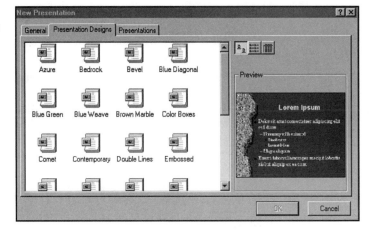

 Q&A *I don't like the way this presentation has turned out. Do I have to start over from scratch?*

When you use the Apply Design Template feature, it only applies a new look to your presentation; you don't lose any of the text or other elements you've added to your slides.

Starting with a blank slate

So, you feel the creative juices flowing? Go ahead, give the Blank Presentation option a try. Nobody's there to hold your hand, and no wizards will be conjured up. But you can't go terribly wrong, and the experience may be enlightening.

Opening an existing presentation

Select this option to open a previously created masterpiece. By default, the File Open dialog box takes you to a folder called My Documents, but you can browse through My Computer and the Network Neighborhood to find a file you previously saved in another folder. If you're unclear on the concepts of saving documents and finding them again, look at Chapter 4.

Starting from nothing

It's that time of year again. You need to get your travel agents pumped up to sell airplane tickets and package tours for next year's Super Bowl. You *could* send out a truckload of brochures and follow up with daily faxes that announce, "Only five months left to the Super Bowl!" Ho-hum. Expensive, and pretty low on the excitability meter, wouldn't you say?

Want to really get results? Invite all those travel agents to brunch, serve them Mai Tais with little parasols in each glass, and knock their socks off with a PowerPoint presentation, accompanied by a Gloria Estefan soundtrack.

How do I create a slide show on my own?

Though the wizards are wonderful design aids, you may find that it's just as thrilling to start with nothing but a blank canvas. Just select the Blank Presentation option from the start-up screen and let your imagination run wild.

 Q&A *I've lost that start-up screen. Do I have to exit PowerPoint and rerun it to get to that screen again?*

There's no way to pull up that helpful dialog box without closing and restarting PowerPoint. But you can choose any of the three options found there without any fuss: Just choose File, New, and use the New

Presentation dialog box. For a blank presentation, look on the General tab. Templates are collected under the Presentation Designs tab, and the AutoContent Wizard lives under the Presentations tab.

Pick a layout, any layout

Take a look at figure 21.4. It looks like you're not on your own here, after all (whew). When you choose to use either a template or a blank presentation, you can pick a layout from the New Slide dialog box. In this example, Title Slide is selected. How do you know? First of all, it has a thicker frame than the rest of the slides. Also, the words `Title Slide` appear in a box at the lower-right side of this dialog box. Click OK to select this layout, or select another one by clicking it (scroll down to view the other slides if necessary). Click OK to add the new slide to your presentation.

Fig. 21.4

To add a new slide, select one of 24 layouts and customize it. If you don't find one you like, pick the closest match, then resize or remove any of its parts until you have the right mix.

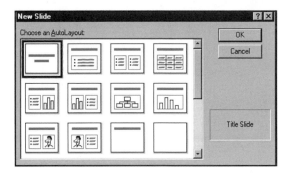

Ready to start typing?

All the slide layouts represented in the New Slide dialog box—except for one labeled `Blank`—feature clearly identified boxes, or **frames**. Their labels invite you to do things: `Click to add title`, for example. To take PowerPoint up on its offer, click anywhere inside a box—like the one in figure 21.5. The instructional message disappears, and a typing insertion point awaits your instructions.

Fig. 21.5

No surprises: your
options on this new
slide are crystal-clear.

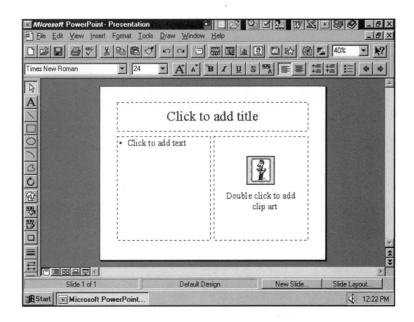

Once you've typed a title or any other text, you can select a different font or
apply special text attributes such as bold, italics, or a different color. But
before you can do anything, you first have to select the text with the mouse.

TIP   **To apply text-format changes to all the text inside a frame, click**
the frame. You can also select some or all of the text inside a frame by
dragging the mouse over the words, just as you would in Word and the
other Office programs.

Now, add special effects to the text

Want to make a lasting impression? Pay special attention to the way your
text is formatted—size, color, and special effects like shadows. These
details are crucial if you want your words and pictures to stand out on the
screen or on the page. Here are several special effects to play around with:

- **To make your text larger**, increase the font size. This can be tricky,
  because if you're not sure what size you need, you may end up wasting
  time trying out different options in the Font Size pop-up list. The easier
  route is clicking the Increase Font Size button, which is located immediately to the right of the Font Size menu. Keep clicking until you're
  happy. If you want to keep the text on a single line, and the words wrap
  around to the next line, you've gone too far.

- Text too big? Click the Decrease Font Size button **to reduce the size of the text** until the text fits on the line.

- **To add more pizzazz to a title**, click the Text Shadow button. These so-called **drop shadows** create the illusion that your letters are floating above the surface.

- **To add color to a title**, click the Text Color button, and select a color. (There's a short list of eight colors that match the current template, or you can click Other Color to choose from a spiffy dialog box with hundreds of available colors.)

- For a dash of excitement, **combine effects**. Pick a different font from the Font pop-up list. Make it bold, even italic. (Note: since bold text is thicker than the plain variety, you may run out of space and the text will wrap around again, so click Decrease Font Size if necessary to adjust it.) See if you can re-create the text in figure 21.6 (hint: you can do *much* better than that).

Fig. 21.6

Apply any fonts and special effects you like, but remember, the ransom-note look is no longer considered respectable.

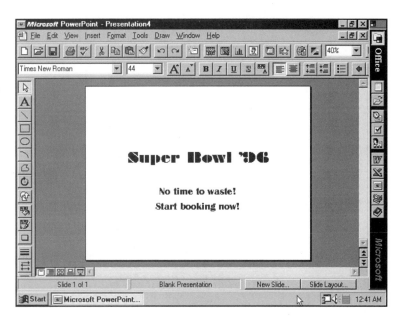

What can I put on a slide?

In an effective presentation, each slide should convey a complete thought or message. Other than text, there are a few elements you can and should add to your slides to make your point come across better or prove your claim (or both):

- **Pictures**. It works every time. Spice up your presentation with graphics, like a dramatic picture or a clever cartoon, and you'll get their attention. Select from one of the dozens of clip-art images included with Office, or find your own.

CAUTION **A little clip art goes a long way. Now that you've discovered** graphics, you'll probably go haywire and want to use one (or more) in every slide. Please fight the temptation, because too much art will make your slide show look amateurish and cluttered. Use graphics sparingly, and only when they help make your point.

- **Charts**. Nothing conveys numeric information more clearly than a well-designed chart. Place a pie chart, bar chart, or column chart in your slide to make the numbers come to life.

- **Tables**. When you have a lot of information to display, the best way to use the limited real estate on the screen is to present your information in a table. The neat, clean grid makes it easy to follow the flow.

I want to add some text

If you've picked one of the predesigned slide arrangements (or **layouts**), such as the Bulleted List layout shown in figure 21.7, click once anywhere in a text frame (any one labeled `Click to add…`), and start typing.

 TIP **If the text is formatted as a bulleted list, you'll get a new** bullet each time you press Enter. Don't want a bulleted list? Select the entire text by pressing Ctrl+A, and click the Bullet On/Off button on the Formatting toolbar. This is called a **toggle** feature: one click turns it on, another click turns it off.

By the way, if you prefer to do your writing in Word, no problem. It's easy to turn a Word document into a PowerPoint presentation. See Chapter 23 for the step-by-step details.

Fig. 21.7
How can you tell if the text is formatted as a bulleted list? Just look for the bullet "•" character to the left of the words `Click to add text`.

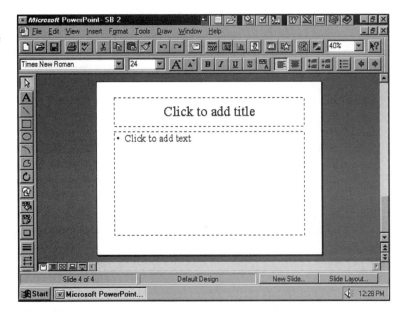

Bite the bullet

Blame it on television, or blame it on junk food, but people have a short attention span. Rather than type a wordy paragraph into a slide, break up your thoughts into short ideas or topics, and point to them with tiny graphic markers called **bullets**. Here are some examples of bullets:

Standard bullet	•
Another common one	■
Beam us up, Scotty...	➢
They went that-a-way!	☞

I sell travel services	✈
Have a nice day!	☺
We're a winning team!	✌
Fun in the sun, anyone?	✹

To replace the standard PowerPoint bullet with a more creative one, click the text frame, choose F_ormat, _Bullet, and click the down arrow next to _Bullets From. Select Wingdings, and a world of wacky graphics is yours to explore. Select the character you want to use for your bullets, then click OK.

I want to turn some numbers into a chart

There are two ways to insert charts into a PowerPoint slide (actually, there are more, but these two are the only ones that don't involve re-inventing the wheel):

Pop in your Excel chart

If you've already created the chart in an Excel worksheet, select it and copy it to the Clipboard (choose Edit, Copy or press Ctrl+C), and then paste it into your slide (choose Edit, Paste). See Chapter 14 for information on creating charts in Excel.

Create a new chart with Microsoft Graph

For simple charts, try creating a custom graph with a special program that comes with Office, called **Microsoft Graph**. Click the Insert Graph button, or double-click the graph icon in a slide. You may feel as though you're still in PowerPoint, but Microsoft Graph takes control of the screen when it's running—you'll notice that the menu and toolbars change.

A spreadsheet-like window called a **datasheet** appears over the current PowerPoint slide. Click the upper-left corner of the datasheet once (the blank, gray rectangle at the intersection of the row and column headings) to select the whole thing. Press the Delete key to clear everything; then type your data as if you were entering it in a spreadsheet, or copy-and-paste it from Word or wherever you've already set up the data. (If you're not familiar with entering data in cells, see the Excel chapters for details.)

Next, choose Format, AutoFormat, select the type of graph you want, and close the dialog box. Finally, use the pull-down menus to dress up the graph the way you want it—change its type, apply legends and titles, and so on. When you're done, click the slide to embed the graph and close the datasheet window by clicking OK.

Using a chart to make your point

Although Microsoft Graph is not as easy to use as the ChartWizard in Excel, for simple charts it's more than adequate.

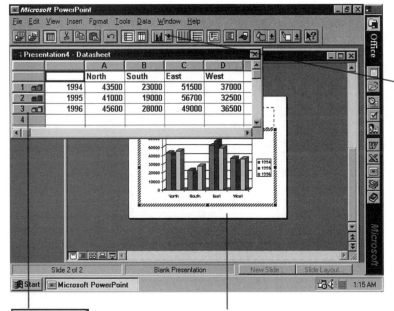

Changing the chart type
But I want a pie chart! To change the chart type, select the chart and just click the Chart Type button. The face of the button will change to show the selected chart type.

What type of chart are you making?
The chart type you've selected is displayed on the datasheet, in case you can't see the underlying slide.

The chart
As you type your data in the datasheet, the underlying screen is redrawn to reflect the changes. For example, when you change a number, watch its corresponding bar get taller or shorter.

Spice things up with a picture

Don't you wish you had a picture of a jet to remind your audience what you're selling? Well, you do. Follow these steps:

1. From the pull-down menus, choose Insert, Clip Art.

2. There are many image categories to choose from. Scroll down the Categories list and click Travel (see fig. 21.8).

Fig. 21.8

Look! Up in the sky! Its a bird! Its a plane! Actually, it's a jet. This may not be the exact image you were looking for, but it's free.

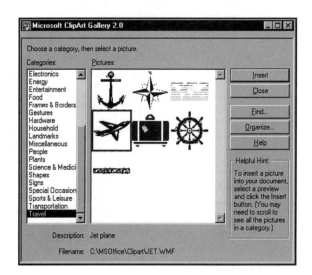

 TIP   **There are hundreds of thousands of graphic images that you can** purchase in any software store or from mail-order catalogs. They are often sold as libraries: packaged by topics such as sports, business, holidays, school, and so on. Since you're creating color slides, look for color graphics. For the more professional look, check out some of the many photo collections (usually sold on CD-ROM). If you can get your hands on a color scanner, scan your own photos or graphics and make your presentations genuinely personal!

3. In the Pictures pane, click the jet graphic (notice the graphic's description and file name beneath the image).

4. Click Insert to add the image to your slide.

5. Is the graphic covering the text? No problem. From the menus, choose Draw, Send to Back; the graphic goes to the background and the text is visible again.

6. You may need to resize or rearrange the graphic object to make the slide look the way you want, as I did in figure 21.9. Click the image and use the handles to adjust as needed.

Fig. 21.9

Text and graphics are stored in separate layers on your slides. Move them around as needed to make sure you get the look you desire.

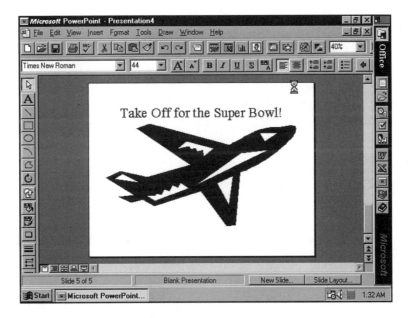

In addition to pictures, PowerPoint also allows you to add sound and video clips to your presentation, which is very cool and makes you a multimedia producer! If you want to explore these options, you'll need special hardware, sound and video files, and monitor-display capabilities. You insert the sound and video as objects through the Insert menu, just as you would a piece of clip media.

You could fill a book with all the details of how to use multimedia with PowerPoint—and, in fact, someone already has. If you want the full story, look for a copy of Que's *Using Microsoft PowerPoint* at your local bookstore.

Different ways to view your presentation

How should you look at your masterpiece? That depends on what you're trying to accomplish. For fine detail work, you'll want to view slides one at a time. To rearrange slides in a lengthy presentation, though, you'll appreciate being able to see the entire collection at once. PowerPoint gives you five distinct views of your presentation, and each one is useful for a different task.

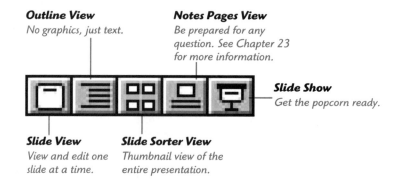

Outline View
No graphics, just text.

Notes Pages View
Be prepared for any question. See Chapter 23 for more information.

Slide Show
Get the popcorn ready.

Slide View
View and edit one slide at a time.

Slide Sorter View
Thumbnail view of the entire presentation.

I want to work on just this slide

There are two ways to view and work on just one slide. The easiest one is to click the Slide View button at the bottom left corner of the screen to switch to **Slide View**. Alternately, choose View, Slides from the menu bar.

How about a panoramic view?

In Hollywood, before anybody ever aims a movie camera at that exploding car, the director must approve the blueprints. These blueprints, called **storyboards** in showbiz lingo, depict tiny frames, with the general layout and action of each scene. Since you're the director (and camera person and producer and caterer) of this slide show, you'll need to refer to a storyboard, too. PowerPoint calls it the **Slide Sorter View**. As you can see in figure 21.10, this is a visual overview of your entire presentation, though you can barely read the text (which is fine because you're looking at global issues, such as layout consistency, not details).

Fig. 21.10

Don't worry. You don't need new glasses. Look at the whole, not the details.

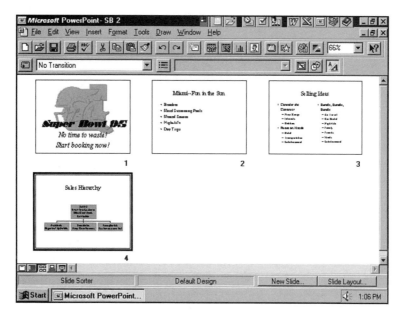

TIP **Not happy with the sequence of your slides? No problem. Click** any slide you want to move, and drag it to its new location.

Time to see the whole presentation

It's the moment we've all been waiting for. It's show time! Click the Slide Show button, and the slide show starts. Any mouse click takes you forward to the next slide, while a right-click moves you back a slide. When you're done, you'll return to Slide View. Don't worry if the show is on the dull side. It'll come to life in Chapter 22.

To stop the presentation while in Slide Show mode, press Esc. This takes you back to Slide View mode.

Stepping with style through a slide show

In case you haven't noticed, there are several ways you can achieve any given task in Office. You can always use the tiny Next Slide and Previous Slide buttons at the bottom of the vertical scroll bar to move around in your PowerPoint presentation. But if you're more comfortable with the keyboard, try these shortcuts instead:

• Press Page Up to go to the previous slide.

• Press Page Down to go to the next.

• Press Ctrl+Home to go to the first slide.

• Press Ctrl+End to go to the last one.

• Slowly slide the vertical scroll bar elevator (no kidding—that's the official name for the sliding button on the scroll bars), and watch the appropriate slide label pop up. Stop scrolling when you get to the desired slide.

Saving your work

If you're happy with the results of your first effort (and even if you're not), select File, Save As, and type a name. Remember, you're not limited to eight characters in Windows 95 applications; you can even use spaces. Don't worry about a file extension; when you save the file, PowerPoint automatically handles that detail.

Before you save, make sure you've selected the folder where you want the file to be stored. See Chapter 4 for more information.

22

Making Great-Looking Presentations

● In this chapter:

- Can I change this background?

- Custom colors, fills, and other great tricks

- Smooth the transitions between slides

- How to make slides dissolve or appear from nowhere

- How can I keep my audience awake?

With a few mouse-clicks, a boring presentation turns into a crowd pleaser. So... lights, camera, action! . . . . ❯

f you're going to climb on stage and give a presentation, you owe it to your audience to mix in some showmanship. Of course you'll start with well-organized ideas, useful information, and a touch of wit and humor. But your audience will listen more intently if you add some sizzle and glitz to the package. That includes readable colors, surprising special effects, relevant graphics, music, and—when all else fails—door prizes.

PowerPoint has all the tools you need to bring your presentation to life: a big selection of interesting backgrounds, dramatic transitions, flying text, you name it.

How to choose a new background

The background image you choose sets the tone for all your slides, and what's right for a motivational talk to a bunch of travel agents might not be appropriate for an undertakers' convention. For the background image on your slides, you can either choose a professionally designed, color-coordinated template, or you can mix and match colors and patterns your-self. The advantage of using the template is clear—it saves energy and time. Even veteran PowerPoint users shouldn't hesitate to rely on this tool.

Spruce up the whole presentation

If your presentation is dull and colorless, it's time for a makeover. Open the presentation you want to modify, and then click the Apply Design Template button (or choose Format, Apply Design Template) to pick from a long list of ready-made designs you can apply to your presentation. Each template contains a color scheme, background, and formatted text, as well as some graphics, like pictures, symbols, lines, and boxes.

Now, the fun begins: tell PowerPoint which background you want for your slides, and you can apply any of the templates in the list to your presenta-tion. Embossed, Metal Bar, or Splatter—a treasure box full of colors, designs, and ideas.

It's easy to window shop: just click any template name that sounds interest-ing—from Azure to World. The names are broadly descriptive, but the best way to see what each one looks like is to click the Preview button in the Apply Design Template dialog box, as shown in figure 22.1. Keep looking until you find a design that's close to what you want; a little later in this chapter I'll show you how to modify the design.

Don't worry if the preview seems a bit grainy and out-of-focus; the actual slide will look much better. When you find the design you like, click Apply, and it will appear on all the slides in the presentation. Now sit back and enjoy your slides.

Fig. 22.1
The preview shows a tiny representation of the actual template. You can easily browse and pick just the look you want.

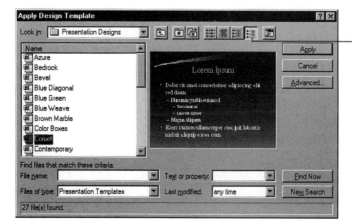

No preview in your dialog box? Click this button.

Q&A *I can't find any of the presentation templates in these examples.*

Whoever installed Office on your PC may have saved disk space by not installing the templates at all. Run the Office setup program again, click the Add/Remove button, highlight PowerPoint, and press the Change Option button. Select the Design Templates box, then click OK and follow the instructions. You may also be looking in the wrong folder. The templates that come with PowerPoint are in the Presentation Designs folder, which you can find in the Templates folder, within the MSOffice folder.

TIP **If you don't like the slides with the new template, you can always** go back to the drawing board. Try picking other design templates until you find the one that's just right for your presentation.

I like this layout, but I *hate* that color!

Every design template combines three separate user-customizable elements:

- **Layout.** Includes graphic elements, frames, lines, and so on.

- **Color.** A wide spectrum of colors is available for you to choose from (providing your monitor can display all these choices).

- **Shade styles.** Colors don't just paint the slide. They can also be placed as **gradients**, with varying dark and light shades of the selected color.

For example, if you select Comet as your template, you can change the sky's color to purple, and have the gradient fill flow from dark at the upper-right corner to light at the bottom-left.

CAUTION **With PowerPoint, you can easily mix and match patterns, colors,** and gradient fills. But you need to develop a good eye for what works. Not every combination is aesthetically acceptable, and one thing you want to avoid at all costs is making your audience nauseous. If you're not sure of your judgment in this matter, designate a friend or colleague as a dry-run audience. Even Hollywood producers arrange these previews before the release of a new movie, which gives them a last chance to redo problem areas.

Adjust the background color

If you want the background to be purple, it's no problem. Right-click anywhere on the background, and from the shortcut menu choose Custom Background. Click the drop-down list underneath the preview window, and you'll see a menu like the one in figure 22.2.

Pick a color, any color? Not quite. PowerPoint begins by suggesting that you pick one of eight colors. Those colors aren't just a random selection, either. They're carefully selected to complement one another so that your text is readable and the colors don't clash. But you *can* choose another color if you wish. Just choose Other Color from the bottom of the list to see the color selector shown in figure 22.3.

Fig. 22.2
Pick a new background color for your slides—your choices also include patterns, textures, and light-to-dark shading.

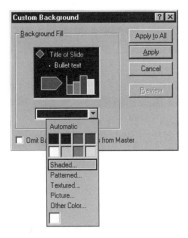

Fig. 22.3
The Colors dialog box gives you a wider selection, and you can click the Custom tab to choose from several **million** options.

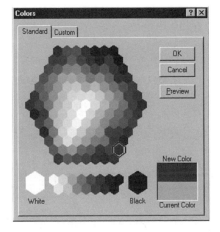

All in all, there are nearly 150 colors (including shades of gray) to choose from. And if you can't find the exact shade of purple you're looking for, you can always click the Custom tab and choose from the resulting rainbow of colors in the Background Color dialog box.

To apply the new background, click OK, and then click Apply to All; the entire presentation changes before your very eyes. If you want to use the new background only with the current slide, click Apply.

TIP **PowerPoint may think the eight colors in each scheme go**
together smashingly. But if you'd prefer to replace one or more of the
colors with alternates of your choosing, go right ahead. Right-click the
background and choose Slide Color Scheme. You can pick one of the
prematched groups or click the Custom tab and build your own, then apply
the new scheme to one or all of your slides.

Change the shading

Everything we've done so far assumes you want to use a solid color as your
background. But most slide backgrounds are more interesting when they
have some variety, such as shading or a texture. A special type of shading
called a **gradient fill** is one of the most impressive and professional-looking
effects you can add to a slide. Look at the Tropical background in figure 22.4
for an example. The dark blue at the top of the slide changes smoothly to a
light blue at the bottom of the slide.

Fig. 22.4
Gradient fills add a flair
to the overall look of
your presentation.

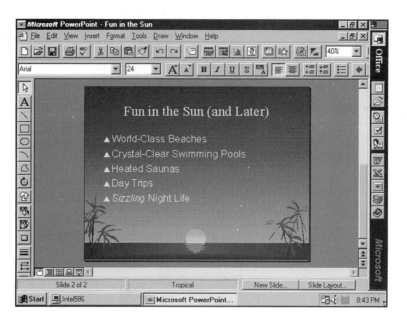

To add a gradient fill to your presentation, choose F<u>o</u>rmat, Custom Background; click the down arrow by the color box, and choose Shaded. You'll
see a dialog box like the one in figure 22.5. Pick any combination of shade

styles and variants to get precisely the effect you're looking for, then choose Apply to modify just the current slide (or Apply To All for the entire presentation).

Fig. 22.5
To fine-tune your gradient fill, play with its three elements: Colors, Shade Styles, and Variants.

Blend a single color from dark to light, blend one color into another, or choose from sixteen preset combinations.

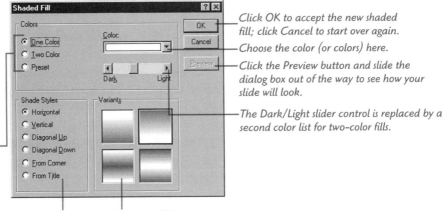

Click OK to accept the new shaded fill; click Cancel to start over again.

Choose the color (or colors) here.

Click the Preview button and slide the dialog box out of the way to see how your slide will look.

The Dark/Light slider control is replaced by a second color list for two-color fills.

Pick a style for the shading, then click one of the variations at the right.

 TIP To explore other options for the background, try experimenting with the Patterned and Textured menu choices. If you'd rather use a piece of clip art for the background, choose Picture and select any Windows-compatible graphic file.

How do I change just a few selected slides?

 Before beginning the editing process, switch to Slide Sorter view. Click the slide you want to modify. If you want to change several slides simultaneously, press Shift, and click each of them (a thick frame appears around each slide you clicked, indicating that it's been selected). Then change the background color, shadows, fills, and so on. Choose Apply (rather than Apply To All) to change just the selected slides.

Simplifying those slides

Background art, extra lines, and other layout elements may look great on a title slide, but they just add clutter to a slide that's already "busy" with graphics and text. To remove all layout elements from a slide, choose

Format, Custom Background, and click the check box labeled Omit Background Graphics from Master. (Click again to remove the check mark and restore the layout elements.)

How do I change a graphic's color?

Suppose the graphic you want to insert clashes with the rest of your color scheme. We can't have that! Just right-click the graphic, and select Recolor from the shortcut menu. In the Recolor Picture dialog box you'll see all the colors used in that piece of art. Use the drop-down color selectors to replace any or all of the original colors (see fig. 22.6).

Fig. 22.6
The dialog box that lets you recolor a piece of clip art works the same as any other color box. You can even choose to fill the picture with a gradient fill.

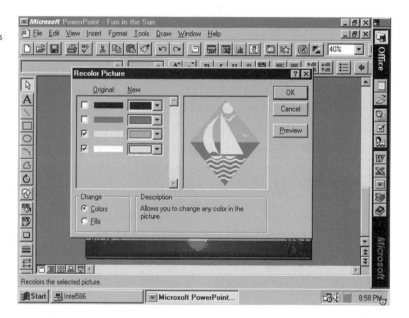

Break-a-leg dress rehearsal

No slide is an island. Your presentation should flow smoothly, with each new slide shifting gracefully into the foreground while the old slide recedes. One way to ensure that your presentation goes swimmingly is to carefully select the transitions between slides. Here are a few things you can do to smooth out the rough edges.

Improve the transitions

In movies and television shows, transitions between scenes have become an art form. It can't be midnight in one scene and bright daylight in the next, a fraction of a second later. There are dozens of techniques to make these transitions smooth and natural, and some are more creative than others.

Sometimes a scene briefly "fades to black" (especially in those juicy love scenes) before the next one appears. Occasionally, you see an overlap between the two scenes, which makes the exiting scene look a bit transparent while the new scene comes into focus.

These effects are added in at the editing phase. And now you can play movie editor, too, because PowerPoint offers 46 different transitions you can use in your presentation. Strictly speaking, there are 13 types of transitions, each with several variations. What they all have in common is the gradual transformation from one slide to the next:

- **Blinds.** Just like your window treatments, these come in the horizontal or vertical variety, gradually opening until you see the entire new slide. *Very impressive.*

- **Box.** A square shrinks into the center of the slide or grows to show the entire slide. *Slick.*

- **Checkerboard.** Small squares cover the new slide, then disappear either sideways or downward. *Three wows.*

- **Cover.** The new slide "flies" in from the top, bottom, sides, or corners, and covers the previous slide. *Oooooh and Aaaaaah.*

- **Cut.** This is a more abrupt transition, lacking the animation of the other transitions. *Yawn.*

- **Dissolve.** Tiny dots that make up the new slide gradually take over the previous one. *Magical.*

- **Fade through black.** A familiar Hollywood "fade-in" effect. The new slide materializes from black. *Classy.*

- **Random bars.** Thick and thin lines (vertical or horizontal) gradually display the new slide. *Dizzying.*

- **Split.** Think of it as pulling curtains over your slide, vertically or horizontally. *Knock their socks off.*

- **Strips.** The new slide reveals itself by covering the previous one in a diagonal direction with a jagged edge. *Interesting.*

- **Uncover.** Unlike Cover, where the new screen flies in all at once, Uncover does a little striptease, peeling off the on-screen elements gradually, in any of eight directions, as the new slide reveals itself. *Teasing.*

- **Wipe.** Slowly reveals the new slide, as if you were gradually sliding a dark cover sheet from in front of a picture (see fig. 22.7). *Smooth.*

- **Random Transition.** Feel like gambling? Select this one—every time you run the show, you'll get different transitions for different slides. *Great if you're trying to annoy your audience.*

- **No Transition.** *No fun.*

Before you can apply a transition to a slide, you have to switch to Slide Sorter view. Once you've done that, you can right-click any slide and choose Slide Transition from the shortcut menu. You'll see a dialog box like the one in figure 22.7. When you add one of these effects, it defines how the slide you're pointing to will make its entrance. To control how a slide leaves the screen, just click the next slide in the presentation.

Fig. 22.7
Take your choice of transitions. The puppy in the preview window shows you what the transition effect will look like.

Apply the same transition to the entire presentation

Switch to Slide Sorter view, and choose Edit, Select All. The thicker frames are your indication that all the slides are selected. Right-click any slide to pop up the Slide Transition Effects dialog box, then select the transition you want to apply. Notice the tiny Transition icon under each slide in figure 22.8 That's your indication that a transition has been applied to that slide.

Fig. 22.8
You can preview the transition by clicking the Transition icon under the slide's thumbnail.

Transition icons

Use a different transition for just one slide

I'll show you how to do this, as long as you promise not to mix-and-match too many different transitions. First, make sure that you've applied one global transition to the entire presentation, and only then override individual slides' settings. While in Slide Sorter view, click the slide you want to affect. It should have a thicker frame. Now click in the Transition Effects pop-up list, and select a transition.

TIP **To apply a different transition to more than one slide, select them** by clicking the first one, then Shift+clicking any additional ones.

That transition went by too fast

So you've put all that effort into selecting just the right transition, but your computer is fast, and those checkerboard squares fly by too fast to impress anybody. No problem. First switch to Slide Sorter view, then select all the slides you want to affect. Click the Slide Transition button to the left of the Slide Transition Effects pop-up list.

Click each of the speed options, and look at the preview screen (the one showing alternating pictures of a dog and a key) to get an idea of how fast they go. This is different from computer to computer, so if you create the presentation on your desktop computer but use a notebook computer to display it, there will be a slight difference.

Keep them in suspense

Seasoned presenters know that no matter how good they are, or how interested the viewers are in the subject matter, minds will wander. To minimize distractions, you need to tease the viewers with the promise of things to come. Imagine telling your best joke of the week, while everybody's busy reading what's on the slide. You won't even get a polite chuckle.

People who use overhead projectors have known the answer to this for years: reveal only one bit of information at a time. What they do is put a piece of paper over the transparency, and slide it down when they need to reveal a new item. And, not surprisingly, PowerPoint can do this for you, in a variety of fun and entertaining ways.

 Plain English, please!

PowerPoint calls the gradual introduction of text to the active slide a build. When you show a slide, each mouse click brings another line or item to full view, building the slide one item at a time.

Select a build

There are ten general build categories, but really only two methods: your words can either fly in, already formed from all directions, or materialize out of thin air and form their shape on-screen.

| No Build Effect |▾|

To select a build, click in the Text Build Effects box, and make your selection. Unlike transitions, there's no way to preview this selection while in Slide Sorter view, so click the Slide Show button to see it live. Every left mouse-click invokes a new line (see Chapter 21 for more information on moving within the presentation). When you've had enough, press Esc to stop the slide show.

You can also automate the unveiling of each item in the build list. Enter all your text on the slide, right-click, and choose Build Slide Text. On the cascading menu, choose Other. In the resulting dialog box, choose a build type, then select the Start when previous build ends check box. Now, when you start your slide show, PowerPoint will automatically unveil each item in sequence without requiring you to click the mouse.

CAUTION **When you first try out the different builds, you'll think they're all** impressive and exciting. However, the honeymoon will soon be over, because once the novelty wears off, some of these effects can be pretty irritating. And if you're weary of them, just imagine how your audience will react (they'll despise you—and they'll *never* buy whatever you're selling). So view them one by one, decide on the ones you like the most, and stick with them. As in the case of transitions, you want to use the same builds throughout the presentation to assure cohesiveness and continuity.

Prevent the viewer from backtracking

It's true what they say: presenters are control freaks. Or at least they should be. If your slide features a bulleted list, you want to display each item only when you're good and ready. But as you progress, you also want to make sure that everybody's attention is focused on the newly displayed items. If you let them, your audience may go back and read previous points (and stop listening to what you're saying now). Here's how to rivet their attention on the line you want them to read:

1 Switch to Slide Sorter view, and make sure that all the slides you want to modify are selected.

2 Choose Tools, Build Slide Text, Other. The Animation Settings dialog box, shown in figure 22.9, appears.

3 Select the After Build Step check box, and choose Hide.

4 You can also choose Other Color, and select a dimming color. For best results, try to find a shade that's similar to, but slightly lighter than, the background color. If the background is dark navy blue, go for a lighter shade of blue.

5 Click OK.

Fig. 22.9
Dimming previous
points is the equivalent
of sliding a piece of
paper over an over-
head transparency to
cover text you don't
want the audience to
notice anymore.

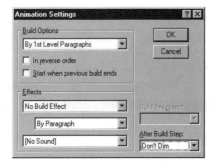

How can I dress up the text?

Text formatting is one of the most powerful tools at your disposal. You can dress up your words with fonts, colors, and drop shadows, as long as you remember two cardinal rules:

- There must be a consistency to the presentation. If you apply a different font to each slide, you'll lose the continuity.

- Too many fonts conjure up images of ransom notes. See Chapter 8 for more information on fonts.

To apply text formatting to an entire layout section, such as a bulleted list, click the frame for that object and then choose Format, Font. PowerPoint lets you change the typeface, its size, and any attributes such as bold or italic. You can add shadows to make your words look as though they're jumping off the page, or you can emboss them so they appear in 3-D glory on the slide surface. And, of course, you can change the color of the type.

You can also apply text formatting to a selected chunk of text—a word, an entire paragraph, or even something as little as one letter. Just make sure to select the text before popping up the formatting dialog box.

CAUTION   I can't say it more strongly: inconsistent formatting will make your carefully planned presentation look like you slapped it together in just a few minutes. To change the overall look of your presentation, choose View, Master, Slide Master. When you make changes here, they'll be reflected on every slide in your presentation.

23

Using Word and Excel with PowerPoint

● In this chapter:

● **Work in the program you like best**

● **How to include a Word table in a slide**

● **I need to add Excel data and a chart to my presentation**

● **Can I use a PowerPoint slide in Word?**

Word, Excel, and PowerPoint are terrific programs on their own—but put 'em together and you've got some real power! . . . .

'll take Software for $300, Alex.

—It's the number one reason for investing in Microsoft Office.

(buzz)

—What is entertainment value?

—Wrong!

(buzz)

—What is integration?

—Right!

Why choose Microsoft Office instead of a bunch of stand-alone programs? OK, the price was right, but the real payoff comes when you can use these powerful programs together. I've said it several times already, but it bears repeating: the unique power of Microsoft Office is its capability to integrate its different components.

Nowhere is this let's-work-together philosophy more evident than in PowerPoint. Word has a great outliner, for example, and Excel has a powerful set of charting tools. How can you put them to work in PowerPoint? It's easy, really.

I'd rather work in Word

If you're like most people who use computers, you feel more at home in one particular program than in any other. Maybe you use Word every day, but you only double-click the PowerPoint icon every six weeks. If that's the case, most of Word's operations have become second nature, while you practically have to take a refresher course each time you start up PowerPoint.

Then, too, some Word and Excel features don't exist in PowerPoint. Yes, there's a spelling checker, but there's no thesaurus. Nor can you use Word styles or macros in a PowerPoint presentation.

PowerPoint's outlining module has enough word processing features to suit some people, whereas others prefer Word's outliner. PowerPoint is gracious enough to let you make your own choice. No matter where the outline originates, you can integrate it into your presentation without too much effort. Here are a few examples.

Create your outlines in Word

Each PowerPoint presentation includes an underlying **outline**. You can build a presentation one slide at a time, or you can create and modify the outline from within PowerPoint, in Outline View. But if you're more comfortable with Word's Outline mode, use it instead. Here's how to turn a Word outline into a presentation:

1 Start PowerPoint (there's no need to open an existing presentation or create a new, blank one). Choose <u>F</u>ile, <u>O</u>pen.

CAUTION   **Unfortunately, you can't work on your outline in Word and PowerPoint simultaneously.** If your Word file is open when you try to bring it into PowerPoint, Office will put up an annoying error message telling you that it can't use the Word document. Close it and try again.

2 Click the down arrow next to the List Files of <u>T</u>ype box, and choose All Outlines, as shown in figure 23.1.

The Open dialog box displays.

3 In the <u>D</u>irectories list box, choose the directory where you keep your Word files.

4 Select the file name, and click OK.

Fig. 23.1

When you open an outline created in Word, PowerPoint translates any text in a Heading style, but ignores whatever you've entered using Normal style.

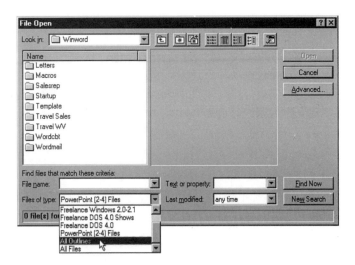

That's it! Your outline appears with each outline element on-screen as a bulleted item, and each bullet represents a slide in your presentation to be formatted and finalized. You're in Outline View, so switch to Slide Sorter View and apply any background, color, and other visual effects you want.

Q&A *I tried to open a Word document in PowerPoint, but some of my text disappeared, and the rest showed up on one slide. What's wrong?*

You can't just start typing in Word and expect it to move gracefully into PowerPoint. Both programs depend on Word's built-in styles. In Word, switch to Outline view and make sure each slide title is formatted with the Heading 1 style. Items in bulleted lists should be Heading 2 or Heading 3. To convert an existing Word document into an outline, switch to Outline view and use the toolbar or the Tab key to promote Normal text into headings.

Fig. 23.2

Before and after: If the original Word document contains the proper outline formatting, it will translate smoothly into a PowerPoint presentation.

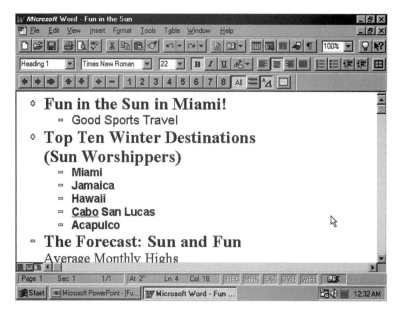

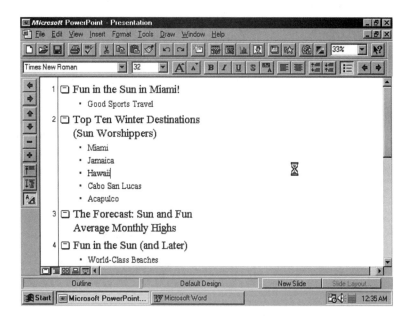

I want to use a Word table

You can create tables in PowerPoint. But if you've already created a table in Word, you can—and should—use it in your presentation. Link your Word table to a slide and take advantage of the two-way street called **OLE**.

 Plain English, please!

> **OLE** (pronounce it oh-LAY) is short for **object linking and embedding**. This Windows trick lets you take a file (or a piece of it) from one program and place that information neatly inside another program. If you **embed** the info, it travels along with the document where it's stored. If it's **linked**, on the other hand, you can store it elsewhere and work on it with another program; the next time you open the document that contains the link, your document will automatically be updated.

There are three advantages to using linked Word tables in PowerPoint:

- Why reinvent the wheel? The table already exists in a Word document, so just use it.

- You can edit the table from within PowerPoint, and all changes will be updated in the source Word document.

- Any change you make to the original Word document will be reflected in your slide—automatically.

Linked Word tables

Creating a PowerPoint table is easy: just choose the AutoLayout that includes a Table object. Adding a Word table to a slide is slightly more complicated. Before you place the table in your slide, you must copy it to the Windows Clipboard, which serves as a temporary storage area for all your programs. Just follow these steps:

1 In Word, select the table by placing the cursor anywhere within the table, and then choose Table, Select Table.

2 Press Ctrl+C or choose Edit, Copy. This copies the selection to the Clipboard.

3 Start PowerPoint, or switch to it if the program is already running. Click the PowerPoint button on the Office Shortcut Bar or use the Start menu and Taskbar.

4 Switch to Slide View and find the slide in which you want to insert the table, or create a new slide using the Object AutoLayout.

5 Choose Edit, Paste Special. This brings up the Paste Special dialog box shown in figure 23.3.

6 Click Microsoft Word Document Object, then select Paste Link. If you select plain Paste, you'll embed the table and cut all ties to the source document.

7 Click OK.

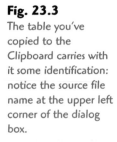

Fig. 23.3
The table you've copied to the Clipboard carries with it some identification: notice the source file name at the upper left corner of the dialog box.

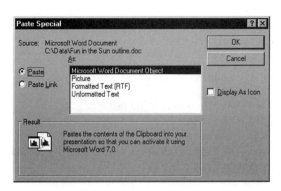

CAUTION **If you close the source document in Word before you paste the** table into a slide, you'll lose the identifying information (file name), and you won't be able to establish a link. So make sure you leave the document open until you've gone through the Paste Special process.

This table is the wrong size!

PowerPoint can't read your mind. So you probably won't like the size and placement of the pasted table. No problem. You can easily resize and move the table as follows:

- To *resize* the table, grab any handle (those tiny squares surrounding the table when you select it by clicking it) and drag it anywhere you can—vertically, horizontally, or diagonally.

- To *move* the table, click anywhere inside the table, and drag the entire selected object to a new location.

You can crop an odd-sized table

Ever taken a shot of your cat and ended up with a print showing mostly your peeling stucco in the background? To correct that unsightly frame, you take your scissors and cut around the cat, so that the print is smaller, but the cat is better positioned in it. Look at figure 23.4. The table is hard to read, and the handles extend well beyond the table's edges, which makes it difficult to resize and move the table.

The Clipboard: tools of the trade

Just like everything else in Windows, you can access Clipboard operations by making menu selections or by using the keyboard. The more you use the Clipboard, the more you'll appreciate the speed and efficiency of the keyboard shortcuts, so here's a cheat sheet. If you never memorize anything else, at least remember these:

Shortcut	Action
Ctrl+C	Copy to Clipboard
Ctrl+X	Cut to Clipboard
Ctrl+V	Paste from Clipboard

Fig. 23.4

You need to crop the extraneous space around the table before you can resize or move it.

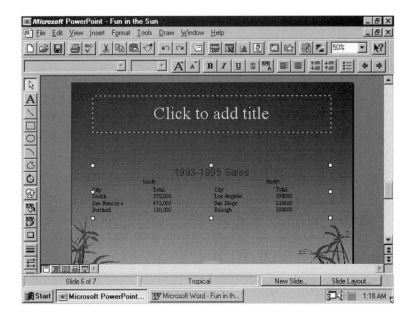

You need to adjust the handles so that they're attached to the table. So get out your electronic scissors, because we're about to **crop** (remove) the extra space around the table:

1 Right-click anywhere within the table.

2 Choose Crop Picture from the shortcut menu. Notice the cropping tool? Place it over a corner handle you wish to adjust (the square gap in the center of the cropping tool should fit perfectly over the frame handle), and drag the edges in diagonally until they properly enclose the table.

3 If you've gone too far and are now missing part of the image, reverse the cropping direction.

4 Click anywhere outside the table to remove the cropping cursor.

5 Now you can resize and move the table.

How do I make changes to the table?

Since that table started in Word, you need to launch Word when you want to modify it or edit information in it. But before you go any further, remember: this is a **linked object**; all you have to do is double-click and Windows will start those applications for you. Just make sure that you're in Slide View and double-click the table. Presto! Word starts up, loads the table, and temporarily takes over the window that you've been working in.

Make your changes and close the document by pressing Ctrl+F4. To return to PowerPoint, select its button on the Office Shortcut bar or the Taskbar. If the recent changes aren't reflected in the slide, don't worry. Right-click the table, and the menu you see in figure 23.5 displays. Select Update Link, and OLE will refresh the table in PowerPoint.

Fig. 23.5
You may need to give OLE a little nudge, to remind it to update the changes in the table.

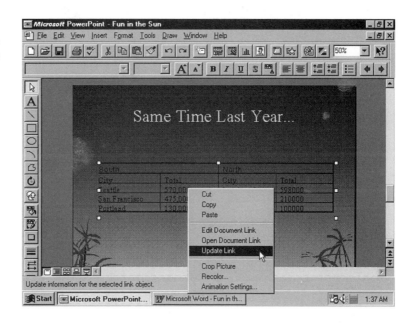

 Q&A *What if I modify my original Word document and PowerPoint isn't running? Will I lose the link?*

Once you've established a link, it's there to stay unless you delete the source document—the Word document that contains the linked table. If you do that, when you next open the PowerPoint presentation, you'll get an error message that a link couldn't be established, but the table itself will still be there. More accurately, all you're left with is a "snapshot" of the table, and you won't be able to edit it any more.

Don't need a link? Copy the table instead

Linking is good whenever you need to go back and edit data in the embedded table. But if you just want to use a table from a Word document, and you don't care whether the new presentation and the old report stay in sync (or you plan to delete the Word document), you don't need the extra baggage that comes with OLE (OLE objects make your data files fatter, and all that extra weight slows you and your software down noticeably, too).

Follow these steps to copy a Word table into your presentation:

1 In Word, select the table by placing the cursor anywhere within the table, and then choosing Table, Select Table.

2 Press Ctrl+C or choose Edit, Copy. This copies the selection to the Clipboard.

3 Switch to PowerPoint.

4 Go to the slide you want to insert the table in, or create a new slide.

5 Switch to Slide View, if you're not already in Slide View.

6 Press Ctrl+V or choose Edit, Paste to paste the selection from the Clipboard.

 TIP **Though you can't edit this table in its originating document, you** can still edit it using Word. Just double-click the table, and... look at your toolbars: are you in PowerPoint or in Word? This is the twilight zone called OLE: these are Word's toolbars, but you're still in PowerPoint. Make your changes, and click anywhere outside the table to save the changes and return to a regular PowerPoint screen.

What about data from Excel?

Let's say you've created a mammoth worksheet in Excel. You've spent hours—no, days, maybe weeks— formatting it so that it looks absolutely perfect. And you've spent an equal amount of time tweaking all the graphs so their statistical impact jumps off the screen at you.

You *could* painstakingly re-create all those graphs in Microsoft Graph. Of course, the Graph applet is much harder to use, and it only does a fraction of what Excel can do, so why make the sacrifice? You don't have to.

The two Excel elements you'd normally want to add to your presentation are:

- **Worksheet.** For obvious reasons (limited screen space), you can use only small chunks at a time. If you have more data to share with your audience, you'll need to resort to—shudder—hard copy.

- **Chart.** True, Microsoft Graph has many of the tools you need to create charts from within PowerPoint, but they're not nearly as easy as using the Excel ChartWizard, or an Excel chart you've already created.

To link or not to link

As with a Word document, you can create a live link to the source worksheet so that all changes in the source document are automatically reflected in your slide. Alternately, you can just paste your worksheet into a slide and cut all links to the originating document. When would you use each method? If you're planning to reuse the presentation over a period of time, the data in the original worksheet may be constantly evolving, so you need to establish a link so that your presentation will reflect the changes. If the presentation is a one-time deal, don't bother creating a link.

How to link an Excel worksheet to a slide

Once again, we're going to rely on the Clipboard to transfer data between the programs. Open your Excel worksheet, and follow these steps:

1 Select the cells you want to copy, and press Ctrl+C to copy the contents to the Clipboard. You should get an animated dashed border around your selection, similar to the one in figure 23.6.

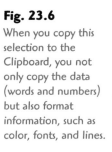

Fig. 23.6

When you copy this selection to the Clipboard, you not only copy the data (words and numbers) but also format information, such as color, fonts, and lines.

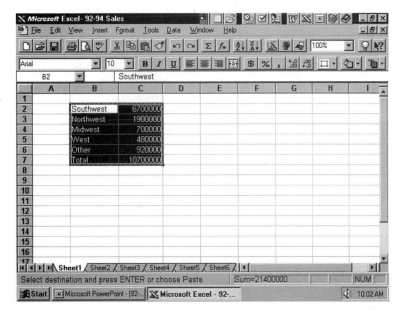

2 Switch to PowerPoint.

3 In Slide Sorter View, go to the slide in which you want to place the worksheet, or create a new one.

4 Choose Edit, Paste Special.

5 Click Microsoft Excel Worksheet Object, and select Paste Link.

6 Click OK.

I don't need it linked

No problem. Follow the same steps for linking a worksheet, but select Paste instead of Paste Link in step 5. Better yet, bypass steps 4, 5, and 6 by pressing Ctrl+V for a quick paste from the Clipboard.

Pop an Excel chart into your slide

Placing an existing Excel chart in a slide is just as easy. All it takes is Clipboard savvy. Here's what you do:

1 In Excel, click once (don't double-click!) on the chart you want to use. You should get handles around its frame, signifying that it's been selected.

2 To copy the chart to the Clipboard, press Ctrl+C.

3 Switch to PowerPoint.

4 In Slide Sorter View, go to the slide in which you want to place the chart, or create a new one.

5 Choose Edit, Paste Special, click Paste or Paste Link, and add the Microsoft Excel Chart Object.

24

It's Showtime! Giving a Great Presentation

● **In this chapter:**

- I need to rehearse my presentation

- Should I run a slide show from the computer?

- How to print handouts

- Can I use an overhead projector?

- What about a slide projector?

Simply put, a PowerPoint presentation is a sales pitch. And nobody ever wants to lose a sale . . . . ●▶

There's an old adage that says that whatever you do, you're always selling something. Sometimes you sell a product or a service, other times you sell an idea, and often you're just selling yourself or the image that you want to project. PowerPoint presentations are used by college students, sales people, executives, and spin doctors of all kinds. They're all trying to get a point across, and sometimes the difference between success and failure is the wrong shade of green in a slide show.

Getting ready

One of the greatest presenters of all time was Demosthenes, who lived in Greece in the 4th century B.C. Of course, he was called an *orator* then, not a *presenter* (because PowerPoint hadn't been written yet), but we can still learn some important lessons from him. Demosthenes developed his reputation as a spell-binding speaker by practicing. He may have gone a bit overboard, though, when, he practiced talking with a mouthful of rocks. Your dentist may not approve of that technique, but you can still prepare yourself for a successful presentation by rehearsing your presentation until you're completely at ease with it.

My name is... my name is...

Forgetting lines is the most common ailment plaguing people who practice any form of public speech. Even great actors freeze on stage every once in awhile. You're on your own—onstage, standing in the spotlight, with an audience of thousands, and you can't remember your name. OK, wake up! There's no need to worry about *that* nightmare. You have PowerPoint—you'll be prepared.

PowerPoint has a couple of tools to help you prepare yourself for the presentation:

- **Rehearse Timing**. Script in hand, you go through a dry run of the presentation, and PowerPoint times how long you take on each slide. When you're finished, you get a report.

- **Notes Pages View**. You can type detailed notes next to each slide. Your audience can't see them, but you can—and writing it down means there's no way you'll forget that witty story or essential factoid.

Pace yourself

To rehearse your timing, switch to Slide Sorter View and click the Rehearse Timings button on the toolbar. The first slide comes up, showing a running digital stopwatch at the bottom left corner (see fig. 24.1). Start talking through the presentation, just as you would in front of a live audience, and PowerPoint will keep track of your progress. Click the left mouse button when you're ready to move to the next slide.

Q&A *When does PowerPoint start timing my presentation?*

As soon as you click the Rehearse Timings button. On some systems, it can take as much as 20 or 30 seconds just to load the presentation, and PowerPoint counts that time. If you don't want it reflected in your running total—then start your pitch.

Fig. 24.1
PowerPoint keeps a running total of your time as you rehearse. Flub a slide? Don't worry—just press Repeat and start over.

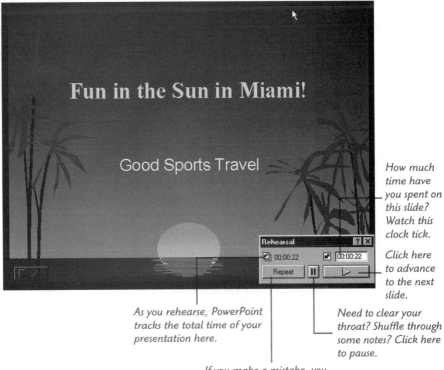

How much time have you spent on this slide? Watch this clock tick.

Click here to advance to the next slide.

As you rehearse, PowerPoint tracks the total time of your presentation here.

Need to clear your throat? Shuffle through some notes? Click here to pause.

If you make a mistake, you don't have to start the entire presentation over. Click here to reset the clock to 0:00 for the current slide.

When you're done, you'll see a dialog box that reports the total length of the presentation and asks whether you want to record the slide timings so that you can see them in Slide Sorter View. If you're happy with the rehearsal results, click Yes.

As you can see in figure 24.2, each slide has a time stamp under it. Now is a good time to fine-tune your presentation. Did the whole thing take too long? Where can you cut out a few seconds or minutes? Adjust your script accordingly, and try again until you fill the time allotted to you perfectly, without rushing the finish.

Fig. 24.2
If you've got exactly fifteen minutes to make your pitch, you'll have to make sure you're spending the right amount of time on each slide.

Time stamp

  If you're having trouble getting through the presentation in the time allowed, consider using Timing options to automatically advance to the next slide at regular intervals. Of course, the trick here is to cut your patter appropriately and keep up with PowerPoint, so you don't end up five slides behind at the end!

The presenter's motto: be prepared

In a perfect world, you're in full control of the audience during your presentation. In reality, though, there's always a wise guy at the back of the room. To prepare yourself for surprise questions, use the Notes Pages View (see fig. 24.3) to write down details that might come in handy when you're giving your presentation.

Fig. 24.3

Print out the Notes Pages View and use it as your script during the live presentation.

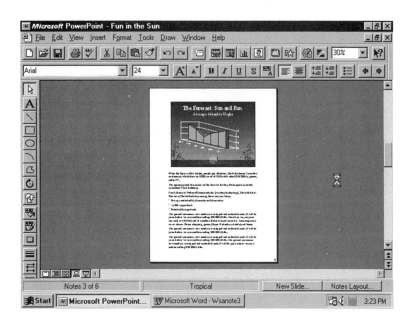

And now, on with the (slide) show!

That's it. You're done. The presentation is perfect. All that's left is, well, the difficult part. Now you need to face your audience and dazzle them. But how? Will you use a computer monitor for the show? Do you need 35mm slides? Are you going to hand out printed copies of the presentation? Or maybe the only equipment available is an overhead projector. Once you establish how you want to show your slides, PowerPoint can generate output to match your specifications.

Your presentation can be informal, with a couple of colleagues looking over your shoulder at your screen. Or it can be the nerve-wracking variety, with 300 customers, coworkers, or rivals waiting for you to slip up. You can't expect hundreds of people to huddle around your computer. For best results, make sure there's a screen projector in place.

What if you need to run your slide show on a different computer?

If your presentation is a computer-based slide show, you need to set it up on a computer. There's a good chance it won't be the same computer you used to create the presentation. Many people run their slide shows from a notebook computer, in fact, because it's easy to move from place to place.

There's only one problem: You might not *want* to install PowerPoint on your notebook, especially if hard disk space is limited.

No problem. You can pack up your presentation to take to another computer quickly and easily using the **Pack and Go Wizard**. To use the wizard, follow these steps:

1 With your presentation on-screen, choose File, Pack and Go. Choose Next in the introductory Wizard box.

2 Now, confirm the presentation you want to take with you; you can take more than one, if you want.

3 Tell the wizard which floppy or network drive you want to use and whether you want to include linked files.

4 Make sure you choose the Embed TrueType Fonts option; you can't be sure the destination computer has the same fonts you used in your presentation.

5 Tell the Wizard you want to take the PowerPoint Viewer with you and click Finish. It may take some time for PowerPoint to assemble your presentation package, especially if you have a lot of linked or embedded files.

PowerPoint copies the file to the floppy disk (or the network destination you specified) and you're ready to go. On the destination computer, insert the floppy disk and open the Run command dialog box. Enter the floppy drive letter and **PNGSETUP.EXE**. Choose OK and tell Pack and Go where to copy the file to. After copying the setup file, you're ready to go.

CAUTION **The Pack and Go Wizard assumes the computer on which you plan** to show the presentation has Windows 95 installed on it. If this isn't the case, you won't be able to run the PowerPoint Viewer, and you'll have to describe your slides to your audience. There is a way to show a presentation on a computer running Windows 3.1, but it takes more work than it's worth.

Running a slide show

To run a slide show from the PowerPoint Viewer, double-click the Power-Point Viewer icon in the Windows Explorer (`Pptview` is the file name). Figure 24.4 shows the resulting dialog box. This is where you can choose to run the presentation continuously—if you're showing it unattended at a trade show booth, for example—or to use automatic timings. If you want to select either, select the appropriate box in the bottom left corner. Select the presentation you want to run from the file list on the left, and click Show.

Fig. 24.4
Think of the PowerPoint Viewer as "PowerPoint Lite." Be prepared for a small surprise: it doesn't recognize your long file names.

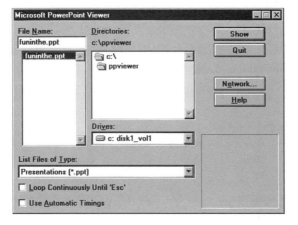

Your secret weapons: hidden slides

There may be some sensitive information you'd rather not talk about unless forced to. For example, if your CEO has disappeared in South America with $5 million from the petty cash fund, you wouldn't want to lie about it, but you don't want to bring the subject up yourself, either. Have a slide ready in case some pesky reporter asks the question, but don't show it until you're cornered.

PowerPoint lets you create these **hidden slides**. They're part of the presentation, but can be displayed at your discretion. To hide a slide, switch to Slide Sorter View, click the slide you want to hide, and click the Hide Slide button on the toolbar. As you can see in figure 24.5, the slide doesn't vanish into thin air, but its number is enclosed in a box with a line across it.

Note: The Hide Slide button appears only while you're in Slide Sorter View. If you want to hide a slide while in Slide View, select Tools, Hide Slide from the menus.

Fig. 24.5
Don't let them catch
you unprepared.
Hidden slides are your
ammunition against
the unexpected.

Q&A   *How do I reveal a hidden slide during my presenta-*
tion?

There are two ways to "unhide" hidden slides:

Mouse. Right-click the slide just before the hidden slide and choose Go To
and Hidden Slide.

Keyboard. If you use the keyboard to advance to the next slide, just type **H**
(or **h**, it doesn't matter) while you're on the slide preceding the hidden
one.

The PowerPoint clicker

Here are the keys you press during your presentation to navigate through the slide show:

If you want to...	Press
Use the Mouse	
Go to the next slide	Left button
Go to the previous slide	Right button
Use the Keyboard	
Go to the next slide	Page Down
Go to the previous slide	Page Up
Go to a specific slide	The slide number, followed by Enter
Stop the show	Esc

"X" marks the spot

During a football game, things can get confusing. Luckily for television audiences, there's John Madden in the broadcast booth, explaining every move and drawing circles and arrows all over the screen. No matter how clear your presentation, there may be times when you need the electronic equivalent of a Magic Marker to highlight an important fact on a slide. Here's how:

1 During the slide show, right-click the screen to display the popup menu. Alternatively, you can press Ctrl+P to show the pen.

2 Choose Pen. Your arrow pointer becomes a pencil pointer. (Press Ctrl+A and the pencil changes back to an arrow icon.)

3 Proceed to draw circles, arrows, or whatever you like (see fig. 24.6) by holding down either mouse button as you draw.

4 If you want to erase your doodles, press **E**. Otherwise, when you move on to the next slide, these annotations disappear by themselves and don't get saved with the presentation.

5 To get the arrow cursor back, press Ctrl+A.

Fig. 24.6

Draw all you want on a slide. As soon as you move on to the next slide, all your annotations will vanish.

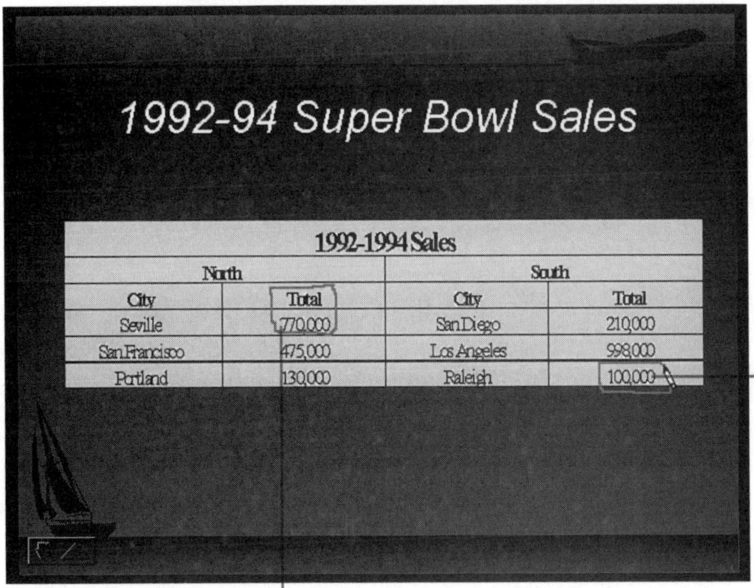

Drawing on the screen can help you call attention to important pieces of information on a slide.

Printing your presentation

Not all PowerPoint presentations are of the high-tech variety. Sometimes you find yourself in a place where setting up a computer is out of the question. But you can still make an effective presentation by handing out printed copies of your slides. In fact, for some meetings you'll get better results preparing the agenda with PowerPoint than you would with Word.

How do I make handouts?

Before you print out your presentation, you need to set it up. Choose File, Slide Setup. In the Slide Setup dialog box (see fig. 24.7), select the paper size and orientation.

 Plain English, please!

Orientation? No, this is not back-to-school week. That term refers to the way your data appears on the printed page. With ordinary paper, portrait orientation means the long margin of the paper goes from top to bottom as you read. Turn the page 90 degrees and you have landscape orientation, which is perfect for displaying wide columns of information. 99

Fig. 24.7
Select any paper size for your printouts (as long as your printer can handle it, that is). Just select the Custom option in the drop-down list, and specify width and height.

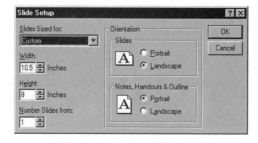

Now choose File, Print. The actual dialog box you see may look different from the one shown in figure 24.8, but the options in the bottom half should be there regardless of what type of printer you use. Make sure the proper printer is selected in the top half of the box, then choose from these options:

- **Print what.** Do you want to print each slide on a separate piece of paper? Do you want to save paper by fitting two, three, or six slides on one sheet? Or do you need the Notes Pages?

- **Number of copies.** Make as many as you want, and collate them if you prefer. Just remember that a photocopier is usually more efficient for making many copies of a presentation.

- **Print Range.** Print the entire presentation or just selected slides.

- **Print Hidden Slides.** If you want your audience to see the hidden slides, select this box.

- **Black & White.** Your colors will be translated into shades of gray.

- **Scale to Fit Paper.** If your slides are larger or smaller than the paper you've chosen to print on, select this box and PowerPoint will try to fill as much of the page as possible.

- **Frame Slides.** Add a thin border around the printed copies of your slides.

Once you've printed one type of item, like handouts, return to this dialog box and print whatever else you need: speakers' notes, outlines, or the slides themselves (see fig. 24.8).

Fig. 24.8
The PowerPoint Print dialog box gives you lots of options. To save paper without giving your audience eyestrain, try printing two slides per page in landscape mode.

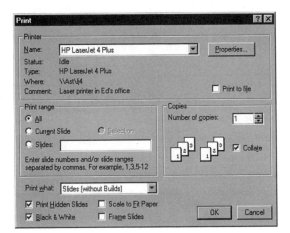

What if I forget my lines?

Earlier in this chapter, we mentioned teleprompters, those wonderful safety nets that any public speaker should have to fall back on. PowerPoint calls them Notes Pages, but we think of them as **cheat sheets**. So now that you have a complete packet of handouts for your audience, make a separate one for yourself, complete with slides and notes. To do so, select Notes Pages under Print <u>W</u>hat in the Print dialog box, and you'll see pages similar to the ones in figure 24.9.

Fig. 24.9

If you tend to forget what you're supposed to say, print out these pages and read them when you make the presentation.

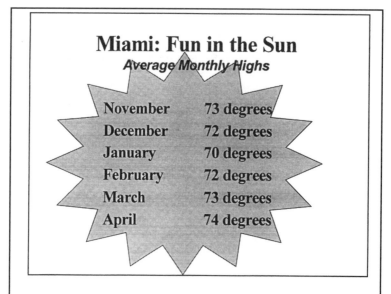

Miami: Fun in the Sun
Average Monthly Highs

November	73 degrees
December	72 degrees
January	70 degrees
February	72 degrees
March	73 degrees
April	74 degrees

Miami is the ultimate winter destination. It's the eternal summer, with temperatures varying from 70 to 74 degrees during the traditionally cold months of the year. No wonder everybody wants to move to Miami when they retire. Here's a rundown of the winter-time weather:

November: a shivering 73

December: a not-so-uncomfortable 72

January: a freezing 70

February: on the rise at 72

March: not too chilling 73

April: a balmy 74

Combine this exciting weather with the rush of the Super Bowl, and you have a winning season. This one will sell itself!

TIP **If you want to skip over the next couple of slides, you'll need to** know which slide you want to skip to. To prepare this cheat sheet, print out the presentation in Outline View.

Can I use an overhead projector?

Before notebook computers, the most popular way to make a business presentation was by using overhead projectors with transparencies. You manually replaced each transparency when you needed to move on, and if you wanted to hide a piece of information or a portion of the text, you covered it with a piece of paper. (Just like the old days, when you had to actually turn a lever around to roll down your car window.)

But there are still plenty of overhead projectors and projection panels out there, and PowerPoint doesn't snub them. If your printer can handle transparencies, you're in luck. Buy a ream of blank transparencies and print just as you normally would. If it's a color printer, make sure the Black & White option in the Print dialog box is *deselected*.

If your printer doesn't support transparencies, you might be able to get good-looking overhead slides if your photocopier can handle transparencies. Print on paper, then copy them onto the transparency stock. Finally, there's the complicated option: You can send your file to Genigraphics, a company that specializes in turning files into printed output, and you'll get them in return mail within a couple of working days. (For more information about how Genigraphics works, fire up the Answer Wizard and type **Tell me about Genigraphics**.)

Can I use a slide projector?

To turn your PowerPoint slide show into the old-fashioned variety with real 35mm color slides, you'll need access to some very expensive and hard-to-use hardware. If your corporate art department has a slide printer, you're in luck. Otherwise, you'll need to send your presentation file to a company that specializes in high-end printing, such as Genigraphics or an up-to-date photo lab.

 TIP It's a good idea to give your audience a hard copy of the presentation if there's important information in it. Nobody's going to retain it, no matter how good a presenter you are. So whether you make an on-screen slide show or use an overhead projector, make printouts of all the slides.

Part V: Beyond the Basics

25

Wrapping Everything Up with Office Binders

● In this chapter:

- **Using binders to keep big projects together**

- **I'd like to create a binder**

- **What can I put in a binder?**

- **The best binder trick: smart printing**

- **Attaching a routing slip to a binder**

Just like the three-ring binders you use to keep your work papers organized, Microsoft Binder keeps files cool and collected in neat, tidy packages . . . .

magine you're going out on a sales call—a command performance before your #1 client. Are you going to just walk in with a boring report? Not on your life. You'll have full-color photos, overhead slides, and several pounds of spreadsheets to keep that report from getting lonely. And to make sure that every piece stays in its place, you'll keep it all safely stored in a thick three-ring binder.

Keeping everything together like that means you never have to turn your office upside-down looking for pieces of the project. It also means you can present each piece of the project in the proper order.

If that level of organization appeals to you, then you're sure to appreciate the new Binder program in Office. It's the computer equivalent to one of those thick three-ring numbers.

What are binders?

A **binder** is a special type of document file specifically designed to store multiple Office files. When you drop files into a **binder,** you tell Office to treat them as if they were sections of a single file. The name of the binder file serves the same function as the label on the spine of a three-ring binder; if you want to know what the individual pieces are called, you'll have to look inside.

With the help of binders, you gather files and perform a task like spell-checking on all of them at once, instead of starting and stopping the same job separately for each file. You can share styles among several files, even if they were created by different applications. And you can print the entire group of files at once, with consecutive page numbers—all by clicking one button.

When you save a binder, you create a single file on your disk. If you look in a folder window or in the Windows Explorer, you'll see its type listed as Microsoft Office Binder (for those of you who care about such things, its MS-DOS file name ends with the OBD extension). This file holds all of the other files (Word documents, Excel spreadsheets and charts, and Powerpoint presentations) contained within your binder.

Binder basics

Office 95 binders help you keep big projects organized. All the files you need for a project—whether they were created in Word, Excel, or PowerPoint—are stored here.

Each file within a binder is called a section. Use this Section menu (found only when you're working within a binder) to rename, rearrange, hide, or perform other tasks with each section.

Click this button to hide the binder pane, letting you see just the file you're working on at the moment

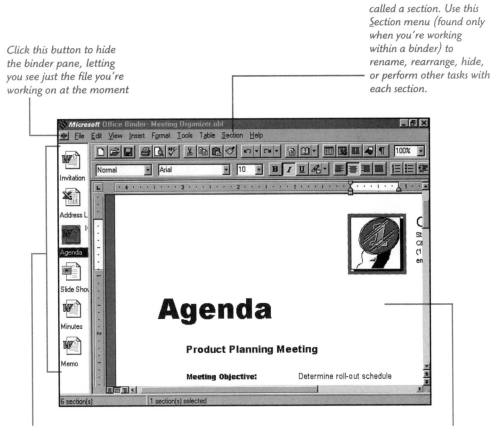

The binder pane shows all the files contained in this binder. This binder includes Word, Excel, and PowerPoint files. To add new files, just drag them from a folder window into this pane.

When you click a binder file's icon, Office automatically opens the application that the file uses. In this example, the toolbars, menus, and rulers tell you you're working with Word.

How do I create and fill a binder?

In your project notebook, you probably have a mix of sections: some blank sheets of paper *and* lots of accumulated notes and memos, letters from vendors, budget updates, and other pieces of information about the project.

An Office binder is no different. You can add new, blank pages to a binder, and you can also drop in files you've already created.

To build a new binder, click the Start a New Document button on the Office Shortcut Bar. On the Binders tab, you'll find ready-made templates for a selection of useful business projects; look on the General tab and you'll find an icon for a Blank Binder. When you click Open, Office opens an empty binder like the one shown in figure 25.1.

Fig. 25.1

A fresh new binder, ready to go. You can fill it with new files and create your project on the fly, or take work you've already done and gather it here.

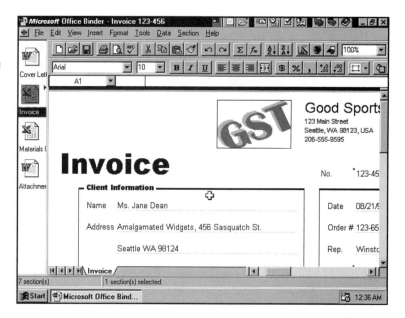

At this point, you have two choices for filling your empty binder:

- **To add a new, blank section,** choose Section, Add. This brings up the dialog box shown in figure 25.2. Choose the type of document you want to add, and click the OK button.

Fig. 25.2
What kind of section do you want to create? Unless you've added a new Office-compatible program to your system, these are your only choices.

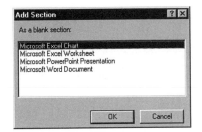

> ***Plain English, please!***
>
> Each **section** of an Office binder is simply a separate file contained within the binder. If you were working with a three-ring binder, sections might be defined by tabs or different types of paperlined graph paper, for example. In an Office Binder, each section has its own icon and file name.

- To add an existing file, choose Section, Add from File. The Add from File dialog box (see fig. 25.3) looks and acts just like a File Open dialog box elsewhere in Office. Select a file, and click Add to insert it into your binder.

Fig. 25.3
Add one file (or several) to a binder in one smooth action. Remember: When you add a file to a binder, you create a copy; editing the original doesn't change the one in the binder.

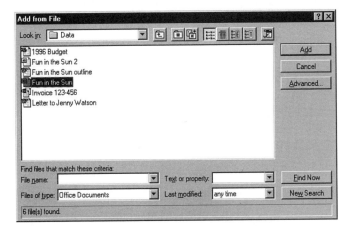

After you click OK, Office creates a blank file and opens the application you'll use to work with it. In the example shown in figure 25.4, you can see that the menus and toolbars for Word have appeared in the Binder window.

Fig. 25.4

When you create a
new section like this
Word file, you can get
to work immediately,
just as if you had
started the application
and then created a
blank file.

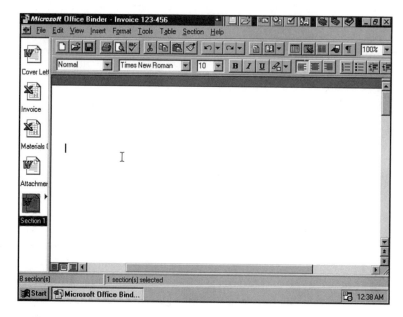

 TIP **When you add a section to a binder, Office gives it a boring name**
like Section 1. To give it a more meaningful name, like Cover page, just
click the icon's label and begin typing. You can also right-click the icon to
change summary information or see its other properties.

Rearranging files in a binder

In a binder stuffed with important pieces of paper, you're constantly reshuf-
fling things—tossing outdated charts, adding new price lists, changing a
word here and a number there.

Moving and deleting files within an Office binder is easy, too—just drag-
and-drop.

- **To move a file...** Simply click the file's icon, and drag it up or down
  within the icon pane at the left of the binder. A small arrow along the
  right edge of this pane indicates where the document will land when
  you release your mouse button.

- **To delete files in a binder...** Just select the file's icon, right-click, and choose <u>D</u>elete from the pop-up menu. When you delete a file from a binder, it's gone for good. No Recycle Bin here, and no Undo, either!

Working with a file outside the binder

Because binders contain many data files, they can get big and cumbersome. How do you take a small file out of the binder? Maybe you want to send a copy of the file to someone else but you'd rather not share the rest of the binder with them. Or maybe you simply want a copy of a file that you can work with at home.

To copy a file from a binder to a separate file on your hard disk, first select the file within the binder. Choose <u>S</u>ection, <u>S</u>ave as File. Move to another folder if you'd like, then type in a name for the new file and click OK. The original file stays inside the binder.

Printing binders

You haven't known true grief until you've tried to put together a report from many parts scattered across multiple files. Normally, there's no easy way to print a gaggle of Word, Excel, and Powerpoint files in one smooth operation. And even when you do get them safely off to the printer, it's nearly impossible to number the pages in the right sequence. Most folks just throw up their hands and write in the page numbers by hand, right before they run the whole mess through the copier.

But not you. Assemble that same group of documents in an Office Binder; let it manage the headaches of printing—choosing what to print, and keeping page numbers in the right position and the right sequence.

To quickly and easily print all the sections of an Office Binder, complete with page numbers, choose <u>F</u>ile, <u>P</u>rint Binder. You'll see the dialog box shown in figure 25.5.

Fig. 25.5

Use the Print Binder dialog box to automatically print all the parts of a binder, or even just the selected parts.

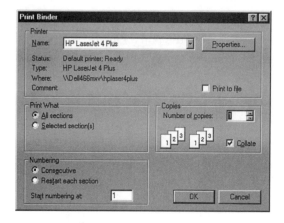

The Print Binder dialog box is reasonably straightforward:

- In the Print What section, tell Office whether you want to print **All sections** or only the **Selected section(s).** (You can select multiple sections by holding down the Ctrl key as you click in the Binder pane.)

- In the Numbering area, choose **Consecutive** to have Office automatically keep track of page numbers, even across different applications and files. **Restart each section,** on the other hand, lets you number individual sections as though they were self-contained files.

26

Making Office Work the Way You Do

● **In this chapter:**

● **I want to display different toolbar buttons**

● **I want to make my own shortcut keys**

● **How else can I change the Office programs?**

● **Will my changes be saved when I exit?**

After you work with Microsoft Office for awhile, you may want to redecorate! Rearrange Office programs until it feels like a comfortable place to work . . . . ❯

If you've ever moved from a cramped cubicle into a real office the kind with walls and windows—you know the feeling. For the first few days (or weeks or months, if it's a *really* nice office), it's a small slice of heaven on earth. Look at all this extra room! Look at all this great new furniture! Look at this view!

And then one day the honeymoon ends. You've run out of space in the filing cabinets. The desk doesn't face the right way, and the chairs make your guests feel like they're in a waiting room at the DMV. And that view isn't so great when the blinding afternoon sun hits you right between the eyes.

After you've worked with Microsoft Office for awhile, you might notice the same phenomenon. The toolbars are arranged all wrong, you can't find what you want on the menus, and there's just not enough room for the stuff you're working on.

In this Office, there's a simple solution: redecorate. With a few clicks here and there, you can rearrange just about every aspect of the Office programs until it feels like a comfortable place to work.

Toolbars: have 'em your way

When you have a new chair delivered to your office, do you let a couple of musclehead delivery guys decide where it goes? Of course not. So when you first install Office, why should you leave all the toolbars arranged the way someone at Microsoft says they should be arranged?

The toolbars work the same in all three Office programs, and it's easy to move buttons around, delete the ones you never use, and add new ones. After you've worked with each program for a while, you'll develop a good sense of where the buttons would be best located for the way you work.

 TIP **You can rearrange the buttons on the Office Shortcut Bar, too.** See Chapter 5 for details.

I never use that button!

I'm not sure why some of the buttons on the default toolbars are there. But after I had gone an entire month without clicking certain buttons, I decided to put them out of sight and out of mind.

From Word's Standard toolbar, I removed AutoText (it's easier to press F3), and Drawing (I have no artistic talent). From the Formatting toolbar, I got rid of the Justify button (because on those rare occasions when I use justified text, I apply it using a style), plus the two indent buttons (because it's easier to just use the ruler).

Why get rid of these unused buttons? For one thing, they're distracting. When the screen is cleaner, I can find the buttons I do use a lot faster. For another, as we'll see in a minute, there are other buttons that deserve a place of honor on the standard toolbars.

Deleting a button, or moving it to a new location on the toolbar, is a simple, three-step process:

1 Right-click any toolbar, and choose Customize from the shortcut menu.

2 Point to the button you want to move or delete. Click and hold the left mouse button—the thick dashed border means you've selected it.

3 To **delete the button**, drag it off the toolbar and release the mouse button (see fig. 26.1). Poof! It's gone.

Or

To **move the button**, drag it to the new place you want it to occupy on the toolbar, then drop it. (This takes practice. If it lands in the wrong place, pick it up and try again.)

Fig. 26.1

If you rarely use a button on one of the standard toolbars, get rid of it. Display the Customize dialog box, then drag the unwanted button off the toolbar.

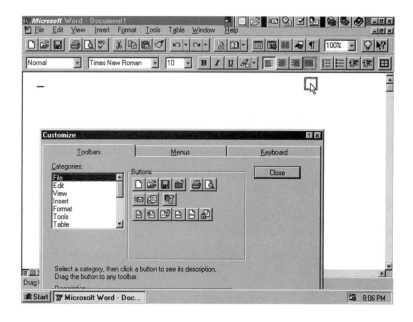

I want to add buttons for things I do a lot

Easily done. Open the Customize dialog box again. All the Office programs have similar dialog boxes that let you scroll through a list of available buttons and drag the ones you want onto any open toolbar (see fig. 26.2). The toolbar buttons are good citizens. When a neighbor moves in or out, they automatically tidy up and adjust their spacing. (Don't add too many, though, or the buttons at the right will disappear off the edge of the screen!)

Fig. 26.2

All the Office programs let you add your own buttons to toolbars. Drag the button you want to add from this dialog box onto the toolbar.

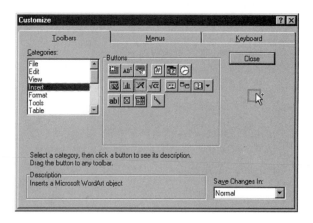

If you're not sure what a button does, just click it, then read about it in the Description section of the Customize dialog box.

 Q&A *My finger slipped and I accidentally created a new toolbar, which I don't really want. How do I get rid of it?*

It's an easy cleanup. Choose Y̲iew, T̲oolbars. From the list, choose the name of the "I didn't mean that" toolbar, and press the D̲elete button. Note that you can only delete toolbars you created. The built-in toolbars are there for good.

I want to see a toolbar (or put one away)

Toolbars come and go in Office programs more often than extras in a Spielberg film. Sometimes it's automatic: if you start drawing a picture, for example, a Drawing toolbar will appear automatically. But you can choose when and where toolbars appear and disappear. To display a list of available toolbars, right-click one that's already visible to display the shortcut menu shown in figure 26.3.

Fig. 26.3
You can have as many or as few toolbars visible on the screen as you want.

 TIP **I find the little ToolTips labels extremely useful, but some people absolutely detest them.** If their constant appearing and disappearing drives you nuts, turn them off. Choose Y̲iew, T̲oolbars, then deselect the S̲how ToolTips box. After you click OK, the labels will no longer appear.

 Q&A *Help! I cleared away all the toolbars, and now I don't know where to click to bring them back. What do I do?*

Fortunately, all the Office programs work alike, and this is an easy problem to fix. Just choose Y̲iew, T̲oolbars to display the list of available toolbars, select the ones you want, then click OK to make them reappear.

Should I redo the menus?

Some people never touch toolbars—they rely on menus for everything. If it works for you, that's fine. If you're tempted to boost your productivity by rearranging menus, I have some disappointing news: you can redo the menus in Word only, not in Excel or PowerPoint.

Frankly, I think it's too much bother to mess around with the pull-down menus. It's also a little dangerous: if you remove a command and then discover later that you need to use that command, even once, you'll have to prowl through the Customize dialog box and add it back to the menu before you can do it.

But the other menus in Word—the shortcut menus that pop up when you click the right mouse button—are worth changing if you use them regularly (and you should). For example, I've added Paste Special to the Text (Shortcut) menu. It comes in handy when I want to move some text from one place to another without changing the formatting in the new location. If you want to do the same, follow these steps:

1 Choose <u>T</u>ools, <u>C</u>ustomize, and click the <u>M</u>enus tab to display the Customize dialog box shown in figure 26.4.

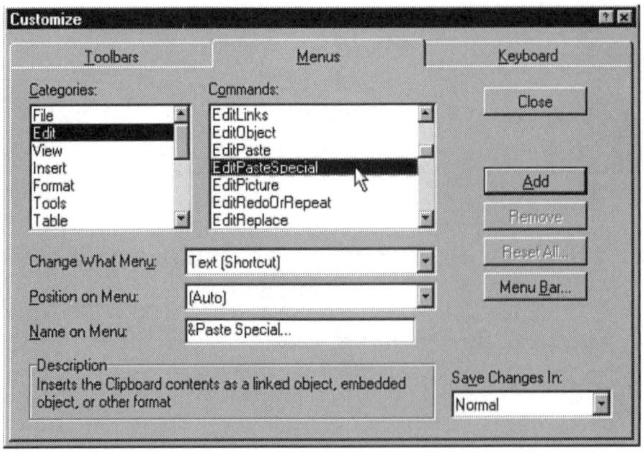

Fig. 26.4
Use this dialog box to change commands on Word's shortcut menus.

2 In the Change What Men<u>u</u> box, pick a menu. Word has 25 shortcut menus, one for every conceivable situation, so be sure you've picked the right one.

3 Pick a category from the left list box and a command from the right.

4 In the Position on Menu box, tell Word where to add the new command: The top of the menu? The bottom? Doesn't matter?

5 In the Name on Menu box, give the new shortcut command a different name, if you'd like. The **ampersand** (&) means the next letter will be underlined so you can use it as a menu shortcut.

6 Be sure to click the Add button before clicking Close.

Figure 26.5 shows a shortcut menu we've modified.

Fig. 26.5
Don't mess with Word's pull-down menus, but feel free to rework the pop-up shortcut menus. In this example, we've added a quick Paste Special option.

Give Word a new set of shortcut keys

When you press a letter or number key, you know what Word will do with it. If you press **C-A-T**, you'll see the word cat on the screen. But what happens when you press some finger-twisting combination like Ctrl+Alt+L? Word doesn't know, so it looks on its list of **keyboard shortcuts**.

You can assign a command, a style, a macro, or even an AutoText entry to a key combination. If you want, you can turn your company logo into an AutoText entry, and then set up Word so the logo will plop into your document every time you press Ctrl+Alt+L. There are hundreds of built-in shortcuts, and you can change them or create new ones with a few clicks and keystrokes:

1 Choose Tools, Customize, then click the Keyboard tab to display the dialog box shown in figure 26.6.

Fig. 26.6

Word lets you take any key (or combination of keys) and do something special with it. Sorry—you can't do this with PowerPoint or Excel.

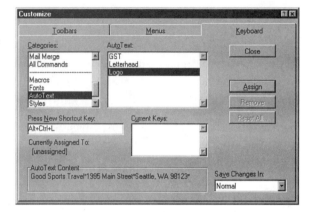

2 Choose a category from the list on the left and an item from the one on the right. You can choose a command, a style, a font, or a special symbol.

3 Click in the Press New Shortcut Key box, then press the key combination you want to use. Word will add the description of whatever you press. The most useful combinations are Ctrl+Shift+*key* and Ctrl+Alt+*key*.

4 Look at the Current keys box to see which key combination(s), if any, are currently assigned to the command you've chosen. There might already be a combination assigned that you don't know about. You can have more than one shortcut for the same command.

5 Look at the Currently Assigned To information to see what the key combination you've chosen does when you press it now. If you don't want to reassign it, try another selection.

6 Click Assign first, then Close to save your new key assignment.

CAUTION **You can actually reassign simple letters and numbers—A,B,C ...** 1,2,3—so that they cause Word to do special functions. But if you do that, you'll have a *lot* of trouble composing a simple memo in English!

Explore those other Office options

When you choose Tools, Options from each of the Office programs, you get wildly different choices. That makes sense, since each program is intended to do wildly different things.

There's a lot of technotrivia buried in these dialog boxes, but there are also a few cool options that help you work faster, smarter, and more comfortably. Here's where to look.

Reworking Word

If you choose the Save tab of the Options dialog box (see fig. 26.7), you see a smattering of ways you can customize Word:

- **Allow Fast Saves** lets you get back to work a little more quickly, but it also makes Word files bigger than they would otherwise be. I turn it off.

- **Prompt to Save Normal Template** lets you decide whether you want to make changes to the standard document style permanent. Good idea.

- **Automatic Save** will annoy you occasionally, but someday, when the lights go out unexpectedly, you'll be glad you put a check mark here.

Fig. 26.7

Some customization options can make your life with Office much more pleasant.

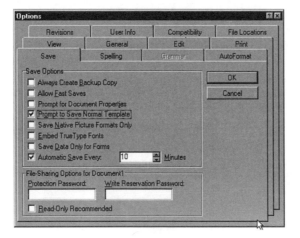

What else can you do with Word? Here are some highlights. Each boldfaced word refers to one of the tabs in that crowded Options dialog box:

- **User Info.** Add your name and address here to have it automatically inserted in letters and printed on envelopes.

- **View.** Decide whether to show tab characters, spaces, paragraph marks, and other oddball characters.

- **General.** Set the number of files (up to 9) to appear on the "recently used file" list.

- **Edit.** Here's where you turn off features like automatic word selection, drag-and-drop text editing, and smart cut and paste.

- **Print.** My ancient laser printer stacks paper face up, which means that page 1 is always on the bottom of the stack. Ugh. So I've selected the Reverse Print Order box here. There's also a box that lets me specify which paper tray to use.

Making an easier Excel

If you choose the General tab of the Options dialog box (see fig. 26.8), you can customize Excel in the following ways:

- **P**rompt for File Properties displays a box so you can add more information every time you save a file. Some people find it annoying; I like it.

- **S**heets in New Workbook starts out at 16, which is too many for me. I've lowered the default number to 4.

- Add a **D**efault File Location here so you don't have to wander through directories every time you want to open or save a file.

- The User **N**ame you enter here is the one Excel will use when you save or mail a worksheet.

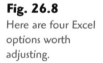

Fig. 26.8

Here are four Excel options worth adjusting.

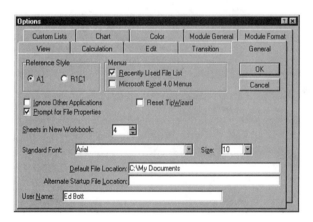

What else can you do to make Excel easier to use? Choose one of these tabs from the dialog box in figure 26.8 to find these useful options:

- **Color.** Choose standard colors to use in worksheets and charts.

- **Transition.** If you know Lotus 1-2-3 inside and out, you can readjust Excel so that the familiar 1-2-3 keystrokes work.

- **Edit.** Lets you turn off in-cell editing and drag-and-drop copies. Set the default number of decimal places Excel uses here, too.

- **Calculation.** If you have a huge worksheet filled with formulas that seem to take forever to recalculate every time you change a value, change automatic calculation to manual here (but don't forget to turn it back on later).

- **View.** Lets you hide the formula bar, gridlines, row and column headers, and just about everything else on the screen.

Personalizing PowerPoint

Now let's look at PowerPoint's Options dialog box (fig. 26.9). Compared with Word and Excel, PowerPoint isn't exactly overwhelming with options, is it? If you use the program a lot, go to the General tab and set the number of recently used files to its maximum of 9. And if the startup dialog boxes bug you, there's an option to turn them off on the same page.

Fig. 26.9

If you've become used to Word's unlimited Undo, reset this PowerPoint option to something higher than 20. The maximum setting is 150.

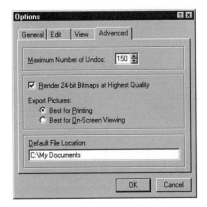

You'll find several useful options on the View tab as well. I like to hide the transparent button that gives me access to the pop-up menu during a slide show (I can use the right mouse button if I need to). And the option to always end with a black slide adds a classy sense of closure to any presentation.

How do I save my setup?

The only thing you have to do to save your new setup is say <u>Y</u>es when the program asks if you want to save changes to the template or the default files or whatever it asks for. Office stores them in a special place along with all your other Windows settings. The next time you open the program, things should be just as you left them.

Of course, there's always a catch. Some of your changes are stored as part of special data files. And someday, if you're a little unlucky, you might lose one of them. Don't despair—it's not the end of the world, but it is a hassle.

The most important of these files is Normal.dot. By default, you'll find it in the Templates folder inside the MSOffice folder. This is where Word stores all your macros, styles, toolbars, and other personal settings. It's *always* a good idea to keep a backup of this file.

27

What Are All Those Little Programs?

● In this chapter:

- I need to create quick charts

- I want to design my own logo

- How do I add cool images to my documents?

- How can I show my company's reorganization in a chart?

Most of the Office programs are small, and, like Hollywood bit players, they have specialized roles to play . . . . ❯

The superstars in the Microsoft Office are easy to spot: Word, Excel, and PowerPoint get all the headlines. But the Office supporting cast is worth a look, too. Most of these programs are small, and like Hollywood bit players, they have specialized roles to play. Because these mini-applications are so small and specialized, they even have a nickname: **applets**.

Meet the Office applets

If you chose the Complete option when you first installed Office, you automatically added five smaller programs to your computer. In every case, these programs allow you to insert **objects** inside your Word documents, Excel worksheets, and PowerPoint presentations. The big program doesn't worry about what's inside the object; it just makes room on the screen for it. So you can have picture objects, graph objects, even sound objects that talk or play music when you double-click them.

Plain English, please!

An **object** is something (a piece of text, graphic object, or sound object) that's created in one program, but can be available and manipulated in another program by a process called embedding. **Embedding** has nothing to do with mattresses: it simply means that the file containing the object lives with the receiving program, and can be moved and resized there. It can also still be opened and modified in the program where it was created.

These mini-programs don't look very much like the big Office programs. The toolbars (for those applets that have them) are different, menus don't match up, and things generally behave just differently enough that it's easy to get confused.

These are the five Office applets:

- **Microsoft Graph** turns numbers into simple charts.

- **Microsoft WordArt** twists words and phrases into unusual shapes for use as logos and letterheads, for example.

- **Microsoft ClipArt Gallery** lets you add canned drawings and cartoons to your documents.

- **Microsoft Organization Chart** lets you sort out who's who (and who answers to whom) in any company.

- **Equation Editor** will be a big help if you're working out a new theory of relativity.

Q&A *I don't have these applets on my computer. Where are they?*

If you (or whoever installed Office on your PC) chose to do a Typical installation, the WordArt, Organization Chart, and Equation Editor applets stayed on the setup disks. To install them now, click the Office icon on the Shortcut Bar and choose Add/Remove <u>O</u>ffice Programs. You'll find all three choices in the Office Tools category.

How do these applets work?

You choose <u>I</u>nsert, <u>O</u>bject, then pick a name from the list of programs that Windows displays. You'll see other programs on the list, in addition to these five, depending on what other kind of software you have on your system.

Three of the applets—Microsoft Graph, Microsoft WordArt, and Microsoft ClipArt Gallery—will only run from inside another program. You can think of them as "servant" applications whose only job is to carry out the requests of a bigger, more powerful program; they never work on their own. The Orgchart and Equation Editor programs can be used by themselves, although you might have to create program items on the desktop or Start menu first.

When you work with one of these applets, it takes over the screen, including the window that your document was in. It's like turning on your VCR: it temporarily takes over the screen for the movie you're showing (and you have to use the VCR controls to make things happen), but the TV programs and controls are still there underneath. Sometimes your document stays there, and only the menus and toolbars change. It's a slightly disorienting experience at first, but you get used to it.

How do you get the regular menus and toolbars back? Click anywhere in your main document outside of the new object. To edit the object, double-click it, and let the applet take over your screen again.

Painting pictures with numbers: Microsoft Graph

For complicated charts, Excel is the best tool for the job. To plop a quick-and-dirty chart into a Word document or a PowerPoint presentation, though, this applet might be a better choice. Think of Microsoft Graph as "Excel Extra Lite."

You enter numbers into a **datasheet** that works like an Excel worksheet. Your chart appears in its own window inside your document. Toolbars and menus let you choose a different chart type, or format labels and numbers on your chart.

Take your choice of two techniques to make a Graph object:

- To start from scratch and enter numbers directly, just choose Insert, Object, choose Microsoft Graph 5.0 Chart, and replace the numbers in the sample datasheet. This is the most common way to insert a chart into PowerPoint (see fig. 27.1).

- If your numbers are already in an Excel worksheet, highlight the relevant cells in the sample datasheet, then click the Import Data button. Your new chart will go in just below the table.

Fig. 27.1
It may look like Excel, but it's really Microsoft Graph.

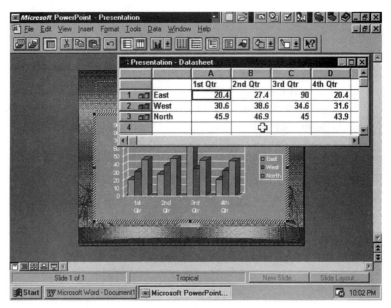

Making your text shine with WordArt

Look at the label on a Coca-Cola can (Classic Coke, of course, not that New stuff). See the flowing script in the logo? It's a work of art that started out as eight letters and a hyphen. A graphic artist took the letters in the name and manipulated them into the most recognized logo on the planet.

Your market might not be as big as the billions and billions of Coke drinkers worldwide, but a good logo can still help your business grow. And the WordArt program, which helps you turn plain text into fancy artwork, is a good place to start.

What is WordArt, anyway?

WordArt is an extremely simple program that takes a few words and lets you stretch, bend, distort, and colorize them. Think of it as the computerized equivalent of what you used to do with Silly Putty and the Sunday comics.

There are a few things you should know before you use WordArt:

- The program won't run by itself. You have to start it from inside another program (like Word or Excel).

- It works only with TrueType fonts. If your printer uses a font that doesn't have a TrueType equivalent, you can't use it in WordArt. (For more on fonts, see Chapter 8.)

- Any object you create with WordArt can be resized, moved, or copied into another document using the Windows Clipboard. It can't be saved as a separate file.

 TIP   **When you insert a WordArt object into a Word document, be sure** to enclose it in a frame after you create it. (Select the WordArt object, click the right mouse button, and choose Frame Picture from the shortcut menu.) Once there's a frame around the picture, you can easily move it where you want it on the page.

How do I create a work of WordArt?

To get started, position the insertion point where you want your masterpiece to appear, and choose Insert, Object. Pick Microsoft WordArt 2.0 from the list. After the program finishes loading, your screen will be transformed. The title bar will still say `Microsoft Word`, but the menus will have changed, and there will be a small box waiting for you to enter some text in it, like the one shown in figure 27.2.

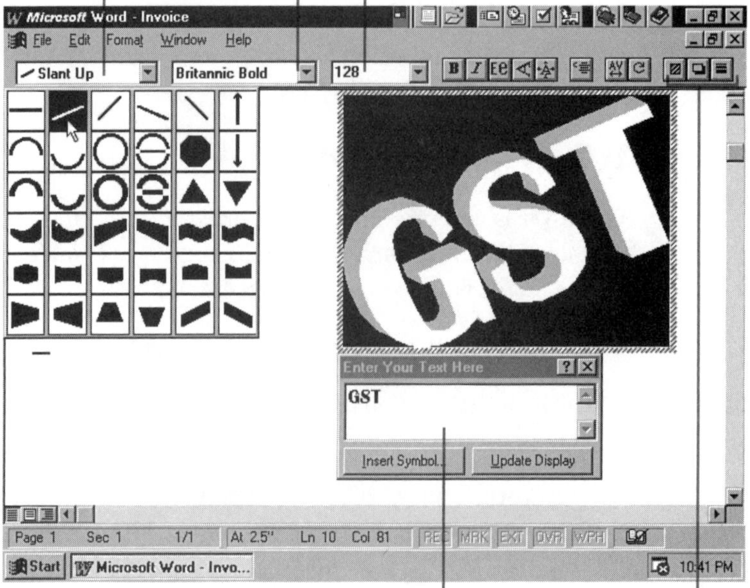
This drop-down palette lets you choose from three dozen special text-distorting effects.
Pick a typeface and a font size here. Sorry, you can't mix and match typefaces.
Microsoft Word - Invoice
File Edit Format Window Help
Slant Up
Britannic Bold
128
GST
Enter Your Text Here
GST
Insert Symbol...
Update Display
Page 1 Sec 1 1/1 At 2.5" Ln 10 Col 81
Start
Microsoft Word - Invo...
10:41 PM
Enter some text here.
Use these buttons to apply special effects like color, shadows, and borders.

Fig. 27.2
To create this logo with WordArt, we used every trick in the book, including shadows and slanted type, to make a dramatic-looking image out of three simple letters.

To return to your document, just click anywhere outside the WordArt object. You can also copy a WordArt object from one document to another. That means you can create and save your WordArt logo in a blank document. When you're satisfied with the way it looks, copy it to the Windows Clipboard and paste it into the document where you want to use it, as shown in figure 27.3. Don't forget to frame it now, so you can move it around the document easily.

Fig. 27.3

With a little fine-tuning and resizing, the logo we created fits perfectly in a variety of Office documents, like this invoice created in Word.

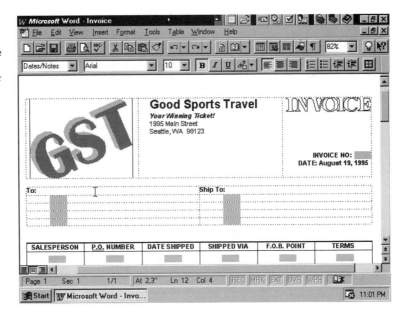

Browsing through the ClipArt Gallery

Most commercially available clip art comes in separate files, disorganized and impossible to find. ClipArt Gallery actually makes it easy to browse through hundreds or thousands of images to find the one you're looking for.

Like all the other applets, this one inserts an editable object in the file you're working on. It doesn't matter whether it's a Word document, an Excel worksheet, or a PowerPoint presentation—the picture sits comfortably in the midst of your work. There are some cool images in the collection (along with some clunkers), but all that clip art comes at a price. If you install it all, as figure 27.4 illustrates, you'll chew up nearly 14 megabytes of hard disk space.

By this time, you should know how to start up this applet. Insert, Object. Microsoft ClipArt Gallery. Right. Don't be surprised if it takes a few minutes the first time you load it.

Once you've started the program, you can do a surprising number of things with it. The simplest is to browse through thumbnail sketches of the images in your collection, organized by category (see fig. 27.5). If you find one you like, click Insert to close the Gallery window and pop back into your program with the new image in place.

Fig. 27.4

You'll need nearly 5 megabytes of disk space to install all the images in the Microsoft ClipArt Gallery. And there are another six-plus megabytes of clip art in the Valupack folder on the Office CD.

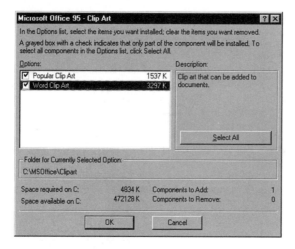

At that point, you can resize the image, put it in a frame, or copy it to the Windows Clipboard to paste into another program.

Fig. 27.5

Sort through collections of clip art until you find the right image, then click OK to insert the picture into your document as an object that can be resized, moved, and copied.

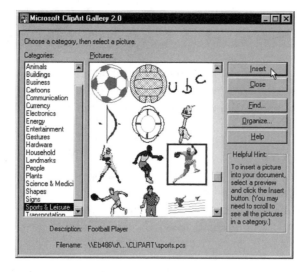

Microsoft Organization Chart

When you start Organization Chart, you get all the tools you need to re-arrange your company's management structure from top to bottom (see fig. 27.6). It only takes a few clicks and drags to move an entire department from one division to another, halfway across the country. The program shows up on the <u>I</u>nsert, <u>O</u>bject list, but it can also be run on its own, and you can save files as separate files, not embedded in another application.

Fig. 27.6

Go ahead—give yourself a promotion with the help of Microsoft Organization Chart.

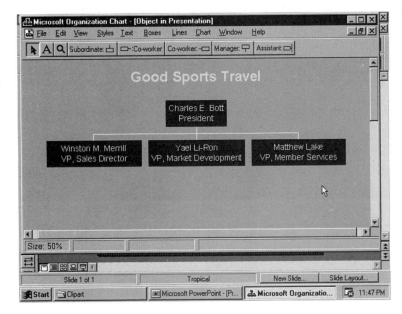

Figuring out Equation Editor

I've been struggling with Stephen W. Hawking's *A Brief History of Time* for more than seven years now. They say it's brilliant, but I can't say for sure. Space, time, physics, math... let's just say I'm no Stephen W. Hawking.

So if you want to insert an equation into your next scientific paper, be my guest. Choose <u>I</u>nsert, <u>O</u>bject, Microsoft Equation 2.0. You'll see an editing window and a set of tools like the ones in figure 27.7. When you figure out what they're for, drop me a line, OK?

Fig. 27.7
"Triple integral with
subscript limit"? Does
that have anything to
do with ice skating? If
you plan to use
Equation Editor, you're
on your own.

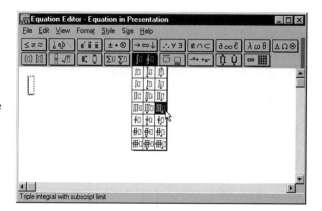

28

Schedule+: Keep Your Life in Order!

● **In this chapter:**

- How do I schedule appointments?

- Can I invite others to this meeting?

- I need to keep the phone numbers of all my contacts

- I need to be reminded of tasks and appointments

Schedule+ is more than just an appointment book. Like a good secretary, it even reminds you to send flowers to your mother on Mother's Day (but you'll need to make that call yourself) . . . . ▶

he newest staff member in the Microsoft Office is Schedule+, a program that helps you organize your work and your life. Schedule+ is just like your organizer: a combination of appointment book, group scheduler, contact manager, to-do list, and more.

But Schedule+ is much more than your paper-based organizer; it's an efficient secretary as well. It reminds you to send flowers to your mother on Mother's Day, it books appointments with other people in your office and accepts invitations to meetings on your behalf. Are you missing a deadline? Schedule+ will remind you, hour after hour, persistently, that you need to turn in that report.

Using the appointment book

When you run Schedule+ for the first time, you'll be prompted to tell the program whether you're creating a new schedule or want to use an existing one. If you opt to create a new schedule, the next dialog box asks you for your name. You might be setting it up for yourself or for your boss or even for a colleague, so enter the appropriate name at the dialog box you see in figure 28.1.

Fig. 28.1
To set up a new appointment book, tell Schedule+ your name, and in which folder you want to save your appointment book.

> **TIP**   **Schedule+ looks for your schedule file in the Schedule folder** inside your Office folder on the hard disk. If you've saved that file elsewhere, select Use an existing schedule.

How do I create a new appointment?

There are several ways to enter new appointments in Schedule+, depending on where you are.

Get yourself together with Schedule+

Schedule+ is like that beer commercial: tastes great, less filling. Take one look at this screen and you'll be able to throw out that one-pound organizer. Everything you need to meet your goals and make your appointments is right here.

Monthly calendar
By default, you get the current month. But you can switch to other months by clicking the right or left arrows. Dates shown in bold mean yes, you have appointments that day.

View
View your information as a daily, weekly, or monthly schedule. Or, for a more panoramic view, select the Planner. You can also look at your to-do list or go to your contact list by clicking these tabs.

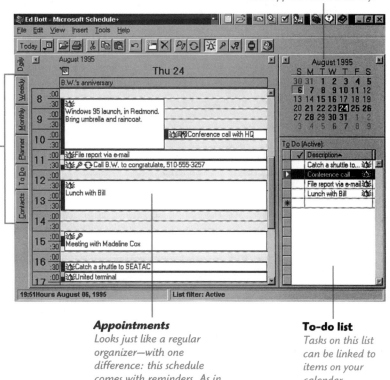

Appointments
Looks just like a regular organizer—with one difference: this schedule comes with reminders. As in loud, annoying beeps, so you don't miss that train.

To-do list
Tasks on this list can be linked to items on your calendar.

- If you're not in Schedule+, click the Make an Appointment button on the Shortcut Bar. This will launch Schedule+ and let you create a new appointment.

- If you're in Schedule+, select the day from the calendar on the right, right-click the right time slot, and select New Appointment.

Type the details of the appointment in the Appointment dialog box you see in figure 28.2.

Fig. 28.2

From this dialog box, you can also invite others to the meeting, or set the meeting as recurring (for example, on the second Monday of every month).

Along with the time and date, Schedule+ gives you lots of other options for each appointment you make:

- **Set reminder:** A pop-up dialog box will remind you of the coming event, even if you're not in Schedule+. And in case your eyes are away from the screen for a while, the alarm also includes a sound effect. Set up the alarm to come up 15 minutes before your appointment, and it'll be your wake-up call. Do you ever get out of bed when your alarm clock goes off? Of course not. You reach for the snooze button and gain 15 more minutes of sleep. Schedule+ gives you that option, too. If you're too busy when you get the reminder, and you're afraid you'll forget the appointment as soon as you click OK on the dialog box, you can tell it to remind you again in a specified number of minutes. See figure 28.3 for an example.

CAUTION **The reminder doesn't pop up when a screen saver is active on your** screen. Even when you return to your desktop (when the screen saver disappears), you won't get that notice. As the old computer saying goes, "Is this a bug or a feature?" It's hard to tell, but until Microsoft fixes this problem, get in the habit of checking your Schedule+ screen whenever you disable a screen saver.

Fig. 28.3
The reminder is patient and polite, and will return in the specified time to harass you. Politely.

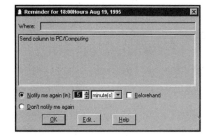

TIP **The default alarm sound is a short beep, but you can change that** to anything you want by opening the Sounds icon in Control Panel, and assigning a different WAV file (from the Media folder or elsewhere on your hard disk) to the event *SchdplusReminder.* Just like an alarm clock, you need to make it really annoying, so you don't snooze and miss the appointment. My sound file says, "I'm late, I'm late, for a very important date!" in a high-pitched voice. I can't ignore that obnoxious alarm.

- **Tentative:** What do you do when you're not sure you can make an appointment? You *pencil it in.* This way, you can erase it if it conflicts with another appointment. In Schedule+ you can pencil something in by selecting Tentative from the Appointment dialog box. The appointment will appear different, with a gray background, so you can tell at a glance whether it's a firm date or not.

- **Private**: If the appointment is confidential or private, you need to protect it from prying eyes. This is especially important if you've assigned access rights to other members of your workgroup (see the section, "Sharing an appointment book with others," later in this chapter). You wouldn't want your colleagues to know that you have a job interview, would you?

How do I invite other people to this meeting?

A meeting is not a huge success if nobody shows up. At least, that's the way it is in my office. How do you invite others to your meeting? You can go around telling them to be at the conference room at 4, and hope they can take their eyes off the Dilbert screen saver long enough to pay attention to you. A much better way is to let Schedule+ invite them via e-mail. When your colleagues get your invitation, they have the option to accept or decline it. Once they accept, the appointment gets added to their own appointment books (assuming, of course, that they're also using Schedule+). Here's how you invite others to your meeting (note that this option is only available if you've configured Schedule+ as a workgroup scheduler):

1 In the Appointment dialog box, click the Attendees tab.

2 Click the Invite Others button.

3 In the Meeting Attendees screen you see in figure 28.4, click the names of people you want to invite, and click the Required or Optional buttons, as appropriate.

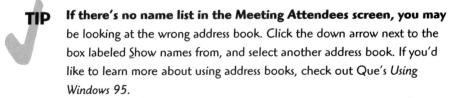 **TIP** If there's no name list in the Meeting Attendees screen, you may be looking at the wrong address book. Click the down arrow next to the box labeled Show names from, and select another address book. If you'd like to learn more about using address books, check out Que's *Using Windows 95.*

4 Now you need a meeting room. You're not expecting a large crowd, so opt for the small conference room. How? In addition to inviting people to your meeting, you can "invite" resources, such as rooms, equipment, and so on. Your system administrator needs to set up your workgroup resources. Once these are set up, they appear on your list of attendees, as if they were people. But how can a room "reply" to your invitation? Simple. There's somebody in your office, perhaps the office manager or receptionist, who's in charge of the resources, and receives all meeting invitations on their behalf.

Fig. 28.4

Invite others and
reserve a meeting
space, all from the
same screen.

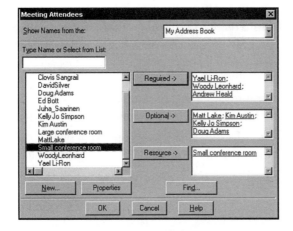

5 When you're done, click OK twice. The next screen lets you compose a
message to the people you've invited, providing them with background
information on the meeting (see figure 28.5). Click the Send button on
the toolbar, and the invitation will be distributed to everybody on your
list.

Fig. 28.5

If you've used the
Inbox in Windows 95,
this screen will look
familiar to you. It's part
of the same system:
Microsoft Exchange.

Send button

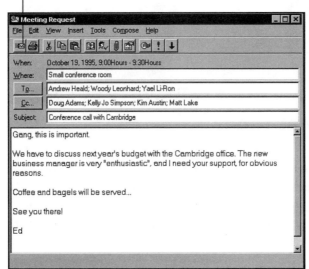

TIP   **If you'd like to learn more about Exchange, double-click the**
Inbox icon on your desktop and press F1 to get the Help screen. This topic
is covered in more detail in Que's *Using Windows 95.*

6 When you're done, the new meeting gets added to your appointment
book. The icons you see in figure 28.6 indicate (in this order) that
you've configured a reminder; that it's a recurring meeting, every
Monday at 9 a.m.—how inconsiderate of you!; that you've invited
others; and that you've reserved a meeting room.

Fig. 28.6

Can't tell what the
meeting is all about?
Double-click this entry
in the appointment
book, and you'll get a
full screen, with all the
information you need.

How can I tell who's available at that time?

To make the scheduling process easier, you can let the Meeting Wizard set
you up. Here's how. Right-click the time slot where you want to add a
meeting, select Make Meeting, and follow the bouncing ball. One advantage
of using the Wizard is that it searches the network for people and resources.
It then immediately displays the results of your invitation, and lets you
select a different date or location if there's a conflict in the others' schedules, or if the meeting room isn't available. See figure 28.7.

Fig. 28.7

One person has a dental appointment, the other's on paternity leave. Well, at least the meeting room is available...

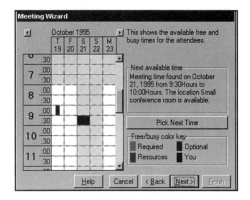

Bad news. It seems that nobody can attend this meeting. Well, at least the meeting room is available...

So why not use the Meeting Wizard every time? The wizard can't read people's minds, that's why. One person's schedule may appear to accommodate you, but in reality, his wife has just had a baby and he's taking a paternity leave. And Schedule+ is none the wiser. It's better to wait for human confirmation, so that you don't end up sitting there, all dressed up, and no meeting to go to.

How do I manage my contact list?

Schedule+ has a contact management module, where you keep names of your clients and friends. There are two ways you can add a name to that list:

- If you're not in Schedule+, click the Add a Contact button on the Shortcut Bar.

- In Schedule+, click the Contacts tab, then the Insert New Contact button.

In the screen you see in figure 28.8, enter the contact information. Click each of the tabs to add as much information as you have. If this is a client, you may want to add his or her birthday and/or anniversary dates, so you can send the obligatory card at the right time.

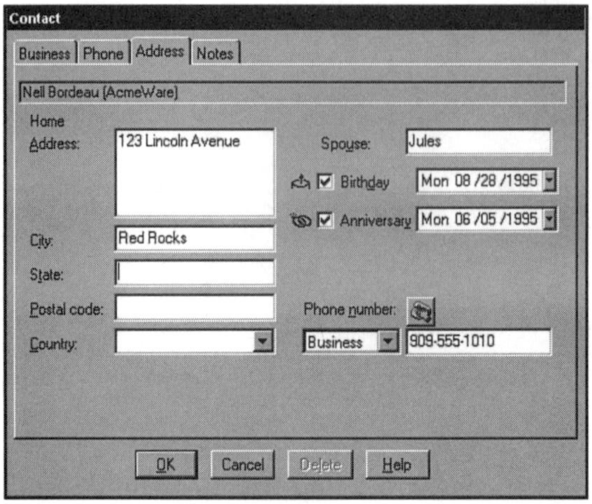

Fig. 28.8

Think of this as a
multi-layered Rolodex
card with brains.

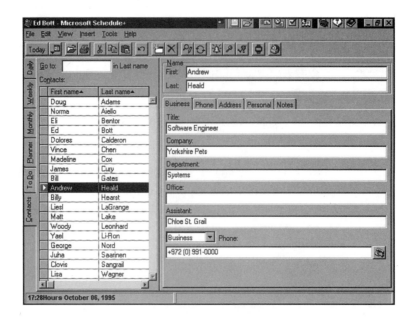

How can I find anything in this list?

As you see in figure 28.9, the contact list is displayed on the left, and the
currently selected name is displayed on the right, in more detail. You can
scroll up and down until you find who you're looking for, but for quicker
results, type the first few characters in the person's name into the Go to box
at the top. Your cursor will jump to the first match. If you type **Jo**, trying to
get to Jones, you may get to Johnson first. Just type an **n** to continue the
search.

Fig. 28.9

The names on the list
at the left side
correspond with the
details on the right.

How to customize the display

If the Contacts screen is cluttered and confusing to you, you're not alone. It's a mess, simple as that. But you don't have to put up with the default display options. Here's what you can do to rearrange the screen:

1 Move your pointer to the line separating the two parts of the screen, until it becomes a double-edged arrow. Click and drag either side to adjust its size to your liking.

2 Right-click the First name or Last name label, select Columns, then Custom.

3 Pick any data column you want to add to the display, select Add to add it to the list, and position it anywhere you want, using the Move Up or Move Down buttons. See figure 28.10.

Fig. 28.10

Which information do you want to get at a glance? Set your preferences here.

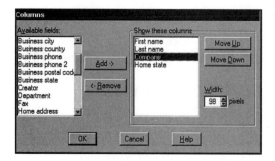

When you're done, the results will be something you can live with. Figure 28.11 is an example of a more usable Contacts screen.

Fig. 28.11
My customized
Contacts screen. It may
not be perfect, but
that's the way I like it.

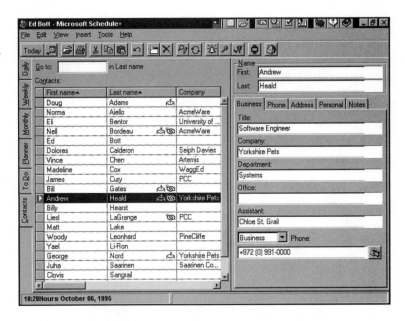

Don't know whether you're coming or going? You need a to-do list!

The to-do list in Schedule+ is a relentless assistant. It'll remind you of your outstanding assignments until you give in and finish them. To enter a new task, use one of the following two methods:

- If Schedule+ isn't running, click the Add a Task button on the Shortcut Bar.

- Inside Schedule+, click the To-Do tab, and then the Insert New Task button.

Enter the details of the task in the dialog box you see in figure 28.12. Pay special attention to the following details:

- **Ends.** That's your deadline. Need I say more?

- **Starts.** When are you going to start working on that task?

- **Project.** Whether this task is part of a project or not, type something here, to categorize the task. It makes it easier to view your to-do list when it's arranged by categories.

- **Priority.** The most urgent task gets a 1. This way, if there's too much on your plate on a given day, you can prioritize your workload by examining the importance of each task. A 4 priority may need to be postponed for a day or two, until you finish your top-priority tasks.

- **Set reminder.** Let Schedule+ remind you to get going on this project.

Fig. 28.12

Do you feel confident that you'll complete the task by the due date? Then select the box next to Mark as done after end date, and Schedule+ will treat the task as done.

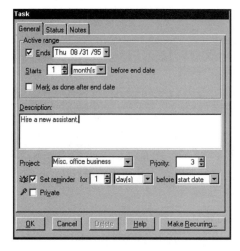

I want to view my to-do list

When you click the To Do tab in Schedule+, you switch to a list view, sorted by category. All your tasks are there, completed, pending, and, of course, you see the dreaded overdue ones. Figure 28.13 shows the completed tasks crossed out, with check marks next to their descriptions. Overdue tasks show up in red on your screen, and get a nasty red exclamation point icon next to them, to put the fear of your editor in you. The rest of the lines represent tasks you're still supposed to finish.

Fig. 28.13

Wait a minute... You've already filed that report! Just click the Completed column (the leftmost one), and the task gets a checkmark and a strikethrough.

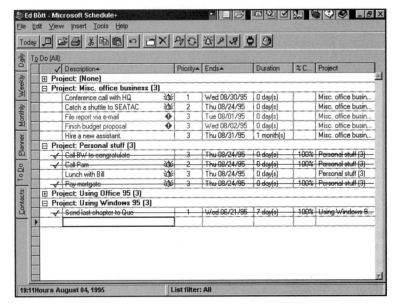

How can I access this information on a business trip?

If you're traveling without your computer, Schedule+ has little advantage for you. In fact, it can be a burden, because you haven't written down any of your contact names or appointments. In short, you're *hosed*. Well, not really. Here's how you *can* take it with you:

You can print out your appointments and contacts, and take them on the road with you. Select the printer button on the Schedule+ toolbar, and, as you can see in figure 28.14, you get more options than in your usual printer dialog box.

Fig. 28.14

You can print out your appointments, to-do list, even contact list. Select an option, and click Preview to make sure that it's what you want.

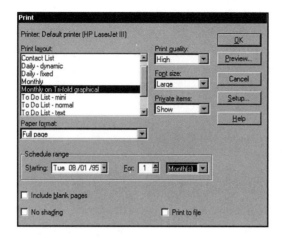

Getting the most from your printouts

You may suffer through several failed attempts to get the right printout out of Schedule+, but for best results, follow these suggestions (because I've been there, and I have piles of wasted paper to show for my suffering):

- **If you're going to scan, fax, or photocopy** this printout, select No Shading. Those gray shades are only nice on the original copy. When you try to copy them, they turn into dark smudges.

- **Always click preview** before committing to a print job.

- **Don't print out the contact list.** It'll go on and on for pages, duplicating a lot of information.

- **To make the text easier to read**, select larger fonts—but you may not be able to fit everything on the page.

- **Select the 5-day option** for weekly schedules whenever possible. Your page will be less cluttered, and the text will be more legible.

Can't I copy this file to my laptop?

If you're taking a portable system while you're traveling, use the Backup option under File to create a copy of your Schedule+ file. While you're on the road, you can modify the information as needed. When you get back to the office, be sure to use the Restore option under the File menu to update your main system.

TIP **If you know how to use the Windows Briefcase, that's even easier** than Backup/Restore for transferring and updating files between two machines. If you'd like to learn more, check out the online Help for Windows 95, under "Briefcase" (under the Index tab). This topic is also covered in Que's *Using Windows 95.*

Playing Dick Tracy

Look at the Schedule+ toolbar, and you'll notice a button adorned with an image of a watch. Click here, and you can download your appointments, to-do lists and contacts, to... your watch. It's true. I kid you not. If you own a Timex DataLink watch ($90 if you know where to shop), this button activates a wizard that walks you through the download process. Just aim your watch at the monitor, and it'll receive up to 15 entries from your appointment book. When Schedule+ is set to sound an alarm, this "Dick Tracy" watch will beep and display the appropriate message.

Just one warning: In certain circles, wearing this watch is considered the ultimate in cool. Elsewhere, you may be dubbed as a technogeek. To confuse things further, the people I work with think it's cool to be a technogeek. Go figure.

29

Using Office with Other People

● **In this chapter:**

- **Sharing files with coworkers**

- **How do I keep track of who does what with a file?**

- **Can I protect my files that are in shared network areas?**

- **We both need to work on the same Excel list!**

- **Create your own custom templates**

You'll get a lot more accomplished if everyone on your team is working together! Here's how to share questions, comments, notes, and much more without any fuss . . . . ➤

T hese days, business is a team sport. It has to be, in a world where faxes and FedEx have trained us to expect that the impossible can absolutely, positively be done overnight. No matter what you do for a living, chances are you occasionally split up those big, we-needed-it-yesterday jobs with your coworkers. One takes the words, the other takes the numbers, and with a little bit of luck it all comes together with minutes to spare.

All the Office applications include features that make it easier for two or more people to work on a single document. There are tools for mailing files from Point A to Point B, for marking up documents with the electronic equivalent of a yellow marker, and even for comparing two versions of the same document to see who changed what.

In this chapter, I'll focus mostly on how these features work across a local area network. But most of them let you accomplish the same ends (with a little extra work) as you would by using floppy disks and a good pair of walking shoes.

Plain English, please!

You'll sometimes hear the word **workgroup** in connection with Microsoft Office. Unless your office is a cave and your business card says Hermit, you probably belong to a workgroup yourself. The members of your workgroup are all attached to the same network file server, and they probably share many of the same files. Workgroup members don't have to be in the same location, but it sure helps.

How can I share Office files with other people?

Sharing files is easy when you simply copy files to a floppy disk and walk down the hall to your coworker's office. As long as that file is locked onto a floppy disk, there's no way two of you can try to work with it at the same time.

The situation changes considerably, though, when two people begin using a shared network hard drive to store files. Let's say you're in your office, feverishly revising the introduction to your annual report. Meanwhile, at the other end of the hall, George in Finance decides he wants to plug the latest profit projections into that same document, so he tells Word to open the file. What happens next?

Your choices are limited when you try to open an Office file that someone else is already working on. How you deal with this situation depends on which application you're using.

In **Word** or **PowerPoint**, you'll see these nearly identical dialog boxes:

Fig. 29.1
The Read-only label is a little misleading. You can make changes to a file you open this way, but you have to give the file a new name.

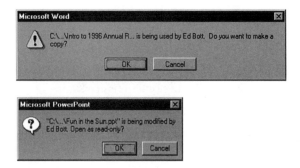

If you're at George's desk, you have three choices when you see this dialog box:

- You can call me and ask when I'll be done. If it's an emergency, I can close the window; otherwise, you'll have to wait until I've finished my work. This option is fine when you simply want to see what's in a document.

- You can cancel the request to open the file and try again later. This is your best bet when you need to make changes to a document.

- You can select OK and open a copy of the document. If you choose this option and make changes to the file, though, you cannot save those changes to the existing file name.

When you try to open an **Excel** workbook that someone else is using, you see a slightly different dialog box, like the one in figure 29.2:

- Excel's Read-Only option works just like Word's option. In both cases, you can make changes to the document but must save them to a new file name.

Fig. 29.2
Don't use the Read-Only option if you need to make changes to a file. It's more trouble than it's worth to consolidate changes from two versions into one document.

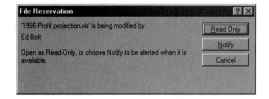

- Press Cancel and try again later if you have the time to wait.

- If you want to look at the file now and have Excel tell you when the other user has closed it, click Notify. Excel immediately opens the workbook in read-only mode. It keeps checking the network every few minutes, though, asking if I'm through with that file yet. When the network sends back the word that I've finally closed that file, you will see a dialog box like the one in figure 29.3.

Click Read-Write and Excel replaces the workbook with the latest version, including any changes the other user made after you opened the read-only copy. If you've made changes, you'll have to decide whether to throw them away and start over or to save them under a new name. In any case, you're now free to make changes and save the file under its original file name.

Fig. 29.3
If you've asked Excel to notify you when another user finishes with a file you want to edit, you'll see this dialog box. Choose Read-Write to open the now available copy.

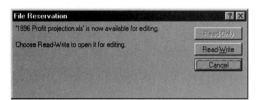

CAUTION **If an Excel workbook is in use by someone else and you click the** Notify button, don't make any changes until after you've been notified that the file is available for Read/Write access. If you and the other user both made changes to the file, you'll have to save your changes under a new name and compare the two versions by sight. It's not worth the headache.

Making your changes stand out

When you work on printed documents, you can take your pick of markup techniques. You can use a bright marker pen to highlight key sections. Your comments and questions go on sticky yellow notes tacked right on the page. To suggest changes, you can cross out the words or numbers on the page and write in your own.

Word includes three features that are directly analogous to these group-editing techniques.

Highlighting: marking up the page

If you want to make a word, sentence, or section stand out on the screen, click Word's Highlight button. The mouse pointer turns to a combination of an insertion point and a pen. As long as that pointer is visible, you can drag it across any text to highlight it with a vivid color. You can see the pointer and the marked text in Fig. 29.4.

Fig. 29.4

When the pointer turns to this marker, you can highlight any part of the screen. If you plan to print the results, be sure to choose a light color.

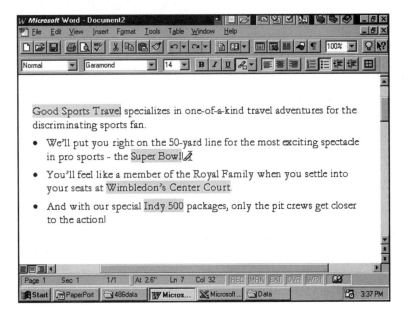

Click the down arrow next to the Highlight button to change marker colors. To stop marking, press Esc or click the Highlight button again.

TIP **Highlighting works best when you're expecting someone to read** the document on a color screen. If you plan to print it out on a black-and-white printer, the marked text turns to a dull gray, and it doesn't have anywhere near the same impact as that vivid yellow or fluorescent green.

Annotations: making notes on the page

Annotations are like sticky notes attached to specific parts of a document's text. Each person types his or her own notes; Word automatically identifies them with the writer's initials (see fig. 29.5). You use annotations to keep track of who is making what changes to a document.

Fig. 29.5

Anyone in your office can use the annotation pane (below) to add comments within a Word file. Anyone reading the document can see all the annotations at once.

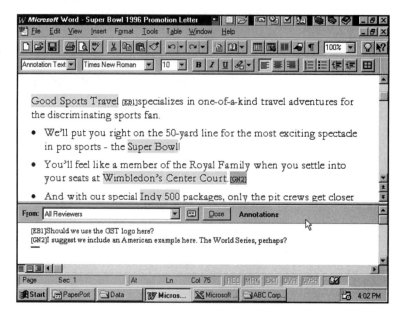

To insert an annotation, click the spot where you want to add a note. Next, choose Insert, Annotation. Word opens the annotation pane in the bottom half of the window. Type your comment in the window provided, then click the Close button to save your note and close the annotation pane. (You can also click in the editing pane to keep the annotation pane open as you work.) Word adds a hidden pointer in the text to mark the annotations.

To see all the annotations in a document, choose Y̲iew, A̲nnotations. You'll see the same window that you used to insert new annotations. Each annotation is indicated with the writer's initials and a sequence number.

TIP   **You can make annotation markers visible. Tools, Options, View** tab, Nonprinting Characters section, Hidden Text. When you see this marker, you can double-click it to open the annotation pane and see the note attached to that marker.

Q&A   *In my department, two of us have the same initials. How do I distinguish my annotations from hers?*

One of you will have to change your initials, at least for use with Word. Choose T̲ools, O̲ptions, and look for the User Info tab. You can create an ID tag of up to eight characters in the I̲nitials box.

What's that button next to the Close button on the annotation pane? If you think it looks like a cassette tape, go to the head of the class. If you have a sound card and a microphone, you can record a note and insert it into a document. Be warned, though: sound files can make a document very, very large.

Revision marks: changing the page

Annotations are the best way to ask questions and make comments. When you're truly working together with another person, though, you'll want to pass different versions of the same file back and forth. The final draft will probably include a little from each version. So how do you see, in perfect detail, all the changes that a second user made to an original document? The secret is to use **revision marks** to automatically highlight changes, additions, and deletions.

Turn on revision marks by selecting T̲ools, Re̲visions, then select the box labeled M̲ark revisions while editing. Now, when you edit the document, the changes you make are easily tracked, as shown in figure 29.6.

TIP   **If you use revision marking often, try this very cool shortcut and** bypass the menus completely. Look on the status bar at the bottom of the screen; roughly halfway across, you'll see the grayed-out letters MRK in a small box. Double-click here to pop up the Revisions dialog box.

Newly added text is marked with an underline

Fig. 29.6
Text additions are underlined and deletions are in strikeout when using revision marks. You can't tell it here, but each author's changes are marked in a different color.

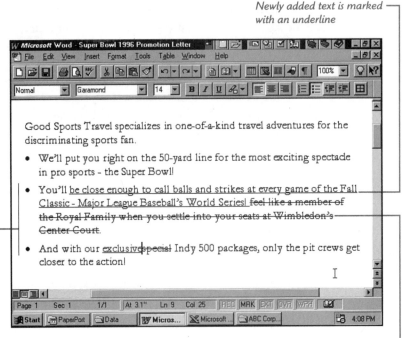

The line in the margin tells you that there's a change in that paragraph

Deletions are marked with a strikeout line through the center

How do you work with a document that someone else has revised? To see all the changes and figure out who made the changes in question, open the document, choose Tools, Revisions, and click Review. In the Review Revisions dialog box (see fig. 29.7), click the Find button to move to each revision in turn. Each change is highlighted in the document, and the Description area of the dialog box tells who made the change and when.

As you view the revisions in a document, you can use this dialog box to accept or reject one or all of the revisions. Just click Accept to incorporate the changed text or Reject to discard it and restore the original. Make sure to save the final document under a new name.

Q&A   ***I'm confused by all the revision marks here. Can I see what the changes will look like before I accept them?***

Yes. Click the Hide Marks button to see what the revisions would look like if you accepted them. When you click that button the text changes, and so does the button. Click the same button with its new Show Marks label to restore the revision marks.

Fig. 29.7
Use the Review Revisions dialog to search for all the changes in a document. You can accept or reject any or all of the changes.

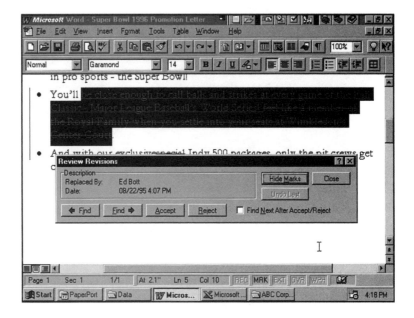

Using e-mail to share the workload

How do you send one or more files to other people? If you only have one or two files, you can attach them to an e-mail message and hope they all make it to their destination. If there are a lot of files, you can drag all those files into an Office binder, insert a Word document as the top section, type a few notes about the files inside, and attach that file to an e-mail message in full confidence that the entire package will get from place to place in one piece.

When you want to send your work out for comments and revisions, you have two choices: send it or route it. In either case, you create a list of other people to work on the file.

- **Sending** the file means that you put it in an electronic envelope and send it (via e-mail) to one or many people, all at the same time. What happens to it after it leaves your computer is completely up to them.

- **Routing** a file means that you attach a cover note to the file and send it to one or more people, either one after another or simultaneously. The routing slip helps you make sure you get the file back when they've all seen the document and added their comments.

CAUTION **The document sending and routing features only work if you have** Exchange configured as your e-mail client software. Installing the Exchange software can be complicated and isn't recommended for novices. Your best bet is to enlist the help of the e-mail expert in your organization well before you need to send your first message. And then practice with a few sample files to give you and your co-workers hands-on experience with how Office and Exchange work together.

Sending files

To send a file to multiple recipients, all at the same time, pull down the File menu and choose Send. (You can use this command from within any of the three big Office applications and from within the Office Binder program.) This starts Microsoft Exchange with your file already attached. Select your recipients and click the Send button to send it to them immediately, as shown in figure 29.8.

Fig. 29.8

When you use Microsoft Exchange to share documents with others, make sure you add an informative Subject line and a brief note explaining why you're sending the file.

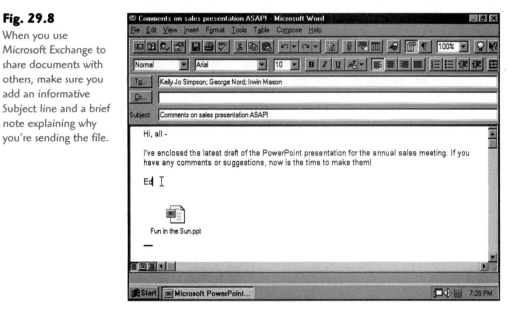

Routing files

Sending a file to someone else usually means you simply want them to see the document you've created. When you absolutely, positively want their comments and suggestions, add a **routing slip** to the document. Choose File, Add Routing Slip to see a dialog box like the one in figure 29.9.

Use the Move buttons to adjust the order in which the document is routed.

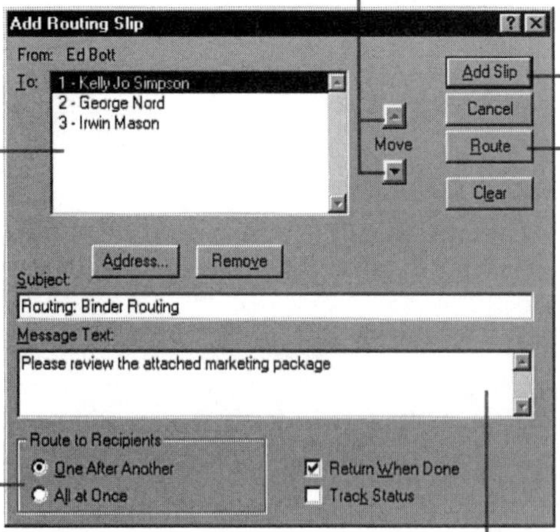

Fig. 29.9

Want to make sure that these three people get their comments back to you on time? Select the Track Status box.

Click here to choose names from the Exchange Address Book.

Choose how the document should be routed, and whether you want to be informed each time it reaches the next name on the list.

Click Add Slip to save the routing slip without sending it.

Click Route to send the file and its routing instructions right now.

Add a subject and informative message text; these will appear in the e-mail message attached to the file.

The routing slip causes the file and its accompanying e-mail message to land in the recipient's mailbox in a special format. All they have to do is double-click to open the file, then choose a simple menu command to send it to the next stop in the routing process. When the document has made it through the entire list, it comes back to you automatically.

TIP **Wondering why it's taking so long for that urgent file to get back** to you? You wouldn't wonder if you had selected the Track Status box. With that option enabled, you'll receive an e-mail message every time the file or files you sent move to the next name on the routing slip.

Part VI: Troubleshooting

Troubleshooting Office 95

Troubleshooting Office 95

● In this chapter:

- **Getting Started**

- **Using Word**

- **Using Excel**

- **Using PowerPoint**

- **Beyond the basics**

Having a problem with Office? Look here to find quick solutions . . . .

Getting Started

Here are some of the common questions that come up while exploring the basic features common to all the Office applications.

I'm trying to install Office, and I get a message that there's not enough memory

If you don't have enough space on your hard drive to install Office, don't even think about running it directly from the CD-ROM. You'll save a few megabytes of hard disk space, but you may end up waiting minutes to complete even the simplest tasks. Better to buy a new hard drive, or try doubling your disk's storage capacity by using a disk-compression utility like Windows 95's DriveSpace (to find it, click on the Start menu, then follow the cascading menus through Programs, Accessories, and System Tools).

When I turned off my computer I lost my document. What happened?

Always close the Office programs and shut down Windows properly before you turn off your PC. If you don't, you run the risk of losing data, and maybe even making such a mess out of Windows or Office that neither one will start up properly. Why take chances? To shut down the right way, click the Start button, choose Shut Down, select one of the options from the Shut Down Windows dialog box, and then click Yes.

I can't find any of my toolbars. How can I get them back?

They're not gone; they're just hidden. When you can't see the regular toolbars, you can't pop up the Toolbars menu by clicking the right mouse button. Instead, pull down the View menu, and choose the Toolbars option. Check the Standard and Formatting boxes to bring back the default toolbars. How can you tell whether a toolbar is hidden or visible? Look for a checkmark next to the toolbar's name on the shortcut menu.

This right mouse button stuff confuses me because I'm left-handed. Any help for me?

When we say "right-click" in this book, we're talking about clicking on the secondary mouse button. To most people, the secondary button is the right one, but if you're a lefty, you can configure the mouse so that the right button is your primary one. To swap the buttons: from the Start menu, select Settings, Control Panel, and double-click on the Mouse icon. (Then, of course, remember to reverse your thinking when we talk about the left and right mouse buttons... but as a lefty, you're probably used to having to do that.)

While using the Find feature, I get about a million files in the search results

Before you click the Find Now button, look at what you're asking for. If you give Office too little information, you won't get meaningful results. Asking it to find every file that contains the letters "the", for example, will probably turn up every file you've ever created. But avoid giving too much information as well: If you enter the word **finance**, for example, you won't find files that contain "financial." When a search doesn't work right, sometimes adding or subtracting a letter will work wonders.

The Office Shortcut Bar doesn't start when I start Windows. Can't I just load it automatically?

Sure. The Office installation program should have done this, but something must have happened on your computer. Click the Start button, and choose Settings, Taskbar. In the Taskbar Properties dialog box, click the Start Menu Programs tab, and click Add. You could type directly into the Command line box, but there's a more foolproof way: click the Browse button, double-click the MSOffice folder, and then the Office folder. Select the MSOffice icon, and choose Open. Click Next. In the folder list, select Startup, and click Next again. Give the shortcut a new name, if you'd like. Click the Finish button, and you're done. The next time you start Windows, the Shortcut Bar should load automatically.

That Office Shortcut Bar is taking up too much space. How can I get it out of sight when I don't need it?

It's true: when the Office Shortcut Bar is anchored to the edge of the screen, it uses up precious working space. To make it duck out of sight when you're not using it, open the Customize dialog box, and deselect Auto Hide between uses. To make it reappear, slide the mouse up to the edge of the screen where the Shortcut Bar lives; slide the mouse back down to the document area, and the toolbar disappears again.

Using Word

Here's where you get quick answers to questions you might have when creating your first Word documents.

This template doesn't look like it did the first time I used it. What could have happened?

Templates are stored in special files, not the standard Word-type files. If you open the original template file by mistake (instead of creating a new document based on it), any changes you make will be saved in the template. From then on, every document you create using that template will include all those changes, whether you want them or not. Avoid this problem by not opening files with a .DOT extension: those are the templates themselves.

I just wanted to add a word, but suddenly I'm typing over stuff I already typed

When you first start Word, you enter text in Insert mode—that is, everything you type "pushes" the text that's already there out of the way. If you hit the Insert key by accident, you'll switch into Overtype mode, where every letter you type gobbles up the one to the right of the insertion point. (If the OVR indicator on the status bar is black instead of gray, you're in Overtype mode.)

If you press the Insert key by accident, click the Undo button on the toolbar to get your old text back.

I'm working in Word in Full Screen, and all my menus disappeared

Your menus are still there, hidden just above the upper edge of the screen. You can still use them, as long as you know the first letter of the menu you want to use. If you want to print the page you're working on, you can press Alt+F to bring down the <u>F</u>ile menu. Once it's visible, use the arrow keys to move left and right, and see all the other menus, too.

When trying to select the first few letters of a word, Word selects the whole thing

Word is trying to read your mind. It thinks you want to select the entire word, so it does that for you. That's actually a very handy shortcut because you can be as sloppy with the mouse as you want, and your selection will still be perfect. But sometimes that selection isn't what you've intended. To show Word that you mean business, and when you say *partial* you don't mean *whole*, select <u>T</u>ools, <u>O</u>ptions, click on the Edit tab, and click next to Automatic <u>W</u>ord Selection to turn it off.

I deleted a paragraph a while ago and now I want to get it back, but I don't want to lose all the work I've done in the meantime. What do I do?

Save your document under another name, then use the Undo button to roll your document back until you can see the lost paragraph. Copy it to the Clipboard, and open the document you just saved. Paste the recovered text into the revised document.

Now for some housekeeping: close the original document (the one you rolled back), resave the revised document to the original document's file name, and delete the revised file.

Someone sent me a document, and the fonts look horrible on my machine. What's wrong?

The other person probably used some fonts that aren't installed on your computer. When that happens, Windows tries to substitute another font for the one your coworker used. Sometimes it works; other times the substitution looks downright ugly. You have two choices: buy the same font and install it on your computer, or change the text formatting to another font that your PC can recognize.

Moving one item in a numbered list didn't work right. The text moved, but the number stayed where it was

To move a bulleted or numbered item properly, you must make sure you've selected the paragraph mark (¶) at the end of the item. (Press the Show/Hide button on the Standard toolbar to make the job easier.) If you don't select the paragraph mark, the bullet formatting stays where it is, and only the text moves.

When working with Mail Merge, there's a lot of gibberish onscreen about Merge Fields

Somehow, you've turned on the View Field Codes option, and Word is showing you the normally hidden codes it uses to track your merge information. If you have the Show Field Codes option turned on for some reason, you'll see {MERGEFIELD FirstName} instead of <<FirstName>>. To shoo those bizarre codes back into hiding where they belong, press Alt+F9.

I'm trying to add a page number, but the command on the <u>I</u>nsert menu is gray

Try it again, and this time look in the status bar at the bottom of the screen for an error message from Word. You're probably working in Outline view. The command you want doesn't work unless you're in Normal or Page Layout View. Get to either of these views using the buttons on the bottom left of your screen, or through the <u>V</u>iew menu.

Pages come out in the wrong order every time I print, with the last page on top and the first page on the bottom

That's just the way your printer works. Fortunately, Word can work with your printer by sending pages to the printer in reverse order. Choose File, Print, and click the Options button. Make sure there's a check in the box labeled Reverse Print Order. Click OK and try it again.

I just sent a long document to the printer. I just realized that I made a mistake. How do I stop printing now?

Quick! Double-click the Printer icon on the taskbar at the bottom of the screen. If you're fast enough, you might be able to stop the job before it reaches the printer.

Using Excel

When you start using Excel, odds are you'll have a few questions about how to make things add up. Here are answers to several frequently asked questions.

The cursor doesn't move when I press Enter

Somebody's been playing with your system settings. Choose Tools, Options, click on the Edit tab, and click next to Move Selection after Enter. Then click on the drop-down arrow, and specify whether you want to progress up, down, or sideways.

The Undo feature in Excel doesn't seem to work like it does in Word. Why not?

Most of the time, pressing Ctrl+Z or clicking the Undo button will bring back the data you accidentally wiped out—as long as it's the last thing you've done.

But...Excel's Undo features aren't the same as Word's, so be careful. Excel's Undo button only keeps track of the very last thing you did. If you delete a row and then reformat another cell, you can undo the formatting but not the deletion.

Trying to move to the upper left corner of a worksheet doesn't work

Check to see if the panes are frozen. You can tell by opening the Window menu. If you see Unfreeze Panes on the menu, the panes are frozen. Just select this menu option to unfreeze them.

I deleted a column, and now some of my formulas don't work any more

When you delete a cell, Excel removes every trace of it. If formulas elsewhere in the worksheet referred to that cell, Excel will get hopelessly confused and say something like #REF! It means Excel has lost track of a reference and can't display the value for the formula. You'll have to put the formula back in with corrected references.

My cell says 1.03E+08—but that's not what I typed. What's going on?

That's **scientific notation**, and Excel uses it when you type a number with more digits than it can display in the General number format. Take the number before the E, and move the decimal eight places to the right (if that were a minus sign, you'd move the decimal to the left). So your number is actually 103,000,000.

I modified my worksheet, but I don't see any changes

If you don't have Excel configured for automatic recalculation, press F9 to refresh the chart; or choose Tools, Options, click the Calculation tab, and select Automatic.

How can I control what part of my spreadsheet prints on a page?

Be sure to define the print area carefully. If most of your worksheets are simple one-page jobs, use Print Preview to confirm that everything fits. Quickly check that the Next and Previous buttons are grayed out. That way, you won't stand by helplessly (as I did once), while 60 pages of nearly blank printout pours out of the printer because you didn't set the print area correctly.

Also, be careful when you ask Excel to print the entire worksheet, especially if you've added formulas, supplementary tables, etc., below or to the right of the main worksheet. Excel considers everything you enter to be part of the worksheet, so you may need to define the print area more precisely.

I have several extra columns between chunks of my data. What happened?

If you have data separated by several spaces, rather than a comma or tab, and you are using a space as your delimiter, you will get blank columns. Be sure to delete any extra blank spaces between the items in your data, or use a different delimiter.

I updated my Excel worksheet, but the numbers in my Word document didn't change. What happened?

Maybe the link broke. That can happen if you rename the source document or move it to a different folder. Try choosing Edit, Links, and click the Change Source button to re-establish the link. If that doesn't work, you'll have to delete the linked range and insert a fresh copy of your worksheet range.

Everytime I show my boss my file, she messes it up. How can I protect Excel spreadsheets I have to share with others?

When you open the file for your boss, choose the Read Only option in the Open dialog box. She'll get a version she can read and print, but not save under that name. This trick is a little safer than actually sharing the file.

Using PowerPoint

Color, pictures, and text add up to powerful presentations—if you know how to use PowerPoint's multitude of features. What follows are some great tips and troubleshooting help.

Everytime I add text, I get a bullet. Is there a way to get rid of those $#@$!! bullets?

 If the text is formatted as a bulleted list, you'll get a new bullet each time you press Enter. To get rid of them, select the entire text by pressing Ctrl+A, and click the Bullet On/Off button on the Formatting toolbar. This is called a **toggle** feature: one click turns it on; another click turns it off.

I can't find any of the standard presentation templates

Whoever installed Office on your PC may have saved disk space by not installing the templates at all. Run the Office setup program again, click the Add/Remove button, highlight PowerPoint, and press the Change Option button. Select the Design Templates box, then click OK and follow the instructions. You may also be looking in the wrong folder. The templates that come with PowerPoint are in the Presentation Designs folder, which you can find in the Templates folder within the MSOffice folder.

I get an error message when I try to work with Word and PowerPoint at the same time

Unfortunately, you can't work on your outline in Word and PowerPoint simultaneously. If your Word file is open when you try to bring it into PowerPoint, Office will put up an annoying error message telling you that it can't use the Word document. Close it and try again.

I tried to open a Word document in PowerPoint, but some of my text disappeared, and the rest showed up on one slide. What's wrong?

You can't just start typing in Word and expect it to move gracefully into PowerPoint. Both programs depend on Word's built-in styles. In Word, switch to Outline view, and make sure each slide title is formatted with the Heading 1 style. Items in bulleted lists should be Heading 2 or Heading 3. To convert an existing Word document into an outline, switch to Outline view, and use the toolbar or the Tab key to promote Normal text into headings.

I created a presentation on one computer but showed it on another, and the PowerPoint Viewer didn't work. Why?

The Pack and Go Wizard assumes that the computer on which you plan to show the presentation has Windows 95 installed on it. If this isn't the case, you won't be able to run the PowerPoint Viewer, and you'll have to describe your slides to your audience.

How do I reveal a hidden slide during my presentation?

There are two ways to "unhide" hidden slides:

Mouse. Right-click the slide just before the hidden slide, and choose Go To and Hidden Slide.

Keyboard. If you use the keyboard to advance to the next slide, just type **H** (or **h**, it doesn't matter) while you're on the slide preceding the hidden one.

Beyond the basics

The answers to these common questions help you take full advantage of the Office environment.

I accidentally created a new toolbar, which I don't really want. How do I get rid of it?

It's an easy cleanup. Choose View, Toolbars. From the list, choose the name of the "I didn't mean that" toolbar, and press the Delete button. Note that you can only delete toolbars you created. The built-in toolbars are there for good.

Help! I cleared away all the toolbars, and now I don't know where to click to bring them back. What do I do?

Fortunately, all the Office programs work alike, and this is an easy problem to fix. Just choose View, Toolbars to display the list of available toolbars, select the ones you want, then click OK to make them reappear.

I don't have any applets on my computer. Where are they?

If you (or whoever installed Office on your PC) chose to do a Typical installation, the WordArt, Organization Chart, and Equation Editor applets stayed on the setup disks. To install them now, click the Office icon on the Shortcut Bar, and choose Add/Remove Office Programs. You'll find all three choices in the Office Tools category.

How do I get this WordArt object to move around the page?

When you insert a WordArt object into a Word document, be sure to enclose it in a frame after you create it. (Select the WordArt object, click the right mouse button, and choose Frame Picture from the shortcut menu.) Once there's a frame around the picture, you can easily move it where you want it on the page.

I thought Schedule+ was going to remind me about a meeting, but it didn't

The reminder doesn't pop up when a screen saver is active on your screen. Even when you return to your desktop (when the screen saver disappears), you won't get that notice. As the old computer saying goes, "Is this a bug or a feature?" It's hard to tell, but until Microsoft fixes this problem, get in the habit of checking your Schedule+ screen whenever you disable a screen saver.

I can't get the formatting in this shared list workbook to change

You *can* change the formatting and formulas in a shared list workbook, but only if you temporarily turn off the shared lists feature (use the File menu's Shared Lists command).

Part VII: Indexes

Action Index

General Office Operations

When you need to...	You'll find help here...
Find help about any topic	p. 45 I don't know what it's called and p. 46 Can't I just ask in plain English?
Create a new file	p. 56 How do I create a new file?
Find and open an existing file	p. 61 I want to work with a file I saved earlier
Tell Office where to save your files	p. 63 Setting up default file locations
Customize the toolbars	p. 416 Toolbars: have 'em your way
Combine several documents into one	p. 408 Organize Your Projects with Office Binder
Share documents with colleagues	p. 454 Word's special workgroup features and Creating a shared list workbook
Share parts of files between programs	p. 332 How do I copy stuff from one place to another? And p.337 How do I create a link? And p.340 How do I stuff a worksheet inside a Word document? And p.379 For using Word and Excel with PowerPoint

Using Word

When you need to...	You'll find help here...
Start typing a new document	p. 88 I just want to start writing and p. 86 Do it yourself with templates
Delete text	p. 90 Deleting text
Move around in a document	p. 91 Moving around in a document
Fit more text on the page	p. 92 How do I adjust the margins? And p. 93 How do I change paper size?

continues

When you need to...	You'll find help here...
Make the on-screen text easy to read	p. 106 I want to make the text look a little bigger
Select part of the document	p. 107 Selecting text
Move a chunk of text somewhere else	p. 110 Moving words around
Change the appearance of the text	p. 118 How do I make my words look more interesting? And p. 128 How can I save my favorite formats and reuse them?
Change this document to double-spacing	p. 123 Adjusting line spacing
Create lists	p. 154 I want to use a bulleted list and p. 156 I want to use a numbered list
Make a table	p. 159 How do I add a table?
Send the same letter to lots of people	p. 177 Mail Merge in a nutshell
Make and print labels	p. 187 I want to make mailing labels
Print envelopes	p. 187 What about these matching 500 envelopes?
Add page numbering	p. 192 How do I create a header or a footer?
Insert a graphic into my document	p. 203 OK, I want to put a picture in this report
Put my text in a box so it stands out	p. 205 How do I make part of my document really stand out?
Print	p. 210 Before you print, preview! p. 213 Enough already! I just want to print and

Using Excel

When you need to...	You'll find help here...
Calculate	p. 256 How do I do calculations with Excel?
Edit, delete, copy or move a bunch of cells	p. 233 What's a range, and why should I care?
Do less data entry	p. 249 Excel's amazing mind-reading tricks: AutoFill, AutoComplete, and AutoCorrect.

When you need to...	You'll find help here...
Add dollar signs to these numbers	P. 267 What's formatting and why should I care?
Calculate dates	P. 271 It's 34731.9583—do you know where your kids are?
Make this column wider	p. 275 I need to resize rows and columns!
Sort a list	p. 282 Sorting your data the easy way
Find something quickly	p. 284 Desperately searching for data
Replace recurring data	p. 288 Search and Replace
Open the same file every time	p. 291 Quick start
Create a graph out of these numbers	p. 295 The Chart Wizard—Just add water
Add labels to parts of the graph	p. 302 I can't tell what these bars represent
View my data by region	p. 309 That section hasn't been written yet, but it'll be something like "How can I view my data by region or country?"

Using PowerPoint

When you need to...	You'll find help here...
Create a new presentation	p. 348, 351 Apply a design template
Apply a different look	p. 351, 354, 366 I want to spruce up the whole presentation and Now I want to add special effects to the text and Apply Design Template
Create better transitions between slides	p. 373 I want smooth transitions
I want this text to pop up only when I'm ready	p. 376 Keep 'em in suspense?
Show my masterpiece	p. 397 Running a slide show
Draw on a slide during a show	p. 399 "X" marks the spot
Print the presentation	p. 400 Printing your presentation

Using Schedule+

When you need to...	You'll find help here...
Schedule an appointment or meeting	p. 438 How do I create a new appointment?
Get others to come to the meeting	p. 442 How can I invite others to this meeting?
Maintain a contact list	p. 445 How do I manage my contact list?
Meet deadlines	p. 448 Don't know whether you're coming or going? You need a to-do list.

Index

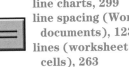

X-Y-Z

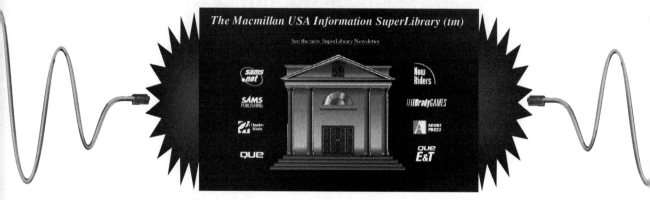

Que's *USING* Series

For the fastest access to the one best way to get things done, check out other *Using* books from Que! These user-friendly references give you just what you need to know to be productive—plus no-nonsense tips and shortcuts in plain English. Whatever the topic, there's a *Using* book to ensure computer confidence!

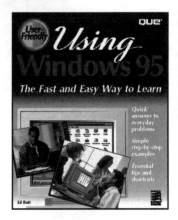

User Identification Level

New   Casual   Accomplished   Expert

Que's *SPECIAL EDITION USING* Series

For accomplished users who desire in-depth coverage, *Special Edition Using* books are the most comprehensive references. These books contain professional tips and advice—as well as valuable tools and software—to optimize results with all major hardware and software topics.

User Identification Level

New   Casual   Accomplished   Expert

Look for Using books and Special Edition Using books at your favorite bookstore!

Complete and Return this Card
for a *FREE* Computer Book Catalog

Thank you for purchasing this book! You have purchased a superior computer book written expressly for your needs. To continue to provide the kind of up-to-date, pertinent coverage you've come to expect from us, we need to hear from you. Please take a minute to complete and return this self-addressed, postage-paid form. In return, we'll send you a free catalog of all our computer books on topics ranging from word processing to programming and the internet.

r. ☐   Mrs. ☐   Ms. ☐   Dr. ☐

me (first) ☐☐☐☐☐☐☐☐☐☐☐☐☐☐   (M.I.) ☐   (last) ☐☐☐☐☐☐☐☐☐☐☐☐☐☐☐☐☐☐

ddress ☐☐☐☐☐☐☐☐☐☐☐☐☐☐☐☐☐☐☐☐☐☐☐☐☐☐☐☐☐☐☐☐☐☐☐☐

☐☐☐☐☐☐☐☐☐☐☐☐☐☐☐☐☐☐☐☐☐☐☐☐☐☐☐☐☐☐☐☐☐☐☐☐

ty ☐☐☐☐☐☐☐☐☐☐☐☐☐☐☐☐☐☐   State ☐☐   Zip ☐☐☐☐☐ ☐☐☐☐

one ☐☐☐ ☐☐☐ ☐☐☐☐   Fax ☐☐☐ ☐☐☐ ☐☐☐☐

mpany Name ☐☐☐☐☐☐☐☐☐☐☐☐☐☐☐☐☐☐☐☐☐☐☐☐☐☐☐☐☐☐☐☐☐☐☐☐

mail address ☐☐☐☐☐☐☐☐☐☐☐☐☐☐☐☐☐☐☐☐☐☐☐☐☐☐☐☐☐☐☐☐☐☐☐☐

Please check at least (3) influencing factors for purchasing this book.

nt or back cover information on book .... ☐
ecial approach to the content .... ☐
mpleteness of content .... ☐
thor's reputation .... ☐
blisher's reputation .... ☐
ok cover design or layout .... ☐
dex or table of contents of book .... ☐
ice of book .... ☐
ecial effects, graphics, illustrations .... ☐
her (Please specify): _____ ☐

How did you first learn about this book?

w in Macmillan Computer Publishing catalog .... ☐
commended by store personnel .... ☐
w the book on bookshelf at store .... ☐
commended by a friend .... ☐
ceived advertisement in the mail .... ☐
w an advertisement in: _____ ☐
ad book review in: _____ ☐
her (Please specify): _____ ☐

How many computer books have you purchased in the last six months?

is book only .... ☐   3 to 5 books .... ☐
ooks .... ☐   More than 5 .... ☐

4. Where did you purchase this book?

Bookstore .... ☐
Computer Store .... ☐
Consumer Electronics Store .... ☐
Department Store .... ☐
Office Club .... ☐
Warehouse Club .... ☐
Mail Order .... ☐
Direct from Publisher .... ☐
Internet site .... ☐
Other (Please specify): _____ ☐

5. How long have you been using a computer?

☐ Less than 6 months   ☐ 6 months to a year
☐ 1 to 3 years   ☐ More than 3 years

6. What is your level of experience with personal computers and with the subject of this book?

	With PCs	With subject of book
New	☐	☐
Casual	☐	☐
Accomplished	☐	☐
Expert	☐	☐

Source Code ISBN:

7. Which of the following best describes your job title?

Administrative Assistant .... ☐
Coordinator .... ☐
Manager/Supervisor .... ☐
Director .... ☐
Vice President .... ☐
President/CEO/COO .... ☐
Lawyer/Doctor/Medical Professional .... ☐
Teacher/Educator/Trainer .... ☐
Engineer/Technician .... ☐
Consultant .... ☐
Not employed/Student/Retired .... ☐
Other (Please specify): _____ ☐

8. Which of the following best describes the area of the company your job title falls under?

Accounting .... ☐
Engineering .... ☐
Manufacturing .... ☐
Operations .... ☐
Marketing .... ☐
Sales .... ☐
Other (Please specify): _____ ☐

Comments: _____
_____
_____

9. What is your age?

Under 20 ....
21-29 ....
30-39 ....
40-49 ....
50-59 ....
60-over ....

10. Are you:

Male .... ☐
Female .... ☐

11. Which computer publications do you read regularly? (Please list)

_____
_____
_____
_____
_____
_____
_____
_____
_____
_____
_____

Fold here and scotch-tape to ma